3rd Workshop on Figurative Language Processing 2022

Abu Dhabi, United Arab Emirates and Online
8 December 2022

ISBN: 978-1-7138-9110-9

Printed from e-media with permission by:

Curran Associates, Inc.
57 Morehouse Lane
Red Hook, NY 12571

CURRAN ASSOCIATES INC.
proceedings.com

Some format issues inherent in the e-media version may also appear in this print version.

Printed with permission by Curran Associates, Inc. (2024)

For permission requests, please contact the Association for Computational Linguistics at the address below.

Association for Computational Linguistics
209 N. Eighth Street
Stroudsburg, Pennsylvania 18360

Phone: 1-570-476-8006
Fax: 1-570-476-0860

acl@aclweb.org

Additional copies of this publication are available from:

Curran Associates, Inc.
57 Morehouse Lane
Red Hook, NY 12571 USA
Phone: 845-758-0400
Fax: 845-758-2633
Email: curran@proceedings.com
Web: www.proceedings.com

FLP 2022

3rd Workshop on Figurative Language Processing

Proceedings of the Workshop

December 8, 2022

Introduction

Welcome to the 3rd Workshop on Figurative Language Processing (FigLang 2022), to be held on December 8, 2022 as part of EMNLP in Abu Dhabi.

The use of figurative language enriches human communication by allowing us to express complex ideas and emotions. Consequently, it is not surprising that figurative language processing has become a rapidly growing area in Natural Language Processing (NLP), including metaphors, idioms, puns, irony, sarcasm, among others. Characteristic to all areas of human activity (from poetic to ordinary to scientific) and, thus, to all types of discourse, figurative language becomes an important problem for NLP systems. Its ubiquity in language has been established in several corpus studies, and the role it plays in human reasoning has been confirmed in psychological experiments. This makes figurative language an important research area for computational and cognitive linguistics, and its automatic identification and interpretation indispensable for any semantics-oriented NLP application. Recent advent of large language model-based NLP has led to novel techniques for understanding, interpreting, and creating figurative language.

This workshop is the third in a series of biannual workshops on Figurative Language Processing (following ACL 2018 and ACL 2020 installments). This new workshop series builds upon the successful start of the Metaphor in NLP workshop series (at NAACL– HLT 2013, ACL 2014, NAACL–HLT 2015, NAACL–HLT 2016), expanding its scope to incorporate the rapidly growing body of research on various types of figurative language such as sarcasm, irony and puns, with the aim of maintaining and nourishing a community of NLP researchers interested in this topic. The workshop features both regular research papers and two shared tasks on euphemism detection and understanding of a variety (e.g., metaphor, simile, idiom, and sarcasm) of figurative language through textual explanations. The workshop is privileged to present two invited talks this year. Penny Pexman and Aline Villavicencio will be presenting talks at this year's workshop.

In the regular research track, we received sixteen research paper submissions and accepted twelve. The featured papers cover a range of aspects of figurative language processing such as metaphor prediction and understanding (Berger; Li et al.; Wachowiak et al.; Dankin et al.; Sengupta et al.), translation of idiomatic expressions (Santing et al.), metaphor-rich translation in fictitious language (Jansen and Boyd-Graber), measure of surprise in humor and metaphor (Bunescu and Uduehi), multimodal metaphor detection in videos (Alnajjar et al.), identifying figurative content in drug lexicon (Reyes and Saldivar), and answering questions from figurative contexts (Rakshit and Flanigan).

The two shared tasks on euphemism detection and understanding of figurative language via textual explanations serve to benchmark various computational approaches to euphemism and different types of figurative language, clarifying the state of this steadily growing field and facilitating further research.

The Shared Task on Euphemism Detection invited teams to submit systems for the following task: given a text containing a potentially euphemistic term (PET), determine whether the PET is being used euphemistically or literally. The dataset used consisted of texts from the GloWbE corpus, human-annotated to be euphemistic (1) or literal (0). The goal of this task was to investigate the performance of current NLP methods on a euphemism-related task, establish a baseline from which to launch future work on euphemisms, and analyze additional enhancements attempted by participants. 46 participants spanning 13 teams attempted the task, and 9 system descriptions were submitted. Teams tested approaches such as transformer models, data balancing, linguistically motivated methods, etc., with the highest F1-scores being around 0.88.

The second shared task on understanding figurative language is designed to challenge the participants to build models to not only identify the type of figurative language but also to explain the decision via natural language. The task is based on the recently developed FLUTE dataset, which is based on four types of figurative language – idiom, sarcasm, metaphor, and simile. Out of all the models submitted, four system papers were submitted to the shared task. Although all the submitted models were based on the transformer architecture, participants did attempt different approaches – such as using elaboration of the situation first as additional contexts, sequential training on a variety of NLI datasets, and conducting multi sequence2sequence tasks. Two participants attained the highest accuracy (accuracy@60) scores of 63.33.

We wish to thank everyone who showed interest and submitted a paper, all of the authors for their contributions, the members of the Program Committee for their thoughtful reviews, the invited speakers for sharing their perspective on the topic, and all the attendees of the workshop. All of these factors contribute to a truly enriching event!

Debanjan Ghosh, Beata Beigman Klebanov, Smaranda Muresan, Anna Feldman, Soujanya Poria, Tuhin Chakrabarty, Workshop Co-Chairs

Organizing Committee

Workshop Organizers

Debanjan Ghosh, Educational Testing Service, USA
Beata Beigman Klebanov, Educational Testing Service, USA
Smaranda Muresan, Columbia University, USA
Anna Feldman, Montclair State University, USA
Soujanya Poria, Singapore University of Technology and Design, Singapore
Tuhin Chakrabarty, Columbia University, USA

Figurative Language Understanding Shared Task Organizers

Tuhin Chakrabarty, Columbia University, USA
Arkadiy Saakyan, Columbia University, USA
Debanjan Ghosh, Educational Testing Service, USA
Smaranda Muresan, Columbia University, USA

Euphemism Detection Shared Task Organizers

Patrick Lee, Montclair State University, USA
Anna Feldman, Montclair State University, USA
Jing Peng, Montclair State University, USA

Program Committee

Program Committee

Tariq Alhindi, Khalid Alnajjar

Yulia Badryzlova, Yuri Bizzoni, Susan Brown

Verna Dankers, Jonathan Dunn

Michael Flor

Katy Gutierrez

Mika Hämäläinen

Hyeju Jang

Valia Kordoni

Mark Lee, Els Lu

Michael Mohler, Elena Musi

Preslav Nakov

Thierry Poibeau

Paul Rayson, Ellen Riloff, Andres Torres Rivera

Farig Sadeque, Eyal Sagi, Vered Shwartz, Oprea Silviu, Carlo Stapparava, Egon Stemle, Kevin Stowe, Tomek Strzalkowski, Stan Szpakowicz

Simone Teufel, Yufei Tian

Tony Veale

Sabine Schulte im Walde

Invited Speakers

Penny Pexman, University of Calgary, Canada
Aline Villavicencio, University of Sheffield, UK

Keynote Talk: Irony Acquisition: How Children Learn to Detect Sarcasm

Penny M. Pexman
University of Calgary

Abstract: One of the challenges children face in learning to navigate the social world is created by the fact that people often speak indirectly, for example, with sarcasm or verbal irony. Research has shown that typically developing children don't usually begin to convey and appreciate ironic intent until the early school years. Children's use and appreciation of ironic language develop over a fairly long developmental window, and are related to their cognitive development and social experiences. Most of these insights have come from research that is focused on the product of interpretation: the understanding that children convey through verbal descriptions, ratings, or yes/no decisions. In a series of studies, we developed methodology that allows us to explore the process of children's irony interpretation. Using a variant of the visual world paradigm, we track children's eye gaze and reaching behavior as they judge speaker intent for ironic language that unfolds in real time. We have used this paradigm to identify factors that make irony particularly challenging for children. Most recently, those studies have helped us to devise a training paradigm to teach children to detect sarcastic speech. I'll discuss what our findings tell us about what it takes to develop a sense of sarcasm.

Bio: Penny Pexman is currently Professor of Psychology and Associate Vice-President (Research) at the University of Calgary. Penny earned her PhD in Psychology at the University of Western Ontario in 1998 and joined the University of Calgary the same year. Her research expertise is in psycholinguistics, cognitive neuroscience, and social-cognitive development. In broad terms, she is interested in how we derive meaning from language, and how those processes are changed by context or experience. Her research investigates several aspects of language understanding, ranging from lexical-semantic processes to figurative language. Penny has published over 150 journal articles and book chapters on those topics. An award-winning mentor and researcher, Penny is an elected Fellow of both the Canadian Psychological Association and the Association for Psychological Science.

Keynote Talk: Modelling Multiword Expressions and Idiomaticity: an Acid Test for Understanding

Aline Villavicencio
University of Sheffield

Abstract: Advances in large-scale word representation models have been successful in capturing distinct (and very specific) word usages in context. However, these models still face a serious challenge when dealing with non-literal or non-compositional language, like that involved in Multiword Expressions (MWEs) such as noun compounds (grandfather clock), light verb constructions (give a talk), and verb particle constructions (give up). MWEs are an integral part of the mental lexicon of native speakers often used to express complex ideas in a conventionalised way accepted by a given linguistic community, but often displaying a wealth of idiosyncrasies, from lexical, syntactic and semantic to statistical which means that they represent a real challenge for current NLP techniques. However, their accurate integration has the potential for improving the precision, naturalness and fluency of downstream tasks like machine translation and text simplification. In this talk, I will present an overview of how advances in word representations have made an impact for the identification and modelling of idiomaticity and MWEs. I will concentrate on what models seem to incorporate of idiomaticity, as idiomatic interpretation may require knowledge that goes beyond what can be gathered from the individual words of an expression (e.g. "dark horse" as an unknown candidate who unexpectedly succeeds).

Bio: Aline Villavicencio is the Chair in Natural Language Processing at the Department of Computer Science, University of Sheffield (UK). Prior to that she was affiliated as a Reader to the Institute of Informatics, Federal University of Rio Grande do Sul (Brazil), and as a Lecturer at the University of Essex (UK). She received her PhD from the University of Cambridge (UK) in 2001, and held postdoc positions at the University of Cambridge and University of Essex (UK). She was a Visiting Scholar at the Massachusetts Institute of Technology (USA, 2011-2012 and 2014-2015), at the École Normale Supérieure (France, 2014), an Erasmus-Mundus Visting Scholar at Saarland University (Germany in 2012/2013) and at the University of Bath (UK, 2006-2009). She held a Research Fellowship from the Brazilian National Council for Scientific and Technological Development (Brazil, 2009-2017). She is a member of the editorial board of Computational Linguistics, TACL and of JNLE. She was a PC Co-Chair of the 60th Meeting of the Association for Computational Linguistics (ACL 2022), and was a PC Co-Chair of CoNLL-2019, Senior Area Chair for ACL-2020 and ACL-2019 among others and General co-chair for the 2018 International Conference on Computational Processing of Portuguese. She is also a member of the NAACL board, SIGLEX board and of the program committees of various ACL and AI conferences, and has co-chaired several ACL workshops on Cognitive Aspects of Computational Language Acquisition and on Multiword Expressions. Her research interests include lexical semantics, multilinguality, multiword expressions and cognitively motivated NLP, and has co-edited special issues and books dedicated to these topics.

Table of Contents

Program

Thursday, December 8, 2022

08:50 - 09:00 *Opening Remarks*

09:00 - 10:30 *Research Track*

Ring That Bell: A Corpus and Method for Multimodal Metaphor Detection in Videos
Khalid Alnajjar, Mika Hämäläinen and Shuo Zhang

Food for Thought: How can we exploit contextual embeddings in the translation of idiomatic expressions?
Lukas Santing, Ryan Jean-Luc Sijstermans, Giacomo Anerdi, Pedro Jeuris, Marijn ten Thij and Riza Batista-Navarro

Distribution-Based Measures of Surprise for Creative Language: Experiments with Humor and Metaphor
Razvan C. Bunescu and Oseremen O. Uduehi

The Secret of Metaphor on Expressing Stronger Emotion
Yucheng Li, Frank Guerin and Chenghua Lin

Back to the Roots: Predicting the Source Domain of Metaphors using Contrastive Learning
Meghdut Sengupta, Milad Alshomary and Henning Wachsmuth

Can Yes-No Question-Answering Models be Useful for Few-Shot Metaphor Detection?
Lena Dankin, Kfir Bar and Nachum Dershowitz

On the Cusp of Comprehensibility: Can Language Models Distinguish Between Metaphors and Nonsense?
Bernadeta Griciūtė, Marc Tanti and Lucia Donatelli

10:30 - 11:00 *Coffee Break*

11:00 - 12:30 *Research Track + Shared Tasks*

A Report on the Euphemisms Detection Shared Task
Patrick Lee, Anna Feldman and Jing Peng

Thursday, December 8, 2022 (continued)

EUREKA: EUphemism Recognition Enhanced through Knn-based methods and Augmentation
Sedrick Scott Keh, Rohit Bharadwaj, Emmy Liu, Simone Tedeschi, Varun Gangal and Roberto Navigli

Detecting Euphemisms with Literal Descriptions and Visual Imagery
Ilker Kesen, Aykut Erdem, Erkut Erdem and Iacer Calixto

A Report on the FigLang 2022 Shared Task on Understanding Figurative Language
Arkadiy Saakyan, Tuhin Chakrabarty, Debanjan Ghosh and Smaranda Muresan

Just-DREAM-about-it: Figurative Language Understanding with DREAM-FLUTE
Yuling Gu, Yao Fu, Valentina Pyatkin, Ian Magnusson, Bhavana Dalvi Mishra and Peter Clark

Effective Cross-Task Transfer Learning for Explainable Natural Language Inference with T5
Irina Bigoulaeva, Rachneet Singh Sachdeva, Harish Tayyar Madabushi, Aline Villavicencio and Iryna Gurevych

Drum Up SUPPORT: Systematic Analysis of Image-Schematic Conceptual Metaphors
Lennart Wachowiak, Dagmar Gromann and Chao Xu

Transfer Learning Parallel Metaphor using Bilingual Embeddings
Maria Berger

12:30 - 14:00 *Lunch Break*

14:00 - 15:00 *Keynote Talk 1: Aline Villavicencio: Modelling Multiword Expressions and Idiomaticity: an Acid Test for Understanding*

15:00 - 15:30 *Research Track*

An insulin pump? Identifying figurative links in the construction of the drug lexicon
Antonio Reyes and Rafael Saldivar

Picard understanding Darmok: A Dataset and Model for Metaphor-Rich Translation in a Constructed Language
Peter A. Jansen and Jordan Boyd-Graber

Thursday, December 8, 2022 (continued)

FigurativeQA: A Test Benchmark for Figurativeness Comprehension for Question Answering
Geetanjali Rakshit and Jeffrey Flanigan

15:30 - 16:00 *Coffee Break*

16:00 - 17:30 *Poster Session (Shared Tasks + Findings)*

TEDB System Description to a Shared Task on Euphemism Detection 2022
Peratham Wiriyathammabhum

A Prompt Based Approach for Euphemism Detection
Abulimiti Maimaitituoheti, Yang Yong and Fan Xiaochao

Euphemism Detection by Transformers and Relational Graph Attention Network
Yuting Wang, Yiyi Liu, Ruqing Zhang, Yixing Fan and Jiafeng Guo

Bayes at FigLang 2022 Euphemism Detection shared task: Cost-Sensitive Bayesian Fine-tuning and Venn-Abers Predictors for Robust Training under Class Skewed Distributions
Paul Trust, Kadusabe Provia and Kizito Omala

An Exploration of Linguistically-Driven and Transfer Learning Methods for Euphemism Detection
Devika Tiwari and Natalie Parde

Adversarial Perturbations Augmented Language Models for Euphemism Identification
Guneet Kohli, Prabsimran Kaur and Jatin Bedi

Exploring Euphemism Detection in Few-Shot and Zero-Shot Settings
Sedrick Scott Keh

SBU Figures It Out: Models Explain Figurative Language
Yash Kumar Lal and Mohaddeseh Bastan

NLP@UIT at FigLang-EMNLP 2022: A Divide-and-Conquer System For Shared Task On Understanding Figurative Language
Khoa Thi-Kim Phan, Duc-Vu Nguyen and Ngan Luu-Thuy Nguyen

Visualizing the Obvious: A Concreteness-based Ensemble Model for Noun Property Prediction
Yue Yang, Artemis Panagopoulou, Marianna Apidianaki, Mark Yatskar and Chris Callison-Burch

Sarcasm Detection is Way Too Easy! An Empirical Comparison of Human and Machine Sarcasm Detection
Ibrahim Abu Farha, Steven Wilson, Silviu Oprea and Walid Magdy

A Unified Framework for Pun Generation with Humor Principles
Yufei Tian, Divyanshu Sheth and Nanyun Peng

It's Better to Teach Fishing than Giving a Fish: An Auto-Augmented Structure-aware Generative Model for Metaphor Detection
Huawen Feng and Qianli Ma

Systematicity in GPT-3's Interpretation of Novel English Noun Compounds
Siyan Li, Riley Carlson and Christopher Potts

PoeLM: A Meter- and Rhyme-Controllable Language Model for Unsupervised Poetry Generation
Aitor Ormazabal, Mikel Artetxe, Manex Agirrezabal, Aitor Soroa and Eneko Agirre

Scientific and Creative Analogies in Pretrained Language Models
Tamara Czinczoll, Helen Yannakoudakis, Pushkar Mishra and Ekaterina Shutova

Cards Against AI: Predicting Humor in a Fill-in-the-blank Party Game
Dan Ofer and Dafna Shahaf

17:30 - 17:55 *Break*

17:55 - 19:00 *Keynote Talk 2: Penny M. Pexman: Irony Acquisition: How Children Learn to Detect Sarcasm*

TEDB System Description to a Shared Task on Euphemism Detection 2022

Peratham Wiriyathammabhum
peratham.bkk@gmail.com

Abstract

In this report, we describe our Transformers for euphemism detection baseline (TEDB) submissions to a shared task on euphemism detection 2022. We cast the task of predicting euphemism as text classification. We considered Transformer-based models which are the current state-of-the-art methods for text classification. We explored different training schemes, pretrained models, and model architectures. Our best result of *0.816* F1-score (*0.818* precision and *0.814* recall) consists of a euphemism-detection-finetuned TweetEval/TimeLMs-pretrained RoBERTa model as a feature extractor frontend with a KimCNN classifier backend trained end-to-end using a cosine annealing scheduler. We observed pretrained models on sentiment analysis and offensiveness detection to correlate with more F1-score while pretraining on other tasks, such as sarcasm detection, produces less F1-scores. Also, putting more word vector channels does not improve the performance in our experiments.

1 Introduction

A shared task on euphemism detection (Gavidia et al., 2022; Lee et al., 2022) is the first installment of a natural language processing (NLP) shared task on a particular figurative language detection, euphemism. Figurative languages, including metaphors, synecdoches, idioms, puns, hyperbole, similes, onomatopoeia, and others, are word uses where the meaning deviates from the literal meaning to convey a complicated, creative and evocative message without directly stating it. In addition, figurative language might use contexts such as relations to other things, actions, social experiences, or images. Figurative languages are ubiquitous since they are filled in countless of our everyday activities without notice (Lakoff and Johnson, 2008).

Euphemisms are mild or indirect words or phrases being used in place of offensive or unpleasant ones. Moreover, euphemisms are used to mark profanity or politely refer to sensitive and taboo topics such as death, disability, or sickness. The applications of euphemisms involve social interactions such as politics or doctor-patient discourses. Euphemisms can also be dangerous since terrorists can use euphemisms for language manipulation and separate message and meaning (Matusitz, 2016). Also, politely calling terrorism results in semantic deviance and attention away from reality for media and government officials which makes citizens lower their guard while in danger.

Table 1: An Example instance from the shared task dataset. The first sentence is more offensive literally. The phrase "collateral damage" should be replaced with politeness. The second sentence was revised by using the phrase "advanced age" to provide more politeness than some possible words or phrases like old, near expiration, or wrinkly.

Sentence	Label
All the deaths were just <collateral damage> in their cause.	[non-euphemistic]
In spite of his <advanced age>, Rollins remains one of jazz's most talented improvisers.	[euphemistic]

Previous works (Gavidia et al., 2022; Lee et al., 2022) utilize RoBERTa models (Liu et al., 2019) for sentiment and offensive ratings because politeness is the aim of euphemisms. Euphemisms should make the sentences more positive in sentiment and less offensive (Bakhriddionova, 2021). Our systems build upon these findings and explore transformer-based models which are pretrained for sentiment analysis or offensive detection.

Our best submission ranks 6th on the leaderboard. The codes for our systems are open-sourced and available at our GitHub repository[1].

[1]https://github.com/perathambkk/euphemism_

Proceedings of the 3rd Workshop on Figurative Language Processing (FLP), pages 1 - 7
December 8, 2022 ©2022 Association for Computational Linguistics

2 Models

2.1 Pretrained Transformers

Huggingface library (Wolf et al., 2020) is an extensive platform for transformer models (Vaswani et al., 2017). Huggingface provides many checkpoints for the pretrained transformer suitable to many tasks as a model hub. TweetEval (Barbieri et al., 2020) is a social NLP benchmark where standardized evaluation protocols and strong baselines and employed on seven Twitter classification tasks. The strong baselines later became pretrained model checkpoints loadable via Huggingface.

Diachronic specialization was shown to be lacking in language models (Loureiro et al., 2022) where changes or evolution in time can break current (synchronic - a language at a moment in time without any histories.) language model performances entirely. For example, pre-COVID19 language models will have no knowledge about the pandemic events completely. Diachrony and synchrony are two complimentary viewpoints that were theorized by linguist Ferdinand de Saussure more than a hundred years ago (De Saussure, 2011). The paper shares many time-specific language model checkpoints (TimeLMs).

Specifically, we employed two RoBERTa language model checkpoints from the papers (TweetEval and TimeLMs), one for sentiment analysis ('cardiffnlp/twitter-roberta-base-sentiment-latest') and another for offensiveness detection ('cardiffnlp/twitter-roberta-base-offensive'), as in (Gavidia et al., 2022; Lee et al., 2022). We finetuned them for euphemism detection as text classification.

2.2 Convolutional Neural Networks Backend

Convolutional Neural Networks (CNN) were primarily introduced for visual tasks, firstly, handwritten digit recognition, given its properties in translation invariance for 2D data (LeCun et al., 1998). KimCNN (Kim, 2014) proposed a little modification that enables on-top finetuning of CNN over pretrained word vectors for sentence classifications. The results in the paper were from a simple CNN with a little parameter tuning and static vectors.

We further performed some modifications by concatenating hidden state outputs from all RoBERTa layers as a word vector and instead finetuning the whole model end-to-end. We also used checkpoints from finetuning the pretrained transformers as RoBERTa starting points. We also attempted to combine two word vectors for a multi-channel KimCNN and finetuning the model with both word vectors for sentiment analysis and offensiveness detection end-to-end in contrast to freezing one word vector channel as in the original paper.

3 Experimental Setup

Our input consists of a three-sentence utterance, the sentence before, after, and the sentence containing the euphemistic term. We did not observe any improvements from removing any special characters including the '<' and '>' symbols around the euphemistic term given in the dataset. We used the maximum input length of 150 tokens since we found that it is the number that fits well as our heuristics with the GPU memory for many reasonable batch sizes ($4-20$ in our cases). Also, it seems to cover most data instances given the histogram plotting in Figure 1. We sampled the model at the end of each epoch. The dataset has 1572 training instances and 393 test instances.

All of our experiments were done in the Google Colab setting on NVIDIA Tesla T4 GPUs. We used the batch size in the range of $4-20$ and the learning rate for an AdamW optimizer (Loshchilov and Hutter, 2018) in the set of $\{2.5e-5, 2e-5, 1e-5, 7.5e-6\}$ for all experiments. We considered linear annealing scheduler and cosine annealing scheduler with restart. The cycle number is in the set of $\{5, 8\}$. Also, adding a warm-up step does not make any difference so we set the warm-up step to zero in all experiments.

3.1 Early Stopping Criterion for Empirical Risk Minimization

We employed the early stopping with zero patience training strategy schema (Prechelt, 1998; Bengio, 2012). We varied the training epoch until the training metric saturated with manual monitoring, and then stopped right at the end of that epoch. We tried to split the training data into training and development sets but empirically we found that the data set size is too small to perform accurate estimations/cross-validations on just an efficient held-out schema. For these reasons, we relied solely on our heuristics on the training set instead.

Theoretically simply speaking, given a small data for finetuning, it is not easy to estimate the

shared_task_emnlp2022

Table 2: Test F1-scores of different pretrained transformers on euphemism detection. (The number in **bold** is for the best score, and in *italic* is for the second best.)

Pretrained Transformer	Test F1-score
'cardiffnlp/xlm-twitter-politics-sentiment'	0.4693
'Hate-speech-CNERG/dehatebert-mono-english'	0.6821
'mrm8488/t5-base-finetuned-sarcasm-twitter-classification'	0.6969
'finiteautomata/bertweet-base-sentiment-analysis'	0.7349
a strong finetuned vanilla baseline: 'roberta-base'	0.7776
'sagteam/covid-twitter-xlm-roberta-large'	0.7776
'cardiffnlp/twitter-roberta-base-offensive'	*0.7838*
another strong finetuned vanilla baseline: 'bert-base-cased'	0.7941
'cardiffnlp/twitter-roberta-base-sentiment-latest' (TimeLMs)	**0.8064**

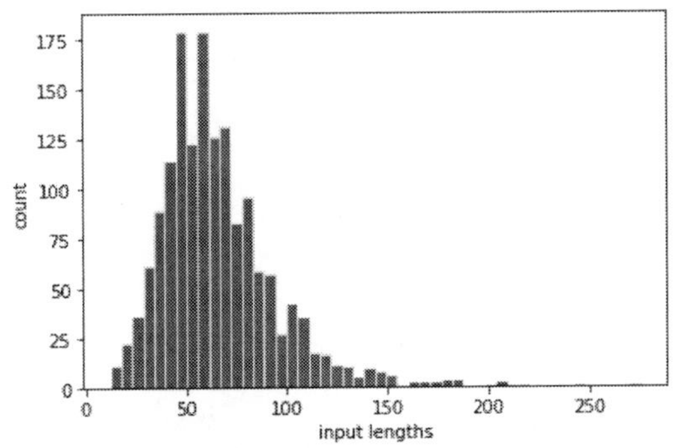

Figure 1: **The distribution of the input length derived from the shared task training set.**

model performance using a held-out validation set. Leave-one-out cross-validation (LOOCV) is appropriate but might need much more computation costs. Even k-fold cross-validation with a high value of k, which is a less extreme case of LOOCV, still needs a lot of computation costs. Additionally, if we split a small data, our model might fit the train split, but not the validation split. That model is very unlikely to perform well on the validation split, especially when the training is still underfitting the task, given a small data to train and a data-hungry model with a large capacity. Therefore, it will certainly have a weak upper bound of its error against a model that fits the whole training data.

This gives us an intuition of training our models just to shatter the whole training data and stop training in a basic train-test setting (empirical risk minimization). In our other simple intuition, it would be weird to withhold some training data from a given small data, implicitly lower the model capacity by (randomly) filtering out some data for an inaccurate generalizability estimation, and let the model predict them wrongly. Also, using more data to train lowers the model variance error term in the bias-variance decomposition framework.

3.2 Finetuning Pretrained Transformers

We compare many available huggingface hub's pretrained checkpoints we feel suitable for the task, which are multilingual Twitter politics sentiment analysis (Antypas et al.), hate speech detection (Aluru et al., 2020), Twitter sarcasm detection (Ghosh et al., 2020; Raffel et al., 2020), Twitter English sentiment analysis (Nguyen et al., 2020; Loureiro et al., 2022), Multilingual Russian-English Twitter COVID-19 report detection (Sboev et al., 2021), and offensiveness detection (Barbieri et al., 2020). The transformer models include BERT (Kenton and Toutanova, 2019), RoBERTa (Liu et al., 2019), XLM (Conneau et al., 2018), XLM-RoBERTa (Conneau et al., 2020) and T5 (Raffel et al., 2020) which are finetuned for the target task and their model parameters are shared on huggingface hub.

From the test F1-scores in Table 2, in which we even report the best result from all model hyperparameter settings in our experiment not reported here for brevity, we tend to confirm the hypothesis in the aforementioned previous works (Gavidia et al., 2022; Lee et al., 2022; Bakhriddionova, 2021) which state that euphemism relates with sentiment and offensiveness because the top-2 best scores in the table are sentiment analysis and offensiveness detection. Also, multilingual pretraining seems not to be helpful in this case of English euphemism detection. The 'cardiffnlp/twitter-roberta-base-sentiment-latest' RoBERTa-base model seems to outperform the 'finiteautomata/bertweet-base-sentiment-analysis' BERTweet model as in the TimeLMs paper (Loureiro et al., 2022) too. Therefore, we further build our models based on these top-2 best scorer pretrained TweetEval/TimeLMs RoBERTa models (Gururangan et al., 2020). We are aware that these top-2 models were among pre-

Table 3: Test F1-scores of different TweetEval pretrained transformers (Barbieri et al., 2020) on euphemism detection. (The number in **bold** is for the best score, and in *italic* is for the second best.)

Pretrained Transformer	Test F1-score
'cardiffnlp/twitter-roberta-base-stance-climate'	0.7238
'cardiffnlp/twitter-roberta-base-sentiment'	0.7238
'cardiffnlp/twitter-roberta-base-stance-feminist'	0.7306
'cardiffnlp/twitter-roberta-base-stance-abortion'	0.7446
'cardiffnlp/twitter-roberta-base-emotion'	0.7588
'cardiffnlp/twitter-roberta-base-emoji'	0.7615
'cardiffnlp/twitter-roberta-base-stance-hillary'	0.7651
'cardiffnlp/twitter-roberta-base-hate'	0.7665
'cardiffnlp/twitter-roberta-base-irony'	*0.7688*
'cardiffnlp/twitter-roberta-base-stance-atheism'	*0.7688*
a strong finetuned vanilla baseline: 'roberta-base'	0.7776
'cardiffnlp/twitter-roberta-base-offensive'	**0.7838**
another strong finetuned vanilla baseline: 'bert-base-cased'	0.7941

trained language models using the most data in TweetEval/TimeLMs.

3.2.1 TweetEval Pretrained Language Models

However, when we additionally compared all TweetEval pretrained RoBERTa-base language models finetuned on the euphemism task using our training scheme in Table 3, we observed that a TweetEval sentiment analysis model does not perform well at all. Besides, it was pretrained using much less data than the one in TimeLMs (45k vs. 138.86M tweets). Still, in Figure 2, the TimeLMs sentiment classification model performs very well given lots of data. The sentiment classification task might have some correlations with euphemism detection when the model learns well, or just lots of data make it work.

The best result in Table 3 is from offensiveness detection with only 11k tweet data. The second best models are irony detection and stance detection in the target domain of atheism. The performances vary based on some degree of euphemisms in the pretrained data. Nevertheless, only the offensiveness detection language model performs better than a finetuned vanilla RoBERTa-base language model. Finally, this is only our evidence-based intuition based on some point estimations of the model performances on euphemism detection.

We observed high sensitivities in hyperparameter settings in these experiments. Changing some hyperparameters such as patience in early stopping, initial learning rate, learning rate scheduler cycle, or even the random seed can result in significant changes in the results as in typical transformer models which are known to be sensitive to perturbations (Dodge et al., 2020). Training the 'cardiffnlp/twitter-roberta-base-sentiment-latest' model until the training metric is saturated but using a linear scheduler for 10 epochs instead of the best 15 epochs and removing special characters can result in 0.6920 test F1-score, using a linear scheduler for 12 epochs and removing special characters can result in 0.7301 test F1-score, which both are significant degradation.

Table 4: Test F1-scores of different classifiers on euphemism detection using vanilla pretrained language models. (The number in **bold** is for the best score.)

Model	RoBERTa-base
Huggingface's classifier	0.5203
sklearn logreg	0.4376
PA classifier	0.4126
3-NN	**0.5446**
MLP	0.4545
Decision Tree	0.4910
Linear SVM	0.4125

Model	BERT-base-cased
Huggingface's classifier	0.4197
sklearn logreg	0.5062
PA classifier	**0.5239**
3-NN	0.4436
MLP	0.4927
Decision Tree	0.4315
Linear SVM	0.4125

Table 5: Validation F1-scores of different classifiers on euphemism detection using vanilla pretrained language models. The split ratio is 0.40. (The number in **bold** is for the best score.)

Model	RoBERTa-base
sklearn logreg	0.5954
PA classifier	0.5929
3-NN	0.6107
MLP	0.6438
Decision Tree	**0.6692**
Linear SVM	0.6260

Model	BERT-base-cased
sklearn logreg	0.5929
PA classifier	0.5700
3-NN	0.5954
MLP	0.6056
Decision Tree	**0.6743**
Linear SVM	0.6031

3.2.2 A Comparison to Vanilla Pretrained Language Models

We additionally conducted experiments on various classifiers using vanilla pretrained language models, like RoBERTa-base and BERT-base-cased, as fixed feature extractors. From Table 4 and Table 5, the validation F1-scores are not good estimations of any test F1-scores. They overestimate all model performances by some large margins of around $0.12 \sim 0.15$ by their best differences or more. Training a classifier on a fixed feature extractor yields us only at most around ~ 0.54 test F1-score. This is a large gap compared to the performance of most finetuned language models. Also, the classifier with the best validation score, a decision tree, performs poorly on the test set. We used default parameters for the classifiers and used the same early-stopping training scheme but with an initial learning rate of $2.5e - 4$.

3.3 Finetuning KimCNNs

We employed the finetuned 'cardiffnlp/twitter-roberta-base-sentiment-latest' RoBERTa from the previous subsection for our KimCNN. We used 100 feature maps and $3, 4, 5$ weight length set input. We use a cross-entropy loss function and cosine annealing scheduler for this model type. Other hyperparameters were the same as in the previous subsection.

We got the best result of 0.8158 test F1-score, approximately 0.01 improvement over the previous model, simply using a KimCNN backend. However, adding another word vector channel using 'cardiffnlp/twitter-roberta-base-offensive', finetuned in the last subsection, reduces the performance as shown in Table 6. We additionally conducted experiments on removing a large language model and used only static word embeddings. A vanilla KimCNN with either word2vec (Mikolov et al., 2013) or glove-twitter (Pennington et al., 2014), trained on euphemism detection, works quite well with 0.6807 and 0.6172 test F1-scores respectively.

Table 6: Test F1-scores of different settings for KimCNNs on euphemism detection. (The number in **bold** is for the best score.)

Model	Test F1-score
KimCNNs	**0.8158**
+ multichannel	0.7980
KimCNNs (word2vec)	0.6807
KimCNNs (glove-twitter)	0.6172

Also, we varied some hyperparameters and observed more stability and faster convergence by simply putting a KimCNN backend on top. The significant degradation in the previous subsection was no longer. The test F1-scores of those models are like 0.8130 or 0.8132 which are very close to the best score. We also observed lower scores and slower convergence from using the 'cardiffnlp/twitter-roberta-base-sentiment-latest' directly from the huggingface's hub for KimCNN. So, another pretraining step to the task by finetuning a model from some relevant task helps improve the overall performance.

4 Conclusion

This report describes our baseline systems for a shared task on figurative language processing 2022, euphemism detection. Our best result is from a single-channel KimCNN model using 'cardiffnlp/twitter-roberta-base-sentiment-latest', pretrained again for euphemism detection, as a feature extractor. We observed more stability and faster convergence from this training schema. Our results on pretrained transformer models are likely to confirm the previous works (Gavidia et al., 2022; Lee et al., 2022; Bakhriddionova, 2021) that euphemism relates with sentiment and offensiveness. Still, we also observed that finetuning a sentiment-based pretrained language model, which pretrained with a rather small dataset, does not perform well.

Limitations

We only sampled a relatively small portion of models and draw conclusions. We also conducted experiments only on one dataset for euphemism detection. We did not perform any strong statistical tests on the models, just point estimations.

The authors are self-affiliated and do not represent any entities.

Acknowledgments

We would like to thank anonymous reviewers for their constructive feedback, and suggestions for additional experiments.

References

Sai Saketh Aluru, Binny Mathew, Punyajoy Saha, and Animesh Mukherjee. 2020. A deep dive into multilingual hate speech classification. In *Machine Learning and Knowledge Discovery in Databases. Applied Data Science and Demo Track: European Conference, ECML PKDD 2020, Ghent, Belgium, September 14–18, 2020, Proceedings, Part V*, page 423–439, Berlin, Heidelberg. Springer-Verlag.

Dimosthenis Antypas, Alun Preece, and Jose Camacho-Collados. Politics, sentiment and virality: A large-scale multilingual twitter analysis in greece, spain and united kingdom. *Spain and United Kingdom.*

Dildora Oktamovna Bakhriddionova. 2021. The needs of using euphemisms. *Mental Enlightenment Scientific-Methodological Journal*, 2021(06):55–64.

Francesco Barbieri, Jose Camacho-Collados, Luis Espinosa Anke, and Leonardo Neves. 2020. Tweeteval: Unified benchmark and comparative evaluation for tweet classification. In *Findings of the Association for Computational Linguistics: EMNLP 2020*, pages 1644–1650.

Yoshua Bengio. 2012. Practical recommendations for gradient-based training of deep architectures. In *Neural networks: Tricks of the trade*, pages 437–478. Springer.

Alexis Conneau, Kartikay Khandelwal, Naman Goyal, Vishrav Chaudhary, Guillaume Wenzek, Francisco Guzmán, Edouard Grave, Myle Ott, Luke Zettlemoyer, and Veselin Stoyanov. 2020. Unsupervised cross-lingual representation learning at scale. In *Proceedings of the 58th Annual Meeting of the Association for Computational Linguistics*, pages 8440–8451, Online. Association for Computational Linguistics.

Alexis Conneau, Ruty Rinott, Guillaume Lample, Adina Williams, Samuel Bowman, Holger Schwenk, and Veselin Stoyanov. 2018. XNLI: Evaluating cross-lingual sentence representations. In *Proceedings of the 2018 Conference on Empirical Methods in Natural Language Processing*, pages 2475–2485, Brussels, Belgium. Association for Computational Linguistics.

Ferdinand De Saussure. 2011. *Course in general linguistics.* Columbia University Press.

Jesse Dodge, Gabriel Ilharco, Roy Schwartz, Ali Farhadi, Hannaneh Hajishirzi, and Noah Smith. 2020. Fine-tuning pretrained language models: Weight initializations, data orders, and early stopping. *arXiv preprint arXiv:2002.06305.*

Martha Gavidia, Patrick Lee, Anna Feldman, and Jing Peng. 2022. Cats are fuzzy pets: A corpus and analysis of potentially euphemistic terms. In *LREC 2022.*

Debanjan Ghosh, Avijit Vajpayee, and Smaranda Muresan. 2020. A report on the 2020 sarcasm detection shared task. *ACL 2020*, page 1.

Suchin Gururangan, Ana Marasović, Swabha Swayamdipta, Kyle Lo, Iz Beltagy, Doug Downey, and Noah A. Smith. 2020. Don't stop pretraining: Adapt language models to domains and tasks. In *Proceedings of the 58th Annual Meeting of the Association for Computational Linguistics*, pages 8342–8360, Online. Association for Computational Linguistics.

Jacob Devlin Ming-Wei Chang Kenton and Lee Kristina Toutanova. 2019. Bert: Pre-training of deep bidirectional transformers for language understanding. In *Proceedings of NAACL-HLT*, pages 4171–4186.

Yoon Kim. 2014. Convolutional neural networks for sentence classification. In *Proceedings of the 2014 Conference on Empirical Methods in Natural Language Processing (EMNLP)*, pages 1746–1751, Doha, Qatar. Association for Computational Linguistics.

George Lakoff and Mark Johnson. 2008. *Metaphors we live by.* University of Chicago press.

Yann LeCun, Léon Bottou, Yoshua Bengio, and Patrick Haffner. 1998. Gradient-based learning applied to document recognition. *Proceedings of the IEEE*, 86(11):2278–2324.

Patrick Lee, Martha Gavidia, Anna Feldman, and Jing Peng. 2022. Searching for pets: Using distributional and sentiment-based methods to find potentially euphemistic terms. In *Proceedings of the Second Workshop on Understanding Implicit and Underspecified Language.*

Yinhan Liu, Myle Ott, Naman Goyal, Jingfei Du, Mandar Joshi, Danqi Chen, Omer Levy, Mike Lewis, Luke Zettlemoyer, and Veselin Stoyanov. 2019. Roberta: A robustly optimized bert pretraining approach. *arXiv preprint arXiv:1907.11692.*

Ilya Loshchilov and Frank Hutter. 2018. Decoupled weight decay regularization. In *International Conference on Learning Representations.*

Daniel Loureiro, Francesco Barbieri, Leonardo Neves, Luis Espinosa Anke, and Jose Camacho-collados. 2022. TimeLMs: Diachronic language models from Twitter. In *Proceedings of the 60th Annual Meeting of the Association for Computational Linguistics: System Demonstrations*, pages 251–260, Dublin, Ireland. Association for Computational Linguistics.

Jonathan Matusitz. 2016. Euphemisms for terrorism: How dangerous are they? *Empedocles: European Journal for the Philosophy of Communication*, 7(2):225–237.

Tomas Mikolov, Ilya Sutskever, Kai Chen, Greg S Corrado, and Jeff Dean. 2013. Distributed representations of words and phrases and their compositionality. *Advances in neural information processing systems*, 26.

Dat Quoc Nguyen, Thanh Vu, and Anh Tuan Nguyen. 2020. BERTweet: A pre-trained language model for English tweets. In *Proceedings of the 2020 Conference on Empirical Methods in Natural Language Processing: System Demonstrations*, pages 9–14, Online. Association for Computational Linguistics.

Jeffrey Pennington, Richard Socher, and Christopher Manning. 2014. GloVe: Global vectors for word representation. In *Proceedings of the 2014 Conference on Empirical Methods in Natural Language Processing (EMNLP)*, pages 1532–1543, Doha, Qatar. Association for Computational Linguistics.

Lutz Prechelt. 1998. Early stopping-but when? In *Neural Networks: Tricks of the trade*, pages 55–69. Springer.

Colin Raffel, Noam Shazeer, Adam Roberts, Katherine Lee, Sharan Narang, Michael Matena, Yanqi Zhou, Wei Li, Peter J Liu, et al. 2020. Exploring the limits of transfer learning with a unified text-to-text transformer. *J. Mach. Learn. Res.*, 21(140):1–67.

Alexander Sboev, Ivan Moloshnikov, Alexander Naumov, Anastasia Levochkina, and Roman Rybka. 2021. The russian language corpus and a neural network to analyse internet tweet reports about covid-19.

Ashish Vaswani, Noam Shazeer, Niki Parmar, Jakob Uszkoreit, Llion Jones, Aidan N Gomez, Łukasz Kaiser, and Illia Polosukhin. 2017. Attention is all you need. *Advances in neural information processing systems*, 30.

Thomas Wolf, Lysandre Debut, Victor Sanh, Julien Chaumond, Clement Delangue, Anthony Moi, Pierric Cistac, Tim Rault, Remi Louf, Morgan Funtowicz, Joe Davison, Sam Shleifer, Patrick von Platen, Clara Ma, Yacine Jernite, Julien Plu, Canwen Xu, Teven Le Scao, Sylvain Gugger, Mariama Drame, Quentin Lhoest, and Alexander Rush. 2020. Transformers: State-of-the-art natural language processing. In *Proceedings of the 2020 Conference on Empirical Methods in Natural Language Processing: System Demonstrations*, pages 38–45, Online. Association for Computational Linguistics.

A Prompt Based Approach for Euphemism Detection

Abulimiti Maimaitituoheti, Yang Yong, Fan Xiaochao
Xinjiang Normal University, China
{1149654712, 68523593, 37769630}@qq.com

Abstract

Euphemism is an indirect way to express sensitive topics. People can comfortably communicate with each other about sensitive topics or taboos by using euphemisms. The Euphemism Detection Shared Task in the Third Workshop on Figurative Language Processing co-located with EMNLP 2022 provided a euphemism detection dataset that was divided into the train set and the test set. We made euphemism detection experiments by prompt tuning pre-trained language models on the dataset. We used RoBERTa as the pre-trained language model and created suitable templates and verbalizers for the euphemism detection task. Our approach achieved the third-best score in the euphemism detection shared task. This paper describes our model participating in the task.

1 Introduction

Euphemism is a common linguistic phenomenon that is indispensable in everyday communication. In daily communication, people often encounter some sensitive topics or taboos that are inconvenient to express directly, such as death, age, income, etc., and need to borrow some synonymous sentences to express them tactfully or use words that are related to the original meaning. The social function of euphemism enables people to express their thoughts more freely and to communicate easily and happily.

Euphemism detection is a classification task in natural language processing and it can be divided into phrase-level euphemism detection and sentence-level euphemism detection. In English, euphemisms consist of one or more words, for example, indigent is a euphemistic word that refers to a poor or needy person; deceased means a person who has died; a sex worker means a prostitute euphemistically. Phrase-level euphemism detection refers to the task of identifying euphemistic phrases in a sentence or paragraph. A model needs to recognize the euphemistic phrases in the target sentences. Phrase-level euphemism detection can be modeled as a token classification task. Sentence-level euphemism detection refers to the task of determining whether a sentence or a paragraph contains a euphemism. For example, the sentence "Give me a moment, I just need to run to the powder room." Contains a euphemistic phrase "powder room" which means toilet, so the sentence could be classified as euphemistic. A model needs to determine whether target sentences contain any euphemistic phrases. Sentence-level euphemism detection can be modeled as a sequence classification task.

The Euphemism Detection Shared Task in the Third Workshop on Figurative Language Processing co-located with EMNLP 2022 is a sentence-level euphemism detection task, which provides a sentence-level euphemism detection dataset based on GloWbE (Davies et al., 2015) dataset. The euphemism detection dataset consists of a total of 1965 sentences, among them 1382 sentences containing euphemistic terms and 777 sentences that don't contain euphemistic terms. The dataset is divided into a train set and a test set, the train set contains 1572 sentences with target labels, and the test set contains 393 sentences without target labels. The task requires participants to develop a model which can determine whether the target sentence contains any euphemistic terms. A model can train on the train set and predict the labels of the test set.

Prompt learning adds additional prompt information to the original input sentence and transforms it into cloze forms to make the pre-trained language model better understand and

Proceedings of the 3rd Workshop on Figurative Language Processing (FLP), pages 8 - 12
December 8, 2022 ©2022 Association for Computational Linguistics

process the sentence. Prompt learning unifies the training of downstream tasks with pre-training processes and avoids the pre-trained language models to forget some of the knowledge and tap more potential of them. By this, prompt learning improves the performance of the models in few-shot and zero-shot, or even full-shot tasks. So we developed a prompt learning-based euphemism detection model, using RoBERTa (Liu et al., 2019) as the pre-trained language model. We trained the model on the train set, then predict the labels of the test set by using it. Our model achieved an F1 score of 85.2% on the test set, the third highest among all participants.

2 Related Works

In recent years, people have made some explorations on euphemism detection, constructed some euphemism detection datasets, and made some efforts to recognize euphemistic phrases and sentences. In this section, we will introduce these works by phrase level and sentence level respectively.

2.1 Phrase-Level Euphemism Detection

Euphemisms consist of phrases, which means that recognizing euphemistic phrases is the direct way of euphemism detection research. So there has been relatively more work on phrase-level euphemism detection.

Magu et al. (2018) made research on euphemistic hate speech. Specifically, they collected 200000 tweets containing euphemistic code words and constructed a dataset, by using the Community detection analysis method they found some unknown euphemistic hate speech code words. Felt et al. (2020) constructed a dataset by manually annotating target phrases as euphemisms, dysphemism, or neutral and made x-phemism classification experiments by using sentiment lexicons and contextual sentiment analysis. As a result, experiments using contextual sentiment analysis achieved better results than experiments using sentiment lexicons. This illustrated that euphemisms are context-dependent and models relying on contexts are more efficient in euphemism detection. Zhu et al. (2021) investigated multi-word euphemistic phrase detection approaches automatically. They extracted suitable phrases from the original data and selected euphemistic phrase candidates utilizing word embedding similarities, then ranked candidate phrases by using Spanbert (Joshi et al., 2020). They achieved significant performance improvement on the euphemistic phrase detection task compared to baseline models. Lee et al. (2022) made an investigation to find potentially euphemistic terms by steps. Firstly, they extracted phrases from original data, then filtered phrases related to sensitive topics by calculating the cosine similarity between the phrases and a list of words representing sensitive topics. After that, they paraphrased quality phrases using the top 25 most similar words as output by word2vec. Finally, they ranked phrases by using a RoBERTa-base model trained on tweets for sentiment analysis and offensive language identification.

2.2 Sentence-Level Euphemism Detection

Sentence-level euphemism detection is another direction in euphemism detection research, which needs to determine whether a sentence contains any euphemism, but there is little research in this direction.

Gavidia et al. (2022) made a list of common euphemistic phrases, which contained a total of 184 euphemistic phrases. Then selected 1382 euphemistic sentences and another 583 not euphemistic sentences according to the list from GloWbE dataset, and constructed a sentence-level euphemism detection dataset. They made sentiment analysis using RoBERTa on the dataset and found that the sentiment and offensiveness of euphemistic phrases have some differences compared to their literal meanings.

3 System Overview

Prompt-tuning is a method of using pre-trained language models, which requires transforming downstream tasks into cloze forms so that the pre-training process of pre-trained language models and the training process of downstream tasks can be unified. The prompt-tuning method can unlock the potential of pre-trained language models and it is a better few-shot learning method compared with the fine-tuning method. Considering these advantages of prompt-tuning, we conducted our euphemism detection experiments using it.

3.1 System Architecture

The architecture of our euphemism detection system is shown in figure 1.

Figure 1: The architecture of the euphemism detection system based on prompt-tuning.

In figure 1, Input refers to the target text inputted into the model. The template is a module that transforms the input text into a cloze form by adding extra characters and <mask> tags to the head and end of the input text. PLM stands for pre-trained Language Model, in this paper we used RoBERTa as the pre-trained language model. Verbalizer is a module that maps predicted words to target labels, it is mainly composed of a word-label dictionary and mapping function. Output is the target label predicted by the model, in our euphemism detection experiment, the output is a label consisting of 0 or 1, 0 stands for not euphemistic, and 1 stands for euphemistic.

3.2 Template For Euphemism Detection

The template is an important module in prompt learning, the quality of the template has a great effect on the performance of the model. So people made a lot of explorations on the method of creating templates, including manually creating, automatically creating, and mixed approaches to the above two methods. We made many experiments using different templates, including manually created templates, prefix-tuning templates (Li et al. 2021), P-tuning templates (Liu et al., 2021), and ptr templates (Han et al., 2021). Through experiments, we found that ptr templates perform better than other templates on the euphemism detection task, so we selected ptr template as the template for our euphemism detection model. Ptr template is a hybrid template using the manually and automatically template-creating methods together. Specifically, a basic template should be created manually, and optimized by logic rules, so we created some candidate basic templates for the euphemism detection task as follows:

<text> Is this euphemistic? <mask>

<text> This is <mask> sentence.

<mask> - <text>

<text> This is <mask>.

In these templates, <text> stands for the original input text, and <mask> is the token that should be predicted by the model. We made experiments using these candidate basic templates and found that template "<text> This is <mask> sentence." achieved the best performance among them, so we selected it as the final basic template for our euphemism detection model.

3.3 Verbalizer For Euphemism Detection

Another important module of prompt learning is the verbalizer, the function of the verbalizer is mapping the predicted words to target labels, in our euphemism detection experiments the verbalizer will map the predicted words into one of the euphemistic or not euphemistic labels. Like the template, there are a lot of ways to create verbalizers, including manually created verbalizer, knowledgeable verbalizer (Hu et al., 2022), and ptr verbalizer (Han et al., 2021). We made euphemism detection experiments using different verbalizers and found that the ptr verbalizer performed better than other verbalizers, so we selected ptr verbalizer as our verbalizer.

In our euphemism detection task, we only need to detect the euphemistic sentences and don't need to detect not euphemistic sentences, so we made some changes to the ptr verbalizer, and determine whether the predicted word is in the words list of the euphemistic label before mapping the predicted words to the target label if it is, then maps the predicted word to euphemistic label, else then maps the predicted word to not euphemistic label. By this, we reduced the burden of the model and we only need to create a word list for the euphemistic labels.

After selecting the ptr verbalizer and making some changes to it, we created some candidate verbalizers as follows:

euphemistic, tactful, periphrastic

yes, yeah

The verbalizer "yes, yeah" is for the template "<text> Is this euphemistic? <mask>" and other templates use the verbalizer "euphemistic, tactful, periphrastic". For example, when we use the template "<text> This is <mask> sentence." and the verbalizer "euphemistic, tactful, periphrastic", if the predicted word is one of the words in the list "euphemistic, tactful, periphrastic", the predicted word will be mapped to euphemistic label, else the predicted word will be mapped to not euphemistic label.

4 Experiments

In this section, we will introduce the specifics of the experiments, including dataset statistics, coding framework, hyperparameters of experiments, results of experiments and analysis, etc.

4.1 Dataset Statistics

There are some hyperparameters like the maximum sentence length inputted the pre-trained language model that has much relations with the dataset features. So we made some statistical

Table 1: Statistics of text length in the dataset

analysis to the dataset. The details of the statistical analysis are shown in table 1.

Dataset	Avg len	Max len	len>192	Total	Percentage
Train	83.13	381	20	1572	1.27%
Test	83.36	247	3	393	0.76%

In table 1, avg len stands for the average number of words in the sentence, max len stands for the number of words in the longest sentence, len>192 stands for the number of sentences that contain words more than 192, and total stands for the total number of the sentence in the dataset, the percentage stands for the ratio of the number of sentences longer than 192 among all the sentences.

4.2 Coding Framework

OpenPrompt (Ding et al., 2022) is an open-source prompt learning framework based on PyTorch (Paszke et al., 2019), which provided the implementation of many templates and verbalizers, including manually created templates, prefix-tuning templates, p-tuning templates, ptr templates, manually created verbalizers, knowledgeable verbalizers, ptr verbalizers, etc. Relying on OpenPrompt, we could implement our prompt learning experiments by conveniently switching among the different templates and verbalizers. So we selected OpenPrompt as our prompt learning framework and coded our model using it.

4.3 Hyperparameters

Table 2: Hyperparameters of the model

From table 1, we can see that the proportion of the sentences containing more than 192 words is about 1%, this means that 192 is a proper value

Hyperparameter	Value
Max sequence length	192
Learning rate	0.00003
Weight decay	0.01
Number warmup steps	500
Number of epochs	5

for the maximum length of the sentence inputted to the
pre-trained language model, so we set it as 192. There are some other hyperparameters like learning rate, weight decay, etc. The details are shown in table 2.

4.4 Results And Analysis

Using RoBERTa-base as our pre-trained language model, we implemented euphemism detection experiments on the euphemism detection dataset. We trained the prompt-based euphemism detection model on the train dataset and let it predict the labels of the test data. By training the model 5 epochs, achieved relatively good results

Table 3: Details of the results of the euphemism detection experiment

on the test data, and ranked third among all participants. The details of the results are shown in Table 3.

Type	Precision	Recall	F1
Euphemistic	0.904	0.924	0.914
Not euphemistic	0.811	0.769	0.789
macro avg	0.858	0.847	0.852

From table 3 we can see that the precision, recall, and fl score of the euphemistic label is better than the not euphemistic label. We think that because the dataset is an unbalanced dataset, contains more euphemistic sentences and fewer not euphemistic sentences, model learning is biased toward euphemistic sentences.

5 Conclusions

In this paper, we described the euphemism detection model based on prompt learning and the details of euphemism detection experiments based on this model. We selected RoBERTa as our pre-trained language model, selected the ptr template and ptr verbalizer, made some reasonable changes to the ptr verbalizer, implemented euphemism detection experiments using this model, and achieved better results on the euphemism detection dataset.

References

Davies, M. and Fuchs, R. 2015. *Expanding horizons in the study of world englishes with the 1.9 billion word global web-based english corpus (glowbe).* English World-Wide, 36(1):1–28.

Yinhan Liu, Myle Ott, Naman Goyal, Jingfei Du, Mandar Joshi, Danqi Chen, Omer Levy, Mike Lewis, Luke Zettlemoyer, Veselin Stoyanov. 2019. *Roberta: A Robustly Optimized BERT Pretraining Approach.* arXiv:1907.11692 [cs.CL].

Rijul Magu, Jiebo Luo. 2018. *Determining Code Words in Euphemistic Hate Speech Using Word Embedding Networks.* Proceedings of the 2nd Workshop on Abusive Language Online (ALW2), pages: 93–100.

Christian Felt, Ellen Riloff . 2020. *Recognizing Euphemisms and Dysphemisms Using Sentiment Analysis.* Proceedings of the Second Workshop on Figurative Language Processing, pages: 136–145.

Wanzheng Zhu, Suma Bhat. 2021. *Euphemistic Phrase Detection by Masked Language Model.* Findings of the Association for Computational Linguistics: EMNLP 2021, pages: 163–168.

Mandar Joshi, Danqi Chen, Yinhan Liu, Daniel S Weld, Luke Zettlemoyer, and Omer Levy. 2020. *Spanbert:Improving pre-training by representing and predicting spans.* Transactions of the Association for Computational Linguistics, 8:64–77.

Patrick Lee, Martha Gavidia, Anna Feldman, Jing Peng. 2022. *Searching for PETs: Using Distributional and Sentiment-Based Methods to Find Potentially Euphemistic Terms.* Proceedings of the Second Workshop on Understanding Implicit and Underspecified Language, pages: 22–32.

Martha Gavidia, Patrick Lee, Anna Feldman, and Jing Peng. 2022. *Cats are fuzzy pets: A corpus and analysis of potentially euphemistic terms.* arXiv preprint arXiv:2205.02728.

Xiang Lisa Li, Percy Liang. 2021. *Prefix-Tuning: Optimizing Continuous Prompts for Generation.* Proceedings of the 59th Annual Meeting of the Association for Computational Linguistics and the 11th International Joint Conference on Natural Language Processing (Volume 1: Long Papers), pages: 4582–4597.

Xiao Liu, Yanan Zheng, Zhengxiao Du, Ming Ding, Yujie Qian, Zhilin Yang, Jie Tang. 2021. *GPT Understands, Too.* arXiv:2103.10385 [cs.CL].

Xu Han, Weilin Zhao, Ning Ding, Zhiyuan Liu, Maosong Sun. 2021. *PTR: Prompt Tuning with Rules for Text Classification.* arXiv:2105.11259 [cs.CL].

Shengding Hu, Ning Ding, Huadong Wang, Zhiyuan Liu, Jingang Wang, Juanzi Li, Wei Wu, Maosong Sun. 2022. *Knowledgeable Prompt-tuning: Incorporating Knowledge into Prompt Verbalizer for Text Classification.* Proceedings of the 60th Annual Meeting of the Association for Computational Linguistics (Volume 1: Long Papers), pages: 2225–2240.

Ning Ding, Shengding Hu, Weilin Zhao, Yulin Chen, Zhiyuan Liu, Haitao Zheng, Maosong Sun. 2022. *OpenPrompt: An Open-source Framework for Prompt-learning.* Proceedings of the 60th Annual Meeting of the Association for Computational Linguistics: System Demonstrations, pages: 105–113.

Paszke, Adam and Gross, Sam and Massa, Francisco and Lerer, Adam and Bradbury, James and Chanan, Gregory and Killeen, Trevor and Lin, Zeming and Gimelshein, Natalia and Antiga, Luca and Desmaison, Alban and Kopf, Andreas and Yang, Edward and DeVito, Zachary and Raison, Martin and Tejani, Alykhan and Chilamkurthy, Sasank and Steiner, Benoit and Fang, Lu and Bai, Junjie and Chintala, Soumith. 2019. *PyTorch: An Imperative Style, High-Performance Deep Learning Library.* Advances in Neural Information Processing Systems 32, pages: 8024—8035.

Transfer Learning Parallel Metaphor using Bilingual Embeddings

Maria Berger
Ruhr University Bochum
maria.berger-a21@rub.de

Abstract

Automated metaphor detection in languages other than English is highly restricted as training corpora are comparably rare. One way to overcome this problem is transfer learning. This paper gives an overview on transfer learning techniques applied to NLP. We first introduce types of transfer learning, then we present work focusing on: i) transfer learning with cross-lingual embeddings; ii) transfer learning in machine translation; and iii) transfer learning using pre-trained transformer models. The paper is complemented by first experiments that make use of bilingual embeddings generated from different sources of parallel data: We i) present the preparation of a parallel Gold corpus; ii) examine the embeddings spaces to search for metaphoric words cross-lingually; iii) run first experiments in transfer learning German metaphor from English labeled data only. Results show that finding data sources for bilingual embeddings training and the vocabulary covered by these embeddings is critical for learning metaphor cross-lingually.

1 Introduction

In the literature, figurative language is instantiated in many different ways. One of the most challenging tasks of figurative language detection, however, is metaphor identification. Dorst (2015) finds that up to almost 20% of words in a text are metaphor-related. However, most work in the field is focused strongly on the English language.

As such, early work on computational metaphor interpretation was performed by Kintsch. Kintsch (2000) uses **Latent Semantic Analysis** to adjust the meaning of a predicate P when it is applied to an argument A. In Kintsch's theory the predicate is what we typically call a metaphor's source (Lakoff and Johnson, 1980) and the argument is its target (e.g., selfies [target] go viral [source]). Before word embeddings were used based on implementations such as word2vec, LSA helped to generate high-dimensional semantic spaces using singular value decomposition for dimension reduction. Kintsch uses cosine similarity to compare a metaphorical predication (i.e., its numerical representation) to some of its semantic surroundings.

Today, semantic information mainly is encoded by word embeddings (Mikolov et al., 2013). Gao et al. (2018) recently presented work of metaphor prediction using an RNN classifier. Together with different types of embeddings vectors, the authors perform **neural metaphor detection**, in a sequence labeling setup, and in a classification setup.

One of the most famous works regarding the development of training and testing data sets is delivered by Steen et al. (2010). The authors present a method for the identification of metaphor in language at the word-level based on methodological and **empirical corpus-linguistic work** in English and Dutch. The method formulates manual instructions and is a refinement based on the metaphor identification procedure (MIP) presented by (Group, 2007). The extended annotation version (MIPVU) is developed at Vrije Universiteit Amsterdam (VUA) and demonstrates case studies addressing metaphor in English and Dutch news amongst others.

While there is a lot of room for improvement in the field of metaphor detection and interpretation, especially languages other than English lack resources and successful algorithms. Transfer learning (TL) is one way to overcome this issue. But work in this field is rare.

Tsvetkov et al. (2014) use lexical semantic features of words participating metaphoric construction. The authors use **transfer learning** based on bilingual dictionaries to find metaphoric expressions across languages. Their work supports the consensus that metaphors are rather conceptual.

More recently, Aghazadeh et al. (2022) perform **probing of metaphor**-annotated data sets. Next to other tasks, they also probe for cross-lingual

Proceedings of the 3rd Workshop on Figurative Language Processing (FLP), pages 13 - 23
December 8, 2022 ©2022 Association for Computational Linguistics

performance using a multilingual pre-trained language model and a data set of four high-resource languages (English, Russian, Spanish, Farsi).

In this paper, we present different strategies to overcome resource gaps using transfer learning strategies. We start with a literature overview before we perform first experiments to assess these techniques for the German language.

2 Literature on transfer learning

2.1 Types of transfer learning

TL in general refers to techniques applied across different domains and languages. Cross-language (CL) learning refers specifically to the transfer from one language to another while domain adaption (DA) rather showcases the transfer of a technique from one domain to another within the same language. In their comprehensive survey, Weiss et al. (2016) differentiate (among others) between instance-based and feature-based techniques of TL.

Instance-based transfer: Instance-based TL infers knowledge based on the behaviour of instances in a source versus target domain. As such, it attempts to reduce the marginal distribution difference ($P(X_t) \neq P(X_s)$, e.g., word freq.) by reweighting the samples in the source domain to correct for distribution differences (Asgarian, 2018).

One example for instance-based TL is Asgarian et al. (2018). For training, the authors only use information from relevant re-weighted instances in the target domain. The target samples are selected upfront based on the uncertainty (distance of sample x to the decision boundary) in a binary model trained on source and target samples. Also, Jiang and Zhai (2007) find relations between different instance distributions in source and target. They formulate requirements for instance distribution and classification function different in source and target. Then, they solve for these differences using semi-supervised instance-weighting. Dai et al. (2008) migrate knowledge—from labeled data—from a source feature space to a target feature space. The authors show that one can use for example labeled text data to train a model for image classification when image labels are rare.

Feature-based transfer: Feature-based TL aims to reduce the gap between the marginal ($P(X_t) \neq P(X_s)$, e.g., word frequencies) and conditional distributions ($P(Y_t|X_t) \neq P(Y_s|X_s)$, typically Y-labels) of source and target domain (Long et al., 2013). In asymmetric feature-based TL, often a transformation ϕ_s/ϕ_t from source to target is employed (Long et al., 2013), which especially works well when both domains share the same label spaces. In symmetric feature based TL, features are transferred from source and target respectively into a common space. Pan et al. (2010) transfer components across domains into a reproducing kernel Hilbert Space using maximum mean discrepancy as a distance measure. In the sub-space represented by that Hilbert Space, data properties are preserved and data distributions of different domains can still remain similar. This enables the training of classifiers in a source domain for use in a target domain. Also Duan et al. (2012) consider the use of source domain and target domain data represented by heterogeneous features of different dimensions. Two projection matrices help to transform data from source and target into a common subspace, and two feature mapping functions use these projections to augment the data in that new space.

2.2 Task-oriented techniques

Following, we give an overview on TL techniques from a more task-driven perspective.

Cross-lingual word embeddings: Often, word embeddings are induced from a source language cross-lingually (CL) into a target language. A such, Upadhyay et al. (2016) perform an empirical comparison of different approaches for inducing CL embeddings, each with a different degree of supervision: First, a simple bilingual Skip-Gram model (Luong et al., 2015) that uses word-aligned corpora to learn contexts for words in different languages; Second, a bilingual compositional model (Hermann and Blunsom, 2014), which finds bilingual embeddings for parallel sentences—each represented by the embedding of its constituent words—using minimized Euclidean length between two candidate sentences; Third, bilingual word vector training based on bilingual documents that upfront were randomly generated from a document-aligned corpora (Vulić and Moens, 2015).

Shi et al. (2015) study matrix co-factorization to learn word embeddings language-independently from distributed meaning. They first induce contexts based on word frequencies from parallel sentences. Then, they maximize similarity of word pairs in multiple languages using probabilistic machine-translation. Results in document classification show that the technique is efficient to encode CL knowledge to create CL word embeddings.

Klementiev et al. (2012) start from an annotated, well-resourced language to study word representations for joint languages. They treat word representation learning as a multitask problem where each task represents a word. Task relatedness is derived from co-occurrence statistics in bi-texts. Their approach partly outperforms MT baselines.

Cross-lingual embeddings can be understood as instance-based transfer since merging data sources from two languages modifies the distribution of words in the new embeddings space. However, when applying it to a classification problem, such as metaphor prediction, it also is an example for feature-based transfer, because we attempt to reduce the cap between the marginal contribution of the words in the embeddings representation following the conditional distributions of the labels.

Using pre-trained models in NLP tasks: Durrani et al. (2021) investigate how fine-tuning of neural models affects the learned knowledge in linguistic downstream tasks. Performing their test on pre-trained models such as BERT and RoBERTa, they use diagnostic classifiers on the layer-level and neuron-level. The authors find out that while linguistic knowledge is distributed in the entire pre-trained network, after fine-tuning it becomes localized in shallower layers, whereas deeper layers are reserved for task specific knowledge. Ahmad et al. (2021) show that explicitly providing language syntax and training mBERT using an auxiliary objective to encode the universal dependency tree structure helps cross-lingual transfer. The authors perform experiments on text classification, QA, NER, and task-oriented semantic parsing. The experiment results show that syntax-augmented mBERT boosts transfer performance with 3.9 and 3.1 points in PAWS-X and MLQA benchmarks.

Typically, TL using transformers is applied together with a fine-tuning on data samples in the target language. Hence, it is a candidate for instance-based transfer learning where the marginal distribution of the source language's instances is reweighted towards the target language.

Transfer learning in neural machine translation: Neural machine translation often approaches TL by first training a "parent" model for a high-resource language pair and then fine-tune it on a low-resource language pair ("child") by simply replacing the training corpus (Kocmi and Bojar, 2018; Zoph et al., 2016). Kocmi and Bojar (2018) find that this child model can perform better than a low-resource trained baseline even for languages with different alphabets. Similarly, Zoph et al. (2016) improve baseline models by 5.6% of BLEU score on low-resource language pairs. In a different setup, Nguyen and Chiang (2017) use parallel data from two related low-resource language pairs. A model is trained on the first language pair, then its parameters are transferred to another model where training is continued. Imankulova et al. (2019) improve TL in a Japanese–Russian pair by more than 3.7 BLEU points over a baseline. English serves as pivot language to train a multilingual model. They then fine-tune on in-domain data. Another translation example is text-to-speech (TTS) generation. To apply TTS for low-resource target languages Tu et al. (2019) transfer knowledge from a high-resource language by mapping linguistic symbols between source and target. This mapping preserves pronunciation information in the transferring process. Experiments show that 15 minutes of paired data is sufficient to build a TTS system.

In this paper, we attempt to classify German language metaphor from training a classifier using English language training data. The English language training data is represented by bilingual embeddings. In future work, we will then also test pre-trained transformers as well as techniques from machine translation.

3 Method Overview

In the following sections (i.e., Sec. 4 to Sec. 7), we present a procedure to TL for metaphor prediction. We start with a description of the metaphor corpus that we use as Gold data. Once it is completely translated and annotated for metaphor source words in the German translation (Sec. 4), we can use it for other evaluation setups too. Right now, we have 500 samples finished and use them for neighborhood retrieval (c.f., Sec. 6) and classification testing (c.f., Sec. 7) In Section 5, we introduce the source data that we build our bilingual embeddings upon and describe a merging strategy of the parallel data. We also present different approaches to handle compound metaphor sources in the target language and how they affect the distance to the English language counterparts (in the embeddings space). The latter is performed on 500 samples of the metaphor corpus. In Sec. 6, we discuss the training of the bilingual embeddings after we perform a retrieval of a metaphoric German language

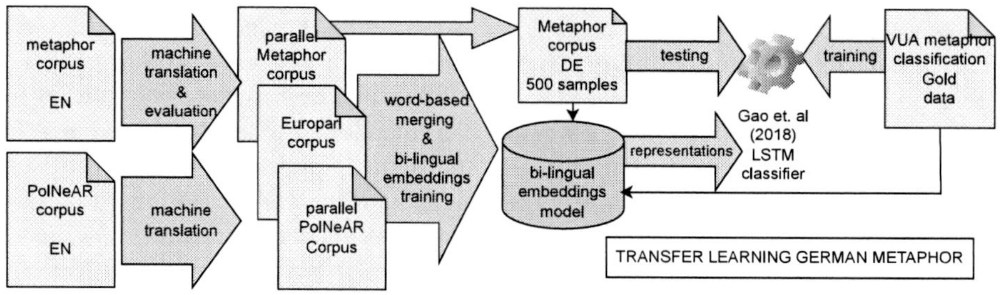

Figure 1: Overview of corpus translation and alignment in order to obtain bilingual embeddings for metaphor prediction training

word within the English language word's embeddings space. In Sec. 7 we present first results on predicting metaphor in a target language when only labeled training data in the source language is available. We use 500 already annotated samples in the target language for testing. Figure 1 shows the overview of the procedure.

4 Metaphor Gold corpus

The corpus: A first step is to create a Gold corpus to have a test set available for all sorts of techniques, be it supervised, unsupervised or transfer. Hence, we start from the corpus of Gordon et al. (2015). It origins from sources such as news articles, blog posts, and online forums. It consists of more than 1700 sentences using metaphoric language. The authors propose the use of conceptual schema to represent scenarios of metaphor usage. They recognize 70 source domains which again are grouped into 14 ontological categories. The corpus is manually validated and contains annotations for a metaphor's target, a metaphor's source, their associated linguistic and conceptual metaphors and the metaphors' lexical trigger. The linguistic metaphor annotation refers to terms from the sentence itself, so we can use this information to find the corresponding figurative label for a term. We prefer this corpus over the famous VUA corpus (Steen et al., 2010), especially because we are also interested in seeing the effect of having training and testing data from different domains (see Sec. 7). Further, having a German-translated and annotated version in place, we can add more diverse data sets to the community. A last reason is that the entire data set (once mirrored to German) offers a good sample size for tuning and evaluating further neural-based classifiers.

Corpus preparation: We prepare the data for our experiments as follows. First, we translate the sentences of the corpus into German making use of contemporary machine translation techniques.[1] We evaluate a sample of 500 sentences manually by one German native. Table 1 shows the results grouping them into three categories; i) high: denoting a perfectly translated sentence that preserves the figurative meaning while not affecting any rule of well-formed syntax nor leading to a "bad" metaphor (c.f. Harati et al. (2021) for criteria judgements on good metaphors); ii) mid: good translation with skipped metaphoric language (15) or a falsely translated (stop) word (31); and iii) low: sentence was not successfully translated (most often the last part of very long sentences). Considering the fact that the majority of sentences is very well translated, in some cases just one word is effected, and only very few translated sentences are ill-formed, we simply work with the entire data set. We also metaphor-annotate these 500 samples. Precisely, we identify the German language metaphor source word.[2]

5 Bi-text for cross-lingual embeddings

Motivation: We follow the idea that metaphoric words often stay robust or conceptual across languages (Stowe et al., 2021; Shutova and Teufel, 2010; Yan et al., 2010). To obtain more resources for languages other than English, we can apply the concept of transfer learning to make use of information of the semantic environment of words (also metaphoric words) to be transferred to the target language. So, starting with an annotated English

[1]Using Google Translate with settings source language English, target language German, and operation type document: `https://translate.google.com/?hl=de&sl=en&tl=de&op=docs`

[2]We plan to annotate the entire German part of that corpus for metaphor sources to fine-tune and evaluate transformer-based models with these Gold data too. When finished, and with the agreement by Gordon et al. (2015) we will also publish this corpus.

quality	example	#
high	EN: I will be out in the city today, feeling the [...] thrust of blood, the apple-red circulation of democracy, [...]	441
	DE: Ich werde heute draußen in der Stadt sein und den [...] Blutstrom spüren, den apfelroten Kreislauf der Demokratie, [...]	
mid	EN: [...] so vital to the smooth flow of taxation within the United States.	46
	DE: [...] die für den reibungslosen Ablauf der Besteuerung in den Vereinigten Staaten so wichtig ist.	
low	EN: [...] to assist the Government of Colombia protect its democracy from United States-designated foreign terrorist organizations [...]	13
	DE: [...] um die kolumb. Regierung beim Schutz ihrer Demokratie vor den USA zu unterstützen. ausgewiesene ausländische Terrororganisa [...]	
total		500

Table 1: Evaluation of a subset of machine translated Metaphor corpus; The medium example is well translated, but does not contain metaphor anymore

metaphor corpus (for example the metaphor corpus by Stowe et al. (2021) or the VUA corpus) and some parallel data, we can predict metaphor in German language text.

Parallel data: We run experiments using our Gold corpus of parallel metaphor to apply the concept of cross-lingual embeddings. As shown above, the technique is efficient for tasks in which semantic knowledge is needed across languages. However, our Gold data is mainly for testing purposes in the classification setup. To train bilingual embeddings, we also need bigger parallel data. We use following bigger corpora:

- The English/German part of Europarl Parallel Corpus (Europarl) (Koehn, 2005)[3]
- The training data share of the Political News Attribution Relations Corpus (PolNeAR) (Newell et al., 2018)[4] to conceive a news corpus which's content is more comparable to the one of the metaphor corpus itself. PolNeAR contains 17,292 sentences. We also translate this corpus using contemporary MT.

We combine the parallel metaphor corpus with the Europarl Parallel corpus and the PolNeAR corpus in different setups. We train the bilingual embeddings using Gensim's word2vec implementation.[5]

Merging procedure: Typically text sources for training bilingual embeddings are in a way aligned or merged (Vulić and Moens, 2015; Luong et al., 2015; Hermann and Blunsom, 2014). We generate bilingual merged text data designing a simple zip-like merging algorithm that takes the words of two sentences (English and German) as arguments. In case one sentence is longer than the other, the factor of this ratio is used to align multiple words from the longer sentence towards the shorter one. See Alg. 1 for details. We remove stop words[6] before applying the zip-merge algorithm to the Metaphor, the PolNeAR, and the whole Europarl corpus.

Algorithm 1: Merging of English and German sentences

Input: $E \leftarrow$ word token list of an English language sentence
Input: $G \leftarrow$ word token list of the German translation
Output: $EG \leftarrow$ merged token list
Ensure: $E \geq G$

```
factor = round(|E|/|G|);
j = 0;
for i in |G| do
    EG = EG ∪ G_i ;    /*i starting with 1*/
    while factor * i > j ≥ factor * (i − 1) do
        EG = EG ∪ E_j;
        j = j + 1
    end
end
```

Handling compounds and derivatives: Handling compounds is a challenging matter. Our target language is famous for shipping with an extraordinary compositional nature especially concerning nouns. We count 68 compounds in our target language data set's metaphor sources (61 nouns and 7 verbs).

Cordeiro et al. (2016) handle English compound words by comparing the embedding of a compound with the embedding of its components' normalized sum. Their hypothesis is that if the angle between both embedding vectors is small then the compound's meaning is literal otherwise its meaning is idiomatic.

We decompose our compounds manually. Then, we retrieve three versions of them in the embeddings spaces that we compare later on with the English language counter word: i) the compound itself[7] (compound std), ii) the averaged vector of its components (components av.), and iii) the nor-

[3] https://www.statmt.org/europarl/

[4] https://github.com/networkdynamics/PolNeAR

[5] https://pypi.org/project/gensim/

[6] For German: https://stopwords.net/german-de/; for English we apply the stop word list delivered with the scikit-learn Python package

[7] This often falls out of vocab

malized sum of its components (Cordeiro et al., 2016) (components norm sum). For derivatives (verbs) we consider i) the finite verb form only (finite), and ii) the infinitive (infinite). We compare these vectors then with the word vector from the metaphor source of the English language text (see next section).

6 Training cross-lingual embeddings

Before we develop a supervised training setup with our data at hand (next section), it is important to learn about the potential contexts offered by cross-lingual embeddings. Therefore, we first test different setups of cross-lingual embeddings to retrieve the distances between a metaphoric word in an English language text and its German counterpart in the target language.

Using 500 manually annotated samples of our (parallel) metaphor corpus, we now retrieve the German counter word given an English language metaphoric word in the embeddings spaces trained from different parallel data setups:

- the metaphor corpus only (Metaphor); train vectors of length 150 with a min. frequency of 2 for 5 epochs
- the metaphor corpus and the PolNeAR corpus (Metaphor+PolNeAR); train vectors of length 150 with a min. frequency of 2 for 5 epochs
- the metaphor corpus & the first 100,000 sentences (to have a comparable data set) of Europarl corpus (Metaphor+Europarl 100K); train vectors of length 150 with a min. frequency of 2 for 5 epochs
- the metaphor corpus & Europarl corpus (Metaphor+Europarl); we train with vectors of length 300 with a min. frequency of 20 for 5 epochs, because this data set is much bigger then the previous data sets

Figure 2 shows the distribution of the German metaphoric word among the nearest neighbors of a metaphoric word from the English data. All corpora except the small metaphor corpus show an inverted bell curve meaning that most of the metaphors have their German counterpart among the 100 nearest neighbors or beyond their 10,000 nearest neighbors. The metaphor data (blue) rather show a bell distribution of the metaphoric words in the target language. However, we only added the blue curve for comparison reasons. The distributions of English and German metaphoric words in

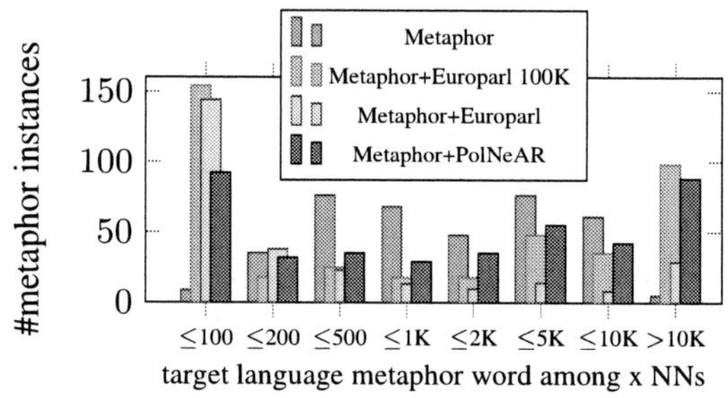

Figure 2: Distribution of metaphors which's German language metaphor source word are within the k-NNs of the English language source words

the embeddings space gives first insights into how they are represented in the bilingual embeddings' vocabulary, and hence, in the language's semantics.

Fig. 3a shows a scatter plot of the distribution of cosine similarities between the metaphors' sources in English and German respectively in the metaphor corpus. The vast majority of values is very close to one. This is especially because the vocabulary of this model is not big, and most words are in close neighborhood of the metaphor source word.

Fig. 3b shows a plot of cosine similarities distributed between the metaphors sources in English and German respectively in the metaphor corpus and PolNeAR. As PolNeAR is about ten times as big as Metaphor, we can see the data points are moving more towards zero being not as similar anymore.

Fig. 3c shows cosine similarities distributed in Metaphor and Europarl 100K. We encounter a much lower oov-rate (min-freq of 2). We also see that the normalized sum for component combination achieves higher similarities with the English metaphor sources than the averages do. Even though we do not have many data points here, we still learn that compounds are somewhat difficult to associate to the English source words. Hence, we plan to test the impact of decomposed compounds in the test data once our entire Gold corpus is finished[8]

In the next section, we use our bilingually trained embeddings[9] in a TL-classification task. We find out experimentally that a mix of Metaphor, PolNeAR, and Europarl with a minimum frequency of 5 and lower-cased embeddings sources covers most

[8]For other corpus combinations we do not show scatter plots since similarity decreases with vocabulary growth.

[9]Using a window of 5, five epochs, and 300 dimensions to match default values

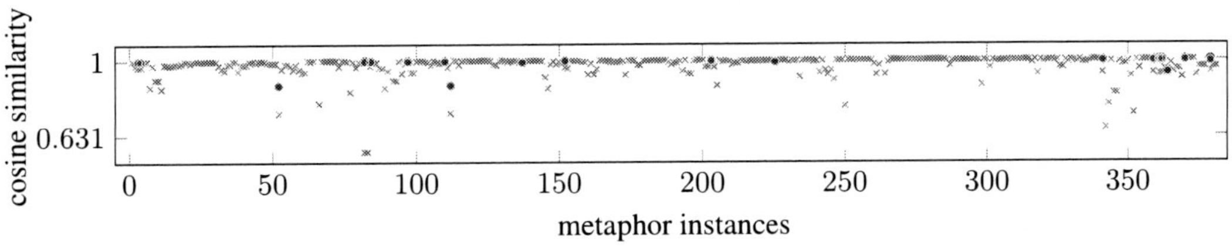

(a) **Metaphor:** 381 data points displayed; 104 oov; 15 no metaphor in target; y-axis logarithmic

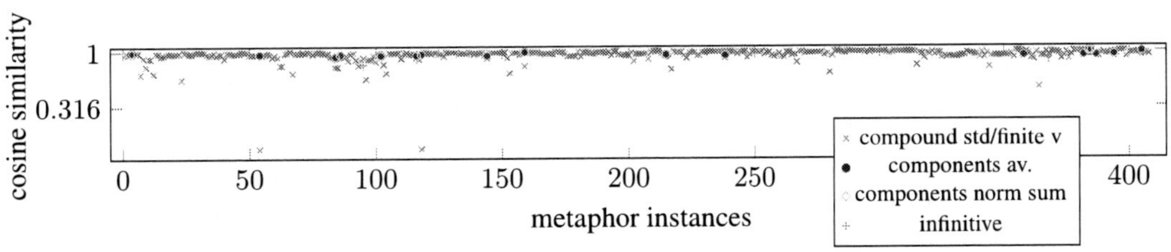

(b) **Metaphor+PolNeAR:** 408 data points displayed; 77 oov; 15 no metaphor in target language; y-axis logarithmic

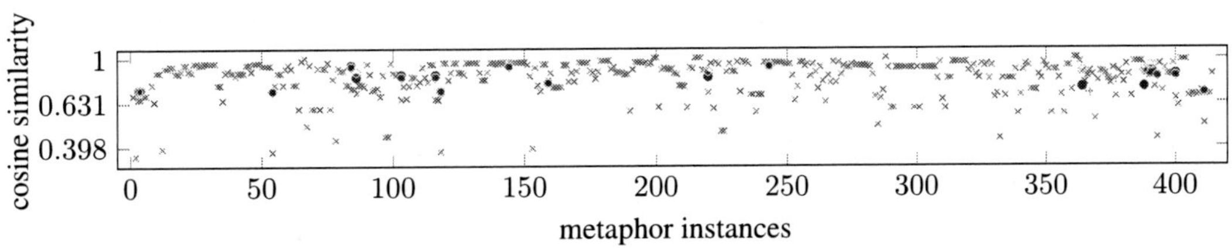

(c) **Metaphor+Europarl 100K:** 414 data points displayed; 71 oov; 15 no metaphor in target; y-axis logarithmic

Figure 3: Distribution of cosine-based similarities between a metaphor source word in EN and DE

of the vocabulary in the training and test data (c.f., Tab. 2).

embedding sources	min f	#voc
Metaphor+PolNeAR	2	42,353
Meta+Europarl 100K lc	5	30,768
Meta+PolNeAR+Euro 100k	5	42,008
Meta+PolNeAR+Euro 100k lc	5	39,229
Meta+Europarl	20	68,506
Meta+PolNeAR+Euro lc	5	139,356

Table 2: Vocab sizes of different embeddings sources; using Metaphor, PolNeAR, Euro(parl) (100,000 sentences) l(ower)c(ased) next to min(imum) f(requnecy) and voc(ab size)

7 TL with cross-lingual embeddings

Experimental setup: Inspired by Gao et al. (2018), we use the VUA corpus (Steen et al., 2010) together with our bilingual embeddings to perform cross-lingual metaphor prediction. This means, we train the model from Gao et al. (2018) as presented in their work (the authors use GloVe embeddings (Pennington et al., 2014) and ELMo embeddings (Peters et al., 1802) with a bidirectional LSTM classifier), then we use our German metaphor data set as test set. Our test data consist of a balanced data set of sentences labeled with 1 (when it contains a main verb that is metaphoric; 259), and with 0 (when it is not; 198). The index of the respective verb is handed over as well.

We run four setups: i) the baseline approach training/testing on VUA using GloVe embeddings (Gao et al., 2018) (no transfer); ii) the same setup using our embeddings instead of GloVe (no transfer); iii) our embeddings testing on the English part of the Metaphor corpus (no transfer); and iv) our embeddings testing on the German part of the Metaphor corpus (transfer).

Results and discussion: Table 3 shows that our embeddings do not address the vocabulary of the training and testing data as well as GloVe does. Still, the bilingual embeddings are capable to represent contexts well as F1-scores rather increase than drop for English (row 2 and 3 compared to row 1). Accuracy, however drops drastically especially

embed	voc addr	voc size	train	sample size	test	sample size	val f1	p	r	f1	ac
GloVe (reprod.)	17,941	18,695	VUA	17,240	VUA	5,873	57	59	53	56	75
M+P+E	11,480	18,695	VUA	17,240	VUA	5,873	52	56	69	62	75
M+P+E	10,862	17,301	VUA	17,240	M-En	480 (284:196)	52	65	66	65	59
M+P+E	11,845	19,567	VUA	17,240	M-De	457 (259:198)	54	60	22	33	48

Table 3: Results (%) of TL classification in metaphor prediction using our embed(dings model): M(etaphor)+P(olNeAR)+E(uroparl) 1.9mio lower-cased; voc(ab) addr(essed); voc(ab) size

while applying the English-trained model in German (row 3 and 4). This might be the case since our testing data set is better balanced than the VUA data set. On the other hand, metaphoric contexts are not as well represented for German as they are for English in the model, especially since we did not word-align the data even though positions of verbs differ in both languages. [10] Looking into samples, we found that the especially low recall is caused by a lot of verbs not used very figuratively, such as "Waffenrechte verteidigen/schützen" (defend/protect gun rights). We plan to investigate these issues in detail to refine our choices and methods for training bilingual embeddings.

We did not use pre-trained bilingual embeddings even though existing work often comes with links to data and code (c.f, Luong et al. (2015); Hermann and Blunsom (2014)). However, these data often is difficult to collect as links are not available, broken or regeneration is laborious. Further, often bilingual embeddings are trained on Europarl which is not necessarily the domain, we can hope to find a lot of metaphoric language—also a problem in our approach as we use Europarl data too. During our work we also learned that adding source data from the news domain to our embeddings data reduces distances in the embeddings space (c.f., Fig. 3b).

8 Next steps

A next step is to predict metaphoric language in a target language using pre-trained transformer models and our Gold data for fine-tuning for example in a classification task. For this task, the embeddings representation of a sentence and the metaphor's source word is given, and the metaphoric word of the target language needs to be predicted.

Another step might be applying TL methods of neural machine translation (e.g., Kocmi and Bojar

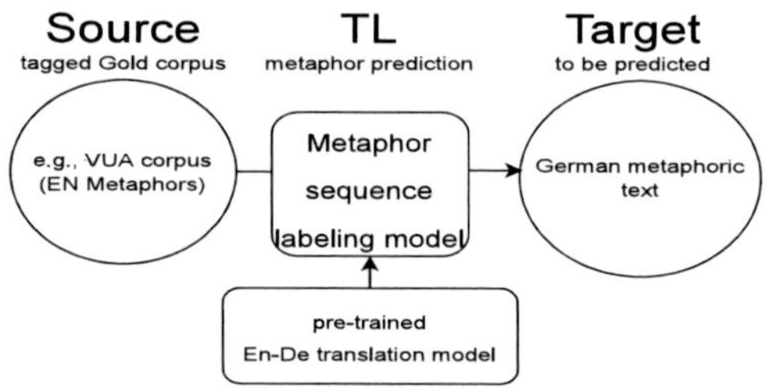

Figure 4: Overview on metaphor detection using a sequence labeling transfer learning technique

(2018)). As we learned in Sec. 2.2 usually a neural model is trained on a high-resource language pair and tested on a low-resource pair. In our setup, we could encounter this using a sequence labeling model trained on an English language metaphor corpus and combine it with a (pre-trained) translation model of English and German. As sources for the translation and evaluation part, we might also consider to use the parallel data from Common Crawl EMNLP (2018). Figure 4 shows an overview on the technique considering language model and tagging model probabilities as common translation setups do.

9 Conclusion

In this paper, we presented an overview of transfer learning techniques structured in a twofold manner: i) types of transfer learning, and ii) transfer learning techniques from a task-oriented perspective. We presented first steps towards the application of modern transfer learning techniques towards metaphor prediction in German language text. The experiments make clear that successfully training bilingual embeddings depends on the vocabulary coverage of the source texts. We furthermore are in the process of annotating a parallel corpus (EN-DE) of metaphor starting from a pre-existing English language corpus, which we plan to use as a Gold data set to test transformer-based models.

[10] We also tested our approach using bilingual embeddings from upfront word-aligned (Jalili Sabet et al., 2020) data. However, test F1-score remains below 10%. We belief that the n:m relations of words make it difficult for the classifier to identify the semantic in the target language well enough.

10 Limitations

Our first results show very low performance considering a guessing baseline of about 50%. We think this is mainly caused by the limited embeddings data we have available. Also, the lack of word alignments might cause difficulties. However, as demonstrated, the task is very complex given all the constrains that need to be fulfilled upfront (such as Gold data set, suitable TL-technique, bilingual resources). We consider to look further for parallel data sources and develop strategies to generate parallel sources, e.g., by back-translation (Dhar et al., 2022) before we go ahead applying other TL-learning techniques. We also need to establish a way to incorporate findings on compound and infrequent words into the creation of the embeddings representation. However, we did not do this yet, because we had to manipulate the primary data for this purpose.

References

Ehsan Aghazadeh, Mohsen Fayyaz, and Yadollah Yaghoobzadeh. 2022. Metaphors in pre-trained language models: Probing and generalization across datasets and languages. In *Proceedings of the 60th Annual Meeting of the Association for Computational Linguistics (Volume 1: Long Papers)*, pages 2037–2050.

Wasi Uddin Ahmad, Haoran Li, Kai-Wei Chang, and Yashar Mehdad. 2021. Syntax-augmented multilingual bert for cross-lingual transfer. In *Proceedings of the 59th Annual Meeting of the Association for Computational Linguistics and the 11th International Joint Conference on Natural Language Processing*, pages 4538–4554. ACL.

Azin Asgarian. 2018. An introduction to transfer learning. Georgian Impact Blog, online. Accessed: Oct. 2022.

Azin Asgarian, Parinaz Sobhani, Ji Chao Zhang, Madalin Mihailescu, Ariel Sibilia, Ahmed Bilal Ashraf, and Babak Taati. 2018. A hybrid instance-based transfer learning method. *arXiv preprint arXiv:1812.01063*.

Silvio Cordeiro, Carlos Ramisch, Marco Idiart, and Aline Villavicencio. 2016. Predicting the compositionality of nominal compounds: Giving word embeddings a hard time. In *Proceedings of the 54th Annual Meeting of the Association for Computational Linguistics (Volume 1: Long Papers)*, pages 1986–1997.

Wenyuan Dai, Yuqiang Chen, Gui-Rong Xue, Qiang Yang, and Yong Yu. 2008. Translated learning: Transfer learning across different feature spaces. *Advances in neural information processing systems*, 21:353–360.

Prajit Dhar, Arianna Bisazza, and Gertjan van Noord. 2022. Evaluating pre-training objectives for low-resource translation into morphologically rich languages. In *The 13th Conference on Language Resources and Evaluation*, pages 4933–4943. European Language Resources Association (ELRA).

Lettie Dorst. 2015. More or different metaphors in fiction? a quantitative cross-register comparison. *Language and Literature*, 24:3–22.

Lixin Duan, Dong Xu, and Ivor Tsang. 2012. Learning with augmented features for heterogeneous domain adaptation. *arXiv preprint arXiv:1206.4660*.

Nadir Durrani, Hassan Sajjad, and Fahim Dalvi. 2021. How transfer learning impacts linguistic knowledge in deep nlp models? *arXiv preprint arXiv:2105.15179*.

EMNLP. 2018. Emnlp 2018 third conference on machine translation (wmt18) - shared task: Machine translation of news. `https://www.statmt.org/wmt18/translation-task.html`. Accessed: Oct. 2022.

Ge Gao, Eunsol Choi, Yejin Choi, and Luke Zettlemoyer. 2018. Neural metaphor detection in context. *arXiv preprint arXiv:1808.09653*.

Jonathan Gordon, Jerry R Hobbs, Jonathan May, Michael Mohler, Fabrizio Morbini, Bryan Rink, Marc Tomlinson, and Suzanne Wertheim. 2015. A corpus of rich metaphor annotation. In *Proceedings of the Third Workshop on Metaphor in NLP*, pages 56–66.

Pragglejaz Group. 2007. Mip: A method for identifying metaphorically used words in discourse. *Metaphor and symbol*, 22(1):1–39.

Parastoo Harati, Chris Westbury, and Milad Kiaee. 2021. Evaluating the predication model of metaphor comprehension: Using word2vec to model best/worst quality judgments of 622 novel metaphors. *Behavior Research Methods*, 53(5):2214–2225.

Karl Moritz Hermann and Phil Blunsom. 2014. Multilingual models for compositional distributed semantics. In *Proceedings of the 52nd Annual Meeting of the Association for Computational Linguistics (Volume 1: Long Papers)*, volume 1, pages 58–68. ACL.

Aizhan Imankulova, Raj Dabre, Atsushi Fujita, and Kenji Imamura. 2019. Exploiting out-of-domain parallel data through multilingual transfer learning for low-resource neural machine translation. In *Proceedings of Machine Translation Summit XVII Volume 1: Research Track*, pages 128–139.

Masoud Jalili Sabet, Philipp Dufter, François Yvon, and Hinrich Schütze. 2020. SimAlign: High quality word alignments without parallel training data using static and contextualized embeddings. In *Proceedings of the 2020 Conference on Empirical Methods in Natural Language Processing: Findings*, pages 1627–1643. ACL.

Jing Jiang and ChengXiang Zhai. 2007. Instance weighting for domain adaptation in nlp. In *Proceedings of the 45th annual meeting of the association of computational linguistics*, pages 264–271.

Walter Kintsch. 2000. Metaphor comprehension: A computational theory. *Psychonomic bulletin & review*, 7(2):257–266.

Alexandre Klementiev, Ivan Titov, and Binod Bhattarai. 2012. Inducing crosslingual distributed representations of words. *Proceedings of COLING 2012*, pages 1459–1474.

Tom Kocmi and Ondřej Bojar. 2018. Trivial transfer learning for low-resource neural machine translation. *arXiv preprint arXiv:1809.00357*.

Philipp Koehn. 2005. Europarl: A parallel corpus for statistical machine translation. In *Proceedings of machine translation summit x: papers*, pages 79–86.

George Lakoff and Mark Johnson. 1980. *Metaphors we live by*. University of Chicago Press.

Mingsheng Long, Jianmin Wang, Guiguang Ding, Sinno Jialin Pan, and S Yu Philip. 2013. Adaptation regularization: A general framework for transfer learning. *IEEE Transactions on Knowledge and Data Engineering*, 26(5):1076–1089.

Thang Luong, Hieu Pham, and Christopher D Manning. 2015. Bilingual word representations with monolingual quality in mind. In *Proceedings of the 1st Workshop on Vector Space Modeling for Natural Language Processing*, pages 151–159.

Tomáš Mikolov, Wen-tau Yih, and Geoffrey Zweig. 2013. Linguistic regularities in continuous space word representations. In *Proceedings of the 2013 conference of the north american chapter of the association for computational linguistics: Human language technologies*, pages 746–751.

Edward Newell, Drew Margolin, and Derek Ruths. 2018. An attribution relations corpus for political news. In *Proceedings of the Eleventh International Conference on Language Resources and Evaluation (LREC 2018)*.

Toan Q Nguyen and David Chiang. 2017. Transfer learning across low-resource, related languages for neural machine translation. *arXiv preprint arXiv:1708.09803*.

Sinno Jialin Pan, Ivor W Tsang, James T Kwok, and Qiang Yang. 2010. Domain adaptation via transfer component analysis. *IEEE transactions on neural networks*, 22(2):199–210.

Jeffrey Pennington, Richard Socher, and Christopher D. Manning. 2014. Glove: Global vectors for word representation. In *Empirical Methods in Natural Language Processing (EMNLP)*, pages 1532–1543.

ME Peters, M Neumann, M Iyyer, M Gardner, C Clark, K Lee, and L Zettlemoyer. 1802. Deep contextualized word representations. arxiv 2018. *arXiv preprint arXiv:1802.05365*, 12.

Tianze Shi, Zhiyuan Liu, Yang Liu, and Maosong Sun. 2015. Learning cross-lingual word embeddings via matrix co-factorization. In *Proceedings of the 53rd Annual Meeting of the Association for Computational Linguistics and the 7th International Joint Conference on Natural Language Processing (Volume 2: Short Papers)*, volume 2, pages 567–572. ACL.

Ekaterina Shutova and Simone Teufel. 2010. Metaphor corpus annotated for source-target domain mappings. In *Proceedings of the Seventh International Conference on Language Resources and Evaluation (LREC'10)*.

Gerard J Steen, Aletta G Dorst, J Berenike Herrmann, Anna A Kaal, and Tina Krennmayr. 2010. Metaphor in usage.

Kevin Stowe, Tuhin Chakrabarty, Nanyun Peng, Smaranda Muresan, and Iryna Gurevych. 2021. Metaphor generation with conceptual mappings. *arXiv preprint arXiv:2106.01228*.

Yulia Tsvetkov, Leonid Boytsov, Anatole Gershman, Eric Nyberg, and Chris Dyer. 2014. Metaphor detection with cross-lingual model transfer. In *Proceedings of the 52nd Annual Meeting of the Association for Computational Linguistics (Volume 1: Long Papers)*, pages 248–258.

Tao Tu, Yuan-Jui Chen, Cheng-chieh Yeh, and Hung-Yi Lee. 2019. End-to-end text-to-speech for low-resource languages by cross-lingual transfer learning. *arXiv preprint arXiv:1904.06508*.

Shyam Upadhyay, Manaal Faruqui, Chris Dyer, and Dan Roth. 2016. Cross-lingual models of word embeddings: An empirical comparison. In *Proceedings of the 54th Annual Meeting of the Association for Computational Linguistics (Volume 1: Long Papers)*, volume 1, pages 1661–1670. ACL.

Ivan Vulić and Marie-Francine Moens. 2015. Monolingual and cross-lingual information retrieval models based on (bilingual) word embeddings. In *Proceedings of the 38th international ACM SIGIR conference on research and development in information retrieval*, pages 363–372. ACM.

Karl Weiss, Taghi M Khoshgoftaar, and DingDing Wang. 2016. A survey of transfer learning. *Journal of Big data*, 3(1):1–40.

Ding Yan, Dirk Noël, and Hans-Georg Wolf. 2010. Patterns in metaphor translation: a corpus-based case study of the translation of fear metaphors between english and chinese. *Using Corpora in Contrastive and Translation Studies. Newcastle: Cambridge Scholars Publishing*, pages 40–61.

Barret Zoph, Deniz Yuret, Jonathan May, and Kevin Knight. 2016. Transfer learning for low-resource neural machine translation. *arXiv preprint arXiv:1604.02201*.

Ring That Bell: A Corpus and Method for Multimodal Metaphor Detection in Videos

Khalid Alnajjar[1], Mika Hämäläinen[1] and Shuo Zhang[2]
[1]University of Helsinki, Finland
[2]Bose Corporation, USA
firstname.lastname@{helsinki.fi or bose.com}

Abstract

We present the first openly available multimodal metaphor annotated corpus. The corpus consists of videos including audio and subtitles that have been annotated by experts. Furthermore, we present a method for detecting metaphors in the new dataset based on the textual content of the videos. The method achieves a high F1-score (62%) for metaphorical labels. We also experiment with other modalities and multimodal methods; however, these methods did not out-perform the text-based model. In our error analysis, we do identify that there are cases where video could help in disambiguating metaphors, however, the visual cues are too subtle for our model to capture. The data is available on Zenodo.

1 Introduction

Figurative language is a challenging topic for computational modeling as the meaning of a figurative expression is non-compositional and typically very context dependent (see Roberts and Kreuz 1994). Metaphor is one of the most important figures of language; it is constantly used in every day language (Steen et al., 2010a) to draw comparisons or to express something difficult and foreign in more familiar terms. Metaphors can be conventional (Traugott, 1985) and they are often found in idioms, but at the same time metaphors are used to create something new (see Kantokorpi et al. 1990).

Given its ubiquitous presence, understanding metaphors is integral in achieving true natural language understanding (NLU) in the real world. Without their successful interpretation, our models are bound to make mistakes whenever anything is expressed in an indirect or creative fashion. Metaphors are often very contextual and their successful detection and interpretation requires a wide range of contextual cues that would be captured in audio (e.g., prosody) and video (e.g., gestures and actions). Therefore, we believe a multimodal dataset is a great contribution to metaphor research within and outside of the field of NLP.

Two important parts of a metaphor are a tenor and a vehicle (see Richards 1936). For example, in the metaphor *life is a journey*, *life* is the tenor and *journey* is the vehicle. How metaphors essentially operate is that a vehicle is used to give some of its attributes to the tenor. In the case above, *journeys* are long and full of adventure, which means that these properties are attributed to *life* in an indirect fashion. The meaning of a metaphor is never literal nor compositional, but rather calls for interpretation on the level of pragmatics (see Rosales Sequeiros 2016).

Meanwhile, multimodality is becoming increasingly important for many tasks (see Castellucci et al. 2020; Mogadala et al. 2020; Declerk et al. 2020). We believe the availability of multimodal datasets for a variety of NLP tasks is lacking, and we hope to contribute to the community with our multimodal metaphor dataset.

In this paper, we present the first fully open expert annotated multimodal dataset for metaphor detection[1]. In addition, we experiment with unimodal and multimodal methods for metaphor detection. Our results indicate that the text-based model achieved the best performance. We discuss the results of our experiments and conduct an extensive error analysis to shed light on what was learned successfully by the model and its shortcomings.

Using CC BY licensed videos in our corpus has been the primary design principle of our data collection so that we can release our corpus without any restrictions in its entirety. This, we believe, is more useful for research purposes than a corpus consisting of short video clips to compile with copyright laws such as the fair use law in the US.

[1]https://doi.org/10.5281/zenodo.7217991

Proceedings of the 3rd Workshop on Figurative Language Processing (FLP), pages 24 - 33
December 8, 2022 ©2022 Association for Computational Linguistics

2 Related Work

Metaphors have, thus far, been computationally detected using only text. In this section, we describe some of the recent approaches for textual metaphor detection, the corpora used to achieve that and some of the multimodal research conducted on NLP tasks other than metaphor detection. There are several takes on metaphor interpretation (Xiao et al., 2016; Rai et al., 2019; Bar et al., 2020) and generation (Hämäläinen, 2018; Terai and Sugyo, 2019; Zheng et al., 2019), but we do not describe them in detail as interpretation is a very different problem.

There are two corpora currently used for metaphor detection, VU Amsterdam (VUA) Metaphor Corpus (Steen et al., 2010b) and Corpus of Non-Native Written English Annotated for Metaphor (Beigman Klebanov et al., 2018). Unlike our corpus, both of these datasets contain textual modality only.

For textual metaphor detection, Gao et al. (2018) has used a bi-directional LSTM (long short-term memory) based model with ELMo embeddings. Similarly, Liu et al. (2020) have used a bi-LSTM model with BERT and XLNet for the same task. Not unlike the previous approaches, Dankers et al. (2020) has also applied bi-LSTM models comparing ELMo and GloVe embeddings to BERT embeddings with global and hierarchical attention models. Traditional machine learning methods, Logistic Regression, Linear SVC (Support Vector Classification) and Random Forest Classifier, have been used recently with feature engineering to detect metaphors (Wan et al., 2020). In DeepMet, proposed by Su et al. (2020), a siamese neural network have been utilized, where textual RoBERTa (Liu et al., 2019) embeddings are computed from the context, the token in question and its part-of-speech and fine-grained part-of-speech. DeepMet was the best performing solution for detecting textual metaphors in the VUA dataset, based on a recent shared task (Leong et al., 2020).

There are several recent works on multimodal detection of a variety of linguistic phenomena. For example, SVMs (Support Vector Machines) with word embeddings and feature extraction have been used for multimodal sarcasm detection (Castro et al., 2019; Alnajjar and Hämäläinen, 2021). Mittal et al. (2020) uses GloVe embeddings, features extracted from audio and facial recognition system output to predict emotion in a multimodal dataset. These multimodal features are fused using a memory fusion network (MFN) (Zadeh et al., 2018). Similarly, Li et al. (2021) detect emotion in a multimodal dataset by modeling the problem from the point of view of the quantum theory. While the field has seen increasing research on multimodal NLP (Tsai et al., 2019; Mai et al., 2020; Sahu and Vechtomova, 2021), no data or model has been proposed for multimodal metaphor detection.

3 Our Metaphor Corpus

In this section, we present our video, audio and textual corpus of manually annotated metaphorical language. Our selection of the video clips includes only CC-BY licensed videos on YouTube that have human authored closed captions in English. The content of the videos presents mainly real people talking, which rules out animations and video game streams. The availability of human authored closed captioning is important as it speeds up our annotation time and provides us with subtitles that are already aligned with video and audio. The CC-BY license was an important selection criterion because it makes it possible for us to release the dataset openly.

We used the filters provided by YouTube to limit our search to videos that were marked as CC-BY and had closed captioning. However, the YouTube filter does not distinguish between automatically generated closed captioning and a human authored one. Fortunately, it is relatively easy to tell these two apart from each other. Automated closed captioning tends to appear one word at a time, whereas human authored closed captioning is visualized more like traditional subtitles. These criteria greatly reduced the number of eligible videos to include in our corpus. Apart from these criteria, we also filtered videos with sensitive and offensive languages. No further restrictions have been explicitly placed on the genres or types of videos, as we do not want to introduce biases for which types of contents are more likely to contain metaphors. Therefore, the availability of the metaphors naturally occurring in the corpus is the result of the ubiquity of the metaphor in everyday language use. All Youtube queries were conducted in incognito mode to avoid biased YouTube suggestions based on our viewing habits.

Figure 1 shows real examples from our corpus where video can be useful in detecting metaphors. On the left, the woman wearing a gray shirt is

sentence
that you can use to really up your <v>game</v>
because while a <t>quick fix</t> can be <v>appetizing</v> and appealing
<t r="domain name">That</t>'s <v>the street address</v> for your website
you're ready to <v>give it a shot</v>

Table 1: Example of the annotations for the metaphor detection corpus.

Figure 1: Metaphors made visible in the video through gestures.

talking about *sprinkling keywords* and showing a sprinkling gesture. On the right, the woman wearing the wine red shirt says *ring that bell* and shows a bell ringing gesture.

Our corpus consists of 27 YouTube videos with a total duration of 3 hours, 53 minutes and 47 seconds of video. For comparison, a recently released multimodal dataset for sarcasm detection (Castro et al., 2019) has the duration of 3 hours, 40 minutes and 47 seconds. The videos belong mostly to a start-up domain and many of them deal with issues of online visibility for a start-up company. This domain was a consequence of our selection criteria for videos. It turns out that YouTube has plenty of high-quality human close-captioned videos released under the CC-BY license that relate to this particular domain.

Our corpus provides linguistics researchers with the ability to study the use of metaphor in a multimodal setting, something that has gained attention in their field of science as well (Müller and Cienki, 2009). This can, indeed, foster a wider interdisciplinary collaboration leading to a deeper understanding of the phenomenon.

3.1 Annotation

Two expert annotators went through the video files and annotated metaphors by surrounding them with *v* tags for vehicles and *t* tags for tenors. The use of experts is motivated by the fact that previous research has found that non-expert annotators struggle with metaphors (Hämäläinen and Alnajjar, 2019).

The annotators followed a simple procedure in annotating the data:

- Is the meaning literal?
- If the meaning of the word is abstract, is it a dictionary meaning?
- Does the potential metaphor express pragmatic insincerity?
- If the answer to all of the questions is no, annotate it as a metaphor.

In other words, if the meaning of a word or a phrase is not literal, it is annotated as a metaphor. However, just the mere fact of a word being used in an abstract way is not enough to mark it as metaphorical. For example, in the sentence *it is tied to revenue*, "tied" is not tagged as a metaphor just because it is used in a more abstract sense than the typical concrete sense of tying one's shoes, for example. If the abstract meaning of a word appears in a dictionary, the word is not considered metaphorical. However, conventional metaphors that consist of multiple words, and are thus idioms, are tagged as metaphors. We do not make a distinction between metaphors and similes.

Pragmatic insincerity (see Grice 1975) is a phenomenon related to sarcasm as one of its preconditions (see Kumon-Nakamura et al. 1995). There is a certain overlap between metaphors and sarcastic expressions in the sense that both use words in their non-literal meaning. In order to ensure that we do not mix these two notions with each other, it is important to avoid annotating pragmatically insincere expressions as metaphorical.

Table 1 shows an example of annotations. The annotations were done directly in the subtitles The utterances are time stamped and aligned with the video. In the table, tenors are indicated with *<t>* and vehicles with *<v>*. For deictic tenors, an *r* attribute is provided to resolve the deixis by indicating the actual tenor that has appeared earlier in the conversation. In the examples, *game* is used metaphorically to talk about marketing, *quick fix* is called *appetizing* as though it was something edible and *domain name* is contrasted to a physical *street address* by direct comparison. *Give it a shot* is a conventional metaphor.

All in all, after multiple annotation iterations, the dataset consists of 304 vehicles and 67 tenors. This totals to 371 metaphorical expressions. They vary in length: the shortest tenor is one word, such as *it*, while the longest tenor is several words *the discovery of those five noble gases to illuminate like that*. The same goes for vehicles where their length varies form one word such as *dive* to multiple words: *the history of the internet itself*. On a token level, we have 672 vehicle tokens and 113 tenor tokens, so altogether 785 metaphorical tokens.

In total, 6% of the expressions in the corpus are metaphorical. While this percentage might appear low, it is natural and more representative of the real usage of metaphors in typical conversations which makes this corpus suitable for building metaphor detection models applicable for real-world scenarios.

Around 55% of the vehicles are conventional metaphors and 45% are novel metaphors. However, it is fairly common that same words appear in the corpus in a metaphorical and non-metaphorical sense. In our corpus, there are two videos that deal with actual cooking, in which many food-related metaphors appear non-metaphorically, such as *sprinkle those in*, said metaphorically about keywords and *a little sprinkle*, said non-metaphorically about sugar. Another example is the use of *house* non-metaphorically as in *come pick it up at my house* and metaphorically as in *think of hosting as your house*, where a metaphorical connection is drawn between *hosting* and a *house*.

3.2 Data preparation

As YouTube serves files in several different formats such as *webm*, *mkv* and *mp4* the first step is to use FFmpeg[2] to convert all videos into mp4 format. We also use the same tool to clip the video files into sentence-length clips based on the time stamps in the subtitles and extract their audio into wav files. This process yielded 6,565 video and audio clips that are aligned with text.

We split the datset randomly so that 70% of sentences that contain metaphors and 70% of sentences that don't contain any metaphors are used for training, 15 % of both types of sentences for validation and 15% of both for testing. This way we ensure that both metaphorical and non-metaphorical sentences are divided proportionally with the same ratios. These splits are used for all the models.

4 Metaphor Detection

We experiment with uni- and multi-modal models for metaphor detection. In this section, we describe the preprocessing steps applied and the experimental setups conducted.

4.1 Preprocessing

For each modality, we make use of the latest advances in neural network models to capture important features that have achieved state-of-the-art results in various NLP tasks. As metaphor detection has been conducted solely based on text, we follow the DeepMet approach by Su et al. (2020) and process the entire textual content using spaCy (Honnibal et al., 2020) to tokenize it and acquire Universal Dependencies style syntactic trees (Nivre et al., 2020) and Penn Treebank parts-of-speech tags (Santorini, 1990). Similarly to the original approach, all of our textual models predict metaphors at the token level given the context surrounding it and its POS tags as input.

We resample the audio to 16kHz. Audio features are extracted using *Wav2Vec2FeatureExtractor* provided by the Transoformers Python library (Wolf et al., 2020).

Video features are obtained by taking equally-distributed 16 frames from a clip and then resize them into 128x171, followed by normalization and center cropping to 112x112.

4.2 Textual model

We train two text-only models, both follow the architecture and approach of DeepMet where we obtain textual embeddings using RoBERTa (Liu et al., 2019) and feed them into two transformer encoding layers which are then combined by applying global average pooling and concatenation. A dense fully-connected layer takes in the combined output of both encoders and predicts whether the token is metaphorical (c.f., Su et al. 2020 for more details).

In our first textual model, we train the model using our corpus, whereas in the second one we train it using VUA corpus (with a learning rate of

[2]https://ffmpeg.org/

0.00001, akin the original paper) and later fine-tune it using our corpus.

4.3 Audio model

We extend and fine-tune Facebook's pretrained multilingual XLSR-Wav2Vec2 large model (Baevski et al., 2020). The model is trained on Multilingual LibriSpeech (Pratap et al., 2020), CommonVoice (Ardila et al., 2020) and Babel (Roach et al., 1996) for speech recognition. We employ this model to encode speech into vector representations from raw audio.

We replace the classification layer of the original model with a dense fully-connected layer that produces two outputs, one for each label. Unlike the textual model, here we classify whether the entire spoken expression contains a metaphor or not (i.e., not on a word level).

4.4 Video model

For our video unimodal model, we incorporate a pretrained model for human action detection. The model is based on the 18 layer deep R(2+1)D network (Tran et al., 2018) and it is trained on the Kinetics-400 (Zisserman et al., 2017) dataset. The intuition behind using this model is that it was able to detect actions (e.g., playing organ), gestures (e.g., pointing) and movements (e.g., waving). Realizing such information is crucial in understanding the context, and would provide further cues for detecting metaphors.

Similar to the audio model, we substitute the original classification layer with a fully connected layer and fine-tune the pretrained model to predict whether a scene is metaphorical or not.

4.5 Multimodal metaphor detection

We test out three multimodal metaphor detection models; 1) text and audio, 2) text and video and 3) text, audio and video. The textual model is the fine-tuned model using the VUA corpus and our textual corpus.

In all of the models, the final classification layer of their sub-models are removed. Unimodal models are combined by concatenating the weights of their last layer, which are then fed to a classification layer.

4.6 Common configuration

All of the models described above share common configurations, unless we explicitly indicate otherwise. Prior to the last classification layer of all of our mono- and multimodal models, we introduce a dropout layer (Srivastava et al., 2014) (with a probability of 20%) to accelerate training, and reduce internal covariate shift and overfitting.

We use the cross entropy loss function along with Adam optimizer (Kingma and Ba, 2014; Loshchilov and Hutter, 2019) to update the weights and train the models. All the fine-tuned models are trained with a learning rate of 0.0001 and for 3 full epochs.

5 Results

In this section, we follow the evaluation metrics commonly used for the metaphor detection task by reporting the precision, recall and F1 scores for the metaphorical label.

Regarding the textual models, we report three sets of results, which are for the models trained on: 1) VUA corpus, 2) our corpus and 3) both the VUA and our corpus. All the models predict metaphoricity on the token level. To ensure that our implementation of the DeepMet approach is correct, we tested the first model on the VUA test dataset of the metaphor detection shared task and achieved an F1-score of 0.68 and 0.73 on all POS and verb subsets of the data, respectively. These results are relatively close to the results reported by the authors.

Table 2 shows the classification results of all three models on the test set. The test set contained 90 metaphorical tokens and 6,961 non-metaphorical tokens. The results indicate that the textual model trained solely on the VUA dataset performed poorly on our test set. In comparison, training the model using our metaphor corpus only resulted in a great increase of correct predictions. Nonetheless, combining both corpora by fine-tuning the first model with our corpus produced the winning model, which managed to spot 76% of the metaphorical tokens correctly.

We believe that the huge differences between the first and second textual models, despite the larger size of VUA's training dataset, are due to the differences in domains. The VUA corpus contains academic texts, conversation, fiction, and news texts, whereas our corpus is dominated by conversations on the web and start-ups. It is evident that by exposing the model to general domains (i.e., VUA's corpus) and, thereafter, concentrating it on the start-up domain, the model was able to identify the highest number of metaphorical usages.

Trained on	Precision	Recall	F1-score
VUA	0.04	0.33	0.07
Ours	0.38	0.63	0.47
VUA + Ours	**0.53**	**0.76**	**0.62**

Table 2: Classification results of the textual monomodal models on the test set of our corpus, for the metaphorical label.

Results from the other models (unimodal or multimodal) that involving audio and video showed that adding these modalities actually did not help improving the model - rather, they are detrimental to the model performance on metaphor detection. We extend two possible explanations for this failure. First, it is possible that because the visual and audio cues of metaphor are subtle, these models failed to learn from such a small amount of annotated data.

Second, it is unclear that the specific models we are using for audio and video modalities encode the information relevant for the metaphor detection task. For instance, whereas it is impossible to completely disentangle what exactly the Wav2Vec model is encoding, we can conjecture that it encodes information about phoneme identity considering it is optimized for the speech recognition task. Therefore, it may not be entirely surprising that the Wav2Vec encoding is not useful for the metaphor detection task because it is adding redundant or irrelevant information to the model. It is our future work (or the future work for the community who utilizes this dataset) to refine our understanding of the multimodal encoding for the metaphor detection task (for instance, employing a model that more directly encodes information about speech prosody from the audio).

5.1 Error analysis

When looking at the results of the text only model, we can see that the model identifies metaphors correctly as metaphors more often than not. There are some metaphorical tokens in metaphors consisting of multiple words that get classified wrong, for example, in *You could think of hosting as your house*, the tenor *hosting* and the determinant *your* of the metaphorical word *house* are not identified as metaphorical, while *house* is correctly identified. Another example is the conventional metaphor *toot their own horn*, where all other words except for *own* are correctly identified as metaphorical.

There are also a fewer number of cases where all words get identified wrongly as non-metaphorical, for example, the model did not predict any metaphorical tokens in *It's where you live*, while in reality *it* is the tenor and *where you live* is the vehicle. Also, individual tenors where the vehicle comes later get often not recognized such as in *Yes, malware you could think of like*, where *malware* is the tenor for a vehicle that appears later in the dialog.

When the tenor and the vehicle co-exist nearby, the model can get all metaphorical tokens right such as in *It's kinda like real estate right?* where both the tenor *it* and the vehicle *real estate* are correctly identified. Also many tenorless expressions are fully recognized correctly as metaphorical, such as *Spreadin' the love*.

There were plenty of cases (61) where the model predicted a metaphor tag for a token while there was no metaphor. Curiously, prepositions were often tagged metaphorical, such as *to* in *ring that bell to see these episodes first*. The actual metaphorical part *ring that bell* ends before the preposition *to* that has a non-metaphorical meaning *in order to*.

We can also see that the model was indeed fooled by cooking terms that were used both metaphorically and non-metaphorically. In *Yeah a little sprinkle*, both *a* and *sprinkle* were classified as metaphors, while the context was about sprinkling sugar. Another similar case was *there's five noble gases that illuminate*, where *noble gases* and *illuminate* were erroneously classified to be metaphorical. This was clearly due to the tenor in the corpus: *the discovery of those five noble gases to illuminate like that* that contained similar words. It is evident that the model relies on word similarities more than reaching to a higher pragmatic representation of the phenomenon, however, this is not an unexpected behavior from a machine learning model.

There are also cases where the model detects a metaphor, that could theoretically be a metaphor, but is not because of the way it was used in the corpus. For example, the model predicts *Give it a go* as metaphorical in the expression *button, "Give it a go."*, where people are talking about a button with a particular text rather than using the expression metaphorically. Another such an example is *flying* in *(money flying)*. Such an expression might be used metaphorically, but in this case this was a note for the hearing impaired as money was actually flying on the video.

6 Discussion and Conclusions

In this work, we have only focused on metaphor as a strictly linguistic phenomenon and we have built a multimodal dataset where these linguistic metaphors have been tagged in terms of tenors and vehicles. However, it is apparent that metaphor is a phenomenon that occurs on a higher level of our cognitive capacities than mere language. There are several cases in our corpus, where we can evidence the existence of a metaphor but it is never expressed verbally. For example in Figure 2, *money flying* cannot be a metaphor when inspected purely from the point of view of language and its relation to the video when money is actually flying in the scene. However, it is a metaphor on a higher level in the sense that the entire scene where money was flying was to indicate someone becoming rich. In other words, stating a fact that is happening is not metaphorical if the fact is literally taking place, however the fact itself might be metaphorical.

Figure 2: Money actually flying on the video.

At the same time, as evidenced by our error analysis, there are certainly cases where video modality could help in disambiguating whether something is said metaphorically or not. For instance, talking about *sprinkling* in a kitchen environment (see Figure 3) is a very strong sign that the word is potentially non-metaphorical. Integrating these weak cues into a multimodal system is, however, not an easy task given that the current methods for video processing are limited in their coverage.

Therefore, in the future, it would be useful to annotate metaphors also in the other modalities. Money flying can be a visual metaphor, and so can a sound effect, and they can exist independently from each other in different modalities. Perhaps the reason why our multimodal attempts failed was that metaphor can be independent of the other modalities. Producing such a dataset where these modal specific metaphors are also annotated for video and audio is definitely a huge undertaking that requires research in its own right.

Figure 3: *Sprinkling* used in a kitchen in reference to sugar.

It is clear that our model can detect metaphors correctly, but also the mistakes it makes highlight that despite using a large RoBERTa model, the meaning representation the model has cannot reach to such a nuanced level as to confidently detect metaphors. Metaphor is a figurative device that cannot be explained by semantics, but rather requires pragmatic inspection. It is not clear based on our research and other contemporary approaches whether the current word or sentence embedding models are sufficient to navigate in the depths of pragmatics and subjective interpretation in any other way than learning some irrelevant co-occurring phenomena from a biased corpus. At the same time there is no such thing as an unbiased corpus, either, given that bias (and mostly heuristics causing it) is a fundamental part of our cognition as human beings.

In this paper, we have presented a new open and multimodal dataset for metaphor detection. Because we have focused strictly on CC-BY licensed videos, we can make the entire dataset available on Zenodo. In our current work, we have not taken the context widely into account when predicting metaphoricity, but rather resorted to a very local context. The fact that the videos can be published in full length makes it possible for any future work to explore different ways of including contextual cues freely.

Acknowledgments

This work was partially financed by the Society of Swedish Literature in Finland with funding from Enhancing Conversational AI with Computational Creativity, and by the Ella and Georg Ehrnrooth Foundation for Modelling Conversational Artificial Intelligence with Intent and Creativity.

References

Khalid Alnajjar and Mika Hämäläinen. 2021. ¡Qué maravilla! multimodal sarcasm detection in Spanish: a dataset and a baseline. *arXiv preprint arXiv:2105.05542*.

Rosana Ardila, Megan Branson, Kelly Davis, Michael Kohler, Josh Meyer, Michael Henretty, Reuben Morais, Lindsay Saunders, Francis Tyers, and Gregor Weber. 2020. Common voice: A massively-multilingual speech corpus. In *Proceedings of the 12th Language Resources and Evaluation Conference*, pages 4218–4222, Marseille, France. European Language Resources Association.

Alexei Baevski, Yuhao Zhou, Abdelrahman Mohamed, and Michael Auli. 2020. wav2vec 2.0: A framework for self-supervised learning of speech representations. *Advances in Neural Information Processing Systems*, 33.

Kfir Bar, Nachum Dershowitz, and Lena Dankin. 2020. Automatic metaphor interpretation using word embeddings. *arXiv preprint arXiv:2010.02665*.

Beata Beigman Klebanov, Chee Wee (Ben) Leong, and Michael Flor. 2018. A corpus of non-native written English annotated for metaphor. In *Proceedings of the 2018 Conference of the North American Chapter of the Association for Computational Linguistics: Human Language Technologies, Volume 2 (Short Papers)*, pages 86–91, New Orleans, Louisiana. Association for Computational Linguistics.

Giuseppe Castellucci, Simone Filice, Soujanya Poria, Erik Cambria, and Lucia Specia, editors. 2020. *Proceedings of the First International Workshop on Natural Language Processing Beyond Text*. Association for Computational Linguistics, Online.

Santiago Castro, Devamanyu Hazarika, Verónica Pérez-Rosas, Roger Zimmermann, Rada Mihalcea, and Soujanya Poria. 2019. Towards multimodal sarcasm detection (an _obviously_ perfect paper). In *Proceedings of the 57th Annual Meeting of the Association for Computational Linguistics (Volume 1: Long Papers)*, Florence, Italy. Association for Computational Linguistics.

Verna Dankers, Karan Malhotra, Gaurav Kudva, Volodymyr Medentsiy, and Ekaterina Shutova. 2020. Being neighbourly: Neural metaphor identification in discourse. In *Proceedings of the Second Workshop on Figurative Language Processing*, pages 227–234, Online. Association for Computational Linguistics.

Thierry Declerk, Itziar Gonzalez-Dios, and German Rigau, editors. 2020. *Proceedings of the LREC 2020 Workshop on Multimodal Wordnets (MMW2020)*. The European Language Resources Association (ELRA), Marseille, France.

Ge Gao, Eunsol Choi, Yejin Choi, and Luke Zettlemoyer. 2018. Neural metaphor detection in context. In *Proceedings of the 2018 Conference on Empirical Methods in Natural Language Processing*, pages 607–613, Brussels, Belgium. Association for Computational Linguistics.

Herbert P Grice. 1975. Logic and conversation. In *Speech acts*, pages 41–58. Brill.

Mika Hämäläinen. 2018. Harnessing nlg to create finnish poetry automatically. In *Proceedings of the ninth international conference on computational creativity*. Association for Computational Creativity (ACC).

Mika Hämäläinen and Khalid Alnajjar. 2019. Let's FACE it. Finnish poetry generation with aesthetics and framing. In *Proceedings of the 12th International Conference on Natural Language Generation*, pages 290–300, Tokyo, Japan. Association for Computational Linguistics.

Matthew Honnibal, Ines Montani, Sofie Van Landeghem, and Adriane Boyd. 2020. spaCy: Industrial-strength Natural Language Processing in Python.

Mervi Kantokorpi, Lyytikäinen Pirjo, and Viikari Auli. 1990. *Runousopin perusteet*. Gaudeamus.

Diederik P Kingma and Jimmy Ba. 2014. Adam: A method for stochastic optimization. *arXiv preprint arXiv:1412.6980*.

Sachi Kumon-Nakamura, Sam Glucksberg, and Mary Brown. 1995. How about another piece of pie: The allusional pretense theory of discourse irony. *Journal of Experimental Psychology: General*, 124(1):3.

Chee Wee (Ben) Leong, Beata Beigman Klebanov, Chris Hamill, Egon Stemle, Rutuja Ubale, and Xianyang Chen. 2020. A report on the 2020 VUA and TOEFL metaphor detection shared task. In *Proceedings of the Second Workshop on Figurative Language Processing*, pages 18–29, Online. Association for Computational Linguistics.

Qiuchi Li, Dimitris Gkoumas, Christina Lioma, and Massimo Melucci. 2021. Quantum-inspired multimodal fusion for video sentiment analysis. *Information Fusion*, 65:58–71.

Jerry Liu, Nathan O'Hara, Alexander Rubin, Rachel Draelos, and Cynthia Rudin. 2020. Metaphor detection using contextual word embeddings from transformers. In *Proceedings of the Second Workshop on Figurative Language Processing*, pages 250–255, Online. Association for Computational Linguistics.

Yinhan Liu, Myle Ott, Naman Goyal, Jingfei Du, Mandar Joshi, Danqi Chen, Omer Levy, Mike Lewis, Luke Zettlemoyer, and Veselin Stoyanov. 2019. Roberta: A robustly optimized bert pretraining approach.

Ilya Loshchilov and Frank Hutter. 2019. Decoupled weight decay regularization. In *International Conference on Learning Representations*.

Sijie Mai, Haifeng Hu, and Songlong Xing. 2020. Modality to modality translation: An adversarial representation learning and graph fusion network for multimodal fusion. In *Proceedings of the AAAI Conference on Artificial Intelligence*, volume 34, pages 164–172.

Trisha Mittal, Uttaran Bhattacharya, Rohan Chandra, Aniket Bera, and Dinesh Manocha. 2020. M3er: Multiplicative multimodal emotion recognition using facial, textual, and speech cues. In *Proceedings of the AAAI Conference on Artificial Intelligence*, volume 34, pages 1359–1367.

Aditya Mogadala, Sandro Pezzelle, Dietrich Klakow, Marie-Francine Moens, and Zeynep Akata, editors. 2020. *Proceedings of the Second Workshop on Beyond Vision and LANguage: inTEgrating Real-world kNowledge (LANTERN)*. Association for Computational Linguistics, Barcelona, Spain.

Cornelia Müller and Alan Cienki. 2009. *Chapter 13. Words, gestures, and beyond: Forms of multimodal metaphor in the use of spoken language*, pages 297–328. De Gruyter Mouton.

Joakim Nivre, Marie-Catherine de Marneffe, Filip Ginter, Jan Hajic, Christopher D Manning, Sampo Pyysalo, Sebastian Schuster, Francis Tyers, and Daniel Zeman. 2020. Universal dependencies v2: An evergrowing multilingual treebank collection. In *Proceedings of The 12th Language Resources and Evaluation Conference*, pages 4034–4043.

Vineel Pratap, Qiantong Xu, Anuroop Sriram, Gabriel Synnaeve, and Ronan Collobert. 2020. Mls: A large-scale multilingual dataset for speech research. *ArXiv*, abs/2012.03411.

Sunny Rai, Shampa Chakraverty, Devendra K Tayal, Divyanshu Sharma, and Ayush Garg. 2019. Understanding metaphors using emotions. *New Generation Computing*, 37(1):5–27.

Ivor Armstrong Richards. 1936. *The Philosophy of Rhetoric*. Oxford University Press, London, United Kingdom.

Peter Roach, Simon Arnfield, W Barry, J Baltova, Marian Boldea, Adrian Fourcin, W Gonet, Ryszard Gubrynowicz, E Hallum, Lori Lamel, et al. 1996. Babel: An eastern european multi-language database. In *Proceeding of Fourth International Conference on Spoken Language Processing. ICSLP'96*, volume 3, pages 1892–1893. IEEE.

Richard M Roberts and Roger J Kreuz. 1994. Why do people use figurative language? *Psychological science*, 5(3):159–163.

Xose Rosales Sequeiros. 2016. Metaphor: Pragmatics, relevance and cognition. *English Studies*, 97(6):656–677.

Gaurav Sahu and Olga Vechtomova. 2021. Adaptive fusion techniques for multimodal data. In *Proceedings of the 16th Conference of the European Chapter of the Association for Computational Linguistics: Main Volume*, pages 3156–3166, Online. Association for Computational Linguistics.

Beatrice Santorini. 1990. Part-of-speech tagging guidelines for the penn treebank project (3rd revision). *Technical Reports (CIS)*, page 570.

Nitish Srivastava, Geoffrey Hinton, Alex Krizhevsky, Ilya Sutskever, and Ruslan Salakhutdinov. 2014. Dropout: A simple way to prevent neural networks from overfitting. *Journal of Machine Learning Research*, 15(56):1929–1958.

GJ Steen, AG Dorst, JB Herrmann, AA Kaal, and T Krennmayr. 2010a. Metaphor in usage. *Cognitive Linguistics*, 21(4):757–788.

GJ Steen, AG Dorst, JB Herrmann, AA Kaal, T Krennmayr, and T Pasma. 2010b. A method for linguistic metaphor identification. from mip to mipvu. *Converging Evidence in Language and Communication Research*, (14).

Chuandong Su, Fumiyo Fukumoto, Xiaoxi Huang, Jiyi Li, Rongbo Wang, and Zhiqun Chen. 2020. DeepMet: A reading comprehension paradigm for token-level metaphor detection. In *Proceedings of the Second Workshop on Figurative Language Processing*, pages 30–39, Online. Association for Computational Linguistics.

Asuka Terai and Taiki Sugyo. 2019. Construction of a corpus-based metaphor generation support system built on japanese literature. In *2019 IEEE 11th International Workshop on Computational Intelligence and Applications (IWCIA)*, pages 1–6. IEEE.

Du Tran, Heng Wang, Lorenzo Torresani, Jamie Ray, Yann LeCun, and Manohar Paluri. 2018. A closer look at spatiotemporal convolutions for action recognition. In *2018 IEEE/CVF Conference on Computer Vision and Pattern Recognition*, pages 6450–6459.

Elizabeth Closs Traugott. 1985. 'conventional'and 'dead'metaphors revisited. *The ubiquity of metaphor: Metaphor in language and thought*, pages 17–56.

Yao-Hung Hubert Tsai, Shaojie Bai, Paul Pu Liang, J Zico Kolter, Louis-Philippe Morency, and Ruslan Salakhutdinov. 2019. Multimodal transformer for unaligned multimodal language sequences. In *Proceedings of the conference. Association for Computational Linguistics. Meeting*, volume 2019, page 6558. NIH Public Access.

Mingyu Wan, Kathleen Ahrens, Emmanuele Chersoni, Menghan Jiang, Qi Su, Rong Xiang, and Chu-Ren Huang. 2020. Using conceptual norms for metaphor detection. In *Proceedings of the Second Workshop on Figurative Language Processing*, pages 104–109, Online. Association for Computational Linguistics.

Thomas Wolf, Lysandre Debut, Victor Sanh, Julien Chaumond, Clement Delangue, Anthony Moi, Pierric Cistac, Tim Rault, Rémi Louf, Morgan Funtowicz, Joe Davison, Sam Shleifer, Patrick von Platen, Clara Ma, Yacine Jernite, Julien Plu, Canwen Xu, Teven Le Scao, Sylvain Gugger, Mariama Drame, Quentin Lhoest, and Alexander M. Rush. 2020. Transformers: State-of-the-art natural language processing. In *Proceedings of the 2020 Conference on Empirical Methods in Natural Language Processing: System Demonstrations*, pages 38–45, Online. Association for Computational Linguistics.

Ping Xiao, Khalid Alnajjar, Mark Granroth-Wilding, Kat Agres, and Hannu Toivonen. 2016. Meta4meaning: Automatic metaphor interpretation using corpus-derived word associations. In *Proceedings of the Seventh International Conference on Computational Creativity*. Sony CSL Paris.

Amir Zadeh, Paul Pu Liang, Navonil Mazumder, Soujanya Poria, Erik Cambria, and Louis-Philippe Morency. 2018. Memory fusion network for multi-view sequential learning. *Proceedings of the Thirty-Second AAAI Conference on Artificial Intelligence*.

Danning Zheng, Ruihua Song, Tianran Hu, Hao Fu, and Jin Zhou. 2019. "love is as complex as math": Metaphor generation system for social chatbot. In *Workshop on Chinese Lexical Semantics*, pages 337–347. Springer.

Andrew Zisserman, Joao Carreira, Karen Simonyan, Will Kay, Brian Zhang, Chloe Hillier, Sudheendra Vijayanarasimhan, Fabio Viola, Tim Green, Trevor Back, Paul Natsev, and Mustafa Suleyman. 2017. The kinetics human action video dataset.

Picard understanding Darmok: A Dataset and Model for Metaphor-Rich Translation in a Constructed Language

Peter A. Jansen
University of Arizona
pajansen@arizona.edu

Jordan Boyd-Graber
University of Maryland
jbg@umiacs.umd.edu

Abstract

Tamarian, a fictional language introduced in the *Star Trek* episode *Darmok*, communicates meaning through utterances of metaphorical references, such as *"Darmok and Jalad at Tanagra"* instead of *"We should work together."* This work assembles a Tamarian-English dictionary of utterances from the original episode and several follow-on novels, and uses this to construct a parallel corpus of 456 English-Tamarian utterances. A machine translation system based on a large language model (T5) is trained using this parallel corpus, and is shown to produce an accuracy of 76% when translating from English to Tamarian on known utterances.[1]

1 Introduction

Science fiction and fantasy literature has long created constructed languages for their characters, from Elvish in *Lord of the Rings* and Klingon in *Star Trek* to Heptapod in *Arrival* (Cheyne, 2008). These languages often have many of the same syntactic or semantic features as human languages, and some (such as Klingon) have been developed to a level where full dictionaries (Okrand, 1992) and online translators are available.[2]

An unconventional language was proposed in an episode of *Star Trek: The Next Generation* called *"Darmok"*, where a race of aliens called the Tamarians speak a language that is communicated exclusively through metaphors. Instead of direct reference (e.g. *"I want to give this to you"*), Tamarians speak in metaphorical references grounded in stories (e.g. *"Temba, his arms wide"*) that (like symbols) have learned associations with their true meaning meaning. In the *Darmok* story, the unusual nature of the language poses a challenge for both the automated translation systems and the characters in the story to learn. The creator of the language, Joe Mendowsky was inspired by the difficulty of translating across cultures (Block and Erdmann, 2012), and Tamarian has since been the subject of repeated informal study (Bogost, 2014) in the 30 years since the episode aired.

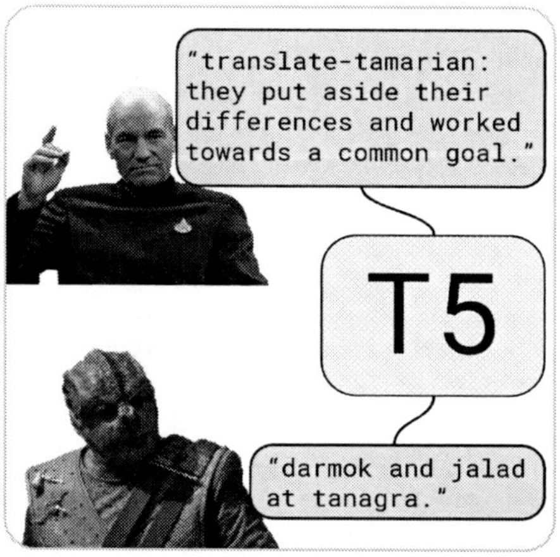

Figure 1: An example of translating English to the metaphor-grounded Tamarian language using T5.

This work investigates the feasibility of translating this artificial metaphor-rich language via our new parallel corpus of English-Tamarian phrases (Figure 1). Our machine translation system based on a large language model (Raffel et al., 2020, T5) has 76% accuracy in translating English phrases to Tamarian metaphorical utterances. This suggests automatically translating metaphor-grounded languages may be feasible, though we discuss several pragmatic challenges in representing complex expressions and generating a parallel corpus preventing scaling the approach.

2 English-Tamarian Parallel Corpus

Comparatively few Tamarian utterances have been authored, effectively limiting the size and scope of the effort. To maximize the number of available utterances, all utterances from the original broadcast

[1]Data and code available at: https://github.com/cognitiveailab/darmok

[2]https://www.translate.com/klingon-english

Proceedings of the 3rd Workshop on Figurative Language Processing (FLP), pages 34 - 38
December 8, 2022 ©2022 Association for Computational Linguistics

	Tamarian Utterance	Inferred Meaning	English Example
1	Darmok and Jalad at Tanagra	Working together	Knowing they would both be needed, they went together.
2	Temba, his arms wide.	Giving	The child offered his toy to his friend.
3	Kira at Bashi.	Story-telling	They described what had happened to those who listened.
4	Chenza at court, the court of silence.	Incontestability	The results were beyond reproach.
5	Zima at Anzo, Zima and Bakor.	Persistence	They continued their task, undeterred from past failures.
6	Fendit, refusing the flame.	Refusing help	She preferred to work alone, without assistance.
7	Chatha and Teribium, the fire warm.	Hospitality	Their household was offered for rest and comfort.
8	Jeral, her arms weary.	Being tired	She was spent at the end of the day.
9	Pirakee, with clouds parted.	Visibility	She turned on a flashlight, making it easier to see.
10	Hammat dancing.	Liking something	It filled them with delight.

Table 1: Example Tamarian utterances, their inferred meaning, and an English example from the parallel corpus.

episode, as well as those in three licensed novels featuring a Tamarian main character were used (Beyer, 2012, 2014, 2015). Approximately twenty utterances are provided in the *Darmok* episode, while an additional forty-eight are used in the novels, for a total of sixty-eight utterances.

Tamarian-to-English dictionary: To create a parallel English-Tamarian corpus, first a Tamarian-to-English dictionary that captures the inferred meaning of each Tamarian utterance was required. The meanings of the twenty broadcast utterances was ascertained from a Reddit thread with extensive discussion of the topic.[3] The meanings of the remaining forty-eight utterances was inferred as best as possible from the surrounding context of where they appeared in their respective novels.

Tamarian-English Parallel Corpus: Training a machine translation system requires a parallel corpus, where utterances of one language are paired with utterances of a second language, where the utterances in both languages have the same meaning. Tamarian utterances abstractly refer to specific types of situations that could be applicable to many circumstances. Thus, for each Tamarian utterance a set of k English examples were manually authored, with ten examples authored for thirty-nine utterances, and five examples authored for eleven utterances. Eighteen Tamarian utterances were not included in the parallel corpus as they have relatively narrow meanings, and generating a large number of parallel examples for them in English proved challenging. The final parallel corpus contains fifty Tamarian utterances, paired with 456 parallel English utterances (Table 1).

[3] `https://www.reddit.com/r/DaystromInstitute/comments/4ggwo5/the_tamarian_language_an_analysis/`

3 Translation Model

Approach: Here, English-to-Tamarian is modeled as a sequence-to-sequence (seq2seq) learning task, using English utterances as the source sentence, and a single Tamarian translation of that English utterance as the target sentence.

Models: Modeling used T5 (Raffel et al., 2020), a large pre-trained multi-task language model. T5 includes pre-training for a variety of tasks, including question answering, summarization, and translation. Several model sizes were explored, including T5-small (66M parameters), T5-base (220M parameters) and T5-large (220M parameters). The model prompt took the form of:

```
translate English to Tamarian:  {src}
```

where *{src}* is the English source sentence to translate (e.g. *"She offered it to them"*). The model then generated a corresponding target sequence corresponding to the Tamarian translation of the source sentence (e.g. *"Temba. His arms wide."*). The model was implemented using the Huggingface Transformers library (Wolf et al., 2020).

Dataset splits: Due to small dataset, we use 5-fold crossvalidation: with 60% of data used for training, 20% for development, and 20% for test. For utterances with ten examples, this corresponds to six train, two development, and two test samples per run, while for utterances with five examples, this corresponds to three train, one development, and one test sample per run.

Evaluation Metrics: Translation performance was evaluated using SACREBLEU (Post, 2018), a metric that measures translation performance using n-grams, while taking partial matches into account. Here, because only fifty Tamarian utterances are

	Model	Dev. BLEU	Dev. Acc.	Test BLEU	Test Acc.
T5	T5-Small	38	34.4%	41	38.0%
	T5-Base	71	72.8%	70	72.4%
	T5-Large	**80**	**82.4%**	**74**	**76.4%**

Table 2: Average English-to-Tamarian translation performance on both development and test sets. BLEU measures per-token accuracy, while *Acc.* refers to the average binary classification accuracy of choosing the correct Tamarian utterance for a given English input sentence.

available, and their surface presentation is generally constant, we also consider evaluating translation as an N*-class* classification task where a given English input sentence can be classified as one of fifty Tamarian utterances.

4 Results

Models were trained until performance (BLEU) asymptoted on the development set, at thirty epochs. The best performing model achieves a translation accuracy of 76% on the unseen test set, which corresponds to translating approximately three out of four English utterances from the corpus correctly into Tamarian (Table 2).

5 Discussion

As a constructed language for a fictional universe, Tamarian is a low resource language with fewer than one hundred known utterances. What might it take to grow Tamarian (or a metaphorically-grounded Tamarian-like language) into a more complete artificial language similar to Klingon? This section attempts to address the challenges of scaling beyond this work in the context of two central difficulties: growing the parallel corpus of metaphors, and challenges associated with the semantics of translating complex ideas in Tamarian.

5.1 Growing the Parallel Corpus

Growing the vocabulary of metaphors in Tamarian presents a unique challenge for constructed languages. Where human languages typically expresses base-level semantics at the level of the morpheme or word, Tamarian's most atomic construction is a single metaphor, making approaches that start with translating a dictionary challenging to adapt. One approach to growing Tamarian would be to continue the current manual approach, identifying a set of atomic events that convey common situations (such as *eating, giving, taking, or helping*),

Tamarian Utterance	**Inferred Meaning**
Gesture/Context Hypothesis	
Temba, his arms wide. *Also: Pointing at item*	Hand me the blue screwdriver I am pointing at
Specificity Hypothesis	
Jeral, her gift.	Give me a blue screwdriver on the left
Modifier Hypothesis	
Temba, his arms wide.	Giving
Paris, in the garage.	Screwdriver
Tolanis painting, in winter.	Blue
Bakor, examining.	Look to the left

Table 3: Examples of the three hypotheses for how fine-grained semantics could be inferred or composed in Tamarian.

and authoring utterances grounded in an expanded Tamarian mythology—for example, *"Timba, his stomach rumbling"* to convey the notion of hunger. The prerequisite for having an exhaustive list of possible event schemas to translate would likely make this approach challenging to scale.

Automatic Generation: An alternate approach was suggested by Picard in *Darmok* – to use the existing body of human literature (such as the *Epic of Gilgamesh*) to build a Tamarian-like language grounded in metaphors inferred from classic literature. Picard suggests that *"Gilgamesh and Enkidu at Uruk"* might be an utterance to represent a central component of the story – two people who were first in conflict coming together in friendship. Such an automatic approach to building a Tamarian-like language is in principle feasible, potentially making use of recent successes in automatic summarization to extract key elements of a story in templated form (e.g. {PERSONX} AND {PERSONY} AT {LOCATION}) to generate novel utterances. One of the challenges with this approach is that narratives often contain many events, specified both at a low-level (e.g. Enkidu entering the city of Uruk) and high-level (e.g. Gilgamesh and Enkidu eventually forming a friendship in spite of their differences), and identifying only a single idea to be represented by the utterance would be difficult.

5.2 The Challenge of Translating Fine-grained Semantics

It has been hypothesized that Tamarian may not be well suited to expressing fine-grained semantics, and would present challenges for translating utterances such as *"Hand me the blue screw driver on the left*" (Bogost, 2014). While the few observed multi-utterance exchanges of Tamarian have (so far) typically conveyed steps in a story, we present three hypotheses for how fine-grained semantics might be achieved, with examples shown in Table 3:

1. *Gesture/Context hypothesis:* The spoken Tamarian language may ground ambiguity through gestures or other situated contextual cues, as the Tamarian captain does when he utters *"Temba, his arms wide" (take)* and gestures to a weapon.
2. *Specificity hypothesis:* Though impractical, the Tamarian language may have many utterances to refer to very specific situations.
3. *Modifier hypothesis:* Unobserved classes of utterances may serve as modifiers, providing additional clarification to an utterance.

There is partial observation of both the *gesture/context* and *modifier* hypotheses provided in the original *Darmok* episode, and we believe the modifier hypothesis likely provides a mechanism for composing larger units of meaning akin to a generative grammar.

The more fundamental challenge of extending Tamarian is that every sentence must be connected to an underlying mythology: if you want to translate a sentence you must first create a universe (Sagan et al., 1983). While we can invent Tamarian sounding proper nouns, a more fundamental challenge is to build a world where there are characters who would have or invent a screwdriver, a character who could successfully use it, a character who would use it incorrectly, and perhaps someone else who could address when you've accidentally stripped the head of the screwdriver.

Thus, the challenge is not just creating enough examples but also building the cultural cannon to support those examples. While this is a unique linguistic challenge for Tamarian, it follows the course of other constructed languages: Quenya was developed alongside the backstory of Middle Earth (Lewis, 1995) and the creator of the Klingon language also ensured that the Klingon mythology was recorded in the Klingon language (Schönfeld et al., 2011). Tamarian foregrounds this challenge of obtaining enough cultural context to translate (Keesing, 1985; Maitland, 2017).

6 Related Work: (Computational) Linguistics for Constructed Languages

The elephant in the room is whether it is worthwhile to study constructed languages at all. This section seeks to answer that question with a resounding yes by discussing the other insights that have come from scholarly investigations of constructed languages.

Tamarian is from the Star Trek Universe, so it is instructive to spend a little time first with the oldest Star Trek language, Klingon. Klingon is often used in NLP education because it has features that are rare in natural languages but it is incredibly regular: a morphological analyzer can get 100% accuracy but still have fascinating properties like affixes for honorifics, completion, and tense (Wicentowski, 2004). Likewise, because Klingon is by construction meant to feel literally alien, its OVS structure can also upend students' part of speech tagging expectations (Boyd-Graber, 2014).

But Klingon is not just a fun exercise for programmers and linguists; the creation of parallel data (as discussed above for Tamarian) also explores the interplay between culture and translation. For the translation of *Hamlet* into Klingon, cultural adaptation (Peskov et al., 2021) is also needed: for example, Fortinbras becomes "the most insuborinate head of the House of Duras" (Kazimierczak, 2010). The art of translation often relies on metaphor (Veale, 2016) and cultural knowledge (Vinay and Darbelnet, 1995), and just as exploring Klingon can reveal limitations of our understanding of affix morphology and OVS word order, Tamarian can help illuminate the limitations of metaphor in communication.

All extant constructed languages are low resource languages, which typically pose challenges for machine translation (Haddow et al., 2021). Like how Klingon can emphasize particular aspects of a language (word order, morphology), Tamarian helps focus attention on the role of mythology, inter-personal relationships, and multiword expressions for translation.

7 Conclusion

This paper is an initial English–Tamarian translation model. This task is difficult because it not only maps words to words but also maps metaphor to typical translation phrases. While Tamarian is a constructed language, it shows large language models' ability and limitations for metaphor.

References

Kirsten Beyer. 2012. *Star Trek Voyager: Eternal Tide*. Pocket Books.

Kirsten Beyer. 2014. *Star Trek Voyager: Acts of Contrition*. Pocket Books.

Kirsten Beyer. 2015. *Star Trek Voyager: Atonement*. Pocket Books.

P.M. Block and T.J. Erdmann. 2012. *Star Trek: The Next Generation 365*. ABRAMS, Incorporated (Ignition).

Ian Bogost. 2014. Shaka, when the walls fell. *The Atlantic*.

Jordan Boyd-Graber. 2014. Homework 5: Qu' bopbe' paqvam.

Ria Cheyne. 2008. Created languages in science fiction. *Science Fiction Studies*, 35(3):386–403.

Barry Haddow, Rachel Bawden, Antonio Valerio Miceli Barone, Jindřich Helcl, and Alexandra Birch. 2021. Survey of low-resource machine translation.

Karolina Kazimierczak. 2010. Adapting shakespeare for "star trek" and "star trek" for shakespeare: "the klingon hamlet" and the spaces of translation. *Studies in Popular Culture*, 32(2):35–55.

Roger M. Keesing. 1985. Conventional metaphors and anthropological metaphysics: The problematic of cultural translation. *Journal of Anthropological Research*, 41(2):201–217.

Alex Lewis. 1995. Historical bias in the making of "the silmarillion". *Mallorn: The Journal of the Tolkien Society*, (33):158–166.

S. Maitland. 2017. *What Is Cultural Translation?* Bloomsbury Advances in Translation. Bloomsbury Academic.

Marc Okrand. 1992. *The Klingon Dictionary: The Official Guide to Klingon Words and Phrases*. Simon and Schuster.

Denis Peskov, Viktor Hangya, Jordan Boyd-Graber, and Alexander Fraser. 2021. Adapting entities across languages and cultures. In *Findings of Empirical Methods in Natural Language Processing*.

Matt Post. 2018. A call for clarity in reporting BLEU scores. In *Proceedings of the Third Conference on Machine Translation: Research Papers*, pages 186–191, Belgium, Brussels. Association for Computational Linguistics.

Colin Raffel, Noam Shazeer, Adam Roberts, Katherine Lee, Sharan Narang, Michael Matena, Yanqi Zhou, Wei Li, and Peter J Liu. 2020. Exploring the limits of transfer learning with a unified text-to-text transformer. *Journal of Machine Learning Research*, 21(140):1–67.

Carl Sagan, Ann Druyan, and Steven Soter. 1983. The lives of the stars. *Cosmos*, 1(9).

Floris Schönfeld, Mar Okrand, Kees Ligtelijn, and Vincent W.J Van Gerven Oei, editors. 2011. *paq'balth: The Klingon Epic*. Punctum Books, Brooklyn, NY.

Tony Veale. 2016. Round up the usual suspects: Knowledge-based metaphor generation. In *Proceedings of the Fourth Workshop on Metaphor in NLP*.

Jean-Paul Vinay and Jean Darbelnet. 1995. *Comparative stylistics of French and English: A methodology for translation*, volume 11. John Benjamins Publishing.

Richard Wicentowski. 2004. Multilingual noise-robust supervised morphological analysis using the WordFrame model. In *Proceedings of the 7th Meeting of the ACL Special Interest Group in Computational Phonology: Current Themes in Computational Phonology and Morphology*, pages 70–77, Barcelona, Spain. Association for Computational Linguistics.

Thomas Wolf, Julien Chaumond, Lysandre Debut, Victor Sanh, Clement Delangue, Anthony Moi, Pierric Cistac, Morgan Funtowicz, Joe Davison, Sam Shleifer, et al. 2020. Transformers: State-of-the-art natural language processing. In *Proceedings of the 2020 Conference on Empirical Methods in Natural Language Processing: System Demonstrations*, pages 38–45.

The Secret of Metaphor on Expressing Stronger Emotion

Yucheng Li [1], Frank Guerin [1], Chenghua Lin [2]*

[1] Department of Computer Science, University of Surrey, UK

{yucheng.li,f.guerin}@surrey.ac.uk

[2] Department of Computer Science, University of Sheffield, UK

c.lin@sheffild.ac.uk

Abstract

Metaphors are proven to have stronger emotional impact than literal expressions. Although this conclusion is shown to be promising in benefiting various NLP applications, the reasons behind this phenomenon are not well studied. This paper conducts the first study in exploring how metaphors convey stronger emotion than their literal counterparts. We find that metaphors are generally more specific than literal expressions. The more specific property of metaphor can be one of the reasons for metaphors' superiority in emotion expression. When we compare metaphors with literal expressions with the same specificity level, the gap of emotion expressing ability between both reduces significantly. In addition, we observe specificity is crucial in literal language as well, as literal language can express stronger emotion by making it more specific.

1 Introduction

Metaphors are widely used in human language, which allows people to communicate not just information, but also feelings and attitudes. It is generally believed that metaphors are especially effective in expressing subjective elements, such as sentiment and attitude. Recent studies in Psychology and Computational Linguistics thus provide a wide range of qualitative evidence which supports the idea that metaphors are closely related to sentiment. For example, Rentoumi et al. (2012) use metaphorical expressions as a feature in sentiment polarity detection and find it can be an effective indicator. Mao and Li (2021) introduce a multitask framework which jointly optimizes a metaphor detection task and aspect-based sentiment analysis and observe considerable improvement on both tasks. More importantly, Mohammad et al. (2016) give the first quantitative finding which shows that 83.6% of annotated metaphors tend to

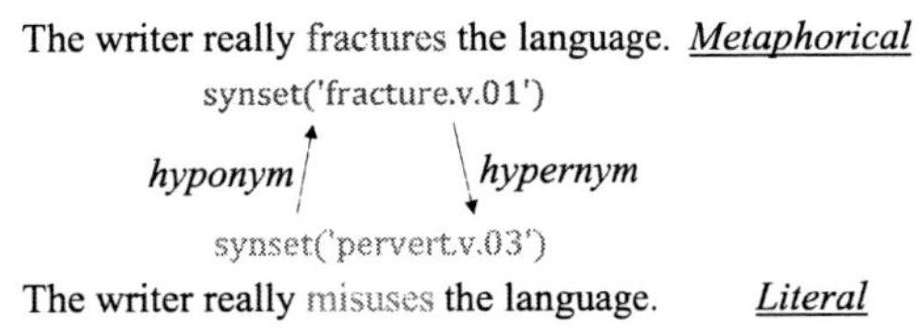

Figure 1: *hypernym* and *hyponym* relation between metaphor and literal expressions. Synset here presents the word sense of the target word based on WordNet sense dictionary. Blue text indicates metaphor and red text indicates literal.

have a stronger emotional impact than their literal counterparts.

However, although researchers conduct fruitful studies showing how metaphors are closely related to sentiment, the reason behind this phenomenon is not well explored. Investigating the mechanism of metaphor sentiment interaction can be quite promising. For instance, understanding how metaphor builds emotional bonds can guide metaphor generation models (Li et al., 2022a,b) producing empathetic and persuading responses. The result can also be helpful for sentiment analysis, especially on metaphor-enriched text (Cabot et al., 2020).

In this paper, we introduce an exploratory answer to the question of how metaphors convey stronger emotion than literal language. To investigate this phenomenon, we manually analyse the metaphor-literal parallel corpus from MOH dataset (Mohammad et al., 2016, see example in Figure 1) where the more emotional expression is marked among each metaphor-literal pair. Our study finds that metaphors might impose emotional impact on readers via giving more specific expressions, i.e., making the expression more precise. First, we find most metaphorical expressions are more specific than their literal counterparts. In other words, literal translations of metaphors usually convey more general meanings. It suits our intuition that metaphors are believed as more vivid. Second,

*Corresponding author

Proceedings of the 3rd Workshop on Figurative Language Processing (FLP), pages 39 - 43
December 8, 2022

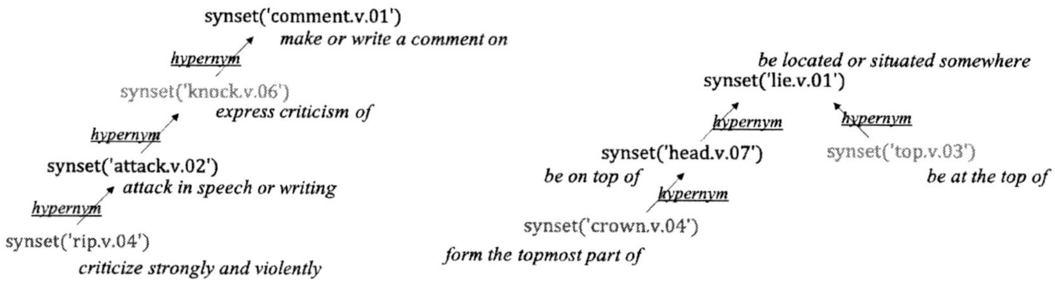

(a) (b)

Figure 2: Two cases illustrating positions of metaphorical and literal synset in the WordNet hierarchy.

we find metaphor's stronger emotional impact is partially from its more specific description. When we compare metaphors and their literal counterparts where both share the same level of specificity, we find the superiority of metaphors in arousing emotional impact drops significantly. When we test the *more-specific* principle on literal expressions, we find more specific literal expressions do surpass general ones on emotional impact.

We use linguistic relation *hypernym* and *hyponym* from WordNet (Miller, 1995) to define the specificity in our analysis. Specifically, *hypernym* denotes a word with a broad meaning yet *hyponym* denotes a word with a more specific meaning. So if a literal term is its metaphorical counterpart's *direct hypernym*, we know the metaphor describes a more specific meaning, or to say in a metaphorical way, draws a more precise picture. The Figure 1 shows an example of the above situation: the synset of the literal expression *misuses language* is the direct hypernym of the metaphorical synset, which means the literal expression is more general and the metaphor is more specific.

In case there is no direct hypernym or hyponym relation between metaphorical and literal expression, we compare the place of both in the WordNet Hierarchy to determine which one is more specific. In Figure 2, we see clearly that from the top to the bottom in the WordNet hierarchy, expressions tend to be more specific. So we can determine the relative specificity of terms by comparing their relative position in the hierarchy.

In summary, our contributions are mainly in two folds: 1) we introduce a novel hypernym-hierarchy method to measure the specificity of language expression and find metaphors are usually more specific than literal counterparts; 2) we find the reason why metaphor express stronger emotion is partially due to its more specific expression. Our code and data can be found in `https://github.com/liyucheng09/Metaphors_are_more_emotional`

Term:	rip
Sense/Synset:	Synset('rip.v.04')
Sentences:	The candidate ripped into his opponent mercilessly.
Literal:	The candidate criticized his opponent mercilessly.
Emotion:	The metaphorical expression is more emotional.

Table 1: The annotation example of verb *rip* in the MOH dataset.

2 The MOH Dataset

Mohammad et al. (2016) create a metaphor dataset in which verb senses are annotated for both metaphoricity and emotionality. In addition, the metaphorical uses are paired with their human-validated interpretations in the form of literal paraphrases (i.e., the metaphor's literal counterpart). In Table 1, we give an example of the MOH annotation for the verb *rip*. There are 171 metaphor-literal parallel annotations in total. We employ the MOH dataset in our study due to its parallel feature.

3 Experimental Setup

This study tests two research hypotheses:

> *Hypothesis 1*: Metaphors are generally more specific than their literal counterparts. In other words, metaphors are lower than their literal counterparts in the WordNet hierarchy.
>
> *Hypothesis 2*: Metaphors' stronger emotional impact is partially from metaphors'

more specific expression. In other words, more precise expression is one of the reasons why metaphors convey stronger sentiment than their literal counterparts.

To compare the specificity of metaphor and its literal counterpart, the hypernym-hierarchy information is assigned to both in parallel.

To explore the role specificity plays in the interaction between emotion and metaphor, we first analyse the correlation between specificity and emotion label of metaphors. We then perform two more experiments to further test how specificity affects emotional impact: 1) labelling which one is more emotional between metaphor and literal counterpart with the same level of specificity; 2) labelling which one is more emotional between a more general literal expression and a more specific literal expression. The first test isolates the influence of specificity in the emotion comparison of metaphor-literal pair; the second tests whether specificity empowers literal expression to convey stronger sentiment.

3.1 Specificity Test

Synset annotation. To access the hypernym relation of metaphor-literal data or locate both in the WordNet hierarchy, synsets of both need to be annotated. A synset in WordNet can be seen as a word sense item thus annotating a synset can be regarded as a word sense disambiguation task. The overall annotation procedure is as follows: 1) query WordNet with lemmatized target words to obtain synsets candidates; 2) determine the best suiting synset for both metaphorical and literal targets based on synset gloss and example sentence. An example of synset annotation is in Figure 1, where target words (i.e., metaphor and its literal counterpart, in colour) are labelled with synset.

Determining Specificity. After obtaining the synsets of metaphor-literal pair, there are two ways to determine the relative specificity of both expressions. For cases where there is a *direct hypernym* or *direct hyponym* relation between metaphorical and literal synset, we can know the relative specificity explicitly: the hypernym is more general yet the hyponym is more specific. For cases where metaphorical and literal synset are not connected with such a relation, we locate both terms in the WordNet hierarchy and compare their relative position. The locating procedure is as follows: 1) find their lowest common hypernym in WordNet hierarchy; 2) compute the number of hops from their common hypernym to both terms.

The example shown in Figure 1 belongs to the first situation that is there is a direct relation linking the two terms. So does the Figure 2 `(a)` case, where the literal term and the metaphoric term are connected via two hops of hypernym relations. So we know the literal term, as it is the hypernym of the metaphoric term, is more general than its metaphoric counterpart. In contrast, examples in Figure 2 `(b)` is the second situation, where the lowest common hypernym has to be found. It takes two hops from the metaphorical synset to reach the common nearest common hypernym, but it only takes one hop for its literal counterpart to arrive at the common hypernym. So we know the lower synset (i.e., the metaphorical one) is relatively more specific than the other. In our experiments, we find the first situation is the dominant cases, which suits around 86% (98 out of 114) of metaphor-literal pairs we tested. And only 14% (16 out of 114) pairs fall in the second situation.

3.2 Emotional Impact Test

To investigate the emotional impact that comes from the specificity of expressions, we analyse the correlation between the specificity and emotion label of metaphors. To further explore the interaction between specificity and emotional impact, we conduct two more manual experiments.

First, we compare which is more emotional between metaphor and its literal counterparts with the same level of specificity. To perform the comparison, we need to make up literal paraphrase same specific as the metaphor. We use the *sister terms* relation in WordNet to realise it. Two terms are sister terms as long as they share the same hypernym in WordNet, which means sister terms are at the same level in the WordNet hierarchy. We manually choose an appropriate literal sister term of the metaphor, and paraphrase the origin sentence with the literal term to form a literal counterpart has the same level of specificity. See line 2 in Table 2 for an example of such a sentence pair. With the paired data, we employ three human annotators with linguistics backgrounds to judge which expression is more emotional.

Second, we compare which is more emotional between more general literal and more specific literal expression. We use the *direct hyponym* relation to realise it. Similarly, we manually choose a direct

Term 1	Sentence 1	Term 2	sentence 2	Specific	Emotion
Synset(rip.v.04)	The candidate ripped into his opponent mercilessly.	Synset(criticize.v.01)	The candidate criticized into his opponent mercilessly.	first	first
Synset(rip.v.04)	The candidate ripped into his opponent mercilessly.	Synset(barrage.v.01)	The candidate admonished his opponent mercilessly.	same	same
Synset(criticize.v.01)	The candidate criticized his opponent mercilessly.	Synset(attack.v.02)	The candidate scolded his opponent mercilessly.	second	second

Table 2: Examples of sentence pairs in three experiments. The specific column denotes which sentence if more specific, and the emotion column indicates which sentence is more emotional. Blue text is metaphor and red text is literal. The three examples are *metaphor vs. literal, metaphor vs. specific literal, and literal vs. more specific literal* respectively.

hyponym term of the literal expression and paraphrase the origin sentence with the more specific literal term to make up the more specific counterpart. See line 3 in Table 2 for such a example sentence pair. We invite the same three annotators to tackle the emotion annotation, where annotators have to decide which express is more emotional, or choose the third option saying that both are similarly emotional.

4 Results

4.1 Metaphor and Specificity

We obtain 114 valid metaphor-literal pairs in the specificity experiment. 54 instances are invalid because we find no common hypernym among the metaphorical and literal terms in WordNet hierarchy. Among all 114 valid cases, 78.9% of metaphors are lower than their literal counterparts in the WordNet hierarchy, which means they are generally more specific. Only 5.2% of pairs show the opposite result, which means the metaphors are more general. 15.7% of metaphor-literal pairs are at the same specificity level. So in summary, we present a quantitative result that shows metaphors are generally more specific than literal expressions. Perhaps that is the reason why metaphors are believed giving more vivid descriptions.

4.2 Specificity and Emotional Impact

Metaphor Specificity and Emotion. Based on both emotion and specificity labels of metaphor-literal pairs, we measure the correlation between these two dimensions. The results are shown in Table 3. According to the table, we find that specificity can be a strong indicator of the emotional impact. Among all 90 more specific metaphors, 91.1% of them express stronger emotion. From the emotional dimension, 84.5% of metaphors that express stronger emotion are also more specific than their literal counterparts.

Metaphors are ..	more specific	more general	same
more emo.	82 (71.9%)	10 (8.7%)	5 (4.4%)
less/same emo.	8 (7.0%)	8 (7.0%)	1 (0.8%)

Table 3: When metaphors are more specific (general) than literal expressions, will they be more (less) emotional at the same time?

Metaphors are ...	vs. Literal	vs. Specific Literal
more emo.	143 (83.6%)	42 (40.0%, ↓ **43.6%**)
less emo.	17 (9.9%)	23 (21.9%, ↑ 12.0%)
similarly emo.	11 (6.4%)	40 (38.1%, ↑ **31.7%**)
Total	171	105

Table 4: Which is more emotional, metaphor or literal? Comparisons made between metaphors vs. normal literals and metaphors vs. more specific literals.

Metaphor and More Specific Literal. To investigate the extent to which specificity influences the emotional impact of metaphors, we perform an experiment to compare metaphors with general literal expressions and literal expressions sharing the same level of specificity with metaphors. We construct 105 valid sentence pairs in total. We fail to make up more because we cannot find a literal synset with the same specificity of the metaphor for those cases. The results are presented in Table 4. The inner-annotator agreement (IAA) score for emotion labelling is 0.77 via Krippendorff's alpha (Krippendorff, 2011). The first column of the Table is obtained from MOH's result. We find that the superiority of metaphors in expressing sentiment drops significantly from 83.6% to 40.0% when metaphors are compared to more specific literal expressions. In contrast, when metaphor-literal pairs share the same specificity, the ratio of expressing similar emotional strength increases noticeably. This results show that specificity is clearly a factor associating with emotional strength. However, metaphors still tend to have more emotional impact than more specific literal expressions. So we believe there are more factors affecting sentiment expressing ability despite specificity. We leave it

# instances that are:	
more specific is more emotional	32 (34.8%)
more general is more emotional	14 (15.2%)
similarly emotional	46 (50.0%)
Total	92

Table 5: Which is more emotional, literals or more specific literals?

to future works.

Literal and More Specific Literal. To test whether the *more-specific* mechanism also applies to literal expressions, we compare literal expressions with more specific literal ones. We construct 92 such sentence pairs in total. The IAA score of emotion labelling in this experiment is 0.82. The results are shown in Table 5, which illustrate that more specific expressions do impose a stronger emotional impact than more general ones. This demonstrates that specificity can be a stronger indicator in sentiment analysis in both figurative language and literal language.

References

Pere-Lluís Huguet Cabot, Verna Dankers, David Abadi, Agneta Fischer, and Ekaterina Shutova. 2020. The pragmatics behind politics: Modelling metaphor, framing and emotion in political discourse. *ACL Anthology*.

Klaus Krippendorff. 2011. Computing krippendorff's alpha-reliability.

Yucheng Li, Chenghua Lin, and Frank Geurin. 2022a. Nominal metaphor generation with multitask learning.

Yucheng Li, Chenghua Lin, and Frank Guerin. 2022b. CM-gen: A neural framework for Chinese metaphor generation with explicit context modelling. In *Proceedings of the 29th International Conference on Computational Linguistics*, pages 6468–6479, Gyeongju, Republic of Korea. International Committee on Computational Linguistics.

Rui Mao and Xiao Li. 2021. Bridging towers of multi-task learning with a gating mechanism for aspect-based sentiment analysis and sequential metaphor identification. In *Proceedings of the AAAI Conference on Artificial Intelligence*, volume 35, pages 13534–13542.

George A Miller. 1995. Wordnet: a lexical database for english. *Communications of the ACM*, 38(11):39–41.

Saif Mohammad, Ekaterina Shutova, and Peter Turney. 2016. Metaphor as a medium for emotion: An empirical study. In *Proceedings of the Fifth Joint Conference on Lexical and Computational Semantics*, pages 23–33.

Vassiliki Rentoumi, George A Vouros, Vangelis Karkaletsis, and Amalia Moser. 2012. Investigating metaphorical language in sentiment analysis: A sense-to-sentiment perspective. *ACM Transactions on Speech and Language Processing (TSLP)*, 9(3):1–31.

Drum Up SUPPORT: Systematic Analysis of Image-Schematic Conceptual Metaphors

Lennart Wachowiak
King's College London
lennart.wachowiak@gmail.com

Dagmar Gromann
University of Vienna
dagmar.gromann@gmail.com

Chao Xu
Shanxi University
c.xu@pku.edu.cn

Abstract

Conceptual metaphors represent a cognitive mechanism to transfer knowledge structures from one onto another domain. Image-schematic conceptual metaphors (ISCMs) specialize on transferring sensorimotor experiences to abstract domains. Natural language is believed to provide evidence of such metaphors. However, approaches to verify this hypothesis largely rely on top-down methods, gathering examples by way of introspection, or on manual corpus analyses. In order to contribute towards a method that is systematic and can be replicated, we propose to bring together existing processing steps in a pipeline to detect ISCMs, exemplified for the image schema SUPPORT in the COVID-19 domain. This pipeline consists of neural metaphor detection, dependency parsing to uncover construction patterns, clustering, and BERT-based frame annotation of dependent constructions to analyze ISCMs.

1 Introduction

Building on the foundation of existing knowledge to structure and explain new experiences is a common, well-known cognitive mechanism that, if depicted as metaphorical projection, can be captured by conceptual metaphors. In the case of image-schematic conceptual metaphors (ISCMs), the structures being transferred are sensorimotor patterns. Natural language is considered a source of evidence for the existence of ISCMs, which has mostly been investigated by a top-down approach of introspectively identifying examples (e.g. Lakoff and Johnson (1999); Kovecses (2010)) or a bottom-up approach of corpus analyses (e.g. Bennett and Cialone (2014)). Automated approaches generally focus on detecting whether a given sequence is metaphoric or not (Leong et al., 2020) rather than identifying the specific type of metaphor, with few exceptions (e.g. Dodge et al. (2015)). However, effective computational tools for metaphor analysis are important as they can play a role in improving machine translation (Mao et al., 2018) and in analyzing the usage and effect of metaphors, e.g. in political discourse (Prabhakaran et al., 2021) or literature (Freeman, 2002). In this paper, we propose a pipeline, depicted in Fig. 1, to automatically detect and identify ISCMs exemplified for the image schema SUPPORT in an English COVID-19 corpus. In contrast to introspective methods, the proposed pipeline promises to be replicable, faster, less subjective and capable of uncovering novel, previously unknown metaphors.

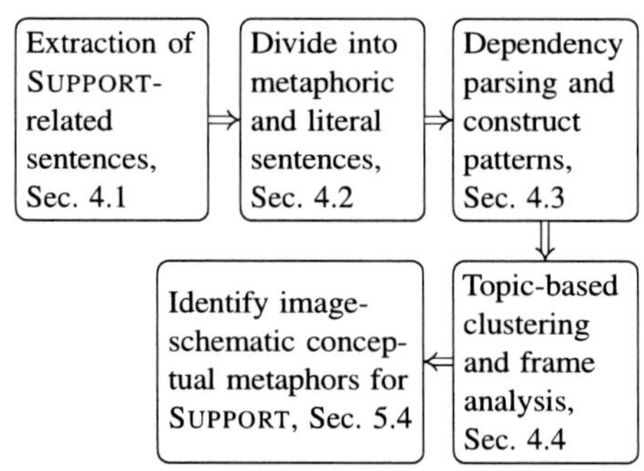

Figure 1: Overview of the proposed ISCMs analysis approach

Image schemas have been proposed by Lakoff (1987) and Johnson (1987) as cognitive building blocks to capture recurring sensorimotor interactions with the physical world. These experiential patterns are said to "reveal features of human thought and language" (Oakley, 2007), since they are mapped onto conceptual structures. ISCMs map these experiential, conceptual structures to the abstract domain. For instance, a person can physically *lean on* a concrete physical entity, e.g. a table, which entails the person pressing their body weight onto an entity that resists the push force. This physical experience can be mapped onto the abstract domain of emotional SUPPORT, such as in *He leans on his friends in these trying times*.

Our approach relies on a series of steps to semi-

Proceedings of the 3rd Workshop on Figurative Language Processing (FLP), pages 44 - 53
December 8, 2022 ©2022 Association for Computational Linguistics

automatically identify ISCMs in natural language: (a) detect whether a sequence is metaphoric or literal, (b) determine its constructional pattern, (c) identify its associated topics, and (d) identify its frames, from which we (e) derive underlying metaphoric projections. We extract sentences from the sample of The Coronavirus Corpus[1] based on seed words related to "support". In order to explore all metaphors related to SUPPORT, we decided to chose a specific, abstract domain, i.e., COVID-19 due to its ongoing relevance, abstract nature and importance to the society at large.

With this first approach to "drum up" SUPPORT for image schemas, this paper contributes a systematic method for detecting and identifying ISCMs in domain-specific natural language. To this end, constructional patterns uncover elements in a sentence that interact with metaphoric seed words, which are then frame annotated to provide evidence of the metaphor type the sentence represents. Furthermore, we contribute to the analysis of conceptual metaphors in natural language in general since the pipeline can equally be applied to other types of metaphors, image schemas and domains.

2 Preliminaries

Within the tradition of embodied cognition, physical experiences are said to shape higher-level cognition, including natural language. For instance, we learn as infants that some objects can support our weight, such as a chair, while others cannot, such as a flower. This physical support can then be transferred in *He leans on his friends in these trying times* to emotional assistance depicted by the metaphor ASSISTANCE IS SUPPORT. The proposed approach relies on theories of semantic frames and image schemas, which we briefly introduce.

2.1 Frames Semantics and Frames

Frame semantics (Fillmore, 1982) has been highly influential in cognitive linguistics as it combines linguistic sequences with knowledge structures to describe cognitive phenomena. Words or phrases, so-called lexical units, are associated with frames based on the common scene they evoke or, as described in FrameNet, their common *situation types*. Fillmore explicitly compares frames to other notions, such as experiential gestalts (Lakoff and Johnson, 1980), stating that frames can refer to a coherent schematization of experience. Thus, widely acknowledged frames provide a theoretically well-founded and practically validated basis for detecting ISCMs in natural language sequences. In fact, an initial yet uncompleted account of image schemas on the highest level of FrameNet can be found (Gangemi and Gromann, 2019). The bottleneck in utilizing frames is the low recall and precision of most existing automated tools to identify frames in natural language, addressed in Section 4.

2.2 Image Schemas

Image schemas capture recurring sensorimotor experiences as so-called gestalts (Johnson, 1987), i.e., structure compositions of parts forming a uniform whole. Image schemas can either be static or dynamic (Lakoff and Núñez, 2000), where the former are classified as orientational (e.g. ABOVE), topological (e.g. CONTACT), or force-dynamic (e.g. SUPPORT). Image schemas are simple spatial events built from spatial primitives (Mandler, 1992). The image schema SUPPORT is built from CONTACT between two objects were one depends on the other (Mandler, 1992; Besold et al., 2017). CONTACT is defined as two objects physically touching and only with force dynamics, i.e., application or exertion of force, constitutes SUPPORT.

Herskovits (1987) proposes that an object supports another if its weight presses or pulls upon it, where the supporting object resists the push or pull force. Prototypically, one entity rests on a horizontal upward-facing SURFACE of the other. SUPPORT can also involve other topological properties (Herskovits, 1987): an object can be hanging from, adhering to or being joined by nails, screws or other devices with the supporting entity. Conceptual metaphors are not merely a linguistic phenomenon, but rather a cognitive mechanism that enables the projection of recurring experiences onto abstract domains and structures our subjective experiences (Lakoff and Johnson, 1999). They can be specialized to image-schematic metaphors (Hedblom et al., 2015), which transfer the skeletal structure of image schemas to abstract target domains.

3 Related Work

Metaphor detection is often framed as binary classification task, in which each word of a sentence is either labeled as being used metaphorically or literally. Tong et al. (2021) provide an overview of architectures used for metaphor detec-

[1] https://www.english-corpora.org/corona/

tion, datasets, and other metaphor-related tasks. Another overview (Rai and Chakraverty, 2020) takes many different approaches to computational metaphor processing into account, additionally, reflecting on the different theoretical and linguistic views on the definition of metaphors. In a recent shared task on metaphor detection, fine-tuning pre-trained language models led to the best results (Leong et al., 2020).

There is, moreover, a tradition of analyzing syntactic patterns of metaphoric language (Sullivan, 2013), e.g. verb-prep-noun in which the verb represents the source domain and the noun the target domain. Such patterns build a core assumption of various researchers with the goal of automatically identifying source-to-target domain mappings. For instance, Shutova et al. (2017) explore unsupervised methods for identifying clusters of source and target concepts as well as the connections between them, limiting their approach to verb–object/subject constructions. Dodge et al. (2015) use multiple constructional patterns to find metaphor candidates that are then further analyzed by identifying evoked frames and checking their relations in MetaNet. Rosen (2018) trains a feed-forward neural network to predict one out of 77 source domains given a target domain referent and dependencies from a contextual sentence deemed as relevant. Compared to conceptual metaphors, image schemas have received little attention from computational linguists. Existing approaches to extract image schemas include unsupervised clustering (Gromann and Hedblom, 2017) and classifying sentences with neural language models (Wachowiak and Gromann, 2022). In terms of method and domain, Wicke and Bolognesi (2020) extract sentences from a COVID-19 corpus also based on seed words and apply topic modeling to analyze the frame WAR. A broader range of COVID-19-related metaphors is considered by Semino (2021).

In contrast to previous work, we do not make any assumptions about syntactic patterns or word classes, but compute statistics on syntactic patterns after we identify metaphoric language with a language model.

4 Method

As shown in Fig. 1, in order to identify image-schematic conceptual metaphors, we first compile a list of seed words related to "support", which we use to extract sentences from an English corpus on COVID-19. Each occurrence of a seed word in the corpus is automatically annotated as literal or metaphoric. With dependency parsing the constructional pattern for each sentence with metaphoric seed words are created. These patterns are important to identify the elements directly related to metaphoric seed words, for which we then obtain frame–semantic relations. The overall topic of each sentence is analyzed by way of clustering and frames and topics serve as a basis to identify its conceptual metaphor.

4.1 Extraction of SUPPORT-Related Sentences

As a first step, we compile a list of seed words related to SUPPORT by taking the top 100 words related to "support" from `relatedwords.org`, which bases its results on combined similarity metrics from resources such as ConceptNet and word embeddings. Moreover, we add words related to physical senses of "support" in WordNet synsets, FrameNet frames, and MetaNet frames. Based on these seed words, we extract sentences related to the image schema SUPPORT from the publicly available sample of The Coronavirus Corpus[2] consisting of 3.2 million words.

Seed words that entirely resulted in sentences unrelated to senses of SUPPORT as defined in Section 2.2 were excluded, e.g. "stomach" only related to the body part and not the related verb or "brook" could only be found in named entities, such as *Brook Park*. The resulting list of seed words with its count of sentences is provided in Section 5.1.

4.2 Automatic Metaphor Detection

Given the list of SUPPORT-related sentences, we automatically labeled each word of a sentence as literal or metaphoric. For this sub-task, we trained a metaphor-detection model on the VU Amsterdam Metaphor Corpus (Steen, 2010), which was annotated at word-level according to the metaphor identification protocol presented in the same paper. Based on the success of large pre-trained language models in a recent shared task on metaphor detection using the same corpus (Leong et al., 2020), we used the multilingual pre-trained language model XLM-RoBERTa (Conneau et al., 2020).

We trained the model with a learning rate of 2e-5 for eight epochs and loaded the model with the best validation performance at the end. We used the same train–test split as in the shared task and used

[2]`https://www.corpusdata.org/formats.asp`

randomly allocated 10% of the training data for validation. Code and model are publicly available[3].

4.3 Dependency Parsing for Comparison of Syntactic Structure

For each seed word, we investigated its syntactic function and relation to other words in the sentence by using the part-of-speech tagger and dependency parser from Stanford's neural NLP library Stanza (Qi et al., 2020). We provide statistics on incoming and outgoing relations to and from the seed words in Table 1. We first identify all dependency relations to and from the seed words, and then remove the relations with the following tags: cc, conj, fixed, flat, list, parataxis, orphan, goeswith, reparandum, punct, root, dep, aux, mark, det. They are considered as having no direct relevance for our purposes, for instance, only indicating function or coordination words. Some seed words used as nouns only have compound relations, with most of the syntactic information being stored in the relations of the compound word. Thus, we also extract the incoming and outgoing relations of the words constituting a compound together with the seed word. All elements identified in this step are then annotated with frames to identify the conceptual metaphor.

4.4 Identifying Topics and Conceptual Metaphors

We clustered the extracted sentences, allowing us to group similar sentences semantically. With this procedure, we quickly explore how SUPPORT is used in a literal and metaphorical sense. We created the clusters by using the BERTopic-library (Grootendorst, 2022). BERTopic represents each sentence using BERT-based sentence embeddings (Reimers and Gurevych, 2019). In a second step, it reduces the dimensionality using UMAP (McInnes et al., 2018), before clustering the resulting data points using the density-based hierarchical clustering algorithm HDBSCAN (McInnes et al., 2017).

Each sentence is automatically annotated with semantic frames by utilizing BERT-for-FrameNet (Minnema and Nissim, 2021) in its configuration of only predicting frames and not jointly predicting also semantic roles, relying on BERT layer 12. Frames related to each seed word and its dependent words or compounds are then manually analyzed and compared. While most frame parsers experience relatively low recall and precision, the BERT-for-FrameNet model returned a considerably higher number of frames than previous approaches. Nevertheless, specific seed words were almost never annotated, which could potentially be alleviated by querying other resources, such as Wikidata. However, for this case study, we opted for analyzing the frame-annotated sentences. The code and data for our approach are publicly available[4].

5 Results and Analysis

5.1 Extraction of SUPPORT-Related Sentences

Our final list of SUPPORT-related seed words and their frequencies is:

> advocacy (54), affirm (19), aid (315), assist (242), assistance (331), back (2154), back up (41), backbone (16), backing (18), backup (17), base (906), bear (142), bear out (2), bolster (37), boost (223), brace (37), bracket (15), buttress (2), commitment (191), corroborate (2), defend (102), endorse (41), endorsement (10), establish (250), financial backing (2), financial support (51), foot (271), help (2985), hold (1169), hold up (40), lifeline (22), livelihood (92), maintain (511), maintenance (95), patronage (5), prop (23), prop up (16), reinforcement (4), resource (563), sponsorship (10), stand (508), subscribe (119), substantiate (4), support (2317), supporter (104), supportive (40), sustain (92), sustenance (11), undercarriage (1), underpin (15), unsupported (10), uphold (34).

5.2 Automatic Metaphor Detection

Our metaphor-detection model achieves an accuracy of 95% on the test set. For the label *literal*, it achieves an F1 score of 0.97 with a precision of 0.96 and a recall of 0.98; and an F1 score of 0.76 for the label *metaphoric* with a precision of 0.82 of and a recall of 0.71. Its performance is, thus, comparable with the best-performing model of the 2020 metaphor-detection task (Leong et al., 2020).

The frequency of seed words in each sentence classified as metaphoric or literal is depicted in Fig. 2, which reveals that some seed words are more regularly used in a metaphoric sense than others. While words like "boost", "maintain", and "hold"

[3]https://github.com/lwachowiak/Multilingual-Metaphor-Detection

[4]https://github.com/lwachowiak/ISCMs/

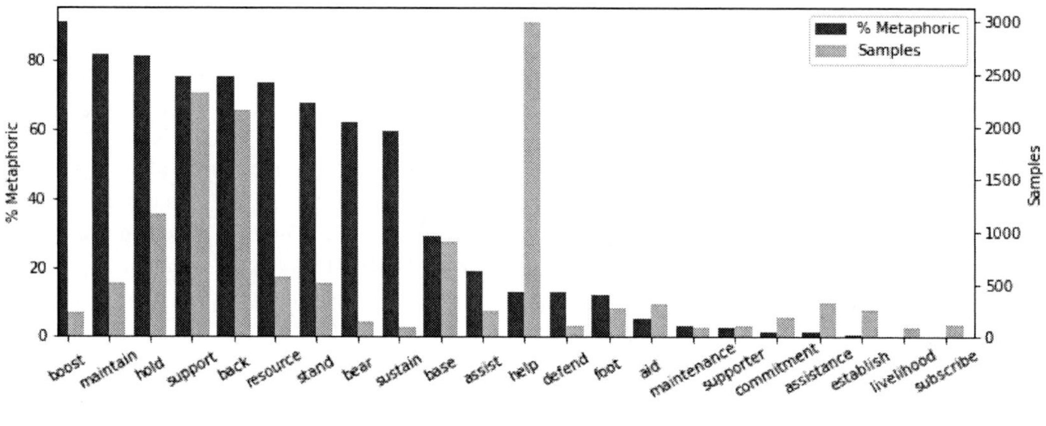

Figure 2: Seed words with over 75 samples ordered by how often they were used metaphorically

are used more than 70% of the time metaphorically, "establish", "livelihood", or "subscribe" are used less than 5% of the time metaphorically. These labels and statistics give us a good indication of which sentences to explore further in order to identify conceptual metaphors based on SUPPORT and which sentences' syntactic structure to investigate.

5.3 Dependency Parsing for Comparison of Syntactic Structure

For each sentence, we compute a constructional pattern centered on the seed word using dependency parsing as described in Section 4.3. For each pattern, we count how many seed words are used metaphorically in that syntactic constellation. Thus, the highest possible count for any pattern is 52 — the number of seed words. Counting all sentences per pattern would dip the statistics towards frequent patterns for a specific seed word that, however, is not necessarily an overall frequent pattern. The resulting most frequent constructional patterns grouped by word class of the seed word and examples are shown in Table 1. Word classes and dependency relations are presented in word order and concatenated by an underscore. If the dependency tag stands after the word class, it is an incoming relation to the seed word, if after the word class, it is an outgoing relation from the seed word, e.g. verb_obj ⟨⟨noun⟩⟩ indicates the relation `obj` going from the verb to the seed noun.

A variety of common patterns was detected for both, verb and noun seed words, where the seed words represent the source domain. The noun seed words appear most frequently as the object of a verb, with only one of the ten most common patterns having the seed word as the subject. Moreover, five of the patterns contain a nominal modifier relation. For verb seed words, the target domain noun frequently occurs as object, frequently co-occurring with a preceding noun or verb. Patterns for adjective and adverb seed words are much rarer, and we did not include those only occurring once.

5.4 Identifying Topics and Conceptual Metaphors

For an exploration of the senses and themes of SUPPORT-related words used in the Coronavirus discourse, we conducted a cluster analysis of different subsets of sentences. To obtain clusters of mostly metaphorical sentences, we clustered all 2,322 samples based on the seed word "support" (76% labeled as metaphoric); to obtain clusters of mostly literal sentences, we clustered all 2,988 samples based on the seed word "help" (13% metaphoric). BERTopic successfully clustered 1,288 sentences with the seed word "support" and 1,442 sentences with the seed word "help", grouping the rest of the sentences in a cluster of outliers. Fig. 3 and 4 show the two resulting cluster hierarchies, with more similar clusters being iteratively grouped together. Each cluster can be identified by the three words representing it best according to their Term Frequency-Inverse Document Frequency (TF-IDF). The TF-IDF value assumes each cluster to be a document and offsets the frequency of a word by the number of clusters containing the same word.

The results show that financial support is one of the most common contexts in which the seed word "support" is being used. A sentence from the cluster 23_billion_package_

Table 1: The most common constructional patterns of metaphorical ⟨⟨seed words⟩⟩. Count indicates how many unique seed words labeled as metaphoric appeared in such a pattern. Abbreviations: prep=preposition, adj=adjective, noun=noun or noun phrase, ppr=personal pronoun, adv=adverb; acl=clausal modifier of noun, advcl=adverbial clause modifier, amod=adjectival modifier, nmod=nominal modifier, nmod:poss=possessive nominal modifier, nsubj=nominal subject, obj=object, obl=oblique nominal, xcmop=open clausal complement

Noun Seed Words		
Dependency Pattern	Language Example (order as in sentence)	Count
verb_obj ⟨⟨noun⟩⟩	give a ⟨⟨lifeline⟩⟩	12
noun_nmod case_prep ⟨⟨noun⟩⟩ nmod_noun	supply on the ⟨⟨back⟩⟩ of demand	11
verb_obj ⟨⟨noun⟩⟩ nmod_noun	form ⟨⟨backbone⟩⟩ (of) speech	10
verb_obj amod_adj ⟨⟨noun⟩⟩	(COVID-19 restrictions) won broad ⟨⟨support⟩⟩	10
verb_obj nmod:poss_ppr ⟨⟨noun⟩⟩	(citizens) strengthen their (politicians) ⟨⟨backbones⟩⟩	9
verb_obl case_prep ⟨⟨noun⟩⟩	put (the industry) on ⟨⟨hold⟩⟩	9
⟨⟨noun⟩⟩ nmod_noun verb_nsubj	⟨⟨backing⟩⟩ (of a) brand becomes (invaluable)	8
verb_obl prep_case amod_adj ⟨⟨noun⟩⟩	(government needs to) get on the "front ⟨⟨foot⟩⟩"	7
⟨⟨noun⟩⟩ nmod_noun	⟨⟨boost⟩⟩ (to) economy	6
verb_obl case_prep ⟨⟨noun⟩⟩ nmod_noun	go (ahead) on ⟨⟨foot⟩⟩ (of) advice	6
Verb Seed Words		
acl_noun ⟨⟨verb⟩⟩ obl_noun	team ⟨⟨standing⟩⟩ (on) the front lines (of the outbreak)	14
verb_xcomp ⟨⟨verb⟩⟩ obj_noun	(war on corruption) continues to ⟨⟨bear⟩⟩ fruits	12
verb_advcl ⟨⟨verb⟩⟩ obj_noun	cut (down on expenses) to ⟨⟨sustain⟩⟩ (these difficult) times	11
nsubj_noun ⟨⟨verb⟩⟩ obj_noun	righteousness ⟨⟨upholds⟩⟩ (the) nation	10
acl_noun ⟨⟨verb⟩⟩ obj_noun	evidence to ⟨⟨back⟩⟩ (this) fear	9
nsubj_noun ⟨⟨verb⟩⟩ obj_noun obl_noun	businesses ⟨⟨bearing⟩⟩ the brunt (for) months	9
verb_ccomp nsubj_noun ⟨⟨verb⟩⟩ obj_noun	ensure everyone ⟨⟨maintains⟩⟩ (stable) housing	9
nsubj_noun ⟨⟨verb⟩⟩ obj_noun	authority ⟨⟨boosts⟩⟩ measures	8
njsub_noun ⟨⟨verb⟩⟩ obj_noun advcl_verb	unit ⟨⟨held⟩⟩ a protest to reiterate (their demands)	8
xcomp_verb ⟨⟨verb⟩⟩ obl_noun	to rebuild (our economy) ⟨⟨based⟩⟩ (on a green energy) future	8
Adjective and Adverb Seed Words		
⟨⟨adj⟩⟩ amod_noun	⟨⟨unsupported⟩⟩ market	3

spending is for example *6bn of new funding to support NHS*. Some clusters revolve around financial, political, and other forms of support for specific groups: artists, football clubs, farmers, businesses, students, children, or journalists. A sample from cluster 20, identified by the keywords "music", "artists", and "great", is simply the phrase *Support for Artists*. Another interesting example from the same cluster shows that support can also go the other way around and music can take the role of the support-giver: ... *the songs they 're turning to right now for support, peace, hope, and inspiration*. Another type of support is life support given in the context of COVID, such as in *To leave the ICU, Dr Monika said Mr Efendi must first be taken off breathing support*. All these examples are covered by the already existing metaphors ASSISTANCE IS SUPPORT and HELP IS SUPPORT in MetaNet. However, the clusters give a more fine-grained overview of what types of assistance and help can be given, as well as who the supporting and the supported entity are.

In comparison to "support", the seed word "help" is used in more diverse contexts in this corpus, resulting in a larger number of clusters. As before, different groups can be identified as giver and receiver of help, e.g. journalists as in *If you can help us, please click the button to ensure we can continue to provide quality independent journalism you can trust*. "Help" is used in a literal way and does not evoke the physical SUPPORT frame. However, in many sentences "help" could be replaced with "support" without changing the meaning of the sentence other than adding a metaphoric sense.

To more closely investigate the types of metaphors, all elements dependency-related to metaphoric seed words were automatically annotated with frames utilizing BERT-for-FrameNet. These frames provide insights into the potential type of metaphor of SUPPORT-related words and were counted once per seed word. Fig. 5 shows the top 14 most frequent frames. From the metaphorically labelled seed words, only 45% were provided with a frame, where the 1,429 examples of "back" and a surprisingly large 1,345 variations of "support" (including supportive, unsupported, etc.) remained without a frame. Nevertheless, an overall picture of types of frames related to SUPPORT can be obtained as shown in Fig. 5.

Besides the typical frames related to ASSISTANCE IS SUPPORT, Fig. 5 shows the interesting case of BODY PARTS as in *get back on their feet*

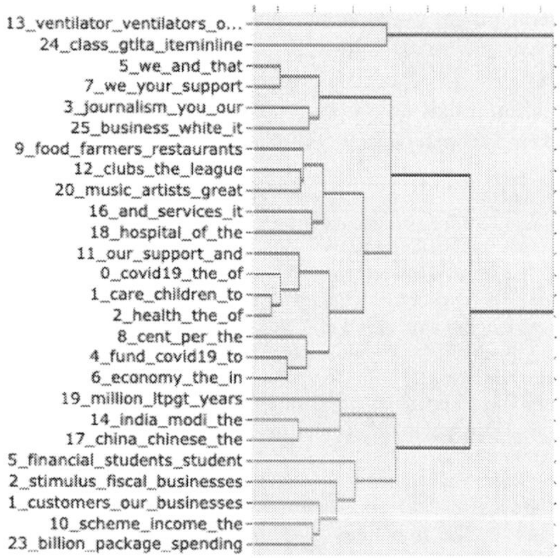

Figure 3: Clusters of sentences containing the word "support'. Clusters have a unique ID, followed by the words representing the cluster based on TF-IDF values.

and *be on the front foot* in the sense of being at an advantage. Adapting MetaNet metaphors, this could be interpreted as RECOVERY IS BODILY SUPPORT since *get back on their feet* means recovery, while *nimble on their feet* indicates endangerment. The orientation here is important since the *front foot* and *best foot forward* represent an advantage and the *back foot* puts one at a disadvantage, which collocates this metaphor with PROGRESS IS FORWARD MOTION. The expression *dragging their feet*, annotated with the frame MANIPULATION, relates it to a lack of support by body parts, i.e., MANIPULATION IS LACK OF BODILY SUPPORT.

The frame TAKING SIDES is mostly related to "support" and "back" as in *backing the campaign* and requires one person to metaphorically push or pull the weight of one side, so TAKING SIDES IS SUPPORT. For SELF MOTION the most frequent contender is "step", where similar to "foot" forward is progress, e.g. *people have stepped forward for this*, and backwards or away is withdrawal of support, e.g. *he backed away from calling for a quarantine*. Thus, a specialization of the PROGRESS IS FORWARD MOTION could be PROGRESS IS SUPPORT BY SELF MOTION, which can be backed by examples of the frames SELF MOTION as well as BODY PARTS, e.g. *put our best foot forward*. The frame COMPLIANCE mostly relates to abide, but provides interesting cases for

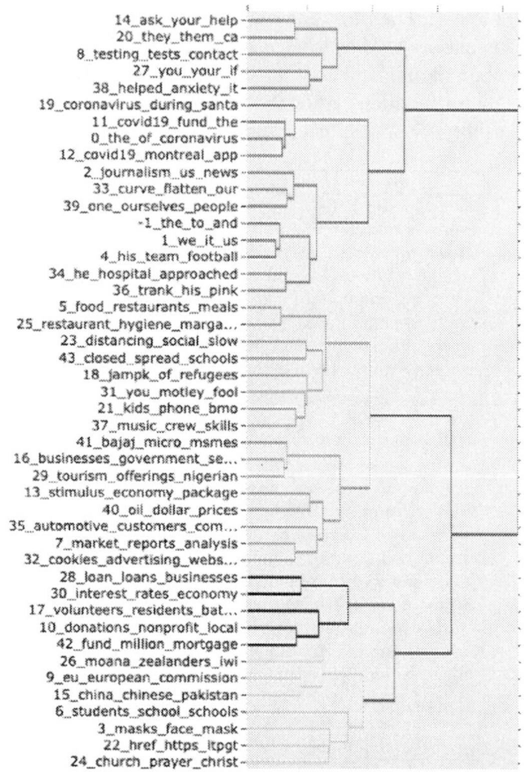

Figure 4: Clusters of sentences containing the seed word "help". Clusters have a unique ID, followed by the words representing the cluster based on TF-IDF values.

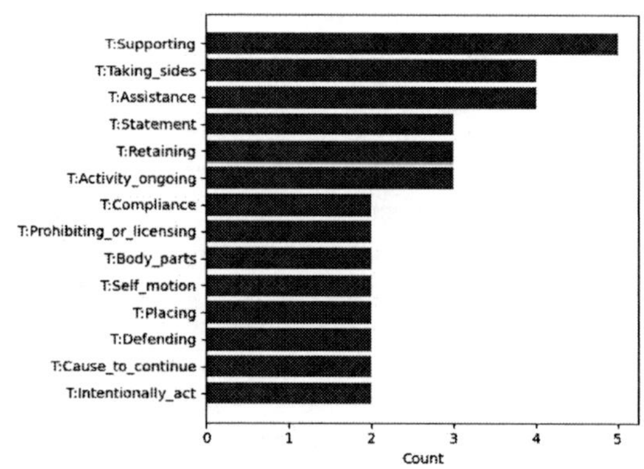

Figure 5: Frequent frames associated with seed words

"upholding" as in *upholding the rule of law* which indicates COMPLIANCE IS SUPPORT, since upholding in its literal sense to keep elevated requires the pulling of weight. One highly frequent frame in terms of occurrence across sentences that, however, only occurs with the two seed words "step" and "boost" is CAUSE CHANGE OF POSITION ON A SCALE. For instance, in the sentence of *He will step down as CEO* it is collocated with ACTIVITY STOP leading to ACTIVITY STOP CAUSES CHANGE OF POSITION ON A SCALE. The seed word "bear" is frequently annotated with TOLERATING as in *patients bear the pain*, indicating that TOLERATING IS SUPPORT.

This frame annotation step provides an excellent method for analyzing the (lack of) semantic richness of seed words, e.g. "aid" always relates to ASSISTANCE and "abide" always to COMPLIANCE. In contrast, the seed word "hold" relates to 13 different frames. While not all meanings of all seed words directly relate to ISCMs of SUPPORT, the above examples show that this method can still facilitate their exploration. Nevertheless, with a representative amount of human-curated data, a more rigorous evaluation can be foreseen, also taking other sources of metaphoric and image-schematic information into account. In any case, the final formulation of ISCMs will most likely always benefit from human refinement.

6 Discussion and Conclusion

In this paper, we presented a method to semi-automatically explore image-schematic conceptual metaphors, their related topics and constructional patterns in natural language. A pipeline returns syntactic patterns, thematic clusters, and frames for seed words related to a specific image schema. This approach enables the analysis of how the image schema SUPPORT is used within the context of COVID-19 in a more systematic and comprehensive way than possible with introspective methods. Besides detecting examples of well-known metaphors, it allowed us to uncover new metaphors, e.g. RECOVERY IS BODILY SUPPORT. To this end, building constructional patterns in a bottom-up manner without prior assumptions was important. In terms of topics, a wide variety of supporters and support recipients could be detected.

To apply the same method to other image schemas, a set of related seed words would need to be compiled as input to the method. For instance, a seed word list for the image schema CONTAINMENT could include words such as "inside", "boundary", or "vessel". One drawback of this seed word approach is that polysemy in the sense of multiple literal or even metaphoric meanings of a seed words is not explicitly considered. Nevertheless, given that no repositories of ISCMs exist and repositories on conceptual metaphors, such as MetaNet, contain a limited number of natural language examples or ISCMs, this semi-automated approach is an important step forward to drum up support of ISCMs.

As a knowledge extraction approach rooted in cognitive science, a natural next step would be to explore the taxonomic structures of frames provided by MetaNet, FrameNet or similar resources to query interdependencies between and relations among ISCMs. Furthermore, existing semantic resources, such as DBpedia and Wikidata, should be utilized to increase the number of annotated frames.

Currently, this approach heavily relies on recent advances of methods in computational linguistics brought together in a pipeline. Errors of one step are then propagated to the next. From the set of analysis steps, the metaphor detection performed best. The part-of-speech tags assigned in the process of dependency parsing are highly problematic for specific seed words, such as "back" that is frequently mistagged as noun or adverb when used as verb, negatively affecting the obtained dependency relations and constructional patterns. Another shortcoming is that the clustering method groups many samples into a cluster of outliers. The number of identified outliers, however, is so large that valuable information is inevitably lost, and only a subpart of the semantic topics is represented in the results. For the frame parsing, the return of frames per sentence was considerably higher than with similar approaches (as also reported in (Minnema and Nissim, 2021)), however, the number of frames for seed words was less than half of the overall count of sentences. Very short, heading-like sequences that lack context were generally not frame-annotated at all, e.g. *standing in line for essentials*. This reinforces the need to supplement frame parsing with other processes and resources.

To improve the pipeline and reduce the amount of manual labor required, it would be beneficial to be able to automatically label the target domains for which a specific image schema is used — a step that currently is mostly done manually with the resulting frames and clusters, due to the lack of frame coverage. In order to automatically identify the target domain, we plan to train a sequence-to-sequence model, e.g. T5 (Raffel et al., 2019), to predict the target domain given a source domain and a contextualizing sentence. For instance, the sample SUPPORT*: He leans on his friends in these trying times* should be labeled as ASSISTANCE.

References

B. Bennett and C. Cialone. 2014. Corpus guided sense cluster analysis: a methodology for ontology development (with examples from the spatial domain). In *The Proceedings of 8th International Conference on Formal Ontology in Information Systems (FOIS)*, pages 213–226. IOS Press.

Tarek R Besold, Maria M Hedblom, and Oliver Kutz. 2017. A narrative in three acts: Using combinations of image schemas to model events. *Biologically Inspired Cognitive Architectures*, 19:10–20.

Alexis Conneau, Kartikay Khandelwal, Naman Goyal, Vishrav Chaudhary, Guillaume Wenzek, Francisco Guzmán, Edouard Grave, Myle Ott, Luke Zettlemoyer, and Veselin Stoyanov. 2020. Unsupervised cross-lingual representation learning at scale. In *Proceedings of the 58th Annual Meeting of the Association for Computational Linguistics*, pages 8440–8451. Association for Computational Linguistics.

Ellen Dodge, Jisup Hong, and Elise Stickles. 2015. MetaNet: Deep semantic automatic metaphor analysis. In *Proceedings of the Third Workshop on Metaphor in NLP*, pages 40–49, Denver, Colorado. Association for Computational Linguistics.

Charles J Fillmore. 1982. Frame semantics. In *Linguistics in the Morning Calm*, pages 111–138. Seoul: Hanshin.

Margaret H Freeman. 2002. Momentary stays, exploding forces: A cognitive linguistic approach to the poetics of emily dickinson and robert frost. *Journal of English Linguistics*, 30(1):73–90.

Aldo Gangemi and Dagmar Gromann. 2019. Analyzing the imagistic foundation of framality via prepositions. In *Proceedings of the Joint Ontology Workshops (JOWO)*.

Dagmar Gromann and Maria M Hedblom. 2017. Kinesthetic mind reader: A method to identify image schemas in natural language. *Advances in Cognitive Systems*, 5:14.

Maarten Grootendorst. 2022. Bertopic: Neural topic modeling with a class-based TF-IDF procedure. *arXiv preprint arXiv:2203.05794*.

Maria M Hedblom, Oliver Kutz, and Fabian Neuhaus. 2015. Choosing the right path: Image schema theory as a foundation for concept invention. *Journal of Artificial General Intelligence*, 6(1):21–54.

Annette Herskovits. 1987. *Language and Spatial Cognition*. Cambridge University Press.

Mark Johnson. 1987. *The Body in the Mind. The Bodily Basis of Meaning, Imagination, and Reasoning*. University of Chicago Press.

Zoltan Kovecses. 2010. *Metaphor: A Practical Introduction*. Oxford University Press.

George Lakoff. 1987. *Women, Fire, and Dangerous Things. What Categories Reveal about the Mind*. The University of Chicago Press.

George Lakoff and Mark Johnson. 1980. *Metaphors We Live By*. University of Chicago Press.

George Lakoff and Mark Johnson. 1999. *Philosophy in the Flesh: the Embodied Mind & its Challenge to Western Thought*. Basic Books.

George Lakoff and Rafael Núñez. 2000. *Where Mathematics Come From: How the Embodied Mind Brings Mathematics into Being*. New York: Basic Books.

Chee Wee (Ben) Leong, Beata Beigman Klebanov, Chris Hamill, Egon Stemle, Rutuja Ubale, and Xianyang Chen. 2020. A report on the 2020 VUA and TOEFL metaphor detection shared task. In *Proceedings of the Second Workshop on Figurative Language Processing*, pages 18–29. Association for Computational Linguistics.

Jean M. Mandler. 1992. How to build a baby: II. conceptual primitives. *Psychological Review*, 99(4):587–604.

Rui Mao, Chenghua Lin, and Frank Guerin. 2018. Word embedding and wordnet based metaphor identification and interpretation. In *Proceedings of the 56th annual meeting of the association for computational linguistics*. Association for Computational Linguistics (ACL).

L. McInnes, J. Healy, and J. Melville. 2018. UMAP: Uniform Manifold Approximation and Projection for Dimension Reduction. *arXiv preprint arXiv:1802.03426*.

Leland McInnes, John Healy, and Steve Astels. 2017. hdbscan: Hierarchical density based clustering. *The Journal of Open Source Software*, 2(11):205.

Gosse Minnema and Malvina Nissim. 2021. Breeding fillmore's chickens and hatching the eggs: Recombining frames and roles in frame-semantic parsing. In *Proceedings of the 14th International Conference on Computational Semantics (IWCS)*, pages 155–165.

Todd Oakley. 2007. Image schemas. In *The Oxford Handbook of Cognitive Linguistics*, pages 214–235. Oxford: Oxford University Press.

Vinodkumar Prabhakaran, Marek Rei, and Ekaterina Shutova. 2021. How metaphors impact political discourse: A large-scale topic-agnostic study using neural metaphor detection. *arXiv preprint arXiv:2104.03928*.

Peng Qi, Yuhao Zhang, Yuhui Zhang, Jason Bolton, and Christopher D. Manning. 2020. Stanza: A Python natural language processing toolkit for many human languages. In *Proceedings of the 58th Annual Meeting of the Association for Computational Linguistics: System Demonstrations*.

Colin Raffel, Noam Shazeer, Adam Roberts, Katherine Lee, Sharan Narang, Michael Matena, Yanqi Zhou, Wei Li, and Peter J Liu. 2019. Exploring the limits of transfer learning with a unified text-to-text transformer. *arXiv preprint arXiv:1910.10683*.

Sunny Rai and Shampa Chakraverty. 2020. A survey on computational metaphor processing. *ACM Computing Surveys (CSUR)*, 53(2):1–37.

Nils Reimers and Iryna Gurevych. 2019. Sentence-BERT: Sentence embeddings using siamese bert-networks. In *Proceedings of the 2019 Conference on Empirical Methods in Natural Language Processing*. Association for Computational Linguistics.

Zachary Rosen. 2018. Computationally constructed concepts: A machine learning approach to metaphor interpretation using usage-based construction grammatical cues. In *Proceedings of the Workshop on Figurative Language Processing*, pages 102–109.

Elena Semino. 2021. "Not soldiers but fire-fighters"–metaphors and covid-19. *Health Communication*, 36(1):50–58.

Ekaterina Shutova, Lin Sun, Elkin Darío Gutiérrez, Patricia Lichtenstein, and Srini Narayanan. 2017. Multilingual metaphor processing: Experiments with semi-supervised and unsupervised learning. *Computational Linguistics*, 43(1):71–123.

Gerard Steen. 2010. *A Method for Linguistic Metaphor Identification: From MIP to MIPVU*. John Benjamins Publishing.

Karen Sullivan. 2013. *Frames and Constructions in Metaphoric Language*. John Benjamins Publishing.

Xiaoyu Tong, Ekaterina Shutova, and Martha Lewis. 2021. Recent advances in neural metaphor processing: A linguistic, cognitive and social perspective. In *Proceedings of the 2021 Conference of the North American Chapter of the Association for Computational Linguistics: Human Language Technologies*, pages 4673–4686. Association for Computational Linguistics.

Lennart Wachowiak and Dagmar Gromann. 2022. Systematic analysis of image schemas in natural language through explainable multilingual neural language processing. In *Proceedings of the 29th International Conference on Computational Linguistics*, pages 5571–5581.

Philipp Wicke and Marianna M Bolognesi. 2020. Framing covid-19: How we conceptualize and discuss the pandemic on twitter. *PLoS ONE*, 15(9):e0240010.

Effective Cross-Task Transfer Learning for Explainable Natural Language Inference with *T5*

Irina Bigoulaeva[1*], **Rachneet Sachdeva**[1*], **Harish Tayyar Madabushi**[2*],
Aline Villavicencio[3] and **Iryna Gurevych**[1]

[1] Ubiquitous Knowledge Processing (UKP) Lab, Technische Universität Darmstadt
[2] Department of Computer Science, The University of Bath
[3] Department of Computer Science, The University of Sheffield

www.ukp.tu-darmstadt.de

htm43@bath.ac.uk, a.villavicencio@sheffield.ac.uk

Abstract

We compare sequential fine-tuning with a model for multi-task learning in the context where we are interested in boosting performance on two tasks, one of which depends on the other. We test these models on the *FigLang2022* shared task which requires participants to predict language inference labels on figurative language along with corresponding textual explanations of the inference predictions. Our results show that while sequential multi-task learning can be tuned to be good at the first of two target tasks, it performs less well on the second and additionally struggles with overfitting. Our findings show that simple sequential fine-tuning of text-to-text models is an extraordinarily powerful method for cross-task knowledge transfer while simultaneously predicting multiple interdependent targets. So much so, that our best model achieved the (tied) *highest score* on the task[1].

1 Introduction and Motivation

The transfer of information between *supervised learning objectives* can be achieved in Pre-trained Language Models (PLMs) using either multi-task learning (MTL) (Caruana, 1997) or sequential fine-tuning (SFT) (Phang et al., 2018). MTL involves simultaneously training a model on multiple learning objectives using a weighted sum of their loss, while SFT involves sequentially training on a set of related tasks. Recent work has extended the SFT approach by converting all NLP problems into text-to-text (i.e., sequence-to-sequence where both input and output sequences are natural text) problems (Raffel et al., 2019). The resultant model – *T5* – has achieved state-of-the-art results on a variety of tasks such as question answering, sentiment analysis, and, most relevant to this work, Natural Language Inference (NLI).

In this work, we focus our efforts on the transfer of information from multiple related tasks for improved performance on a different set of tasks. In addition, we compare the effectiveness of SFT with that of MTL in a context where one of the target tasks is dependent on the other. Given the dependence of one of the target tasks on the other, we implement an end-to-end multi-task learning model to perform each of the tasks sequentially: an architecture referred to as a *hierarchical feature pipeline* based MTL architecture (*HiFeatMTL*, for short) (Chen et al., 2021). While HiFeatMTL has been previously used in different contexts (see Section 3), it has, to the best of our knowledge, *not* been used with, or compared to, text-to-text models. This is of particular importance as such models are known to enable transfer learning (Raffel et al., 2019) and it is crucial to determine if traditional MTL methods can boost cross-task knowledge transfer in such models.

Specifically we participate in the FigLang2022 Shared Task[2], which extends NLI to include a figurative-language hypothesis and additionally requires participants to output a textual explanation (also see Section 2). FigLang2022 is ideally suited for the exploration of knowledge transfer, as PLMs have been shown to struggle with figurative language and so any gains achieved are a result of knowledge transfer. For example, Liu et al. (2022) show that in the zero- and few-shot settings, PLMs perform significantly worse than humans. This is especially the case with idioms (Yu and Ettinger, 2020; Tayyar Madabushi et al., 2021), on which T5 does particularly poorly (see Section 4). Additionally, FigLang2022's emphasis on explanations of the predicted labels provides us with the oppor-

*Equal Contribution

[1]To ensure reproducibility and to enable other researchers to build upon our work, we make our code and models freely available at https://github.com/Rachneet/cross-task-figurative-explanations

[2]https://figlang2022sharedtask.github.io/

Proceedings of the 3rd Workshop on Figurative Language Processing (FLP), pages 54 - 60
December 8, 2022

tunity to test cross-task knowledge transfer in a setting where one target task depends on the other (HiFeatMTL) – this is especially so given the evaluation methods used (detailed in Section 2).

We evaluate the effectiveness of boosting performance on the target tasks through the transfer of information from two related tasks: a) eSNLI, which is a dataset consisting of explanations associated with NLI labels, and b) IMPLI, which is an NLI dataset (without explanations) that contains figurative language. More concretely, we set out to answer the following research questions:

1. Can distinct task-specific knowledge be transferred from separate tasks so as to improve performance on a target task? Concretely, can we transfer explanations of literal language from eSNLI and figurative NLI without explanations from IMPLI?
2. Which of the two knowledge transfer techniques (SFT or HiFeatMTL) is more effective in the text-to-text context?

2 The FigLang2022 Shared Task

FigLang2022 is a variation of the NLI task which requires the generation of a textual explanation for the NLI prediction. Additionally, the hypothesis is a sentence that employs one of four kinds of figurative expressions: *sarcasm, simile, idiom,* or *metaphor*. Additionally, a hypothesis can be a *creative paraphrase*, which rewords the premise using more expressive, literal terminology. Table 1 shows examples from the task dataset.

Entailment	
Premise	I respectfully disagree.
Hypothesis	I beg to differ. *(Idiom)*
Explanation	To beg to differ is to disagree with someone, and in this sentence the speaker is respectfully disagreeing.
Contradiction	
Premise	She was calm.
Hypothesis	She was like a kitten in a den of coyotes. *(Simile)*
Explanation	A kitten in a den of coyotes would be scared and not calm.

Table 1: An entailment and contradiction pair from the FigLang2022 dataset.

FigLang2022 takes into consideration the quality of the generated explanation when assessing the model's performance by use of an *explanation score*, which is the average between BERTScore and BLEURT and ranges between 0 and 100. The task leaderboard is based on NLI label accuracy at an explanation score threshold of 60, although the NLI label accuracy is reported at three thresholds of the explanation score (i.e. 0, 50, and 60) so as to provide a glimpse of how the model's NLI and explanation abilities are influenced by each other.

3 Related Work

NLI is considered central to the task of Natural Language Understanding, and there has been significant focus on the development of models that can perform well on the task (Wang et al., 2018). This task of language inference has been independently extended to incorporate explanations (Camburu et al., 2018) and figurative language (Stowe et al., 2022) (both detailed below). Chakrabarty et al. (2022) introduced *FLUTE*, the Figurative Language Understanding and Textual Explanations dataset which brought together these two aspects.

Previous shared tasks involving figurative language focused on the identification or representation of figurative knowledge: For example, FigLang2020 (Klebanov et al., 2020) and Task 6 of SemEval 2022 (Abu Farha et al., 2022) involved sarcasm detection, and Task 2 of SemEval 2022 (Tayyar Madabushi et al., 2022) involved the identification and representation of idioms.

The generation of textual explanations necessitates the use of generative models such as BART (Lewis et al., 2020) or T5 (Raffel et al., 2019). Narang et al. (2020) introduce WT5, a sequence-to-sequence model that outputs natural-text explanations alongside its predictions and Erliksson et al. (2021) found T5 to consistently outperform BART in explanation generation.

Of specific relevance to our work are the IMPLI (Stowe et al., 2022) and eSNLI (Camburu et al., 2018) datasets. IMPLI links a figurative sentence, specifically idiomatic or metaphoric, to a literal counterpart, with the NLI relation being either entailment or non-entailment. Stowe et al. (2022) show that idioms are difficult for models to handle, particularly in non-entailment relations. The eSNLI dataset (Camburu et al., 2018) is an explanation dataset for general NLI. It extends the Stanford Natural Language Inference dataset (Bowman et al., 2015) with human-generated text explanations.

Hierarchical feature pipeline based MTL architectures (*HiFeatMTL*) use the outputs of one task as a feature in the next and are distinct from hierarchical *signal* pipeline architectures wherein the outputs are used indirectly (e.g., their probabilities) (Chen et al., 2021). HiFeatMTL has previously been used variously (Fei et al., 2019; Gong et al., 2019; Song et al., 2020), including, for example, to provide PoS and other syntactic information to relatedness prediction, the output of which is, in addition to the syntactic features, passed to an entailment task (Hashimoto et al., 2017) (see also the survey by Chen et al. (2021)). To the best of our knowledge, this is the first work to use HiFeatMTL with, and to compare against, text-to-text models and their ability to transfer knowledge across tasks.

4 Methods

We set out to answer the research questions in Section 1 by evaluating the effectiveness of SFT and HiFeatMTL on the transfer of task-specific knowledge from separate tasks, namely, explanations from eSNLI and figurative language from IMPLI. We use T5 for all our experiments as it has been shown to be effective in explanation generation (Erliksson et al., 2021). We run all our hyperparameter optimisation and model variations using T5-base (evaluated on a development split consisting of 10% of the training data) before then transferring over the best performing settings to T5 large (trained on all of the training data) which is used to make predictions on the test set. While we find this method adequate in finding a good set of hyperparameters, the best setting for a smaller model need not necessarily be a good setting for larger models, especially given that some capabilities emerge only in larger models (Wei et al., 2022).

4.1 Exploratory Experiments

The first phase of our experiments was dedicated to using our development split to determining the best hyperparameters for T5, specifically the learning rate, and the number of beams, the two parameters that we found T5 to be extremely sensitive to. We do not experiment with prompt optimisation, but rather our prompts are based on what T5 was trained on (See listing 1).

```
Source_text:
    figurative hypothesis: <hypothesis> premise:
        <premise>
target_text:
    <label> explanation: <explanation>
```

Listing 1: Our default prompt used for T5.

An additional consideration of this initial phase was whether it was more effective to independently perform the task of NLI before subsequently generating explanations. However, we find that incorporating the gold inference labels does not improve the quality of explanations generated.

Knowledge Transfer To determine those forms of figurative language that T5 finds challenging and how effective knowledge transfer is, we test T5 fine-tuned just on FigLang2022, and sequentially on IMPLI followed by FigLang2022. The results of these experiments are presented in Table 2, which correspond to the observations made by Stowe et al. (2022) that idioms are particularly challenging for NLI models. Crucially, we find that the performance of the model *does* improve when first trained on IMPLI, thus establishing that knowledge transfer is possible in T5 through SFT.

Type	FigLang	IMPLI → FigLang
Metaphor	81.97	**83.61 (+ 2.0%)**
Simile	**65.38**	**66.92 (+ 1.5%)**
Idioms	**72.50**	**78.13 (+ 6.0%)**
Creative Paraphrase	98.36	98.36
Sarcasm	100	99.54 (- 0.5%)

Table 2: T5 performance (acc) on the various labels of FigLang2022, before and after training on IMPLI.

Importantly, we found that training for more epochs on the IMPLI dataset led to improved inference label accuracy but led to poorer explanations, which suggests knowledge transfer as oppsed to, for example, the advantage of additional training data. Since we were more interested in transferring figurative information from IMPLI, we optimise on Acc@0 (label accuracy) when training on IMPLI and Acc@60 (the evaluation metric relevant to the task) when training on the final FigLang dataset.

4.2 Experimental Setup

Training Regime In establishing the most effective method of knowledge transfer, we compare SFT with HiFeatMTL trained on: a) FigLang, b) eSNLI → FigLang, c) IMPLI → FigLang, d) eSNLI → IMPLI → FigLang, and e) IMPLI → eSNLI → FigLang. The training sets of both eSNLI and IMPLI are truncated to the same length as that of FigLang to ensure that the model does not over-fit on those other tasks.

4.3 Sequential Fine-Tuning

In SFT, we fine-tune the model on each of the relevant datasets in sequence. When training on the IMPLI dataset, which does not have associated explanations, we use the same prompt (Listing 1) but with no associated explanation. The number of training epochs is established based on the change in loss on the development set and was found to be 3 for IMPLI and 10 for the other two datasets.

4.4 Multi-Task Learning

We experiment with a *hierarchical feature pipeline* for multi-task learning as the output inference label is likely to be important in generating the explanation. This involved creating an end-to-end model wherein, during the forward pass, T5 is used to predict the inference labels based on the hypothesis and the premise. This label, in addition to the hypothesis and premise are then used as input to T5 to generate an explanation. During the backward pass, the overall loss of the model is calculated as the weighted sum of the loss associated with each of the two steps above. Importantly, the weights of the T5 model used in the two steps are shared. Figure 1 provides an illustration.

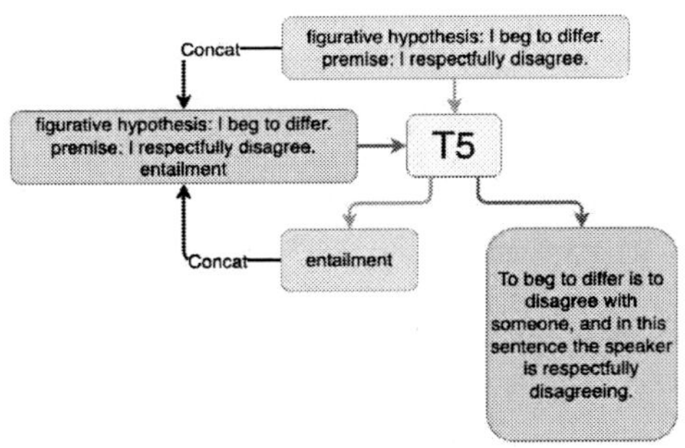

Figure 1: Our HiFeatMTL architecture. Note that we do not use GPT in our experiments, although it is possible to use GPT in place of T5.

As in the case of SFT, we fine-tune the model on each of the relevant datasets in sequence. When training on the FigLang dataset, we found it effective to train the model twice: fist with a higher weight to the loss associated with the inference (90%) and a second time with a higher weight to the loss associated with explanations (also 90%). Due to the summing of losses, we found that the model loss was not a good indicator of overfitting and instead determined the number of training epochs experimentally (10 for all datasets).

5 Results and Discussion

Table 3 shows the full shared task results from the CodaLab leaderboard[3] as of the competition's end date of 20 Aug, 2022. Our results (Team UKPChefs) are highlighted in bold.

[3]Our CodaLab submissions appear under the name "rachneet": `https://codalab.lisn.upsaclay.fr/competitions/5908`

Rank	Team Name	Acc@0	Acc@50	Acc@60
***1st**	**UKPChefs**	**0.925**	**0.869**	**0.633**
*1st	TeamCoolDoge	0.947	0.889	0.633
2nd	vund	0.936	0.865	0.607
3rd	hoho5702	0.911	0.854	0.548
4th	yklal95	0.847	0.779	0.517
5th	tuhinnlp	0.443	0.443	0.443
6th	peratham.bkk	0.590	0.203	0.033
	Shared Task Baseline	*0.817*	*0.748*	*0.483*

Table 3: Shared task results from all teams (ours – UKPChefs – in bold). Asterisks represent tied results.

The results of our experiments using SFT and HiFeatMTL are presented in Table 4. The results on the development set and those on the test set are not directly comparable: not only do we use different models, we also train on all the complete training data before evaluating on the test set. The drop in performance of the HiFeatMTL model on the test set on Acc@60, which consistently outperforming SFT on Acc@0 across both the development and the test sets is surprising. This seems to indicate that HiFeatMTL, while an effective way of boosting performance on the earlier of multiple dependent objectives, seems to be less effective on subsequent tasks (in this case, explanation generation). Additionally, HiFeatMTL also seems prone to overfitting, as the FigLang test set introduced novel idioms and similes previously unseen in the training set, into the test set.

While the gain in accuracy when using the additional datasets could be due to the corresponding addition of training data, it should be noted that IMPLI does not have explanations and eSNLI contains no figurative language. As such, the improved scores indicate the transfer of figurative information from one task (IMPLI) and explanation generation capabilities from another (eSNLI).

As such, in addressing the research questions, our results indicate that: a) distinct task-specific knowledge (i.e. explanations or figurative language) can indeed be transferred from separate tasks so as to improve performance on a target task, and b) SFT seems to be a more effective way of transferring knowledge across tasks when we are concerned with the latter of a sequence of tasks (as in this case), while HiFeatMTL seems effective in boosting the performance of the first.

	Dataset 1	Dataset 2	Dataset 3	Acc@0		Acc@50		Acc@60	
				Dev	Test	Dev	Test	Dev	Test
SFT	FigLang	-	-	84.99	93.27	78.49	87.80	56.18	61.74
	eSNLI	FigLang	-	86.06	92.67	80.74	87.20	57.77	63.27
	IMPLI	FigLang	-	86.59	93.20	80.74	87.33	56.97	60.93
	eSNLI	IMPLI	FigLang	86.32	92.47	80.08	86.87	58.17	63.33
	IMPLI	eSNLI	FigLang	84.99	92.73	79.42	87.33	55.38	62.00
HiFeatMTL	FigLang	-	-	91.24	94.67	82.07	86.54	55.11	55.13
	eSNLI	FigLang	-	91.50	94.14	82.07	86.40	55.91	53.80
	IMPLI	FigLang	-	89.50	N/A	81.27	N/A	55.78	N/A
	eSNLI	IMPLI	FigLang	90.97	94.54	80.35	85.94	53.92	54.27
	IMPLI	eSNLI	FigLang	89.37	N/A	80.34	N/A	53.52	N/A
Shared Task Baseline				-	*81.70*	-	*74.80*	-	*48.30*

Table 4: Results of the SFT and HiFeatMTL models on the development and test splits of the FigLang2022 task. Experiments on the dev set were performed using T5-Base and those on the test set on T5-Large trained on the complete training set. Results marked N/A were not obtained due to the limits on the number of submissions.

6 Knowledge Transfer vs Bias

Recent works on NLI have shown that for some datasets, models are able to correctly predict the label using only the hypothesis, without considering the premise (Glockner et al., 2018; Gururangan et al., 2018; McCoy et al., 2019). This is caused by the model exploiting spurious correlations or patterns in the data, rather than acquiring task-relevant knowledge. As such, we wish to analyse if this is the case with our models: namely, whether our models employ figurative language knowledge from the hypothesis when predicting NLI labels.

We perform the following experiments using T5 large on our validation set: we train only the hypothesis, only on the premise, and compare these results with a model trained on both (the standard training regime). The results (Table 5) indicate that, while the model *can* achieve reasonable accuracy while relying solely on the hypothesis, the significant improvement in accuracy (on both Acc@0 and Acc@60) when considering both the hypothesis and the premise indicates that, to a certain extent, the model is using knowledge of figurative language to predict the NLI labels and corresponding explanations.

Setting	Acc@0	Acc@50	Acc@60
Regular	92.16	87.92	66.14
Hyp-Only	65.47	60.96	45.95
Prem-Only	56.31	47.81	33.74

Table 5: T5-large performance on the FigLang dataset with either the hypothesis or premise removed.

7 Conclusions and Future work

In this work we set out to establish the possibility of effectively transferring knowledge across tasks in the context where we are interested in boosting the performance of two dependent tasks. As such, we evaluate the effectiveness of SFT and HiFeatMTL for transferring distinct task-specific knowledge from different tasks and find that both of these methods are good at achieving this: SFT on the last task and HiFeatMTL on the first. We find that using SFT to transfer information across tasks is, in this instance, so effective that we are *ranked first* on the FigLang 2022 task.

In extending this work, we intend to test these methods on a variety of sequentially dependent tasks as well as incorporating the use of more efficient MTL methods including AdapterFusion (Pfeiffer et al., 2021) and AdapterDrop (Rücklé et al., 2021).

Acknowledgements

This work was made possible through a research visit hosted by the UKP Lab[4] and funded by the Alan Turing Institute[5] through their Post-Doctoral Enrichment Award granted to HTM while at the University of Sheffield. In addition, this work was also partly supported by the UK EPSRC grant EP/T02450X/1, the European Regional Development Fund (ERDF), the Hessian State Chancellery – Hessian Minister of Digital Strategy and Development (reference 20005482, TexPrax), the State of Hesse in Germany (project 71574093, CDR-CAT), the German Federal Ministry of Education and Research and the Hessian Ministry of Higher Education, Research, Science and the Arts within their joint support of the National Research Center for Applied Cybersecurity ATHENE.

[4]https://www.informatik.tu-darmstadt.de/ukp/ukp_home/

[5]https://www.turing.ac.uk/

Limitations

This work only deals with English, and since English makes up a majority of the training data for PLMs, performance may drop across other languages. Additionally, we only address figurative language within the context of the NLI task, and thus do not make broader claims about our model's ability to handle figurative language, to generate explanations or generalise across other generative models. This also extends to the comparisons between models that we present.

Model Explanations This work is involved in the generation of explanations associated with language inference predictions. Importantly, there is no guarantee (and very unlikely) that the generated explanations are indeed faithful to the process of predicting inference labels (also see Jacovi and Goldberg (2020)).

Carbon Footprint All initial experiments are performed on smaller models and the best performing model architectures and parameters are transferred over to larger models to minimise the carbon footprint of our experiments. Despite this, the use of large language models does contribute to the climate crisis.

References

Ibrahim Abu Farha, Silviu Vlad Oprea, Steven Wilson, and Walid Magdy. 2022. SemEval-2022 task 6: iSarcasmEval, intended sarcasm detection in English and Arabic. In *Proceedings of the 16th International Workshop on Semantic Evaluation (SemEval-2022)*, pages 802–814, Seattle, United States. Association for Computational Linguistics.

Samuel Bowman, Gabor Angeli, Christopher Potts, and Christopher D Manning. 2015. A large annotated corpus for learning natural language inference. In *Proceedings of the 2015 Conference on Empirical Methods in Natural Language Processing*, pages 632–642.

Oana-Maria Camburu, Tim Rocktäschel, Thomas Lukasiewicz, and Phil Blunsom. 2018. e-snli: Natural language inference with natural language explanations. In *Advances in Neural Information Processing Systems*, volume 31. Curran Associates, Inc.

Rich Caruana. 1997. Multitask learning. *Machine learning*, 28(1):41–75.

Tuhin Chakrabarty, Arkadiy Saakyan, Debanjan Ghosh, and Smaranda Muresan. 2022. Flute: Figurative language understanding and textual explanations.

Shijie Chen, Yu Zhang, and Qiang Yang. 2021. Multitask learning in natural language processing: An overview. *CoRR*, abs/2109.09138.

Karl Fredrik Erliksson, Anders Arpteg, Mihhail Matskin, and Amir H Payberah. 2021. Cross-domain transfer of generative explanations using text-to-text models. In *International Conference on Applications of Natural Language to Information Systems*, pages 76–89. Springer.

Hongliang Fei, Shulong Tan, and Ping Li. 2019. Hierarchical multi-task word embedding learning for synonym prediction. In *Proceedings of the 25th ACM SIGKDD International Conference on Knowledge Discovery & Data Mining*, KDD '19, page 834–842, New York, NY, USA. Association for Computing Machinery.

Max Glockner, Vered Shwartz, and Yoav Goldberg. 2018. Breaking NLI systems with sentences that require simple lexical inferences. In *Proceedings of the 56th Annual Meeting of the Association for Computational Linguistics (Volume 2: Short Papers)*, pages 650–655, Melbourne, Australia. Association for Computational Linguistics.

Yu Gong, Xusheng Luo, Yu Zhu, Wenwu Ou, Zhao Li, Muhua Zhu, Kenny Q. Zhu, Lu Duan, and Xi Chen. 2019. Deep cascade multi-task learning for slot filling in online shopping assistant. In *Proceedings of the Thirty-Third AAAI Conference on Artificial Intelligence and Thirty-First Innovative Applications of Artificial Intelligence Conference and Ninth AAAI Symposium on Educational Advances in Artificial Intelligence*, AAAI'19/IAAI'19/EAAI'19. AAAI Press.

Suchin Gururangan, Swabha Swayamdipta, Omer Levy, Roy Schwartz, Samuel Bowman, and Noah A. Smith. 2018. Annotation artifacts in natural language inference data. In *Proceedings of the 2018 Conference of the North American Chapter of the Association for Computational Linguistics: Human Language Technologies, Volume 2 (Short Papers)*, pages 107–112, New Orleans, Louisiana. Association for Computational Linguistics.

Kazuma Hashimoto, Caiming Xiong, Yoshimasa Tsuruoka, and Richard Socher. 2017. A joint many-task model: Growing a neural network for multiple NLP tasks. In *Proceedings of the 2017 Conference on Empirical Methods in Natural Language Processing*, pages 1923–1933, Copenhagen, Denmark. Association for Computational Linguistics.

Alon Jacovi and Yoav Goldberg. 2020. Towards faithfully interpretable NLP systems: How should we define and evaluate faithfulness? In *Proceedings of the 58th Annual Meeting of the Association for Computational Linguistics*, pages 4198–4205, Online. Association for Computational Linguistics.

Beata Beigman Klebanov, Ekaterina Shutova, Patricia Lichtenstein, Smaranda Muresan, Chee Wee, Anna

Feldman, and Debanjan Ghosh, editors. 2020. *Proceedings of the Second Workshop on Figurative Language Processing*. Association for Computational Linguistics, Online.

Mike Lewis, Yinhan Liu, Naman Goyal, Marjan Ghazvininejad, Abdelrahman Mohamed, Omer Levy, Veselin Stoyanov, and Luke Zettlemoyer. 2020. Bart: Denoising sequence-to-sequence pre-training for natural language generation, translation, and comprehension. In *Proceedings of the 58th Annual Meeting of the Association for Computational Linguistics*, pages 7871–7880.

Emmy Liu, Chen Cui, Kenneth Zheng, and Graham Neubig. 2022. Testing the ability of language models to interpret figurative language. *arXiv preprint arXiv:2204.12632*.

Tom McCoy, Ellie Pavlick, and Tal Linzen. 2019. Right for the wrong reasons: Diagnosing syntactic heuristics in natural language inference. In *Proceedings of the 57th Annual Meeting of the Association for Computational Linguistics*, pages 3428–3448, Florence, Italy. Association for Computational Linguistics.

Sharan Narang, Colin Raffel, Katherine Lee, Adam Roberts, Noah Fiedel, and Karishma Malkan. 2020. Wt5?! training text-to-text models to explain their predictions. *arXiv preprint arXiv:2004.14546*.

Jonas Pfeiffer, Aishwarya Kamath, Andreas Rücklé, Kyunghyun Cho, and Iryna Gurevych. 2021. AdapterFusion: Non-destructive task composition for transfer learning. In *Proceedings of the 16th Conference of the European Chapter of the Association for Computational Linguistics: Main Volume*, pages 487–503, Online. Association for Computational Linguistics.

Jason Phang, Thibault Févry, and Samuel R. Bowman. 2018. Sentence encoders on stilts: Supplementary training on intermediate labeled-data tasks. *CoRR*, abs/1811.01088.

Colin Raffel, Noam Shazeer, Adam Roberts, Katherine Lee, Sharan Narang, Michael Matena, Yanqi Zhou, Wei Li, and Peter J. Liu. 2019. Exploring the limits of transfer learning with a unified text-to-text transformer. *CoRR*, abs/1910.10683.

Andreas Rücklé, Gregor Geigle, Max Glockner, Tilman Beck, Jonas Pfeiffer, Nils Reimers, and Iryna Gurevych. 2021. AdapterDrop: On the efficiency of adapters in transformers. In *Proceedings of the 2021 Conference on Empirical Methods in Natural Language Processing*, pages 7930–7946, Online and Punta Cana, Dominican Republic. Association for Computational Linguistics.

Wei Song, Ziyao Song, Lizhen Liu, and Ruiji Fu. 2020. Hierarchical multi-task learning for organization evaluation of argumentative student essays. In *Proceedings of the Twenty-Ninth International Joint Conference on Artificial Intelligence, IJCAI-20*, pages 3875–3881. International Joint Conferences on Artificial Intelligence Organization. Main track.

Kevin Stowe, Prasetya Utama, and Iryna Gurevych. 2022. IMPLI: Investigating NLI models' performance on figurative language. In *Proceedings of the 60th Annual Meeting of the Association for Computational Linguistics (Volume 1: Long Papers)*, pages 5375–5388, Dublin, Ireland. Association for Computational Linguistics.

Harish Tayyar Madabushi, Edward Gow-Smith, Marcos Garcia, Carolina Scarton, Marco Idiart, and Aline Villavicencio. 2022. SemEval-2022 task 2: Multilingual idiomaticity detection and sentence embedding. In *Proceedings of the 16th International Workshop on Semantic Evaluation (SemEval-2022)*, pages 107–121, Seattle, United States. Association for Computational Linguistics.

Harish Tayyar Madabushi, Edward Gow-Smith, Carolina Scarton, and Aline Villavicencio. 2021. AStitchInLanguageModels: Dataset and methods for the exploration of idiomaticity in pre-trained language models. In *Findings of the Association for Computational Linguistics: EMNLP 2021*, pages 3464–3477, Punta Cana, Dominican Republic. Association for Computational Linguistics.

Alex Wang, Amanpreet Singh, Julian Michael, Felix Hill, Omer Levy, and Samuel Bowman. 2018. GLUE: A multi-task benchmark and analysis platform for natural language understanding. In *Proceedings of the 2018 EMNLP Workshop BlackboxNLP: Analyzing and Interpreting Neural Networks for NLP*, pages 353–355, Brussels, Belgium. Association for Computational Linguistics.

Jason Wei, Yi Tay, Rishi Bommasani, Colin Raffel, Barret Zoph, Sebastian Borgeaud, Dani Yogatama, Maarten Bosma, Denny Zhou, Donald Metzler, Ed H. Chi, Tatsunori Hashimoto, Oriol Vinyals, Percy Liang, Jeff Dean, and William Fedus. 2022. Emergent abilities of large language models. *Transactions on Machine Learning Research*. Survey Certification.

Lang Yu and Allyson Ettinger. 2020. Assessing phrasal representation and composition in transformers. In *Proceedings of the 2020 Conference on Empirical Methods in Natural Language Processing (EMNLP)*, pages 4896–4907, Online. Association for Computational Linguistics.

Detecting Euphemisms with Literal Descriptions and Visual Imagery

Ilker Kesen[1,2] **Aykut Erdem**[1,2] **Erkut Erdem**[1,3] **Iacer Calixto**[4,5]
[1] Koç University, KUIS AI Center [2] Koç University, Computer Engineering Department
[3] Hacettepe University, Computer Engineering Department
[4] Amsterdam UMC, University of Amsterdam, Department of Medical Informatics
[5] Amsterdam Public Health, Methodology & Mental Health, Amsterdam, The Netherlands

Abstract

This paper describes our two-stage system[1] for the Euphemism Detection shared task hosted by the 3rd Workshop on Figurative Language Processing in conjunction with EMNLP 2022. Euphemisms tone down expressions about sensitive or unpleasant issues like addiction and death. The ambiguous nature of euphemistic words or expressions makes it challenging to detect their actual meaning within a context. In the first stage, we seek to mitigate this ambiguity by incorporating literal descriptions into input text prompts to our baseline model. It turns out that this kind of direct supervision yields remarkable performance improvement. In the second stage, we integrate visual supervision into our system using *visual imageries*, two sets of images generated by a text-to-image model by taking terms and descriptions as input. Our experiments demonstrate that visual supervision also gives a statistically significant performance boost. Our system achieved the second place with an F1 score of 87.2%, only about 0.9% worse than the best submission.

1 Introduction

Recent advances in large pretrained language models allowed the computational linguistics community to tackle more knowledge-intensive tasks which require commonsense reasoning (Talmor et al., 2019; Bisk et al., 2020; Lin et al., 2021), and figurative language understanding (Pedinotti et al., 2021; Liu et al., 2022). In this work, we focus on a figurative language understanding task called *euphemism detection*. Euphemisms attempt to smooth harsh, impolite, or blunt expressions about taboo or sensitive topics like death and unemployment (Holder, 2008). For instance, when we speak of older people we often refer to *senior citizens* instead of a direct expression that can be seen as offensive.

Identifying euphemisms is challenging due to their natural ambiguity, i.e., the meaning of the term shifts depending on the context: '*Over the hill*' could either mean someone or something is *physically* over some hill (*literal*), or someone or something is *old*, past one's prime (*figurative*) (Lee et al., 2022). One cannot distinguish these two different senses without sufficient context. Thus, these terms are referred as *potentially euphemistic terms* (PETs) (Gavidia et al., 2022). Here, we propose a two-stage method for the Euphemism Detection shared task hosted by the 3rd Workshop on Figurative Language Processing at EMNLP 2022.

In the first stage, we manually collect literal descriptions for each PET. We then incorporate these descriptions into input text prompts to help the model distinguish figurative from literal usage. We demonstrate that this kind of extraneous linguistic supervision improves a strong baseline by a large margin. In the second stage, we attempt to answer the question, *"Is visual supervision also useful to infer the meaning behind a PET?"* To answer this question, we use a text-to-image model which takes terms and descriptions as input, and we generate two sets of images, which we denote as *visual imageries*. Our experiments show that using visual imagery provides the best results. A paired t-test points out that the improvement is statistically significant. Our qualitative analysis also suggests visual imageries are beneficial for analyzing PETs.

The rest of this paper is organized as follows. Section 2 describes our proposed solution. In Section 3, we share the details of our evaluation setup and design choices. Section 4 reports our experimental results. In Section 5, we briefly review the relevant literature. Section 6 outlines our conclusions and discuss the limitations of our approach.

2 Approach

In this section, we first formulate the euphemism detection task by describing a simple baseline

[1]Code is available at github.com/ilkerkesen/euphemism

Proceedings of the 3rd Workshop on Figurative Language Processing (FLP), pages 61 - 67
December 8, 2022

model, and then explain how we extend it with the literal term descriptions and visual imagery.

2.1 Vanilla Baseline

Given a textual context C with a potentially euphemistic term (PET) T, the aim of euphemism detection is to decide whether the candidate term T is euphemistic ($y = 1$) or not ($y = 0$). Here, we only pick a sentence $S = [w_1, w_2, ..., w_n]$ which contains a candidate term T, and ignore the rest of the context C at first. We use a pretrained language model LM as our initial baseline as below.

$$\begin{aligned} e_i &= \text{EMBED}(w_i), \\ \hat{p} &= \text{LM}(e_1, e_2, ..., e_n), \end{aligned} \quad \hat{y} = \begin{cases} 1 & \hat{p} \geq 0.5, \\ 0 & \text{otherwise.} \end{cases}$$

e_i denotes the word embedding of the ith token w_i, $\hat{p}$ is the probability that the candidate term T is euphemistic, and $\hat{y}$ is the predicted label. EMBED is the embedding layer and LM denotes the language model that produces the probability $\hat{p}$.

2.2 Literal Descriptions

We extend the baseline model by supplying extra supervision with literal descriptions D for each candidate term T (which we collect manually). To make use of the literal descriptions, we create a textual prompt $X = [x_1, x_2, ..., x_n]$ for each sentence S, term T and description D as below.

$$X = [\text{Term: } T, \text{ Description: } D, \text{ Sentence: } S].$$

Then, we change the formulation,

$$\begin{aligned} e_i &= \text{EMBED}(x_i) \\ \hat{p} &= \text{LM}(e_1, e_2, ..., e_n), \end{aligned}$$

where e_i is the embedding for the ith token of the input prompt X.

2.3 Visual Imagery

We subsequently move beyond the text-only baselines by integrating visual modality into the Literal Descriptions baseline in the form of *visual imagery*. To accomplish this, we generate two sets of images $I_T = [I_T^{(1)}, I_T^{(2)}, ..., I_T^{(k)}]$ and $I_D = [I_D^{(1)}, I_D^{(2)}, ..., I_D^{(k)}]$, for each term and description pair, respectively. We denote these set of images as visual imageries. To obtain the visual imageries, we feed a text-to-image model T2I with terms and descriptions as input language,

$$I_T^{(k)} \sim \text{T2I}(T), \qquad I_D^{(k)} \sim \text{T2I}(D).$$

Next, we use a pretrained visual encoder (VE) to embed visual imageries.

$$v_T = \frac{1}{K}\sum_{k=1}^{K} \text{VE}(I_T^{(k)}), \quad v_D = \frac{1}{K}\sum_{k=1}^{K} \text{VE}(I_D^{(k)})$$

where v_T denotes the visual imagery embedding of the candidate term T and v_D denotes the visual imagery embedding of the corresponding literal description D. K is the number of images per term T and description D. Thus, we reformulate the literal descriptions baseline as follows,

$$\begin{aligned} e_i &= \text{EMBED}(x_i) \\ \hat{p} &= \text{LM}(f_p(v_T), f_p(v_D), e_1, e_2, ..., e_n) \end{aligned}$$

We make sure visual imagery embeddings are compatible with the word embeddings and language model LM by applying a linear projection layer f_p. We train each baseline using the negative log-likelihood objective.

3 Data and Implementation

Data. The euphemism detection dataset consists of two separate splits for training and testing purposes with 1573 and 394 examples, respectively. The test split is unlabeled. The whole data includes 131 different PETs. Since there is no data supplied for validation, we reserve 20% of the training data for this purpose. We only select the sentences with PETs and remove repetitive patterns of punctuation "@ @ @ ..." to decrease computational requirements by shortening the input language. We manually collect literal descriptions within 6 hours, and try to avoid impolite expressions like insults or slang phrases.

Implementation. We use DeBERTa-v3 base and large as our language model (He et al., 2021a,b). We generate the visual imageries I_T and I_D by using an open-source DALL-E implementation (Ramesh et al., 2021; Dayma et al., 2021).[2] The number of images per visual imagery K is set to 9. We extract visual imagery embeddings v_T and v_D using CLIP's ViT-L/14 as our visual encoder (Radford et al., 2021). f_p is a single linear layer, and we randomly initialize its weights. We use Adam optimizer with weight decay (Kingma and Ba, 2015; Loshchilov and Hutter, 2018). The learning rate is set to $5e^{-6}$ and $3e^{-6}$ for the experiments

[2] https://github.com/kuprel/min-dalle

Model	LM	*validation*	*test*
Vanilla Baseline	Base	79.84 ±2.23	-
+ Desc.	Base	86.39 ±1.05	83.58
+ Desc.	Large	88.89 ±1.35	85.74
+ Desc. + Imag.	Large	**90.11** ±1.59	**87.16**

Table 1: Quantitative results on the labeled data using F1 as evaluation metric. The last two columns respectively show the average score over different *validation* splits, and the ensemble performance achieved on the *test* split.

with DeBERTa-v3-base and DeBERTa-v3-large, respectively. We train our models for a maximum of 50 epochs using Tesla V100s and mixed precision. A typical experiment takes less than one hour with a batch size of 16. Due to the small dataset size, we perform multiple experiments and reserve a different portion of the labeled data for validation in each experiment. We report mean and standard deviation over all experiments, and use ensembling to evaluate our system on the test set.

4 Experimental Analysis

4.1 Quantitative Results

Table 1 presents the quantitative results of our experiments as ablation studies. We perform several experiments in a curriculum, where each following experiment activates a different feature (e.g. literal descriptions). We first implement a vanilla baseline using DeBERTa-v3-base, which lacks descriptions and imagery.

Using Literal Descriptions. In our first ablative analysis, we incorporate the literal term descriptions into the vanilla baseline described in Section 2.2. Integrating this supervision results in substantial performance improvement, i.e. ≈ 6.5 points using F1 as evaluation metric.

Larger Language Model. We implement the literal descriptions model using a larger language model which is the large architecture of the DeBERTa-v3 model. Using a bigger LM gives 2 points performance improvement.

Visual Imagery. We now report on the visual imagery model explained in Section 2.3. This model additionally uses two different visual embedding vectors, denoted as visual imageries, which are generated by a text-to-image model using terms and descriptions. By using this extra visual supervision, we obtain 1.22 and 1.42 F1 score increments in validation and testing phases. A paired t-test is applied to determine the significance of the results: We obtained a p-value of 0.032, which points out that this improvement is statistically significant ($p < 0.05$).

4.2 Qualitative Analysis

Figure 1 wraps up our qualitative analysis, where we share the collected descriptions and the generated visual imageries for some euphemistic terms. The first two examples show that if a term has a dominant literal meaning, the text-to-image V2I model produces images conveying the literal meaning instead of the figurative one. V2I can also produce visuals based upon individual word meanings as a consequence of being completely unconscious to the figurative meaning. This can be seen on the third example, where the model generates *lunch* images instead of vomiting for phrase '*lose one's lunch*'. Moreover, V2I can generate unrelated images for some terms as one can see on the *pro-life* and *able-body* examples. On the other hand, the text-to-image model V2I is well aware of some euphemism candidates as in the case with the last two examples. This phenomenon arises when the term has just one single meaning which is euphemistic.

In summary, a text-to-image model can be a complementary tool for analyzing figurative language: one can observe how models process these expressions. By looking at the produced images, we can recognize the terms with dominant literal meanings (e.g. *late*) or single euphemistic meaning (e.g. *lavatory*).

5 Related Work

Euphemisms. Recently, euphemisms have attracted the attention of the natural language processing community. Zhu et al. (2021) and Zhu and Bhat (2021) extract euphemistic phrases by using masked language modeling. A few work practices sentiment-oriented methods to recognize candidate euphemism phrases (Felt and Riloff, 2020; Gavidia et al., 2022; Lee et al., 2022). Most notably, Gavidia et al. (2022) replace PETs with their literal meanings and observe how the sentiment scores change. They demonstrate that using literal meanings produces higher scores for offensive speech and negative sentiment. Similarly, we also put literal meanings to use, but differently, by creating a textual input prompt. In this work, we also use the euphemism dataset they created.

Knowledge-augmented Language Understand-

Term	Description	I_T	I_D
late	old person, elderly		
pass on	death, dying	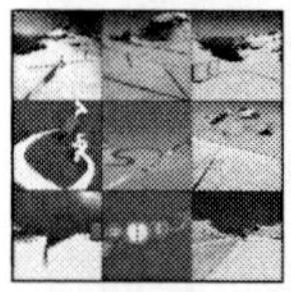	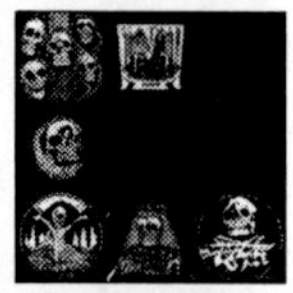
lose one's lunch	vomit, vomiting, throwing up	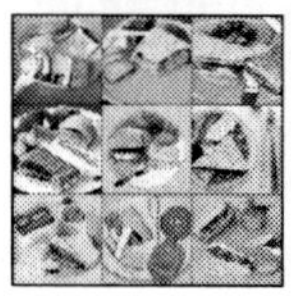	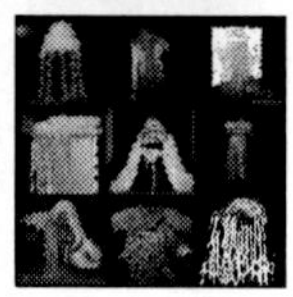
pro-life	a person opposes abortion		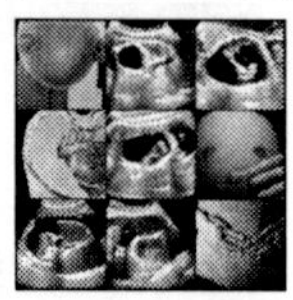
able-body	not disabled	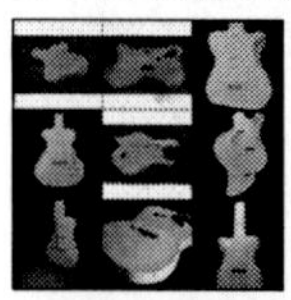	
lavatory	restroom, toilet		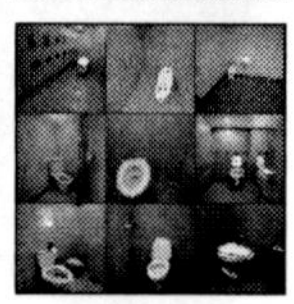
senior citizen	old person, elderly		

Figure 1: Examples of collected literal descriptions for euphemistic terms and their visual imageries.

ing. External knowledge[3] can be either unstructured (i.e. text) or structured (i.e. graph). To benefit from unstructured knowledge, a text retriever collects related entries from an external corpus (Karpukhin et al., 2020; Guu et al., 2020). Conversely, structured knowledge integration may happen in two ways: explicit methods prefer to use knowledge in their input (Weijie Liu, 2020; Zhang et al., 2019), and implicit methods try to learn knowledge in their objective (Xiong et al., 2019; Shen et al., 2020). Some exceptions (Yu et al., 2022a; Shangwen Lv and Hu, 2020) combines both: they learn to predict graph embeddings and use these embeddings as input in their model concurrently. Similar to us, Yu et al. (2022b); Xu et al. (2021); Chakrabarty et al. (2021) also insert descriptions into their textual inputs.

[3]Please check Zhu et al. (2022) for a comprehensive review of the related literature.

Visually-aided Language Understanding. Several methods have been proposed to aid language learning with external visual knowledge. Most of these methods experiment on machine translation (MT). Calixto et al. (2019) propose a latent variable model for multi-modal MT, to learn an association between an image and its target language description. Long et al. (2021); Li et al. (2022) first synthesize an image conditioned on the source sentence, then use both the source sentence and the synthesized image to produce translation. Caglayan et al. (2020) obtain a lower latency in simultaneous MT by supplying visual context. Differently, Vokenization (Tan and Bansal, 2020) extend BERT (Devlin et al., 2019) by implementing visual token prediction objective to learn a mapping between tokens and associated images. Most relevantly, Lu et al. (2022) improve text-only language understanding performance in low-resource settings by using generated imagination as visual supervision.

6 Conclusion

In this paper, we described our two-stage method for the euphemism detection task. We first collected literal descriptions for PETs, inserted these descriptions into the model input, and showed that such linguistic supervision greatly boosts performance. We then supplied extra visual supervision using a text-to-image model, where we denote this kind of supervision as visual imageries. We achieved a statistically significant performance increase by using visual imageries in addition to the term descriptions. Our qualitative analysis on visual imageries also suggests that a text-to-image model can be a functional tool to break down how models interpret figures of speech.

Limitations. Due to working with a small-scale dataset, we were able to manually collect descriptions for the PETs. Collecting these descriptions using an automatic retrieval system would be more sophisticated. We also did not perform a detailed analyses of the results, which could help shed light on the contribution of each model component.

Acknowledgements. This work was supported in part by an AI Fellowship to I. Kesen provided by the KUIS AI Center, GEBIP 2018 Award of the Turkish Academy of Sciences to E. Erdem, and BAGEP 2021 Award of the Science Academy to A. Erdem. This publication is based upon work from COST Action Multi3Generation CA18231, supported by COST (European Cooperation in Science and Technology).

References

Yonatan Bisk, Rowan Zellers, Jianfeng Gao, Yejin Choi, et al. 2020. Piqa: Reasoning about physical commonsense in natural language. In *Proceedings of the AAAI conference on artificial intelligence*, volume 34, pages 7432–7439.

Ozan Caglayan, Julia Ive, Veneta Haralampieva, Pranava Madhyastha, Loïc Barrault, and Lucia Specia. 2020. Simultaneous machine translation with visual context. In *Proceedings of the 2020 Conference on Empirical Methods in Natural Language Processing (EMNLP)*, pages 2350–2361, Online. Association for Computational Linguistics.

Iacer Calixto, Miguel Rios, and Wilker Aziz. 2019. Latent variable model for multi-modal translation. In *Proceedings of the 57th Annual Meeting of the Association for Computational Linguistics*, pages 6392–6405, Florence, Italy. Association for Computational Linguistics.

Tuhin Chakrabarty, Debanjan Ghosh, Adam Poliak, and Smaranda Muresan. 2021. Figurative Language in Recognizing Textual Entailment. In *Findings of the Association for Computational Linguistics: ACL-IJCNLP 2021*, pages 3354–3361, Online. Association for Computational Linguistics.

Boris Dayma, Suraj Patil, Pedro Cuenca, Khalid Saifullah, Tanishq Abraham, Phúc Lê Khc, Luke Melas, and Ritobrata Ghosh. 2021. Dall·e mini.

Jacob Devlin, Ming-Wei Chang, Kenton Lee, and Kristina Toutanova. 2019. BERT: Pre-training of deep bidirectional transformers for language understanding. In *Proceedings of the 2019 Conference of the North American Chapter of the Association for Computational Linguistics: Human Language Technologies, Volume 1 (Long and Short Papers)*, pages 4171–4186, Minneapolis, Minnesota. Association for Computational Linguistics.

Christian Felt and Ellen Riloff. 2020. Recognizing euphemisms and dysphemisms using sentiment analysis. In *Proceedings of the Second Workshop on Figurative Language Processing*, pages 136–145, Online. Association for Computational Linguistics.

Martha Gavidia, Patrick Lee, Anna Feldman, and Jing Peng. 2022. CATs are Fuzzy PETs: A Corpus and Analysis of Potentially Euphemistic Terms. *arXiv preprint arXiv:2205.02728*.

Kelvin Guu, Kenton Lee, Zora Tung, Panupong Pasupat, and Mingwei Chang. 2020. Retrieval augmented language model pre-training. In *International Conference on Machine Learning*, pages 3929–3938. PMLR.

Pengcheng He, Jianfeng Gao, and Weizhu Chen. 2021a. Debertav3: Improving deberta using electra-style pretraining with gradient-disentangled embedding sharing.

Pengcheng He, Xiaodong Liu, Jianfeng Gao, and Weizhu Chen. 2021b. Deberta: Decoding-enhanced bert with disentangled attention. In *International Conference on Learning Representations*.

Robert W Holder. 2008. *Dictionary of euphemisms*. Oxford University Press.

Vladimir Karpukhin, Barlas Oguz, Sewon Min, Patrick Lewis, Ledell Wu, Sergey Edunov, Danqi Chen, and Wen-tau Yih. 2020. Dense passage retrieval for open-domain question answering. In *Proceedings of the 2020 Conference on Empirical Methods in Natural Language Processing (EMNLP)*, pages 6769–6781, Online. Association for Computational Linguistics.

Diederik P. Kingma and Jimmy Ba. 2015. Adam: A method for stochastic optimization. In *ICLR (Poster)*.

Patrick Lee, Martha Gavidia, Anna Feldman, and Jing Peng. 2022. Searching for PETs: Using Distributional and Sentiment-Based Methods to Find Potentially Euphemistic Terms. In *Proceedings of the Second Workshop on Understanding Implicit and Underspecified Language*, pages 22–32, Seattle, USA. Association for Computational Linguistics.

Yi Li, Rameswar Panda, Yoon Kim, Chun-Fu (Richard) Chen, Rogerio S. Feris, David Cox, and Nuno Vasconcelos. 2022. VALHALLA: Visual Hallucination for Machine Translation. In *Proceedings of the IEEE/CVF Conference on Computer Vision and Pattern Recognition (CVPR)*, pages 5216–5226.

Bill Yuchen Lin, Haitian Sun, Bhuwan Dhingra, Manzil Zaheer, Xiang Ren, and William Cohen. 2021. Differentiable open-ended commonsense reasoning. In *Proceedings of the 2021 Conference of the North American Chapter of the Association for Computational Linguistics: Human Language Technologies*, pages 4611–4625, Online. Association for Computational Linguistics.

Emmy Liu, Chenxuan Cui, Kenneth Zheng, and Graham Neubig. 2022. Testing the ability of language models to interpret figurative language. In *Proceedings of the 2022 Conference of the North American Chapter of the Association for Computational Linguistics: Human Language Technologies*, pages 4437–4452, Seattle, United States. Association for Computational Linguistics.

Quanyu Long, Mingxuan Wang, and Lei Li. 2021. Generative imagination elevates machine translation. In *Proceedings of the 2021 Conference of the North*

American Chapter of the Association for Computational Linguistics: Human Language Technologies, pages 5738–5748, Online. Association for Computational Linguistics.

Ilya Loshchilov and Frank Hutter. 2018. Decoupled weight decay regularization. In *International Conference on Learning Representations*.

Yujie Lu, Wanrong Zhu, Xin Wang, Miguel Eckstein, and William Yang Wang. 2022. Imagination-Augmented Natural Language Understanding. In *Proceedings of the 2022 Conference of the North American Chapter of the Association for Computational Linguistics: Human Language Technologies*, pages 4392–4402, Seattle, United States. Association for Computational Linguistics.

Paolo Pedinotti, Eliana Di Palma, Ludovica Cerini, and Alessandro Lenci. 2021. A howling success or a working sea? testing what BERT knows about metaphors. In *Proceedings of the Fourth BlackboxNLP Workshop on Analyzing and Interpreting Neural Networks for NLP*, pages 192–204, Punta Cana, Dominican Republic. Association for Computational Linguistics.

Alec Radford, Jong Wook Kim, Chris Hallacy, Aditya Ramesh, Gabriel Goh, Sandhini Agarwal, Girish Sastry, Amanda Askell, Pamela Mishkin, Jack Clark, et al. 2021. Learning transferable visual models from natural language supervision. In *International Conference on Machine Learning*, pages 8748–8763. PMLR.

Aditya Ramesh, Mikhail Pavlov, Gabriel Goh, Scott Gray, Chelsea Voss, Alec Radford, Mark Chen, and Ilya Sutskever. 2021. Zero-shot text-to-image generation. In *Proceedings of the 38th International Conference on Machine Learning*, volume 139 of *Proceedings of Machine Learning Research*, pages 8821–8831. PMLR.

Jingjing Xu Duyu Tang Nan Duan Ming Gong Linjun Shou Daxin Jiang Guihong Cao Shangwen Lv, Daya Guo and Songlin Hu. 2020. Graph-based reasoning over heterogeneous external knowledge for commonsense question answering. In *The Thirty-Fourth AAAI Conference on Artificial Intelligence, AAAI 2020, New York, USA*, pages 8449–8456. AAAI Press.

Tao Shen, Yi Mao, Pengcheng He, Guodong Long, Adam Trischler, and Weizhu Chen. 2020. Exploiting structured knowledge in text via graph-guided representation learning. In *Proceedings of the 2020 Conference on Empirical Methods in Natural Language Processing (EMNLP)*, pages 8980–8994, Online. Association for Computational Linguistics.

Alon Talmor, Jonathan Herzig, Nicholas Lourie, and Jonathan Berant. 2019. CommonsenseQA: A question answering challenge targeting commonsense knowledge. In *Proceedings of the 2019 Conference of the North American Chapter of the Association for Computational Linguistics: Human Language Technologies, Volume 1 (Long and Short Papers)*, pages 4149–4158, Minneapolis, Minnesota. Association for Computational Linguistics.

Hao Tan and Mohit Bansal. 2020. Vokenization: Improving language understanding with contextualized, visual-grounded supervision. In *Proceedings of the 2020 Conference on Empirical Methods in Natural Language Processing (EMNLP)*, pages 2066–2080, Online. Association for Computational Linguistics.

Zhe Zhao Zhiruo Wang Qi Ju Haotang Deng Ping Wang Weijie Liu, Peng Zhou. 2020. K-BERT: Enabling language representation with knowledge graph. In *Proceedings of AAAI 2020*.

Wenhan Xiong, Jingfei Du, William Yang Wang, and Veselin Stoyanov. 2019. Pretrained encyclopedia: Weakly supervised knowledge-pretrained language model. In *International Conference on Learning Representations*.

Yichong Xu, Chenguang Zhu, Ruochen Xu, Yang Liu, Michael Zeng, and Xuedong Huang. 2021. Fusing context into knowledge graph for commonsense question answering. In *Findings of the Association for Computational Linguistics: ACL-IJCNLP 2021*, pages 1201–1207, Online. Association for Computational Linguistics.

Donghan Yu, Chenguang Zhu, Yiming Yang, and Michael Zeng. 2022a. Jaket: Joint pre-training of knowledge graph and language understanding. *Proceedings of the AAAI Conference on Artificial Intelligence*, 36(10):11630–11638.

Wenhao Yu, Chenguang Zhu, Yuwei Fang, Donghan Yu, Shuohang Wang, Yichong Xu, Michael Zeng, and Meng Jiang. 2022b. Dict-BERT: Enhancing language model pre-training with dictionary. In *Findings of the Association for Computational Linguistics: ACL 2022*, pages 1907–1918, Dublin, Ireland. Association for Computational Linguistics.

Zhengyan Zhang, Xu Han, Zhiyuan Liu, Xin Jiang, Maosong Sun, and Qun Liu. 2019. ERNIE: Enhanced language representation with informative entities. In *Proceedings of ACL 2019*.

Chenguang Zhu, Yichong Xu, Xiang Ren, Bill Yuchen Lin, Meng Jiang, and Wenhao Yu. 2022. Knowledge-augmented methods for natural language processing. In *Proceedings of the 60th Annual Meeting of the Association for Computational Linguistics: Tutorial Abstracts*, pages 12–20, Dublin, Ireland. Association for Computational Linguistics.

Wanzheng Zhu and Suma Bhat. 2021. Euphemistic phrase detection by masked language model. In *Findings of the Association for Computational Linguistics: EMNLP 2021*, pages 163–168, Punta Cana, Dominican Republic. Association for Computational Linguistics.

Wanzheng Zhu, Hongyu Gong, Rohan Bansal, Zachary Weinberg, Nicolas Christin, Giulia Fanti, and Suma Bhat. 2021. Self-supervised euphemism detection and identification for content moderation. In *42nd IEEE Symposium on Security and Privacy*.

Distribution-Based Measures of Surprise for Creative Language: Experiments with Humor and Metaphor

Razvan C. Bunescu
Department of Computer Science
University of North Carolina at Charlotte
Charlotte, NC 28223
razvan.bunescu@uncc.edu

Oseremen O. Uduehi
School of EECS
Ohio University
Athens, OH 45701
ou380517@ohio.edu

Abstract

Novelty or surprise is a fundamental attribute of creative output. As such, we postulate that a writer's creative use of language leads to word choices and, more importantly, corresponding semantic structures that are unexpected for the reader. In this paper we investigate measures of surprise that rely solely on word distributions computed by language models and show empirically that creative language such as humor and metaphor is strongly correlated with surprise. Surprisingly at first, information content is observed to be at least as good a predictor of creative language as any of the surprise measures investigated. However, the best prediction performance is obtained when information and surprise measures are combined, showing that surprise measures capture an aspect of creative language that goes beyond information content.

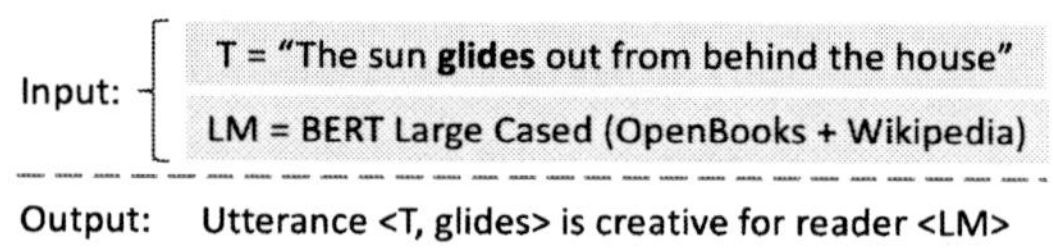

Figure 1: Creative language detection requires as input not only the Text (T), but also the Reader (LM).

1 Introduction

Language is used primarily as a means for communicating information. It is thus appropriate that information theory (Shannon, 1948) has provided the foundation for numerous studies into properties of natural language, as in (Shannon, 1951; Hale, 2001; Piantadosi et al., 2011; Gibson, 2019), among many others. Under the information theory framework, a communication channel is posited between the speaker and the listener, and correspondingly the goal of the speaker is to employ the channel as efficiently as possible while also minimizing the risk of miscommunication. Maximizing the use of the communication channel is achieved when speakers choose their words such that their information rate is close to the channel capacity, which can be seen as determining speakers to construct utterances such that information is spread uniformly across them. This is known as the Uniform Information Density (UID) hypothesis (Fenk and Fenk-Oczlon, 1980; Jaeger and Levy, 2006), operationalized as a tendency for regression towards the mean information content across the language (Meister et al., 2021). The UID hypothesis can explain a variety of linguistic phenomena, such as the optional omission of syntactic relativizers (Jaeger and Levy, 2006), or the shortened phonetic duration of highly predictable language units (Aylett and Turk, 2004). UID has also been construed to imply that speakers avoid producing words with an *information content*[1] that is too high or too low (Meister et al., 2022) relative to the expected information rate of the channel, or the entire language. While this holds true for most communicative uses of language, there are at least two types of situations when words have an information content much higher than expected, as illustrated in Figure 1.

First, there is the case when the listener has no clear expectation of what the speaker will utter next, such as when introducing a new discourse entity through a definite or indefinite article, especially at the beginning of a story when not much context is available. In this case, the next word distribution has a high entropy, all words have a relatively low probability, hence high information content. The word 'sun' in the sentence[2] shown in Figure 1 is in this category. Second, there are situations when language is used in creative ways, when speakers deliberately produce words or phrases that are interesting or unexpected, often with the purpose of inducing particular kinds of emotion in the listener, as is the case with the word 'glides' in Figure 1. In this paper, we aim to characterize such creative use of language solely through distribution-based

[1]Computed as negative log of word probability $-\log p(x)$.
[2]First line in a poem by Tomas Tranströmer.

Proceedings of the 3rd Workshop on Figurative Language Processing (FLP), pages 68 - 78
December 8, 2022

measures that are designed to discriminate creative language from normal language. In both situations discussed above the information content is high, therefore, at least theoretically, information content alone is not sufficient to discriminate between the two. As such, we propose that *surprise* be used as the main discriminating factor. We emphasize that determining whether an input text exhibits creativity or surprise requires specifying a *reference reader*, as shown in the example from Figure 1, which distinguishes the task explored in this paper from related tasks such as humor detection or figurative language classification, where novelty with respect to a reference reader is not a concern.

2 Definitions and Measures of Surprise

The ability to produce surprising outputs is a cornerstone of creativity, which in turn is widely considered to be an essential component of intelligent behavior (Boden, 1991). Surprise is a powerful driver for creativity and discovery. As such, surprise has been used to guide search algorithms in models of computational creativity and discovery (Yannakakis and Liapis, 2016). Owing to its importance for the creative process, surprise has also become one of the core criteria for the evaluation of creative artifacts (Maher et al., 2013). As reviewed in (Itti and Baldi, 2009), surprise is an essential concept in many studies on the neural basis of behavior, with surprising stimuli shown to be strong attractors of attention. Surprise, or violation of expectation, has also been hypothesized to be an essential mechanism through which music and stories elicit emotion. According to (Meyer, 1961), the principal emotional content of music arises from the composer's manipulation of expectation. Composers build expectations in time, which then they purposely violate in order to elicit tension, prediction, reaction, and appraisal responses (Huron, 2008). In text and narratives, surprise can be employed with substantial emotional impact at multiple levels, spanning from word-level, as in "Elon Musk has just blasted the world 's most powerful rocket into landfill" where the original word "space" was purposely replaced with "landfill" for humorous effect, to story-level, as in the various types of plot twists that are used to draw the reader emotionally in the story, e.g. *peripeteia* or *deux ex machina*.

In this section, we attempt to characterize word-level surprise using probability distributions computed by language models. We first consider a number of measures of surprise in the context of a general probability distribution p over an event space X, followed by more specialized surprise measures that are targeted to the special case of X being a language vocabulary. As such, we are interested in measuring how surprising the occurrence of an event $x \in X$ is for the audience p. An event x is improbable if its probability $p(x)$ is very small. Since improbable events are rare, it is tempting to consider the occurrence of an improbable event as being surprising. Weaver (1948) pondered on whether low probability implies surprise, *"an improbable event is often interesting. But is an improbable event always interesting?"*, and concluded *"we shall see that it is not"*, providing a simple, prototypical example in which improbable events are intuitively not surprising: a uniform distribution over an event space that has a large cardinality, as in dealing off a single bridge hand of thirteen cards from a shuffled pack of cards. There are more than 635 billion configurations of thirteen cards, all equally likely. Whatever bridge hand is dealt, although its probability is very small, it will not be, or feel, surprising. *"Any hand that occurs is simply one out of a number of exactly equally likely events, some one of which was bound to happen"*. What makes an event interesting or surprising is not that its probability is small in an absolute sense, it is that it is small in comparison to the probabilities of the other alternative events.

Weaver's insight is also in agreement with the interpretation of *"surprise as violation of expectation"*, which is hypothesized to be a major factor underlying emotion in music (Meyer, 1961). In this context, the term *expectation* refers to the kind that is engineered by composers in their music or by writers in their stories. Informally, a strong expectation is created when one or more potential outcomes are much more likely than other outcomes. More formally, an expectation regarding a random variable x is created when, prior to its value being observed, its context h makes a potential outcome $x = j$ more likely than other outcomes, as measured through the probability $p(x = j|h)$. Upon observing outcome $x = k$, we call it surprising if it confounds the expectation of seeing outcome $x = j$, i.e. $p(x = k|h) \ll p(x = j|h)$. Like in Weaver's argument above, the relative likelihood requirement for creating expectations immediately rules out uniform distributions.

The intuitive lack of surprise when observing

events sampled from a uniform distribution makes Shannon's *surprisal* inadequate as a measure of surprise. It is thus important that the notion of *surprise* is not equated with *surprisal*. The surprisal of an event x is an information-theoretic quantity defined as the negative log probability of x, i.e. $-\log p(x)$. Since surprisal is based solely on the event probability, monotonically decreasing with it, using surprisal to model surprise has the same conceptual deficiency as saying that rare events are surprising, as originally observed by Weaver (1948). Henceforth, to avoid confusion, we will refer to $-\log p(x)$ as the *information content* of x.

2.1 Quantifying Surprise

In this section, we describe a number of measures of surprise that are meant to capture the notion of small relative probability associated with surprising events. These measures are summarized in Table 1.

One of the first measures of surprise was the *surprise index* λ_1 proposed by Weaver (1948):

$$\lambda_1(p, x) = \frac{E[p]}{p(x)} \quad (1)$$

Weaver's surprise index is multiplicative: if X and Y are independent with distributions p and q, then the surprise index of the joint event $[x, y]$ is $\lambda_1(pq, [x, y]) = \lambda_1(p, x)\lambda_1(q, y)$.

Observing that the numerator $E[p]$ with which $p(x)$ is compared is somewhat arbitrary, Good (1956) generalized Weaver's surprise index to the following multiplicative (λ_c) and additive (Λ_c) versions, for $c > 0$:

$$\lambda_c(p, x) = \frac{(E[p^c])^{1/c}}{p(x)} \quad (2)$$

$$\Lambda_c(p, x) = \log \lambda_c(p, x) \quad (3)$$

Of all possible values for c, Good recommended as the most natural λ_0 and λ_1, together with their logarithmic versions Λ_0 and Λ_1, respectively:

$$\lambda_1(p, x) = \frac{E[p]}{p(x)} \quad (4)$$

$$\Lambda_1(p, x) = \log E[p] - \log p(x) \quad (5)$$

$$\lambda_0(p, x) = \frac{exp(E[\log p])}{p(x)} \quad (6)$$

$$\Lambda_0(p, x) = E[\log p] - \log p(x) \quad (7)$$

The additive measure Λ_0 is appealing because it can be interpreted in information theoretic terms as the difference between the Shannon information content $I(p, x) = -\log p(x)$ and the Shannon entropy $H(p)$:

$$\Lambda_0(p, x) = -\log p(x) - E[-\log p] \quad (8)$$

$$= I(p, x) - H(p) \quad (9)$$

Howard (2009) observes that Weaver's index can be written as $\lambda_1(p, x) = E\left[\frac{p}{p(x)}\right]$, whereas Good's index can be written as the mean of the log of the same variable, i.e. $\Lambda_0(p, x) = E\left[\log \frac{p}{p(x)}\right]$.

Observing that additive surprise indexes like Λ_0 more easily exceed a given value when the dimensionality is increased, Good (1988) advocated for using the tail-area probability as a surprise measure:

$$t(p, x) = \sum_{x': p(x') \leq p(x)} p(x') \quad (10)$$

However, the tail-area does not necessarily select outcomes that occur with small *relative probability*, for example when there are n alternative outcomes with slightly different probabilities that are all close to $1/n$. Howard (2009) points out that this behavior is connected to the fact that tail-area is not continuous in the outcome probabilities $p(x)$ and proposes a new measure of surprise called *s-value*:

$$sv(p, x) = 1 - \sum_{x'} min(p(x'), p(x)) \quad (11)$$

$$= 1 - [t(p, x) + n_x \cdot p(x)] \quad (12)$$

where n_x is the number of discrete outcomes with probability greater than $p(x)$. The s-value is continuous in $p(x)$ and, unlike the tail-area, selects for outcomes that conform with the basic intuition of small relative probability. It is equivalent with the probability mass contained in the area under the *pdf* curve that is above the $p(x)$ level.

If we use the term expectation with its psychological meaning of anticipation of an occurrence that may take place in future, a number of alternative definitions of surprise quantify the gap between the *psychological expectation* of a future event, i.e. the probability of the most likely event m_p, and its *realization*, i.e. the probability of the actual event x that happened. Correspondingly, the Expectation Realization (ER) gap can be defined as:

$$\psi(p, x) = \textit{Expectation} - \textit{Realization}$$

$$= \max_{x'} p(x') - p(x)$$

$$= p(m_p) - p(x) \quad (13)$$

Name	Formula	Unit
Good's surprise index	$\Lambda_0(p,x) = -\log p(x) - H(p)$	Information (bits)
Howard's s-value	$sv(p,x) = 1 - \sum_{x'} min(p(x'), p(x))$	Probability mass
Mode ER gap	$\Psi_m(p,x) = -\log p(x) + \log p(m_p)$	Information (bits)
Core ER gap	$\Psi_C(p,x) = -\log p(x) + \log p(C_p)$	Information (bits)

Table 1: Selected measures of surprise that capture the notion of small relative probability.

where $m_p = \arg\max_x p(x)$ is the largest mode of the distribution p, i.e. the expected, most likely outcome. Similar to Weaver and Good's surprise indexes, one can define a *multiplicative* version:

$$\begin{aligned}\psi(p,x) &= \textit{Expectation}/\textit{Realization} \\ &= p(m_p)/p(x)\end{aligned} \tag{14}$$

as well as an *additive* version:

$$\begin{aligned}\Psi_m(p,x) &= \log \textit{Expectation} - \log \textit{Realization} \\ &= \log p(m_p) - \log p(x) \\ &= I(p,x) - I(p,m_p)\end{aligned} \tag{15}$$

The ER measures for surprise are continuous in $p(x)$ and conform to the basic intuition of a surprising event having a small relative probability. We note that the simple ER gap from 14 has been previously proposed by Macedo et al. (2004), who found it to correlate well with human ratings of surprise. We prefer the additive version from 15 due to its information theoretic interpretation.

The measures of surprise proposed so far are summarized in the top 3 rows of Table 1. The measures were selected based on their properties, as follows: Good's surprise index and the Mode ER gap for their information-theoretic interpretation, and Howard's s-value for its probability mass interpretation. Of the 3 measures, the s-value and the mode ER gap also have the desirable property that they are non-negative for any outcome x, and become zero when x is the most likely outcome.

2.1.1 The Core Expectation Realization Gap

In this paper, we estimate surprise using the probability distribution computed by a language model. However, this creates a mismatch between the lexical level used to support the distribution and the semantic level that was used to annotate the creative examples. Most often, creativity implies surprise in terms of meaning, not necessarily in terms of the particular words chosen to express that meaning. Thus, the use of lexical distributions to estimate semantic surprise can lead to poor estimates of surprise in cases where a strong semantic expectation can be expressed with a large number of words. For example, to determine that "Congressmen" is surprising in the metaphor "an infestation of [Congressmen]", it is not sufficient that the realization $x =$ "Congressmen" in the context "an infestation of x" has a low probability. We also need a measure that tells us there is a strong expectation for what x is anticipated to be in the phrase "an infestation of x". In this example, the expectation is especially strong in terms of the semantic category of x, i.e. the reader strongly expects to see an instance from the PESTS category. Because this is a large category, there is a large set of words that can be reasonably expected in this context, resulting in a weak word-level expectation. Hence, the mode of the distribution used by the ER gap Ψ_m will not have a sufficiently high probability to make the Ψ_m pass a surprise threshold. The partition of the category expectation into many small word-level expectations leads to an increase in entropy, which adversely affects Good's surprise index Λ_0 as well.

For lack of an effective LM-based approach to compute probability distributions over semantic spaces, we designed an alternative version of the ER gap measure called Core ER gap, where the largest mode of the distribution m_p is replaced with the *Core* of the distribution C_p, comprising all the events $x \in X$ whose probability passes a predefined threshold, i.e. $C_p = \{x \in X | p(x) > \tau\}$. By appropriately setting the lower bound τ, we expect to capture in the core C_p all words belonging to the most expected semantic categories in a given context. Due to its information theoretic interpretation, we consider only the *additive* version:

$$\begin{aligned}\Psi_C(p,x) &= \log \textit{Expectation} - \log \textit{Realization} \\ &= \log p(C_p) - \log p(x) \\ &= I(p,x) - I(p,C_p)\end{aligned} \tag{16}$$

This version of the new Core ER gap measure is listed at the bottom of Table 1.

3 Datasets of Creative Language

We built two datasets of creative language examples: a HUMOR dataset and a METAPHOR dataset. The humor examples were extracted from the Humicroedit dataset (Hossain et al., 2019), which consists of regular English news headlines paired with versions of the same headlines that contain simple replacement edits designed to make them funny. Each funny headline was scored by five judges, resulting in a curated dataset of over 15,000 headline pairs. As positive examples for humor, we randomly selected 400 examples from a subset of the humorous headlines that were originally created using single-word replacements and that had an average annotator score of 1.8 or higher. The positive examples for metaphor were extracted from the English section of the LCC Metaphor dataset (Mohler et al., 2016) where the average annotator rating was 3.0 or above and where the source field of the metaphor was a single word. Furthermore, as explained below, we further applied a filtering step designed to preserve only metaphors that are novel to the language model, leaving a total of 268 positive examples of metaphor.

While a metaphor may appear creative to a person hearing it for the first time, it will sound completely unoriginal to a listener who has heard it and used it so many times that it has become part of their normal use of language. Similarly, a line that triggered laughter upon its first utterance, when repeated multiple times will normally get a smile at best from an audience already habituated to it. Therefore, it is important that creativity be determined with reference to a listener's experience. In general, judgements of creativity require specifying a reference model, e.g. the listener, the reader, or the audience, consuming the output produced by the speaker, the writer, or the composer, respectively. Consequently, based on the premise that creativity requires novelty, building an evaluation dataset annotated with creative uses of language requires fixing a *reference reader* and ensuring that examples annotated as creative are 1) novel for this reader and 2) evaluated with respect to the same reader. Since the proposed measures of surprise will necessitate access to the reader's contextual word distributions, in this paper we set the reference reader to be a generic reader whose knowledge of language is modeled by a large language model (LM), such as BERT (Devlin et al., 2019) if both the left and the right context of a word are used, or OPT (Zhang et al., 2022) if only using the previous discourse as context. Given that BERT was trained on the BooksCorpus and English Wikipedia, it is safe to assume that its pre-training data was not contaminated with any of the humorous headlines from Humicroedit, and therefore the humorous headlines appear novel to the reader modeled by BERT. However, we cannot say the same for the metaphor examples, as many of them are commonly used and likely to be found in BERT's pre-training corpus, e.g. "floating ideas", "deep understanding", "stealing dreams", "crushing insurgencies", "leap of faith", "seeds of discontent", to list just a few. To ensure that the metaphor examples included in the dataset are novel with respect to the reader modeled by BERT, since we did not have access to the exact pre-training data, we devised a conservative filtering where the base metaphor phrases were filtered out if a Google search returned less than 25 documents containing the phrase or its variations. For example, given the annotated metaphor "the bureaucracy barrier", we removed the article and also searched for "bureaucratic barrier" and "barrier of bureaucracy". Furthermore, we removed examples where the source word is repeated in the sentence context, as in "this [prison]$_s$ is the prison of [poverty]$_t$".

In terms of negative examples, for humor we used the 400 original titles corresponding to the 400 humorous examples. We further augmented these negative examples with nouns (as tagged by NLTK's POS tagger) selected at random from news articles downloaded from the CNN website in July 2022, such that the number of positive examples represents 10% of the total number of examples in each dataset. Regular news articles are expected to use regular language, without novel humor or novel metaphors. This is not to say the news articles do not contain metaphors, but when that happens they are metaphors that are commonly used and thus unsurprising for a generic reader. To summarize, the label distribution in the two datasets is as follows:

1. The Humor dataset, 4000 examples:
    (a) 400 positive examples, one-word substitution in news headlines that made them humorous, extracted from examples in the Humicroedit dataset with high inter-annotator agreement.
    (b) 400 negative examples, using the substituted word from the original titles used in the 400 positive examples above.

(c) 3200 negative examples, using random content words from CNN news articles.

2. The Metaphor dataset, 3760 examples:

   (a) 268 positive examples, the annotated one-word source domain field of metaphors from the LCC Metaphor dataset that had high inter-annotator agreement and were rare on the internet.

   (b) 2412 negative examples, a subset of the 3200 selected at 1.(c) above.

The imbalanced label distribution was meant to address the fact that instances of creative language are relatively rare, although the exact proportion in general is hard to estimate due to the fact that certain types of text, e.g. poetry, are expected to be substantially more creative than other types, e.g. news articles. We note that the labels in the resulting dataset are likely to be noisy: metaphors that we annotated as creative, even though uncommon ad litteram on the internet, may still have been present in the LM's pre-training data in a different form, such as using a synonym for any of the words in the expression. Furthermore, it is possible that the CNN news articles included in the dataset contain instances of creative language, albeit very few. Overall though, it is expected that a good measure of surprise would show substantial discriminative power between the soft positive vs. soft negative examples in this dataset. Hardening the dataset would require the development of feasible annotation guidelines for determining whether the reference LM (the reference reader) has been exposed (through its pre-training data) to any given expression, and then going over each example and using the annotation criteria to determine the label.

4 Experimental Evaluation

All the distribution-based measures of surprise evaluated in this section were calculated using the probability distributions computed by the BERT Large model (cased) available on the HuggingFace website[3]. This is done by taking the word that is labeled in the dataset, masking it, and asking BERT to output the token distribution at the masked position, using a context size of 15 tokens to the left and to the right. Due to the WordPiece subword tokenization used by BERT, sometimes the word that need to be labeled is split into multiple tokens, where the first token is distinguished from the continuation tokens using the double hashtags '##', as for example 'disrespect' = 'di' + '##s' + '##res' + '##pect'. In these cases, we use the probability of the first token as a proxy for the probability of the entire word – preliminary experiments where the simple product or the geometric mean of all the token probabilities were used did not show a significant difference in the results, likely due to the fact that continuation tokens often receive a very high probability.

A starting assumption in these experiments is that the input text is well formed, e.g. it does not contain ungrammatical phrases or typos. While we recognize that real text may contain ill formed language that could be incorrectly detected as surprising by the various surprise measures proposed in this paper, we do not consider this to pose a significant challenge as such text could be feasibly detected and filtered out using current state-of-the-art NLP tools. Furthermore, a simple way to filter out ill formed language and typos is to ignore tokens that belong to the tail of the LM distribution, a procedure that we will investigate in future work.

The support of the raw LM distribution is modified to exclude *continuation tokens*, *non-content words*, and *punctuation symbols* for the reasons explained below, after which the probabilities of the remaining tokens are renormalized so that their total probability mass is still 1. Continuation tokens sometimes receive a high probability at the masked position. For example, in the annotated metaphor "$[\text{tax}]_t$ $[\text{sorcery}]_s$ is a mystery to me", when the source word "sorcery" is masked the continuation token "##ation" receives the highest probability, corresponding to the reasonable completion "taxation is a mistery to me". Since the masked word cannot be continuation in our task, all continuation tokens are eliminated from the distribution support. Depending on the context, non-content words such as determiners and prepositions may receive a high probability at the masked position, as for example in the metaphor text "we had our own little electoral “irregularities” down here in Portsmouth's First Ward, where we suffer from $[\text{constipated}]_s$ $[\text{democracy}]_t$". Determiners such as 'a' or 'the' receive a relatively high probability for occurring at the masked position for the source field. Since metaphors and one-word humorous word substitutions are content words, we remove non-content words from the distribution support. Punctuation symbols may also receive a relatively

[3]https://huggingface.co/bert-large-cased

Measures		creative Humor P	R	F_1	F_{1m}	AuC	creative Metaphor P	R	F_1	F_{1m}	AuC
Random baseline		10.0	50.0	16.7	–	–	10.0	50.0	16.7	–	–
All positive baseline		10.0	100.0	18.2	–	–	10.0	100.0	18.2	–	–
Information content	$I(p, x)$	32.0	86.5	46.7	50.3	46.2	27.6	79.2	40.8	47.8	38.2
Good's surprise index	$\Lambda_O(p, x)$	28.2	73.5	40.7	45.2	39.4	27.8	75.6	40.5	47.3	33.8
Howard's s-value	$sv(p, x)$	22.5	85.3	35.5	43.9	38.1	21.9	85.9	34.8	47.3	34.3
Mode ER gap	$\Psi_m(p, x)$	30.7	82.5	44.7	48.6	44.1	27.8	78.7	41.0	47.6	35.9
Core ER gap	$\Psi_C(p, x)$	31.6	85.8	46.2	49.8	45.6	27.8	79.2	41.1	48.1	38.3
Info ∧ Entropy	$[I(p, x), H(p)]$	32.7	87.8	47.6	53.4	47.4	27.4	80.8	40.8	47.7	37.2
Info ∧ Mode Info	$[I(p, x), I(p, m_p)]$	31.7	86.3	46.4	52.7	46.4	27.6	80.0	40.9	47.8	37.9
Info ∧ Core Info	$[I(p, x), I(p, C_p)]$	33.0	88.3	48.0	53.2	49.3	27.7	79.5	41.0	48.1	38.2
Info ∧ Entropy ∧ Mode Info ∧ Core Info		33.4	88.0	48.4	53.6	49.5	29.8	82.7	43.6	53.1	42.3
Contextual Embeddings + 2-layer FCN		80.3	89.8	84.5	87.1	91.2	93.7	94.1	93.7	95.1	95.6

Table 2: Results from comparative evaluation of surprise measures on detecting creative use of language.

high probability in some contexts, as such they are excluded as well from the distribution support. In the metaphor example "communism thrives on an empty stomach and $[\text{democracy}]_t$ $[\text{relaxes}]_s$ on a full one", symbols such as commas ',' and the dashes '–' are predicted with a high probability at the masked source position.

4.1 Quantifying Discriminative Power

To estimate the discriminative power of the various surprise measures, we use them as input features for a simple binary binary logistic regression model. During training of this linear classifier, given the imbalanced label distribution, positive examples are given 9 times the weight of negative examples in the cross-entropy cost function. Evaluation is done in a 10-fold setting, where each dataset is shuffled and partitioned into 10 equally-sized folds, then 9 folds are used as training and the remaining fold as testing. This training-testing procedure is repeated 10 times so that test results are obtained for each fold. Care was taken to ensure that test folds are not contaminated with information from training. Thus, metaphor examples that had the same target word were always placed in the same fold. The original title and the humorous title obtained by one-word substitution were also always placed in the same fold. Precision (P), recall (R), and F_1-measure are computed by pooling results across the 10 folds. Furthermore, by varying a threshold over the probabilistic output of the classifier, we create precision vs. recall graphs and use them to calculate two additional scores: the maximum F_1 measure across all confidence thresholds (F_{1m}) and the area under the curve (AuC).

4.2 Results and Discussion

For each dataset, Table 2 show the performance of 2 simple baselines, 5 standalone distribution-based measures, and 4 combinations of information-based measures. The 'random' baseline assigns labels uniformly at random, whereas the 'all positive' baseline labels every example as positive. In terms of combinations, for each of the 3 information measures we used the two terms in the measure as separate features. Therefore, since Good's surprise index is written as information content minus entropy, we evaluated a binary classifier that uses information content and entropy as two separate features. Similarly, the information content and mode information combination corresponds to the Mode ER Gap, whereas the information content and core information combination corresponds to the Core ER Gap. Finally, we use all these information terms as features in an overall combination, as shown at the bottom of the table.

The results show that all standalone measures do much better than random, showing that they do capture an important signal in terms of creative use of language. Somewhat surprisingly, no surprise measure does better than information content, despite the proven theoretical deficiency of using information content to model surprise. Of the 4 surprise measures, the Core ER Gap performs the best, being slightly under information content on Humor and slightly better than information content on Metaphor. We hypothesize that an important reason for the lower performance of standalone surprise measures is the fact that the LM probabilities are miscalibrated. While calibration of probability distributions for classification tasks downstream of LM has been investigated in a number of recent works (Wang et al., 2020; Desai and Durrett, 2020; Park and Caragea, 2022), we are not aware of any work targeting calibration of the LM distribution itself. It is known for example that the tail of the LM distribution is unreliable (Holtzman et al., 2019), giving too much probability mass to words that should not be acceptable in the given context, e.g. resulting in ungrammatical phrases. The Mode and Core ER gaps ignore the the tail of the distribution completely, which may explain their relatively better performance when compared with Good's surprise index and Howard's s-value.

Since theoretically the average, mode, and core information are important for quantifying the level of surprise, instead of adding them directly to information content as was done in the surprise measures, we aimed to alleviate the miscalibration issue by training a linear model to optimize the trade-off between each of them and information content. The results in Table 2 show that, overall, when all types of information-based measure are combined, there is a substantial 3% increase in overall performance (AuC) over information content alone, on both datasets. The improvements in F_1 measure are statistically significant at $p < 0.01$, as measured using a one-tailed paired T-test over the results from the 10 folds. Overall, these results empirically support the theoretical observation that surprise measures capture aspects of creative language use that go beyond simple information content.

Finally, although the focus of this paper is on the discriminative power of surprise measures that are based solely on word-level distributions, the last line of Table 2 shows the performance of a classifier that uses the contextual representations produced by the frozen LM as input to a fully connected network (FCN) consisting of 2 hidden layers and one output logistic regression node. Unsurprisingly, the use of contextual embeddings as input to the FCN leads to much better results, likely due to its better capacity for modeling semantic-level surprise.

Humor* $\vee$ *Metaphor* $\not\Rightarrow$ *Creative We would like to emphasize here that the detection of creative language evaluated in this section, although using examples drawn from humor and metaphor datasets, is quite different from the metaphor or humor detection tasks pursued in related work. The metaphor detection task (Leong et al., 2020) is unconcerned with whether the metaphor is commonly used vs. novel or surprising to the reader. In comparison, as argued in Section 3, creative language detection requires specifying a *reference reader* and the examples that are annotated as creative, be they humor or metaphor, need to be novel to this reader.

4.3 Error Analysis

Upon looking at the errors in which the trained classifier had the most confidence, we discovered a few major sources of errors. First, in terms of false negative, sometimes the metaphor word that is tagged as the source is made highly predictable by the presence of other words in the context, as in "[democracy]$_t$ is the thinly gloved [hand]$_s$ of repressive power", where the likelihood of hand is high due to the preceding 'gloved'. A possible solution could be to mask the entire phrase 'thinly gloved hand' when asking the LM to compute the probability distribution, and utilizing an encode-decoder LM such as T5 to produce a probability distribution over phrases. There also also instances of parallel metaphors in the same sentence, where one metaphor is highly predictive of the other, as in ""If [poverty]$_t$ is a [fire]$_s$ and aid is a firefighter, good governance is the water".

In terms of false positive, there are words that are associated with high information content because BERT does not have knowledge of named entities or types of events mentioned in the text. For example, in the title "Texas church [shooter] was Atheist, thought Christians stupid", the word shooter had a very low probability, likely due to BERT not having been trained on text referencing shootings in places of worship. Likewise, 'Harvey' receives a very low probability in the sentence "Trump has pledged $1 million to [Harvey] relief". In a way, these examples, although they were considered as negative by default, they are indeed surprising for the reference reader modeled by BERT.

5 Related Work

Owing to its essential role in our daily lives, there have been numerous computational approaches to humor recognition, as reviewed for example in (West and Horvitz, 2019; Hossain et al., 2019). Humor generation has presented a challenging problem in AI since the early 1990s, leading to the development of various template-based and neural approaches (Amin and Burghardt, 2020). The important role that surprise plays in humor generation has been previously recognized in theories of humor, such as the surprise theory of laughter (Toplyn, 2014) and other prominent models that posit humor is evoked by incongruity within a text, such as the two-stage model of Suls (1972). According to incongruity theories of humor, a text conveys at least two interpretations, of which one is more salient. As readers process the text, the salient interpretation is activated until a text segment is encountered that contradicts it and thus promotes the previously unexpected interpretation. Surprise arises from his sudden revision of understanding.

Metaphors are pervasive in everyday communication, as well as in creative writing such as novels and poetry. Metaphors enhance the communicative aspects of language by connecting concepts from new domains, often abstract, with more familiar ones, usually concrete (Lakoff and Johnson, 1980). Metaphorical expressions have many uses, from helping frame an issue in order to emphasize some aspects of reality (Boeynaems et al., 2017), to creating a strong emotional effect (Blanchette and Dunbar, 2001; Citron and Goldberg, 2014). The ubiquity of metaphors means their computational treatment (Veale et al., 2016) has received significant attention in the NLP community, as surveyed by Shutova (2015) and more recently Tong et al. (2021). A distinction is made in the literature between *conventional* metaphors, which are entrenched in the conceptual system, and *novel* metaphors, which are unfamiliar. In this paper, we further recommend that novelty judgements be made relative to a *reference reader*. Our use of a large LM to model the reference reader is supported by the fact that pre-trained LMs encode conventional metaphorical information, as shown recently in the probing study of Aghazadeh et al. (2022). Even though metaphor is widely seen as a creative tool and surprise is an essential component of creative artifacts, we are not aware of any work investigating the role of surprise in discriminating between conventional vs. novel metaphors.

Computational approaches to humor and metaphor are part of a larger inquiry into identifying and formalizing the basic processes underlying human creativity. In the growing field of computational creativity[4], surprise has been proposed as one of the major criteria for the evaluation of creative artifacts (Maher et al., 2013). Surprising outputs were shown to attract the attention of the observer (Itti and Baldi, 2006), but also to guide the creative process itself: in a study of the creative design process followed by architects (Suwa et al., 2000), surprising discoveries in design sketches were observed to cause reformulations of design goals, which in turn led to further unexpected discoveries, due to designers reading more off a sketch than what they originally intended to put there (Schon and Wiggins, 1992). In this paper we emphasize that surprise, and by extension creativity, needs to be defined relative to a reference reader or audience. Consequently, generative architectures that aim to learn patterns of surprise and expectation from data need to contain a separate model for the reference reader, as implemented in the composer-audience models from (Bunescu and Uduehi, 2019) for binary sequences and (Uduehi and Bunescu, 2021) for basic geometrical shapes.

6 Conclusion and Future Work

Aiming to characterize creative language, we introduced a number of measures of surprise that are based solely on the probability distributions computed by a reference LM, considered to model a reference reader. Experimental evaluations show that, in combination with information content, the surprise measures improve detection of novel metaphors or humor, providing empirical evidence for the role of surprise in creative use of language. The code and data will be made publicly available[5].

Future work includes refining the datasets, calibrating the LM probabilities, developing semantic-level measures of surprise, and evaluating the proposed measures with respect to a reference reader that only knows the literal meaning of words. An interesting future extension to other types of word-level humor such as puns was suggested by a reviewer, where surprise measures would be combined with measures of character-level similarity such as edit distance.

Acknowledgements

We would like to thank the anonymous reviewers for their suggestions and constructive feedback.

[4]https://computationalcreativity.net

[5]https://github.com/uoseremen/SurpriseCreativeLanguage

References

Ehsan Aghazadeh, Mohsen Fayyaz, and Yadollah Yaghoobzadeh. 2022. Metaphors in Pre-Trained Language Models: Probing and Generalization Across Datasets and Languages. In *Proceedings of the 60th Annual Meeting of the Association for Computational Linguistics (Volume 1: Long Papers)*, pages 2037–2050, Dublin, Ireland. Association for Computational Linguistics.

Miriam Amin and Manuel Burghardt. 2020. A survey on approaches to computational humor generation. In *Proceedings of the The 4th Joint SIGHUM Workshop on Computational Linguistics for Cultural Heritage, Social Sciences, Humanities and Literature*, pages 29–41, Online. International Committee on Computational Linguistics.

Matthew Aylett and Alice Turk. 2004. The smooth signal redundancy hypothesis: A functional explanation for relationships between redundancy, prosodic prominence, and duration in spontaneous speech. *Language and Speech*, 47(1):31–56. PMID: 15298329.

Isabelle Blanchette and Kevin Dunbar. 2001. Analogy use in naturalistic settings: The influence of audience, emotion, and goals. *Memory & Cognition*, 29(5):730–735.

Margaret A. Boden. 1991. *The Creative Mind: Myths and Mechanisms*. Basic Books, Inc., New York, NY, USA.

Amber Boeynaems, Christian Burgers, Elly Konijn, and Gerard Steen. 2017. The impact of conventional and novel metaphors in news on issue viewpoint. *International Journal of Communication*, 11(0).

Razvan Bunescu and Oseremen Uduehi. 2019. Learning to surprise: A composer-audience architecture. In *ICCC*, pages 41–48.

Francesca M. M. Citron and Adele E. Goldberg. 2014. Metaphorical sentences are more emotionally engaging than their literal counterparts. *Journal of Cognitive Neuroscience*, 26(11):2585–2595.

Shrey Desai and Greg Durrett. 2020. Calibration of pre-trained transformers. In *Proceedings of the 2020 Conference on Empirical Methods in Natural Language Processing (EMNLP)*, pages 295–302, Online. Association for Computational Linguistics.

Jacob Devlin, Ming-Wei Chang, Kenton Lee, and Kristina Toutanova. 2019. BERT: Pre-training of deep bidirectional transformers for language understanding. In *Proceedings of the 2019 Conference of the North American Chapter of the Association for Computational Linguistics: Human Language Technologies, Volume 1 (Long and Short Papers)*, pages 4171–4186, Minneapolis, Minnesota. Association for Computational Linguistics.

August Fenk and Gertraud Fenk-Oczlon. 1980. Konstanz im kurzzeitgedächtnis - konstanz im sprachlichen informationsfluß? *Zeitschrift für experimentelle und angewandte Psychologie*, 27:400–414.

Futrell R. Piantadosi S. P. Dautriche I. Mahowald K. Bergen L. Levy R. Gibson, E. 2019. How efficiency shapes human language. *Trends in cognitive sciences*, 23(5):389—407.

I. J. Good. 1956. The Surprise Index for the Multivariate Normal Distribution. *The Annals of Mathematical Statistics*, 27(4):1130 – 1135.

I. J. Good. 1988. Surprise index. *Encyclopedia of Statistical Sciences*, 7(1):1–5.

John Hale. 2001. A probabilistic Earley parser as a psycholinguistic model. In *Second Meeting of the North American Chapter of the Association for Computational Linguistics*.

Ari Holtzman, Jan Buys, Li Du, Maxwell Forbes, and Yejin Choi. 2019. The Curious Case of Neural Text Degeneration.

Nabil Hossain, John Krumm, and Michael Gamon. 2019. "president vows to cut <taxes> hair": Dataset and analysis of creative text editing for humorous headlines. In *Proceedings of the 2019 Conference of the North American Chapter of the Association for Computational Linguistics: Human Language Technologies, Volume 1 (Long and Short Papers)*, pages 133–142, Minneapolis, Minnesota. Association for Computational Linguistics.

J. V. Howard. 2009. Significance testing with no alternative hypothesis: A measure of surprise. *Erkenntnis (1975-)*, 70(2):253–270.

David Huron. 2008. *Sweet Anticipation: Music and the Psychology of Expectation*. MIT.

Laurent Itti and Pierre Baldi. 2009. Bayesian surprise attracts human attention. *Vision Research*, 49(10):1295 – 1306.

Laurent Itti and Pierre F. Baldi. 2006. Bayesian surprise attracts human attention. In *NIPS*. MIT Press.

T. Jaeger and Roger Levy. 2006. Speakers optimize information density through syntactic reduction. In *Advances in Neural Information Processing Systems*, volume 19. MIT Press.

George Lakoff and Mark Johnson. 1980. *Metaphors we Live by*. University of Chicago Press, Chicago.

Chee Wee (Ben) Leong, Beata Beigman Klebanov, Chris Hamill, Egon Stemle, Rutuja Ubale, and Xianyang Chen. 2020. A report on the 2020 VUA and TOEFL metaphor detection shared task. In *Proceedings of the Second Workshop on Figurative Language Processing*, pages 18–29, Online. Association for Computational Linguistics.

Luis Macedo, R. Reisezein, and A. Cardoso. 2004. Modeling forms of surprise in artificial agents: empirical and theoretical study of surprise functions. In *Proceedings of the 26th Annual Meeting of the Cognitive Science Society*.

Mary Lou Maher, Katherine A. Brady, and Douglas H. Fisher. 2013. Computational models of surprise in evaluating creative design. In *Proceedings of the Sixth International Conference on Computational Creativity (ICCC)*.

Clara Meister, Tiago Pimentel, Patrick Haller, Lena Jäger, Ryan Cotterell, and Roger Levy. 2021. Revisiting the Uniform Information Density hypothesis. In *Proceedings of the 2021 Conference on Empirical Methods in Natural Language Processing*, pages 963–980, Online and Punta Cana, Dominican Republic. Association for Computational Linguistics.

Clara Meister, Tiago Pimentel, Gian Wiher, and Ryan Cotterell. 2022. Typical Decoding for Natural Language Generation. *arXiv:2202.00666 [cs]*. ArXiv: 2202.00666.

Leonard Meyer. 1961. *Emotion and Meaning in Music*. University of Chicago.

Michael Mohler, Mary Brunson, Bryan Rink, and Marc Tomlinson. 2016. Introducing the LCC metaphor datasets. In *Proceedings of the Tenth International Conference on Language Resources and Evaluation (LREC'16)*, pages 4221–4227, Portorož, Slovenia. European Language Resources Association (ELRA).

Seo Yeon Park and Cornelia Caragea. 2022. On the Calibration of Pre-trained Language Models using Mixup Guided by Area Under the Margin and Saliency. In *Proceedings of the 60th Annual Meeting of the Association for Computational Linguistics (Volume 1: Long Papers)*, pages 5364–5374, Dublin, Ireland. Association for Computational Linguistics.

Steven T. Piantadosi, Harry Tily, and Edward Gibson. 2011. Word lengths are optimized for efficient communication. *Proceedings of the National Academy of Sciences*, 108(9):3526–3529.

Donald A Schon and Glenn Wiggins. 1992. Kinds of seeing and their functions in designing. *Design studies*, 13(2):135–156.

C. E. Shannon. 1948. A mathematical theory of communication. *The Bell System Technical Journal*, 27(3):379–423.

C. E. Shannon. 1951. Prediction and entropy of printed english. *The Bell System Technical Journal*, 30(1):50–64.

Ekaterina Shutova. 2015. Design and Evaluation of Metaphor Processing Systems. *Computational Linguistics*, 41(4):579–623. _eprint: https://direct.mit.edu/coli/article-pdf/41/4/579/1807226/coli_a_00233.pdf.

Jerry M. Suls. 1972. Chapter 4 - A Two-Stage Model for the Appreciation of Jokes and Cartoons: An Information-Processing Analysis. In JEFFREY H. GOLDSTEIN and PAUL E. McGHEE, editors, *The Psychology of Humor*, pages 81–100. Academic Press, San Diego.

Masaki Suwa, John Gero, and Terry Purcell. 2000. Unexpected discoveries and s-invention of design requirements: Important vehicles for a design process. *Design Studies*, 21(6):539–567.

Xiaoyu Tong, Ekaterina Shutova, and Martha Lewis. 2021. Recent advances in neural metaphor processing: A linguistic, cognitive and social perspective. In *Proceedings of the 2021 Conference of the North American Chapter of the Association for Computational Linguistics: Human Language Technologies*, pages 4673–4686, Online. Association for Computational Linguistics.

Joe Toplyn. 2014. *Comedy Writing for Late-Night TV: How to Write Monologue Jokes, Desk Pieces, Sketches, Parodies, Audience Pieces, Remotes, and Other Short-Form Comedy*.

Oseremen O. Uduehi and Razvan C. Bunescu. 2021. Adversarial learning of expectation and surprise: Experiments with geometric shapes. In *ICCC*, pages 286–290.

Tony Veale, Ekaterina Shutova, and Beata Beigman Klebanov. 2016. Metaphor: A Computational Perspective. *Synthesis Lectures on Human Language Technologies*, 9(1):1–160. Publisher: Morgan & Claypool Publishers.

Shuo Wang, Zhaopeng Tu, Shuming Shi, and Yang Liu. 2020. On the inference calibration of neural machine translation. In *Proceedings of the 58th Annual Meeting of the Association for Computational Linguistics*, pages 3070–3079, Online. Association for Computational Linguistics.

Warren Weaver. 1948. Probability, rarity, interest, and surprise. *The Scientific Monthly*, 67(6):390–392.

Robert West and Eric Horvitz. 2019. Reverse-Engineering Satire, or "Paper on Computational Humor Accepted despite Making Serious Advances". *Proceedings of the AAAI Conference on Artificial Intelligence*, 33(01):7265–7272. Number: 01.

Georgios N. Yannakakis and Antonios Liapis. 2016. Searching for surprise. In *Proceedings of the Seventh International Conference on Computational Creativity*, pages 25–32, PAris, France.

Susan Zhang, Stephen Roller, Naman Goyal, Mikel Artetxe, Moya Chen, Shuohui Chen, Christopher Dewan, Mona Diab, Xian Li, Xi Victoria Lin, Todor Mihaylov, Myle Ott, Sam Shleifer, Kurt Shuster, Daniel Simig, Punit Singh Koura, Anjali Sridhar, Tianlu Wang, and Luke Zettlemoyer. 2022. Opt: Open pre-trained transformer language models.

Euphemism Detection by Transformers and Relational Graph Attention Network

Yuting Wang, Yiyi Liu, Ruqing Zhang, Yixing Fan, Jiafeng Guo
CAS Key Lab of Network Data Science and Technology, Institute of Computing Technology,
Chinese Academy of Sciences, Beijing, China
University of Chinese Academy of Sciences, Beijing, China
{liuyiyi17s,wangyuting22g,zhangruqing,fanyixing,guojiafeng}@ict.ac.cn

Abstract

Euphemism is a type of figurative language broadly adopted in social media and daily conversations. People use euphemisms for politeness or to conceal what they are discussing. Euphemism detection is a challenging task because of its obscure and figurative nature. Even humans may not agree on if a word expresses euphemism. In this paper, we propose to employ bidirectional encoder representations transformers (BERT), and relational graph attention network in order to model the semantic and syntactic relations between the target words and the input sentence. The best performing method of ours reaches a macro F_1 score of 84.0 on the euphemism detection dataset of the third workshop on figurative language processing shared task 2022.

1 Introduction

Euphemism is a sophisticated language phenomenon in which one usually uses a polite word or expression instead of a more direct one to avoid shocking or upsetting someone[1]. For example, *"We are very sorry that he has passed away"*. Here, *"pass away"* does not mean dissipation intuitively, but death, which can make unpleasant things sound more polite. Due to its obscure and figurative nature, euphemism detection which aims to predict a text as euphemism or non-euphemism becomes a particularly challenging classification task. With the usage of euphemisms becoming prevalent on social media and in daily conversation, euphemism detection has received growing research attention to facilitate the understanding of natural language's sentiment and semantics.

Felt and Riloff (2020) make the first attempt to recognize euphemisms and dysphemisms. They identify synonym phrases of given seed euphemism-related phrases by a weakly supervised bootstrapping algorithm and then classify the phrases using sentiment cues and contextual sentiment analysis. With the advent of Pre-trained Language Models (PLMs), euphemism detection methods based on PLMs such as BERT (Devlin et al., 2019) have been proposed. Zhu and Bhat (2021) propose an automatic euphemistic phrase detection method without human effort. They first extract quality phrases and select euphemistic phrase candidates by computing embedding similarities. Then they use SpanBERT to rank and classify all candidates.

Despite existing work have achieved promising results, there are still several challenges to tackle. On the one hand, existing euphemism detection work mainly focus on mining characteristics of target words/phrases that triggered the euphemism phenomenon. They emphasize too much the euphemism of target words while ignoring the context circumstances where the target words sit. On the other hand, the first step of these methods is often to extract euphemism candidate words or phrases based on domain expertise or existing data annotations. If the first step is not done well, it will influence the subsequent classification and ranking, which may cause error propagation and lead to poor performance. We observe that euphemisms are essentially polysemy. In this sense, we argue that the meanings of euphemism target words/phrases are closely related to the context in which they are located semantically and syntactically.

Shed light on the great performance achieved by BERT and Graph Neural Network (Veličković et al., 2017) on the aspect-based sentiment analysis task, we propose to employ BERT and Relational Graph Attention Network (RGAT) (Wang et al., 2020) to deal with euphemism detection. Specifically, our model contains two isolated sub-models, BERT-Concat and RGAT-BERT. For BERT-Concat, the model's input is the concatenation of the input sentence and target words. We use BERT-Concat to enhance the information of target words and

[1] https://www.ldoceonline.com/dictionary/euphemism

Proceedings of the 3rd Workshop on Figurative Language Processing (FLP), pages 79 - 83
December 8, 2022 ©2022 Association for Computational Linguistics

capture the sequential semantic knowledge of the input sentence and target words. RGAT-BERT is adopted mainly to capture the syntactic information between target words and their corresponding contexts. The graph is built on the dependency tree. To enhance the syntactic connections between target words and the essential contexts, RGAT reshapes the dependency tree in which target words are root. It also prunes the reshaped tree to avoid the noise that unimportant contexts bring. Finally, we design a voting mechanism to ensemble the results of the two sub-models, which can leverage the advantages of the two.

We conduct experiments on the euphemism detection dataset. Empirical experimental results demonstrate the effectiveness of our proposed method. We ended up fourth in the third workshop on figurative language processing shared task 2022.

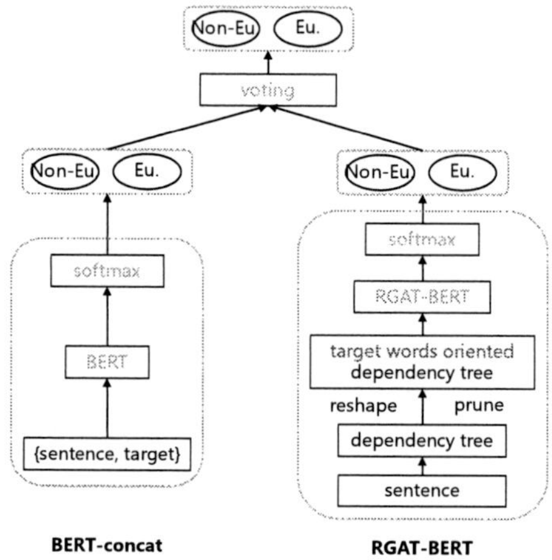

Figure 1: Structure of our model, which contains BERT-Concat(left) and RGAT-BERT(right). Eu. and Non-Eu. denote euphemism and non-euphemism classes respectively.

2 Related Work

In this section, we briefly review the related work on euphemism detection.

Existing work mainly focus on identifying euphemistic words. Magu and Luo (2018) provide an unsupervised word embedding's similarity method to identify euphemisms (code words) in hate speech. Felt and Riloff (2020) use sentiment analysis to recognize the euphemistic and dysphemistic language. They adopt a bootstrapping algorithm for finding near-synonym phrases and then classify the collected phrases as euphemistic, dysphemistic, or neutral using lexical sentiment cues and contextual sentiment analysis.

With the advent of pre-trained language models, a lot of euphemism detection methods based on PLMs have been proposed. Zhu et al. (2021) propose a self-supervised euphemistic detection method. They first extract candidate phrases from a base corpus and then filter out ones associated with euphemistic seed phrases through embedding similarity computing. Finally, they use pre-trained language models to classify these phrases. Similar to (Felt and Riloff, 2020), Zhu et al. (2021) rely on a set of predefined seed phrases, which may not be generalized to different datasets. Zhu and Bhat (2021) improve Zhu et al. (2021)'s approach by adding an automatic paraphraser. Kapron-King and Xu (2021) investigate gender differences in euphemism usage and they find that women do not use euphemisms more than men through empirical analysis. Gavidia et al. (2022) present a corpus of potentially euphemistic terms, which promotes the development of euphemism detection. We observe that most work on euphemism detection focus on euphemistic terms. They pay less attention to the contexts and the connections between euphemistic terms and their corresponding contexts in a sentence, which may lose important information.

3 Model

In this section, we introduce our method for euphemism detection in detail. The overview of our proposed method is shown in Figure 1. We first introduce the pre-processing of the dataset, and then the BERT model and the RGAT-BERT model. Finally we elucidate the model ensembling process.

3.1 Data Pre-processing

The original data includes text IDs, utterances, and euphemistic labels. We pre-process the text to (1) extract target words and their position, (2) remove the unexpected punctuation. Since the target is marked with "<>" symbols, for the convenience of subsequent model implementation, we extract the target and mark the position of the left character start point and the right character endpoint. Then we remove the unexpected punctuation marks "@@@@@@@@@@", "<" and ">". "@@@@@@@@@@" is a feature of GloWbE corpus that obscures spans of text. The removal of the above marks will not affect the meaning of the input utterance. The input sentence is denoted as $s = \{w_1^s, w_2^s, ..., w_n^s\}$ and the corresponding target words is represented as $t = \{w_i^t, w_{i+1}^t, ..., w_k^t\}$. n is the length of the input sentence. k is the length of target words.

3.2 BERT-Concat

We design the BERT-Concat model to enhance the information of target words and capture the sequential semantic knowledge of the input sentence and target words. The input of BERT-Concat is $\{s, t\}$. Note that the concatenation happens at the sequence length, not the hidden dimension. We also try to concatenate the input sentence and target words at the hidden dimension, but the experimental results are not good. The reason may be that the hidden size of the new representation is too large after concatenating, which may increase the complexity of the model and introduce irrelevant noisy information.

The training objective is to minimize the cross-entropy loss of the euphemism label probability distribution.

$$L_{CE}(\theta) = \sum \text{cross-entropy}(y, P(\hat{y})),$$

where y is the ground-truth of the euphemism label, and $P(\hat{y})$ is the predicted score. θ is the parameter set of the model.

3.3 RGAT-BERT

The syntactic structure is an important tool for understanding natural language. The relationships between words can be denoted with directed edges and labels. Sometimes the context that is important to understand target words may not be found in the sequence structure but in the syntactic structure. Therefore, the use of graph neural networks and syntactic trees can solve the mistakes caused by sequential attention mechanisms. We leverage RGAT-BERT to capture the syntactic information between target words and their corresponding contexts.

Firstly, we extract the original dependency graph by syntax parsing tools. Note that the root of the current dependency graph may not be target words. Then the structure of the dependency tree is rooted in the euphemism target words by reshaping and pruning the ordinary dependency analysis tree. The new dependency tree is encoded by the relational graph attention network(RGAT) model.

The reconstructed tree can be represented by a graph G with N nodes, where each node is a word in the utterance, and the edges of the graph represent the dependencies between words. The neighborhood nodes of node i are N_i. The graph attention network(Veličković et al., 2017) iteratively updates each node by aggregating the representation of neighborhood nodes with multiple heads of attention. Training the BERT model can obtain the hidden layers. The whole RGAT formula comes from (Wang et al., 2020). The attention formula is as follows:

$$h_{att_i}^{l+1} = ||_{k=1}^{K} \sum_{j \epsilon N_i} \alpha_{ij}^{lk} W_k^l h_j^l \quad (1)$$

$$\alpha_{ij}^{lk} = attention(i, j), \quad (2)$$

where l means the number of the layer and i and j mean the number of the node. And $h_{att_i}^{l+1}$ means the attention head, $||_{k=1}^{K} x_i$ is the concatenation of vectors from x_1 to x_k, α_{ij}^{lk} is a dot-product attention which comes from $attention(i, j)$ computed by the k-th attention at layer l, W_k^l is an input transformation matrix. K means the number of attention headers.

The graph attention mechanism aggregates the representations of neighborhood nodes along the dependency path. However, neighborhood nodes with different dependencies should have different effects. Therefore, RGAT uses additional relationship headers to expand the original network. The dependency relationship is mapped into a vector representation to calculate a relationship header. RGAT contains M relationship headers. The calculation formula is as follows:

$$h_{rel_i}^{l+1} = ||_{m=1}^{M} \sum_{j \epsilon N_i} \beta_{ij}^{lm} W_m^l h_j^l \quad (3)$$

$$g_{ij}^{lm} = \sigma(relu(r_{ij} W_{m1} + b_{m1}) W_{m2} + b_{m2}) \quad (4)$$

$$\beta_{ij}^{lm} = \frac{exp(g_{ij}^{lm})}{\sum_{j=1}^{N_i} exp(g_{ij}^{lm})}, \quad (5)$$

where r_{ij} is the relation embedding between nodes i and j. The final representation of each node is as follows:

$$x_i^{l+1} = h_{att_i}^{l+1} || h_{rel_i}^{l+1} \quad (6)$$

$$h_i^{l+1} = relu(W_{l=1} x_i^{l+1} + b_{l+1}). \quad (7)$$

The hidden representation is then passed through a fully connected softmax layer and mapped to probabilities over the euphemistic labels. BERT is used as a basic encoder in the RGAT-BERT model. The training objective of RGAT-BERT is also to minimize cross-entropy loss. For a more detailed description of RGAT, please refer to the original paper (Wang et al., 2020).

Dataset	Eu.	Non-Eu.	Total	Avg ℓ
Train	1106	466	1572	65.7
Test	/	/	393	65.8

Table 1: The detailed statistics of the dataset. Eu. and non-Eu. mean the number of euphemism and non-euphemism samples respectively. Avg ℓ denotes the average length of texts in the number of tokens.

3.4 Model Ensembling

We adopt a voting strategy for ensembling the results of BERT-Concat and RGAT-BERT. Specifically, there is a set of predicted labels by different models. For each sample, if more than half models saying that the sample belongs to the euphemistic class, then the voting result is euphemism. On the contrary, if more than half models saying that the sample belongs to the non-euphemistic class, then the voting result is non-euphemism.

4 Experiment

In this section, we will introduce the dataset and experimental settings, and then analyze the results.

4.1 Dataset

We use the official euphemism dataset provided by the third workshop on figurative language processing shared task 2022. The statistics are shown in Table 1. We observe that the training dataset is unbalanced. The number of euphemistic samples is more than twice as large as the number of non-euphemistic samples. The original dataset does not contain a validation set. We randomly choose 200 samples from the training set as a validation set to fine-tune the parameters. In the validation set, there are 133 euphemism and 67 non-euphemism.

4.2 Baselines

We adopt LSTM (Hochreiter and Schmidhuber, 1997), RGAT (Wang et al., 2020), and BERT (Devlin et al., 2019) as the baseline methods for comparison. Each utterance in the given dataset contains only one euphemism, there is no case of multiple euphemisms mixed in one utterance. So we take the sentences as input directly for the above baseline models.

4.3 Experimental Settings

We train our models on Nvidia Telsa V100-16GB GPUs. For the BERT-Concat model, we set the learning rate to $5e-5$, the batch size to 16, and the maximum sequence length to 512. We implement RGAT-BERT for euphemism detection based on the released source code [2] in their paper. For the RGAT-BERT model, the learning rate is set to $5e-5$, the batch size is 8, and the dropout is 0.3. For other parameters of RGAT-BERT, we use the default settings in the source code. For each method, we train them with five seeds among $\{2022, 2021, 2019, 142, 42\}$. The difference between macro F_1 scores of different seeds is within 2%. For model ensembling, we selected 7 highest results of the two models and vote on the final labels. We use BERT-base as the backbone model.

Method	Precision	Recall	Macro F_1
LSTM	73.4	71.0	71.7
RGAT	77.6	73.5	73.9
BERT	78.4	76.9	77.5
BERT-Concat	76.7	81.4	78.4
RGAT-BERT	81.1	83.4	82.1
Ensembled	**84.2**	**83.8**	**84.0**

Table 2: The precision, recall, and macro F_1 (%) on the test set. Best results as bold.

4.4 Experimental Results

The overall experimental results are shown in Table 2. We observe that: (1) RGAT model outperforms LSTM model, which shows that involving syntactic information is more effective than relying solely on sequential information intra-sentence. (2) Fine-tuning with pre-trained language models performs better than traditional deep neural models. By using only BERT model, the macro F_1 score reaches 78.4. It demonstrates the power of large-scale pre-trained language models. This indicates that though euphemisms are obscure, they are commonly used, so euphemism detection tasks can make better use of the knowledge in the pre-trained language models. (3) There is a slight improvement using BERT-Cocat compared to the basic BERT model. RGAT-BERT outperforms BERT-Concat with a large margin of 3.7 on the macro F_1 score. This demonstrates that syntactic connections between target words and their corresponding contexts can better understand the meaning of euphemism. (4) Ensembling the two models achieves the best performance since model ensembling can leverage the advantages of the two models.

5 Conclusion

In this paper, we have proposed to leverage transformers and relational graph attention networks to detect euphemisms. Specifically, on the one hand,

[2] https://github.com/shenwzh3/RGAT-ABSA

we utilize BERT-Concat to capture sequential semantic information between target words and their corresponding contexts. On the other hand, we adopt RGAT-BERT to learn the syntactic connections between target words and essential contexts. Experimental results show that ensembling the two sub-models can achieve promising performance on the euphemism detection shared task of the third workshop on figurative language processing.

Limitations

At present, we view euphemism detection from the perspective of the task itself and specific datasets. Our model is not much integrated with the euphemistic theory linguistically. Later, we will explore the different meanings between original target words and their euphemistic usage by text matching strategies.

References

Jacob Devlin, Ming-Wei Chang, Kenton Lee, and Kristina Toutanova. 2019. BERT: Pre-training of deep bidirectional transformers for language understanding. In *Proceedings of the 2019 Conference of the North American Chapter of the Association for Computational Linguistics: Human Language Technologies, Volume 1 (Long and Short Papers)*, pages 4171–4186, Minneapolis, Minnesota. Association for Computational Linguistics.

Christian Felt and Ellen Riloff. 2020. Recognizing euphemisms and dysphemisms using sentiment analysis. In *Proceedings of the Second Workshop on Figurative Language Processing*, pages 136–145, Online. Association for Computational Linguistics.

Martha Gavidia, Patrick Lee, Anna Feldman, and Jing Peng. 2022. CATs are Fuzzy PETs: A Corpus and Analysis of Potentially Euphemistic Terms. *arXiv e-prints*, page arXiv:2205.02728.

Sepp Hochreiter and Jürgen Schmidhuber. 1997. Long short-term memory. *Neural Comput.*, 9(8):1735–1780.

Anna Kapron-King and Yang Xu. 2021. A diachronic evaluation of gender asymmetry in euphemism. In *Proceedings of the 2nd International Workshop on Computational Approaches to Historical Language Change 2021*, pages 28–38, Online. Association for Computational Linguistics.

Rijul Magu and Jiebo Luo. 2018. Determining code words in euphemistic hate speech using word embedding networks. In *Proceedings of the 2nd Workshop on Abusive Language Online (ALW2)*, pages 93–100, Brussels, Belgium. Association for Computational Linguistics.

Petar Veličković, Guillem Cucurull, Arantxa Casanova, Adriana Romero, Pietro Liò, and Yoshua Bengio. 2017. Graph Attention Networks. *arXiv e-prints*, page arXiv:1710.10903.

Kai Wang, Weizhou Shen, Yunyi Yang, Xiaojun Quan, and Rui Wang. 2020. Relational graph attention network for aspect-based sentiment analysis. In *Proceedings of the 58th Annual Meeting of the Association for Computational Linguistics*, pages 3229–3238, Online. Association for Computational Linguistics.

Wanzheng Zhu and Suma Bhat. 2021. Euphemistic phrase detection by masked language model. In *Findings of the Association for Computational Linguistics: EMNLP 2021*, pages 163–168, Punta Cana, Dominican Republic. Association for Computational Linguistics.

Wanzheng Zhu, Hongyu Gong, Rohan Bansal, Zachary Weinberg, Nicolas Christin, Giulia Fanti, and Suma Bhat. 2021. Self-supervised euphemism detection and identification for content moderation. In *2021 IEEE Symposium on Security and Privacy (SP)*, pages 229–246.

Just-DREAM-about-it: Figurative Language Understanding with *DREAM-FLUTE*

Yuling Gu, Yao Fu, Valentina Pyatkin, Ian Magnusson, Bhavana Dalvi Mishra, Peter Clark

Allen Institute for AI, Seattle, WA

yulingg@allenai.org

Abstract

Figurative language (e.g., "he flew like the wind") is challenging to understand, as it is hard to tell what implicit information is being conveyed from the surface form alone. We hypothesize that to perform this task well, the reader needs to mentally elaborate the scene being described to identify a sensible meaning of the language. We present *DREAM-FLUTE*, a figurative language understanding system that does this, first forming a "mental model" of situations described in a premise and hypothesis before making an entailment/contradiction decision and generating an explanation. *DREAM-FLUTE* uses an existing scene elaboration model, DREAM, for constructing its "mental model." In the FigLang2022 Shared Task evaluation, *DREAM-FLUTE* achieved (joint) first place (Acc@60=63.3%), and can perform even better with ensemble techniques, demonstrating the effectiveness of this approach.[1] More generally, this work suggests that adding a reflective component to pretrained language models can improve their performance beyond standard fine-tuning (3.3% improvement in Acc@60).

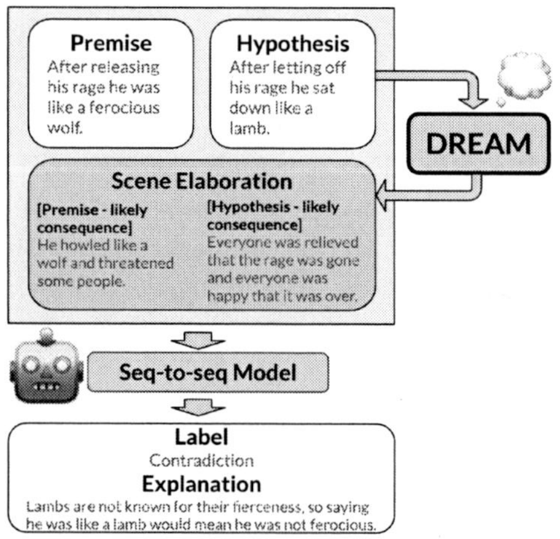

Figure 1: Overview of *DREAM-FLUTE*: It first uses DREAM (Gu et al., 2022) to generate an elaboration of the situation in the premise and hypothesis (separately), then uses this additional context for entailment classification and explanation generation. *DREAM-FLUTE* (consequence), using the "likely consequence" elaboration dimension as additional context, achieved top scores. Such systems also form the building blocks of *DREAM-FLUTE* (ensemble), our best system.

1 Introduction

Understanding figurative language is a particularly challenging problem in NLP since the underlying meaning of the utterance is very different from the surface meaning of its constituent words (Stowe et al., 2022). In this paper we focus on the task of recognizing and explaining textual entailment between a premise and hypothesis involving figurative language (FigLang 2022 Shared Task in Chakrabarty et al., 2022). We propose *DREAM-FLUTE*,[2] a system that makes use of scene elaboration for building a "mental model" of the situations presented in the premise and hypothesis to detect textual entailment between them (see Figure 1).

The design of *DREAM-FLUTE* builds upon the scene elaboration model, DREAM, presented by Gu et al. (2022). DREAM uses a T5-based (Raffel et al., 2020) sequence-to-sequence model to generate additional, pertinent details about each given situation in the input text, along key conceptual dimensions informed by cognitive science, story understanding and planning literature (Minsky, 1974; Dyer, 1983; Mueller et al., 1985; Mueller, 1990). Using such scene elaboration as additional context has been shown to improve question-answering (QA) performance on different models and across different downstream tasks such as ETHICS (Hendrycks et al., 2021), CODAH (Chen et al., 2019) and Social IQA (Sap et al., 2019).

[1]We make our code and models publicly available at https://github.com/allenai/dream.

[2]Using DREAM (Gu et al., 2022) on FLUTE: Figurative Language Understanding through Textual Explanations (Chakrabarty et al., 2022).

Proceedings of the 3rd Workshop on Figurative Language Processing (FLP), pages 84 - 93

To adapt it for the figurative language understanding shared task, we made three significant extensions to using DREAM that have not been previously explored. First, we incorporate DREAM for elaborating the premise and hypothesis in a natural language inference (NLI) task involving figurative language understanding (Chakrabarty et al., 2021; Stowe et al., 2022). We hypothesize that such additional, pertinent details could also improve a model's ability to judge whether there is an entailment or contradiction between the premise and hypothesis. This could be especially helpful for the instances that use figurative language, where the underlying meaning might be opaque to the model: further elaborating the context can make certain inferences more explicit. Second, beyond improvements on label prediction accuracy (i.e. choosing from multiple-choice options) shown in Gu et al. (2022), our work uncovers the use of such additional context for improving explanation quality. And lastly, we exploit the dimensions in DREAM to train different models for an ensemble system representing a cognitive continuum (Figure 2), further improving accuracy and explanation quality.

Our approach is easily adaptable to other language models, and task-agnostic in format (e.g. QA or NLI) and domain (e.g. ethical decisions or figurative language understanding). We demonstrate the effectiveness of our single model system in terms of achieving top scores in the task, as well as the flexibility of implementing an ensemble system that not only yields further improvements for this task but also allows customization to suit the requirements of different downstream applications.

2 Approach

We first describe our single model systems in Section 2.1. Next, we present a two-step "classify then explain" pipeline in Section 2.2. In Section 2.3, we take advantage of all information learned by the different models and propose an ensemble approach inspired by cognitive science.

2.1 Single Model Systems

Given an input <Premise, Hypothesis> sentence pair, the task has two goals: (1). first classify the relationship between the premise and hypothesis (*entailment* or *contradiction*); then (2). generate a textual explanation about why the premise entails/contradicts the hypothesis. Figure 1 shows an example. We further consider two additional pieces of information for performance improvements: (1). the type of the figurative language (*simile*, *metaphor*, *sarcasm*, *idiom*, and *creative paraphrase*) which is provided in the training data (but not the test data); (2). the elaboration of situations in the premise-hypothesis pair provided by DREAM, which gives additional information about the *consequence*, *emotion*, *motivation*, or *social norm* of the input. In Appendix A, we provide intuitive examples showing why such additional information could help this figurative language task.

System 1: Using original data Given the <Premise, Hypothesis, Label, Explanation> in the original data, we first trained a sequence-to-sequence model for the figurative language task using the following input-output format:

Input <Premise> <Hypothesis>
Output <Label> <Explanation>

System 2: Jointly predicting the type of figurative language Using type of figurative language provided as part of the training set (Chakrabarty et al., 2022), one of our models jointly predicts the type of figurative language, together with the target label and explanation:

Input <Premise> <Hypothesis>
Output <Figurative-Language-Type> <Label> <Explanation>

Systems 3: *DREAM-FLUTE* - Providing DREAM's different dimensions as input context We adapt DREAM's scene elaborations (Gu et al., 2022) for the figurative language understanding NLI task by using the DREAM model to generate elaborations for the premise and hypothesis separately. This allows us to investigate if similarities or differences in the scene elaborations for the premise and hypothesis will provide useful signals for entailment/contradiction label prediction and improving explanation quality. Figure 1 gives an overview of such systems and the input-output format is:

Input <Premise> <Premise-elaboration-from-DREAM> <Hypothesis> <Hypothesis-elaboration-from-DREAM>
Output <Label> <Explanation>

where the scene elaboration dimensions from DREAM are: *consequence*, *emotion*, *motivation*, and *social norm*. We also consider a system incorporating all these dimensions as additional context.

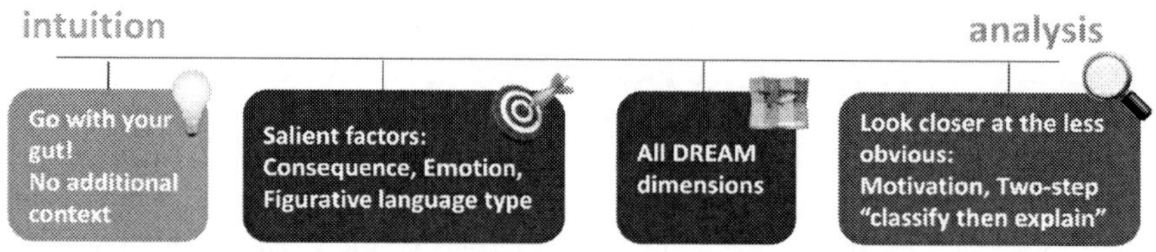

Figure 2: A cognitive continuum implemented to account for different levels of intuition and analysis.

2.2 Two-step System: Classify then explain

In contrast to Systems 1 to 3 where the entailment/contradiction label and associated explanation are predicted jointly, System 4 uses a two-step "classify then explain" pipeline. Previous work on generating explanations have discussed the difference between predicting and generating respective rationalizations in a pipeline vs. jointly. Wiegreffe et al. (2021) showed that for reasoning tasks pipelines work less well than models which jointly predict and explain. Hase et al. (2020) compared rationalizing methods (first predict label and then the explanation) to reasoning methods (predict the explanation first), and showed that rationalization methods perform better. It is therefore of interest to compare such different approaches for explanation generation also for the figurative language task.

2.3 Ensemble System: A cognitive continuum

We take advantage of ensembling to use information learned by Systems 1 to 4 together in *DREAM-FLUTE* (ensemble). For entailment/contradiction label prediction, the top 5 system variants were chosen based on validation Acc@0 (Table 1 *green italicized*) scores, and used for majority voting.

Brachman and Levesque (2022) note that several psychologists claim "there is a *cognitive continuum* between endpoints that they call *intuition* and *analysis*." Likewise, in rationalizing, our different system variants can be viewed as different points on this continuum. For generating explanations, Systems 1 to 4 were used as building blocks for *DREAM-FLUTE* (ensemble) (excluding the model with social norm due to its low scores on the validation set) to implement such a continuum that includes various levels of intuition and analysis (Figure 2). Specifically, given the entailment label from majority voting, the ensemble looks for the first of the ordered models that agrees with the ensemble label, then uses its explanation.

Our approach first considers more salient factors (Systems 2, 3 (consequence, emotion)) which can inform the content and style of explanation: likely consequence of the actions and the emotions of characters, which can possibly tease apart whether the sentence pairs entail/contradict,[3] as well as type of figurative language which can inform the style of explanation.[4] Next, we take a step back and look at the bigger picture, in considering all DREAM dimensions (Gu et al., 2022) (System 3 (all dimensions)). Then we examine some of the less salient dimensions more closely (Systems 3 (motivation), 4). And finally, we use the explanation in the case when there is no context at all (System 1). More details about this ordering and the pseudocode for ensembling can be found in Appendix C.

3 Experiment Settings

Data This shared task has a two-phases timeline: the development phase then the test phase. During the development phase, ~7500 samples are provided as the training set. We used a 80-20 split to create our own training (6027 samples) and validation (1507 samples) partitions on which we build our models. Later at the test phase, separate 1500 test samples (without gold labels) are released on which all models are tested. Note that our model is primarily developed during the training phase without having access to the test data.

Model We train all models with a T5-3B backbone using the data formats detailed in Section 2.1. The size of the model is the same as the officially provided fine-tuned T5 baseline. We use the Huggingface implementation (Wolf et al., 2019, 2020), based on PyTorch (Paszke et al., 2019). For each system, we fine-tune the 3B version of T5 (Raffel et al., 2020) for 3 epochs using an Adam Optimizer and a learning rate of 5e-05, selecting the best checkpoint based on the lowest validation loss.

[3] E.g. If one situation involves an action leading to good outcome whereas another leads to bad outcome, that is a clear sign (that gives you strong intuition) for contradiction. Whereas, if the premise and hypothesis both describe situations where a person would be happy, that provides intuition for entailment. See Table 2 for examples from task data.

[4] See Appendix A and Table 3.

	System	Our validation partition			Official test partition		
		Acc@0	Acc@50	Acc@60	Acc@0	Acc@50	Acc@60
	T5-3B (official baseline)	–	–	–	76.7	69.1	44.3
1	Original data	*94.8*	89.0	66.9	94.7	88.7	60.4
2	+ Figurative language type	*94.9*	89.8	66.5	94.6	87.8	61.3
3	*DREAM-FLUTE*						
	emotion	94.2	89.3	65.0	93.9	88.3	61.7
	motivation	*95.4*	90.2	66.2	94.5	87.7	60.3
	consequence	94.3	90.1	65.8	94.7	88.9	**63.3**
	social norm	93.1	88.3	64.2	92.3	86.4	60.6
	all 4 dimensions	*95.2*	89.4	66.6	94.3	87.7	60.0
4	Classify then explain	*95.0*	90.5	66.6	95.1	89.4	61.1
5	*DREAM-FLUTE* (ensemble)	**96.4**	**92.1**	**67.0**	**95.9**	**89.8**	**63.7**

Table 1: Results on our validation set and the official test set. Amongst the non-ensemble methods, System 3 with likely consequence, i.e. *DREAM-FLUTE* (consequence), performed the best on the test set in terms of Acc@60 which was used for ranking submissions on the leaderboard. This system was already ranked first, but further gains can still be achieved using ensembling in System 5, *DREAM-FLUTE* (ensemble). *Green italics* indicates systems selected for label prediction in the ensemble system, using validation Acc@0.

A more detailed list of hyperparameters used can be found in Appendix D.

Evaluation There are two major evaluation metrics: (1). *accuracy*, which measures if predicted NLI labels are correct; (2). *explanation score*, which measures if generated explanations are of high quality. The explanation score is computed as the average of BERTScore (Zhang et al., 2020) and BLEURT (Sellam et al., 2020) on the generated explanation against given references. The overall performance metric, Acc@s (Table 1), is a combination of *accuracy* and *explanation score* where a prediction (label and explanation) counts as correct only when: (a) the label is correct, and (b) the explantion score is at least s (where $s = 0, 50$ and 60). On the official leaderboard, all models are ranked according to Acc@60.

4 Results and Discussion

4.1 Better explanation quality

Table 1 shows the performance of our systems. Based on test Acc@60, the following strategies improve explanation quality compared to the setup with just the original data: predicting figurative language type, using emotion, likely consequence, social norm, two-step "classify then explain" pipeline, and ensembling. Each non-ensemble system can be seen as guiding the model to focus on a particular direction when reasoning about the entailment/contradiction relationship between a sentence pair. Table 2 and Appendix F present examples of how each DREAM dimension helps uncover implicit meaning in the input. *DREAM-FLUTE* (consequence), by incorporating the likely consequence scene elaboration from DREAM, was already ranked first based on test Acc@60,[5] which requires explanations to be of high quality. Figure 1 shows another example of how elaborating along this dimension can be useful. On top of that, *DREAM-FLUTE* (ensemble), an ensemble system that makes further use of context achieves further improvements (Acc@60 = 63.7%). The ensemble approach allows for considering these different directions and rationalizing with varying levels of intuition and analysis, then choosing one that fits the current sentence pair, potentially boosting explanation quality.

4.2 Better label prediction accuracy

This ensemble system is also our best submission overall with Acc@0 = 95.9%, Acc@50 = 89.8%, where Acc@0 is equivalent to computing label accuracy alone. The better label prediction accuracy could be attributed to using the different individual systems for majority voting, which mimics arriving at a decision by considering different perspectives, ultimately leading to a more well-thought decision.

4.3 Effect of DREAM generated context

We qualitatively analyze how DREAM-generated context helps in the figurative language understanding task. Table 2 presents examples from our validation set for DREAM dimensions "consequence" and "emotion" comparing predictions from System

[5]See results of shared task at `https://codalab.lisn.upsaclay.fr/competitions/5908#results`.

Premise	Hypothesis	Gold label	T5's answer + explanation	DREAM context	*DREAM-FLUTE*'s answer + explanation
My decision-making skills are not purely based on emotions and gut.	My personal feelings color my judgment in this case.	(C)	(E): My personal feelings color my judgment in this case means that I am influenced by my emotions and gut when making decisions.	**[Consequence]** **Pre:** I make more balanced and informed decisions. **Hypo:** I make a decision that is not in the best interests of the company.	(C): To have personal feelings color one's judgment means to make decisions based on them, but this context describes making decisions based on facts and not emotions.
We laid in the field of green grass and relaxed.	We laid in fields of gold.	(E)	(C): Gold is a type of metal that is used to make jewelry, while green grass is a type of grass that is used for lawns and gardens.	**[Emotion]** **Pre:** I (myself)'s emotion is happy. **Hypo:** I (myself)'s emotion is happy.	(E): Gold is a color that is associated with happiness, so the fields of gold are associated with happiness.

Table 2: Examples from the validation set where DREAM generated context consisting of consequence and emotion helped our proposed model *DREAM-FLUTE* (System 3) in figurative language understanding. For both the examples a T5-based model that did not have access to additional context (System 1) gave wrong label prediction. DREAM context helped improve both answer accuracy and explanation quality. Labels: (E), (C) refer to Entailment, Contradiction respectively. (Appendix F presents examples where motivation, social norm helped *DREAM-FLUTE*.)

1 (trained using just original data) with those from System 3 (*DREAM-FLUTE*, which uses scene elaboration from DREAM). These examples illustrate that similarities and differences along the scene elaboration dimensions provide useful signals to guide entailment/contradiction label prediction and improve explanation quality.

4.4 More flexibility beyond FigLang2022

The day-to-day mental activities of humans take place on different parts of the cognitive continuum (Brachman and Levesque, 2022). DREAM's scene elaborations give us the different building blocks to implement to such a continuum, and therefore use various levels of intuition and analysis to better come to a decision and rationalize. This approach also allows customization to suit the requirements of different downstream applications, by changing the order of factors to consider on the continuum (e.g. social norm may be more salient for ethical decisions) and considering different pertinent factors (i.e. in place of the figurative language type).

5 Conclusion

In this work we showed how *DREAM-FLUTE*, a competitive system for the figurative language understanding NLI task, can be built by utilizing scene elaborations from an existing model, DREAM. Compared to a model without such scene elaborations, *DREAM-FLUTE* makes use of scene elaboration for building a "mental model" of situations in the premise and hypothesis to make inferences more explicit, thus improving label prediction accuracy and explanation quality. *DREAM-FLUTE* (ensemble) uses different elaborations to form building blocks for implementing a continuum with varying levels of intuition and analysis, modeling deriving answers and rationalizing by considering different positions on a cognitive continuum. This novel use of DREAM not only obtained the highest scores for the figurative language understanding shared task, but could also easily be applied to the situational QA tasks in Gu et al. (2022), and beyond. Our approach is easily adaptable to other language models, and task-agnostic in format (e.g. QA or NLI) and domain (e.g. ethical decisions or figurative language understanding). More generally, our work demonstrates that adding a reflective component helps to improve answer accuracy and explanation quality in pretrained language models.

Limitations

Our approach is designed for applications involving natural language understanding for short text (around 1-3 sentences), e.g. in the figurative language NLI task and situational QA tasks tackled in the original DREAM paper. Building on a better understanding for short text, we hope our work can inspire future efforts towards extending the approach for long text too. The current approach presented also requires the use of GPU resources for model training. However, we also demonstrate that using DREAM scene elaboration as additional context yields improvements on label prediction accuracy for an off-the-shelf NLI model, without any training (Table 4 in Appendix E).

Ethics Statement

Like any other large-scale language model, despite the best intentions, there is a risk of our models producing biased or offensive statements as part of the free-form rationalization. We release our models for research purposes only.

Acknowledgements

We would like to thank the entire Figurative Language Understanding Shared Task organizing committee for organizing this shared task. We thank the anonymous reviewers for their helpful comments. This work was done as part of a Hackathon project during AI2's 2022 Hackathon. We are grateful to the Hackathon organizers, Caitlin Wittlif and Carissa Schoenick, for the great 3-day Hackathon that led to this work.

References

R.J. Brachman and H.J. Levesque. 2022. *Machines like Us: Toward AI with Common Sense*. MIT Press.

Tuhin Chakrabarty, Debanjan Ghosh, Adam Poliak, and Smaranda Muresan. 2021. Figurative language in recognizing textual entailment. In *Findings of the Association for Computational Linguistics: ACL-IJCNLP 2021*, pages 3354–3361, Online. Association for Computational Linguistics.

Tuhin Chakrabarty, Arkadiy Saakyan, Debanjan Ghosh, and Smaranda Muresan. 2022. Flute: Figurative language understanding through textual explanations.

Michael Chen, Mike D'Arcy, Alisa Liu, Jared Fernandez, and Doug Downey. 2019. CODAH: An adversarially-authored question answering dataset for common sense. In *Proceedings of the 3rd Workshop on Evaluating Vector Space Representations for NLP*, pages 63–69, Minneapolis, USA. Association for Computational Linguistics.

Michael G. Dyer. 1983. The role of affect in narratives. *Cogn. Sci.*, 7:211–242.

Yuling Gu, Bhavana Dalvi, and Peter Clark. 2022. DREAM: Improving situational QA by first elaborating the situation. In *Proceedings of the 2022 Conference of the North American Chapter of the Association for Computational Linguistics: Human Language Technologies*, pages 1115–1127, Seattle, United States. Association for Computational Linguistics.

Peter Hase, Shiyue Zhang, Harry Xie, and Mohit Bansal. 2020. Leakage-adjusted simulatability: Can models generate non-trivial explanations of their behavior in natural language? In *Findings of the Association for Computational Linguistics: EMNLP 2020*, pages 4351–4367.

Dan Hendrycks, Collin Burns, Steven Basart, Andrew Critch, Jerry Li, Dawn Song, and Jacob Steinhardt. 2021. Aligning ai with shared human values. *ICLR*.

Yinhan Liu, Myle Ott, Naman Goyal, Jingfei Du, Mandar Joshi, Danqi Chen, Omer Levy, Mike Lewis, Luke Zettlemoyer, and Veselin Stoyanov. 2019. Roberta: A robustly optimized bert pretraining approach.

Marvin Minsky. 1974. *A framework for representing knowledge*.

Erik T Mueller. 1990. *Daydreaming in humans and machines: a computer model of the stream of thought*. Intellect Books.

Erik T Mueller, Michael G Dyer, et al. 1985. Daydreaming in humans and computers. In *IJCAI*, pages 278–280.

Adam Paszke, Sam Gross, Francisco Massa, Adam Lerer, James Bradbury, Gregory Chanan, Trevor Killeen, Zeming Lin, Natalia Gimelshein, Luca Antiga, Alban Desmaison, Andreas Kopf, Edward Yang, Zachary DeVito, Martin Raison, Alykhan Tejani, Sasank Chilamkurthy, Benoit Steiner, Lu Fang, Junjie Bai, and Soumith Chintala. 2019. PyTorch: An Imperative Style, High-Performance Deep Learning Library. In H. Wallach, H. Larochelle, A. Beygelzimer, F. d'Alché-Buc, E. Fox, and R. Garnett, editors, *Advances in Neural Information Processing Systems 32*, pages 8024–8035. Curran Associates, Inc.

Colin Raffel, Noam Shazeer, Adam Roberts, Katherine Lee, Sharan Narang, Michael Matena, Yanqi Zhou, Wei Li, and Peter J. Liu. 2020. Exploring the limits of transfer learning with a unified text-to-text transformer. *Journal of Machine Learning Research*, 21(140):1–67.

Maarten Sap, Hannah Rashkin, Derek Chen, Ronan Le Bras, and Yejin Choi. 2019. Social IQa: Commonsense reasoning about social interactions. In *Proceedings of the 2019 Conference on Empirical Methods in Natural Language Processing and the 9th International Joint Conference on Natural Language Processing (EMNLP-IJCNLP)*, pages 4463–4473, Hong Kong, China. Association for Computational Linguistics.

Thibault Sellam, Dipanjan Das, and Ankur Parikh. 2020. BLEURT: Learning robust metrics for text generation. In *Proceedings of the 58th Annual Meeting of the Association for Computational Linguistics*, pages 7881–7892, Online. Association for Computational Linguistics.

Kevin Stowe, Prasetya Utama, and Iryna Gurevych. 2022. IMPLI: Investigating NLI models' performance on figurative language. In *Proceedings of the 60th Annual Meeting of the Association for Computational Linguistics (Volume 1: Long Papers)*, pages 5375–5388, Dublin, Ireland. Association for Computational Linguistics.

Sarah Wiegreffe, Ana Marasović, and Noah A Smith. 2021. Measuring association between labels and free-text rationales. In *Proceedings of the 2021 Conference on Empirical Methods in Natural Language Processing*, pages 10266–10284.

Thomas Wolf, Lysandre Debut, Victor Sanh, Julien Chaumond, Clement Delangue, Anthony Moi, Pierric Cistac, Tim Rault, R'emi Louf, Morgan Funtowicz, and Jamie Brew. 2019. HuggingFace's Transformers: State-of-the-art Natural Language Processing. *ArXiv*, abs/1910.03771.

Thomas Wolf, Lysandre Debut, Victor Sanh, Julien Chaumond, Clement Delangue, Anthony Moi, Pierric Cistac, Tim Rault, Rémi Louf, Morgan Funtowicz, Joe Davison, Sam Shleifer, Patrick von Platen, Clara Ma, Yacine Jernite, Julien Plu, Canwen Xu, Teven Le Scao, Sylvain Gugger, Mariama Drame, Quentin Lhoest, and Alexander M. Rush. 2020. Transformers: State-of-the-Art Natural Language Processing. In *Proceedings of the 2020 Conference on Empirical Methods in Natural Language Processing: System Demonstrations*, pages 38–45, Online. Association for Computational Linguistics.

Tianyi Zhang, Varsha Kishore, Felix Wu, Kilian Q. Weinberger, and Yoav Artzi. 2020. Bertscore: Evaluating text generation with BERT. In *8th International Conference on Learning Representations, ICLR 2020, Addis Ababa, Ethiopia, April 26-30, 2020.*

A Examples from training set

We randomly sampled around 100 examples from the training set and manually looked at the targeted explanations to get a sense of how explanations for this task look like. We observed that the explanation style may depend on the type of figurative language involved. Table 3 shows some of these examples. For instance, when the type of figurative language is sarcasm, the explanation often starts by describing what is usually the case and then goes into how one of the sentences describes an unusual or unexpected situation. Whereas, if the type is idiom, then the explanation often involves elucidating what the idiom means. This motivated the design of System 2.

Further, we noticed that the gold explanations often involve elements like emotion and motivation of characters. In the first example in Table 3, for example, identifying the emotions in the premise and hypothesis directly helps us identify the contradiction — in that the person's emotion is scared in one case and fearless in another. Therefore, we explored elaborating the situations in the given premise and hypothesis along such dimensions using DREAM (Gu et al., 2022). By using DREAM to generate scene elaborations and using that as additional context to the input, we have the different variations of *DREAM-FLUTE* (System 3).

B Details of input prompt

In training our T5 based sequence-to-sequence models, whenever the target output is the entailment/contradiction label and explanation, we append the question "Is there a contradiction or entailment between the premise and hypothesis?" to the input to prompt the model for the NLI task. In the case of System 2, where the model jointly predicts the type of figurative language then the label and explanation, we first append the question "What is the type of figurative language involved?" to the input, then append the usual contradiction or entailment question.

C Algorithm for ensembling

The order of systems used in rationalizing when implementing the cognitive continuum described in Section 2.3 is as follows: likely consequence, emotion, type of figurative language, all DREAM dimensions, motivation, two-step "classify then explain," no context. Algorithm 1 shows more details on how to obtain the ensemble label and explanation from the individual systems.

Algorithm 1: Ensemble - a cognitive continuum

```
Input: Individual systems' predicted label and
       explanation
Output: Ensemble label; Ensemble explanation
ensemble_label =
  majority_vote(top5_Acc@0_systems_labels)
  ensemble_explanation = None
 // ordered_systems takes an order
  described in Section C
for system_prediction ∈ ordered_systems do
    if system_prediction.label == ensemble_label
     then
        ensemble_explanation =
          system_prediction.explanation
        break
    end
end
```

Note that beyond the figurative language understanding task, this ensembling approach representing a cognitive continuum could be applied to other tasks, with the possibility of modifying the order of component systems to better suit different applications.

D Hyperparamters used during training

The following hyperparameters were used during training:

- learning_rate: 5e-05
- train_batch_size: 1
- eval_batch_size: 1
- seed: 42
- distributed_type: multi-GPU
- num_devices: 2
- total_train_batch_size: 2
- total_eval_batch_size: 2
- optimizer: Adam with betas=(0.9,0.999) and epsilon=1e-08
- lr_scheduler_type: linear
- num_epochs: 3.0

Type of figurative language	Premise	Hypothesis	Gold label	Gold Explanation
Sarcasm	Yesterday two gangs were fighting just in front of my home.	Yesterday I saw two gangs fighting right in front of my house and it totally didn't make me scared at all.	Contradiction	The sight of two gangs fighting **is often** very violent and can invoke fear in people, **so** someone who saw it and wasn't scared is not being truthful.
Idiom	If you want fresh food, just go with your gut feeling and you will find villagers happy to sell or trade what they have.	If you want fresh food, just follow your noses and you will find villagers happy to sell or trade what they have.	Entailment	To **follow your nose means** to trust one's instinct, which is what you would need to do in order to find fresh food.

Table 3: Examples from Chakrabarty et al. (2022)'s training set. Text in bold illustrate how the style of explanation may depend on the type of figurative language involved.

E Baseline: Off-the-shelf MNLI model

Without any training on the task data, we can similarly achieve better label prediction accuracy if we provide additional context from DREAM as input. Table 4 shows that with the off-the-shelf RoBERTa MNLI model (Liu et al., 2019), we achieve improvements in accuracy when providing the emotion of characters, and even more improvements if we provide all 4 dimensions generated by DREAM. Since this model is unable produce any explanations, we measure only Acc@0 scores.

System	Our validation partition		
	Acc@0	Acc@50	Acc@60
RoBERTa MNLI	73.9	–	–
+ DREAM emotion	77.4	–	–
+ DREAM 4 dimensions	79.3	–	–
DREAM-FLUTE(ensemble) (our model)	**96.4**	**92.1**	**67.0**

Table 4: Comparing off-the-shelf RoBERTa MNLI model (Liu et al., 2019) to our proposed model on our validation set.

F Analysis: Effect of DREAM generated context

Table 5 presents validation set examples for DREAM dimensions "motivation" and "social norm" where this additional context helped the model correct its prediction.

Premise	Hypothesis	Gold label	T5's answer + explanation	DREAM context	*DREAM-FLUTE*'s answer + explanation
After years of service & contribution to the company, he was finally promoted.	The company released him after many years of service.	(C)	(E): The company released the employee after many years of service.	**[Motivation]** **Pre:** Company's motivation is to recognize his hard work. **Hypo:** Company's motivation is to get someone else to work.	(C):To release someone means to let them go from a position, while to promote someone means to give them a higher position.
Sure, he snorted just to make me feel even better about the already great situation.	Sure, he snorted, just rub it in.	(C)	(E): To rub it in means to make someone feel better about an already great situation, which is what he did by snorting.	**[Social Norm]** **Pre:** It's good to make people feel better about a situation. **Hypo:** It's rude to rub something in someone's face when they don't want to.	(C):To rub it in means to make someone feel bad about themselves, but in this sentence he is making the speaker feel better about the already great situation.

Table 5: Examples from the validation set where DREAM generated context consisting of motivation and social norm helped our proposed model *DREAM-FLUTE* (System 3) in figurative language understanding. For all these examples a T5-based model that did not have access to additional context (System 1) gave wrong label prediction. DREAM context helped improve both answer accuracy and explanation quality. Labels: (E), (C) refer to Entailment, Contradiction respectively.

Bayes at FigLang 2022 Euphemism Detection shared task: Cost-Sensitive Bayesian Fine-tuning and Venn-Abers Predictors for Robust Training under Class Skewed Distributions

Paul Trust
University College Cork
Cork, Ireland

Kadusabe Provia
Worldquant University
Louisiana, USA

Kizito Omala
Makerere University
Kampala, Uganda

Abstract

Transformers have achieved a state of the art performance across most natural language processing tasks. However, the performance of these models often degrades when being trained on data that exhibits skewed class distributions (class imbalance) common social media data. This is because training tends to be biased towards head classes that have majority of the data points . Most of the classical methods that have been proposed to handle this problem like re-sampling and re-weighting often suffer from unstable performance, poor applicability and poor calibration. In this paper, we propose to use Bayesian methods and Venn-Abers predictors for well calibrated and robust training against class imbalance. Our proposed approach improves $f1-$score over the baseline RoBERTa (A Robustly Optimized Bidirectional Embedding from Transformers Pretraining Approach) model by about 6 points (79.0% against 72.6%) when training with class imbalanced data.

1 Introduction

The phenomena of skewed class distribution also known as class imbalance is ambiguous and common in most real-world datasets and natural language processing (NLP) tasks (Tayyar Madabushi et al., 2019). Instead of preserving an ideal uniform distribution over each category of labels, most large-scale datasets exhibit skewed class distributions with a long tail having some target distributions with significantly more observations than others (Yang and Xu, 2020).

Although transformer-based models (Vaswani et al., 2017) have achieved a state of the art performance across several tasks in NLP, their performance tends to degrade when trained on long-tailed data. The main challenge lies in the sparsity of tail classes leading to estimation of the decision boundaries severely biased towards head classes (classes with more observations) (Pan et al., 2021a).

Class imbalance problem can be tackled at either model training or model inference phases. Approaches to handle class imbalance at training phase can be classified into re-weighting or re-sampling and those at model inference phase are mostly calibration techniques (Menon et al., 2020; Tian et al., 2020) which adjusts a classifier's confidence scores without changing the internal weights or architectures (Pan et al., 2021b) of the underlying models.

Post-processing calibration techniques have been found to be efficient since they requires no further training of the model and are effective on multiple class imbalanced classification benchmarks in computer vision (Kang et al., 2020; Pan et al., 2021b). Inspired by the success of post-processing calibration techniques, we experiment with techniques that are theoretically known to produce well calibrated predictions; Bayesian inference for neural networks (Blundell et al., 2015; Wen et al., 2018; Gal and Ghahramani, 2016) and Venn-Abers predictors (Vovk and Pctcj, 2014, 2012).

We test these methods by participating in the shared task at the third Workshop on Figurative Language Processing 2022 at EMNLP 2022 (Conference on Empirical Methods in Natural Language Processing). The training dataset exhibited a long tail distribution with 70% of the training texts containing euphemism (Gavidia et al., 2022; Lee et al., 2022).

Euphemisms are mild or indirect expressions that are used in place of more unpleasant or offensive ones common in social media data. They are used to show politeness when discussing sensitive topics or as a way to make unpleasant things sound better for example saying "laid to rest" instead of "buried" or "armed conflict" instead of "war" (Lee et al., 2022). With the need to curb inappropriate material on social media, people use these euphemisms to bypass media censoring software and thus automatically identifying texts containing

Proceedings of the 3rd Workshop on Figurative Language Processing (FLP), pages 94 - 99
December 8, 2022

these statements is a timely task. Several computational techniques have been proposed for the euphemism task (Gavidia et al., 2022; Lee et al., 2022; Zhu and Bhat, 2021). To the best of our knowledge, this is the first attempt to combine Bayesian transformers and Venn-Abers predictors for this task. The contributions of this work are:

- We show that fine-tuning transformers with Bayesian methods boosts performance over naive training in imbalanced class setting.
- We propose an an approach to combine Bayesian transformers and Venn Predictors for long tail distribution learning.
- We propose a euphemism detection method with considering of the class imbalance.

2 Background and Related Work

2.1 Euphemism Detection

Machine learning approaches have been proposed for euphemism detection (Kapron-King and Xu, 2021; Magu and Luo, 2018; Gavidia et al., 2022; Lee et al., 2022). Sentiment analysis methods have been utilized to recognize and classify euphemistic language in text (Felt and Riloff, 2020; Lee et al., 2022). Magu and Luo, 2018 used word embeddings and network analysis to identify euphemisms in the context of hate speech (Magu and Luo, 2018). Self supervised methods (Zhu and Bhat, 2021; Zhu et al., 2021) have also been employed. Our methodology is different from methods in literature in that we consider the long tailed distribution nature of the task and we also present apply novel techniques from Bayesian inference and Venn predictors which have not been used before in this task.

2.2 Learning under skewed class distributions

The dominant solutions to learning data with long-tailed distributions can be classified into re-sampling, re-weighting, confidence calibration and regularization. Re-sampling strategies flatten the data distribution, popular techniques are over-sampling (Buda et al., 2018; Byrd and Lipton, 2019; Shen et al., 2016) and under-sampling (He and Garcia, 2009; Haixiang et al., 2017). However, under-sampling may discard most of the data points and over-sampling results into over-fitting on the minority classes.

Cost sensitive learning (loss re-weighting) is another widely used method which works by assigning weights for different training samples. class-balanced loss assigns weights to classes proportional to the inverse of their frequency in the dataset (Huang et al., 2016, 2019). But optimizing deep learning models with this method under extreme class class imbalance may deteriorate performance (Zhong et al., 2021). Focal loss (FL) is a weighted version of cross-entropy loss with sample-specific weight. Label distribution-aware margin loss (LDAM) derives a generalization error bound for imbalanced training and proposes a margin-aware weighted cross-entropy loss (Cao et al., 2019) by minimizing margin-based generalization bound achieving significant performance boost over unweighted cross-entropy loss.

Post-processing methods of handling class imbalances re-calibrate the posterior distribution from the predicted confidence scores at test time. Examples of the methods are are logit adjustment (Menon et al., 2020) and posterior calibration (PC) (Tian et al., 2020).

2.3 Bayesian modeling with transformers

Deep learning models especially those based on the transformer architecture (Vaswani et al., 2017) have achieved a state-of-the-art performance across several tasks. BERT (Devlin et al., 2019) (Bidirectional Embedding from Transformers) and RoBERTa (Liu et al., 2019) (Robustly Optimized BERT Pretraining Approach) are among the most influential transformer variants in NLP. Despite their impressive performance, deep learning models tend to be produce over-confidence scores that are not calibrated which may deteriorate performance in imbalanced learning settings (Blundell et al., 2015).

Unlike the traditional neural networks trained with Maximum Likelihood Estimation (MLE) that fit a point estimate for the neural network's weights, Bayesian inference puts a prior distribution $p(w)$ over the weights and approximates the posterior distribution $p(w|D) \propto p(w)p(D|w)$. The predictive distribution of an unknown label $\tilde{y}$ of a test data item $\tilde{x}$ is given by $p(\tilde{y}|\tilde{x}) = E_{p(w|D)}[p(\tilde{y}|\tilde{x}, w)]$, we observe that taking an expectation over the posterior distribution of the weights is equivalent to using an ensemble of unaccountably infinite number of neural networks which would results into a boost in performance over a single neural network

Model	Precision	Recall	f1-score
BERT-base	0.712	0.714	0.713
RoBERTa-base (Baseline)	0.745	0.719	0.726
RoBERTa-Platt Scaling	0.702	0.710	0.706
RoBERTa-Venn-Abers	0.736	0.728	0.731
RoBERTa-bayesian	0.732	0.761	0.743
RoBERTa-LDAM	0.769	0.779	0.774
RoBERTa-bayesian-LDAM	0.769	0.819	0.787
RoBERTa-Bayesian-LDAM-Venn-Abers (Ours)	**0.794**	**0.786**	**0.790**

Table 1: Accuracy, precision and $f1-$score in percentages on the test data set for baseline model (RoBERTa-base) and our proposed approach (RoBERTa-Bayesian-LDAM-Venn-Abers), LDAM stands for label-distribution-aware margin loss

(Blundell et al., 2015).

However computing the posterior distribution over the weights often involve high dimensional integrals that are intractable and cannot be obtained in closed form. Popular approaches that have been proposed to produce approximates of these distribution are based on monte-carlo estimates and variational inference. Popular methods that utilise Bayesian principles for approximating the posterior distribution over neural networks are Bayes by Backprop (Blundell et al., 2015) and Flipout (Wen et al., 2018) and monte-carlo dropout (Gal and Ghahramani, 2016).

Flipout (Wen et al., 2018) is an efficient method for decorrelating the gradients within a mini-batch by implicitly sampling pseudo-independent weight perturbations for each example. Bayes by Backprop (Blundell et al., 2015) learns a probability distribution on the weights of the neural networks by minimizing the expected lower bound on the marginal likelihood. Monte Carlo dropout (Gal and Ghahramani, 2016) casts dropout training during training of neural networks as approximate Bayesian inference in deep Gaussian processes.

2.4 Venn-Abers Prediction

Venn-Abers predictors (Vovk and Petej, 2012) are a special case of Venn predictors (Vovk and Petej, 2014) which are distribution-free probabilistic predictors that have a guarantee of being valid under a sole assumption of the training examples being exchangeable. They work by transforming the output of a scoring classifier which in our case is a machine learning model into a multi-probabilistic prediction that has calibration guarantees.

More formally, assume we are given training samples $D = \{(x, y)\}_{i=1}^{n}$ consisting of two components; a data point $x \in X$ and its label $y \in Y$. Given a test data point x_{n+1}, the Venn predictor outputs a multi probabilistic prediction in the form of a probability distribution over possible values of the label.

A venn taxonomy B is a measurable function B that assigns to each $n \in \{1, 2, ...\}$ and each sequence $(d_1, ...d_n) \in D^n$ an equivalence relation $\sim$ on $\{1, ..., n\}$. The relation has to be equivariant in the sense that for each n and each permutation ϕ of $\{1, ..., n\}$,

$$(i \sim j | d_1, ...d_n) \Rightarrow (\phi(i) \sim \phi(j) | d_{\phi(1)}, ..., d_{\phi(n)}) \tag{1}$$

where $(i \sim j | d_1, ...d_n)$ means that i is equivalent to j under the relation assigned by B to $(d_1, ...d_n)$. A venn predictor with a Venn taxonomy B outputs a pair (p_0, p_1) where

$$p_y = \frac{|\{i \in B(n+1|d_1, ..., d_n, (x_{n+1}, y)) | y_i = 1\}|}{|B(n+1|d_1, ...d_n, (x_{n+1}, y))|} \tag{2}$$

where $B(j|d_1, .., d_n)$ the class of the equivalence of j is defined as follows:

$$B(j|d_1, .., d_n) = \{i \in \{1, ..., n\} | (i \sim j | d_1, ...d_n)\} \tag{3}$$

p_0 and p_1 express the predicted probabilities of the test object x_{n+1} belonging to a certain class.

3 Methodology

The dataset $D = \{(x, y)\}_{i=1}^{n}$ is divided into 3 splits; D_{train} for training the model, $D_{validation}$ for selecting the best models and calibration step, D_{test} for testing our approaches. We fine-tune RoBERTa (Liu et al., 2019) with standard cross entropy loss and with label-distribution-aware margin loss (LDAM) function (Cao et al., 2019). We first experiment with training our models in non-

Bayesian way using the standard maximum likelihood estimation and also in a Bayesian way by applying Bayesian layers in our neural network. The Bayesian layers used for our experimentation are Monte carlo dropout (Gal and Ghahramani, 2016).

To calibrate our predictions, we perform inference on the validation dataset $D_{validation}$ of size k with our trained model and obtained uncalibrated confidence scores denoted as $\{z_1, ..., z_k\}$ for each test data point x. Venn-Abers predictors proceeds by fitting an isotonic regression on the set $(z_1, y_1), ...(z_k, y_k), (z, 0)$ and the computing the score $s(x_i)$ for each calibration data points (x_i, y_i). Let g be an increasing function on the set $s(x_1), ...s(x_k)$ that maximizes the likelihood $\prod_{i=1}^{k} p_i$ where:

$$p_i = \begin{cases} g(s(x_i)) & \text{if } y_i = 1 \\ 1 - g(s(x_i)) & \text{if } y_i = 0 \end{cases} \tag{4}$$

Thus the multi-probabilistic prediction for x is the pair

$$(p_0, p_1) = (g_0(s_0(x)), g_1(s_1(x))) \tag{5}$$

The estimated label for a text data point x is the probability that minimizes the regret of the loss function calculated as in Equation 6.

$$p = \frac{p_1}{1 - p_0 + p_1} \tag{6}$$

4 Results and Discussion

4.1 Datasets

The dataset used for experiments is an Euphemism detection (ED) dataset (Gavidia et al., 2022; Lee et al., 2022) released by Third Workshop on Figurative Language Processing 2022 at EMNLP 2022 shared task on Euphesim Detection. This was a binary classification problem for identifying text expression that was euphemistic. The training data consisted of 1572 training points and test data consisted of 393 texts. Of the 1572 training texts, only 466 (30%) were did not contain euphemism.

4.2 Experimental Setup

We conduct experiments with pretrained transformer language models; RoBERTa (Liu et al., 2019), Bayesian methods and Venn-Abers predictors . Experiments are done for 50 epochs, max length of 512, batch size of 50 and the learning rate was set at 0.0005. The final submission were evaluated using $f1$-score. Transformers are implemented using hugging-face transformer library (Wolf et al., 2019), bayesian layers are implemented using Bayesian torch and baal (Krishnan and Tickoo, 2020; Atighehchian et al., 2022) and conformal predictors were implemented using reliabots (Shafer and Vovk, 2008).

4.3 Discussion

To assess the impact of Bayesian fine-tuning and Venn predictors, we perform experiments on the euphemisms detection dataset (Lee et al., 2022) described in section 4.1. Table 1 shows a combination of different models and their results on the test set. F1-score, recall and accuracy measures were used to evaluate the performance of different models as shown in Table 1. RoBERTa achieves a a slightly better performance compared to BERT (72.6% versus 71.3%). The observation is re-enforced by the impact of the architecture design of the pre-trained model on downstream tasks.

Experiments results on the test as shown in Figure 1 reveal that calibrating confidence scores of RoBERTa using Venn Abers predictors improves performance of the model by 1.2%. This is consistent with other results that report improved performance with post-hoc posterior calibration but naive calibration using platt scaling degrades performance of the model (Tian et al., 2020). Finetuning RoBERTa with a Bayesian layer boosts performance (about 2%) compared to the traditional fine-tuning, This is because Bayesian layers in a neural networks can be seen an ensemble of many networks at test time.

The biggest performance boost comes from training our models with a label distribution aware margin loss function (LDAM) and differed weighting, and this demonstrated the importance of cost sensitive learning when the data distribution is skewed. Finally our best system which we submitted for competition to the euphemism shared tasks was a combination of RoBERTa, Bayesian learning, cost sensitive learning and Venn Abers Predictors (*RoBERTa-bayesian-LDAM-Venn-Abers*) with an $f1-$score of 79% as shown in Table 1.

5 Conclusion

In this work, we have presented an approach for improving classification performance of transformer model when the data exhibits skewed class distributions. Data exhibits skewed class distribution when majority of the data points belong to some classes while other classes have very few data points. The situation makes naive training of neural networks hard since they tend to biased towards head classes. Our approach is based on cost sensitive Bayesian learning with Venn predictors for robust training against the class imbalance. Experiments the Euphemisms detection dataset which had class imbalance show that this method improves over traditional fine tuning by about 6% in terms of $f-$score (79.0% versus 72.6%). As future work, we would like to investigate how these finding extend beyond the euphemisms detection dataset.

6 Acknowledgements

We thank Science Foundation Ireland (SFI) Center for Research Training in Advanced Networks and Future communications at University College Cork for funding this research and Irish Centre for High-End Computing (ICHEC) for providing access to computing power for running some of our experiments.

References

Parmida Atighehchian, Frederic Branchaud-Charron, Jan Freyberg, Rafael Pardinas, Lorne Schell, and George Pearse. 2022. Baal, a bayesian active learning library. https://github.com/baal-org/baal/.

Charles Blundell, Julien Cornebise, Koray Kavukcuoglu, and Daan Wierstra. 2015. Weight uncertainty in neural network. In *International conference on machine learning*, pages 1613–1622. PMLR.

Mateusz Buda, Atsuto Maki, and Maciej A Mazurowski. 2018. A systematic study of the class imbalance problem in convolutional neural networks. *Neural networks*, 106:249–259.

Jonathon Byrd and Zachary Lipton. 2019. What is the effect of importance weighting in deep learning? In *International Conference on Machine Learning*, pages 872–881. PMLR.

Kaidi Cao, Colin Wei, Adrien Gaidon, Nikos Arechiga, and Tengyu Ma. 2019. Learning imbalanced datasets with label-distribution-aware margin loss. *Advances in neural information processing systems*, 32.

Jacob Devlin, Ming-Wei Chang, Kenton Lee, and Kristina Toutanova. 2019. BERT: Pre-training of deep bidirectional transformers for language understanding. In *Proceedings of the 2019 Conference of the North American Chapter of the Association for Computational Linguistics: Human Language Technologies, Volume 1 (Long and Short Papers)*, pages 4171–4186, Minneapolis, Minnesota. Association for Computational Linguistics.

Christian Felt and Ellen Riloff. 2020. Recognizing euphemisms and dysphemisms using sentiment analysis. In *Proceedings of the Second Workshop on Figurative Language Processing*, pages 136–145, Online. Association for Computational Linguistics.

Yarin Gal and Zoubin Ghahramani. 2016. Dropout as a bayesian approximation: Representing model uncertainty in deep learning. In *international conference on machine learning*, pages 1050–1059. PMLR.

Martha Gavidia, Patrick Lee, Anna Feldman, and Jing Peng. 2022. Cats are fuzzy pets: A corpus and analysis of potentially euphemistic terms. *arXiv preprint arXiv:2205.02728*.

Guo Haixiang, Li Yijing, Jennifer Shang, Gu Mingyun, Huang Yuanyue, and Gong Bing. 2017. Learning from class-imbalanced data: Review of methods and applications. *Expert systems with applications*, 73:220–239.

Haibo He and Edwardo A Garcia. 2009. Learning from imbalanced data. *IEEE Transactions on knowledge and data engineering*, 21(9):1263–1284.

Chen Huang, Yining Li, Chen Change Loy, and Xiaoou Tang. 2016. Learning deep representation for imbalanced classification. In *Proceedings of the IEEE conference on computer vision and pattern recognition*, pages 5375–5384.

Chen Huang, Yining Li, Chen Change Loy, and Xiaoou Tang. 2019. Deep imbalanced learning for face recognition and attribute prediction. *IEEE transactions on pattern analysis and machine intelligence*, 42(11):2781–2794.

Bingyi Kang, Saining Xie, Marcus Rohrbach, Zhicheng Yan, Albert Gordo, Jiashi Feng, and Yannis Kalantidis. 2020. Decoupling representation and classifier for long-tailed recognition. In *International Conference on Learning Representations*.

Anna Kapron-King and Yang Xu. 2021. A diachronic evaluation of gender asymmetry in euphemism. In *Proceedings of the 2nd International Workshop on Computational Approaches to Historical Language Change 2021*, pages 28–38, Online. Association for Computational Linguistics.

Ranganath Krishnan and Omesh Tickoo. 2020. Improving model calibration with accuracy versus uncertainty optimization. In *Advances in Neural Information Processing Systems*, volume 33, pages 18237–18248.

Patrick Lee, Martha Gavidia, Anna Feldman, and Jing Peng. 2022. Searching for PETs: Using distributional and sentiment-based methods to find potentially euphemistic terms. In *Proceedings of the Second Workshop on Understanding Implicit and Underspecified Language*, pages 22–32, Seattle, USA. Association for Computational Linguistics.

Yinhan Liu, Myle Ott, Naman Goyal, Jingfei Du, Mandar Joshi, Danqi Chen, Omer Levy, Mike Lewis, Luke Zettlemoyer, and Veselin Stoyanov. 2019. Roberta: A robustly optimized bert pretraining approach. *arXiv preprint arXiv:1907.11692*.

Rijul Magu and Jiebo Luo. 2018. Determining code words in euphemistic hate speech using word embedding networks. In *Proceedings of the 2nd Workshop on Abusive Language Online (ALW2)*, pages 93–100, Brussels, Belgium. Association for Computational Linguistics.

Aditya Krishna Menon, Sadeep Jayasumana, Ankit Singh Rawat, Himanshu Jain, Andreas Veit, and Sanjiv Kumar. 2020. Long-tail learning via logit adjustment. *arXiv preprint arXiv:2007.07314*.

Tai-Yu Pan, Cheng Zhang, Yandong Li, Hexiang Hu, Dong Xuan, Soravit Changpinyo, Boqing Gong, and Wei-Lun Chao. 2021a. On model calibration for long-tailed object detection and instance segmentation. *Advances in Neural Information Processing Systems*, 34:2529–2542.

Tai-Yu Pan, Cheng Zhang, Yandong Li, Hexiang Hu, Dong Xuan, Soravit Changpinyo, Boqing Gong, and Wei-Lun Chao. 2021b. On model calibration for long-tailed object detection and instance segmentation. In *Advances in Neural Information Processing Systems*, volume 34, pages 2529–2542. Curran Associates, Inc.

Glenn Shafer and Vladimir Vovk. 2008. A tutorial on conformal prediction. *Journal of Machine Learning Research*, 9(3).

Li Shen, Zhouchen Lin, and Qingming Huang. 2016. Relay backpropagation for effective learning of deep convolutional neural networks. In *European conference on computer vision*, pages 467–482. Springer.

Harish Tayyar Madabushi, Elena Kochkina, and Michael Castelle. 2019. Cost-sensitive BERT for generalisable sentence classification on imbalanced data. In *Proceedings of the Second Workshop on Natural Language Processing for Internet Freedom: Censorship, Disinformation, and Propaganda*, pages 125–134, Hong Kong, China. Association for Computational Linguistics.

Junjiao Tian, Yen-Cheng Liu, Nathaniel Glaser, Yen-Chang Hsu, and Zsolt Kira. 2020. Posterior recalibration for imbalanced datasets. *Advances in Neural Information Processing Systems*, 33:8101–8113.

Ashish Vaswani, Noam Shazeer, Niki Parmar, Jakob Uszkoreit, Llion Jones, Aidan N Gomez, Łukasz Kaiser, and Illia Polosukhin. 2017. Attention is all you need. *Advances in neural information processing systems*, 30.

Vladimir Vovk and Ivan Petej. 2012. Venn-abers predictors. *arXiv preprint arXiv:1211.0025*.

Vladimir Vovk and Ivan Petej. 2014. Venn-abers predictors. In *Proceedings of the Thirtieth Conference on Uncertainty in Artificial Intelligence*, UAI'14, page 829–838, Arlington, Virginia, USA. AUAI Press.

Yeming Wen, Paul Vicol, Jimmy Ba, Dustin Tran, and Roger Grosse. 2018. Flipout: Efficient pseudo-independent weight perturbations on mini-batches. *arXiv preprint arXiv:1803.04386*.

Thomas Wolf, Lysandre Debut, Victor Sanh, Julien Chaumond, Clement Delangue, Anthony Moi, Pierric Cistac, Tim Rault, Rémi Louf, Morgan Funtowicz, et al. 2019. Huggingface's transformers: State-of-the-art natural language processing. *arXiv preprint arXiv:1910.03771*.

Yuzhe Yang and Zhi Xu. 2020. Rethinking the value of labels for improving class-imbalanced learning. In *Conference on Neural Information Processing Systems (NeurIPS)*.

Zhisheng Zhong, Jiequan Cui, Shu Liu, and Jiaya Jia. 2021. Improving calibration for long-tailed recognition. In *Proceedings of the IEEE/CVF conference on computer vision and pattern recognition*, pages 16489–16498.

Wanzheng Zhu and Suma Bhat. 2021. Euphemistic phrase detection by masked language model. In *Findings of the Association for Computational Linguistics: EMNLP 2021*, pages 163–168, Punta Cana, Dominican Republic. Association for Computational Linguistics.

Wanzheng Zhu, Hongyu Gong, Rohan Bansal, Zachary Weinberg, Nicolas Christin, Giulia Fanti, and Suma Bhat. 2021. Self-supervised euphemism detection and identification for content moderation. In *2021 IEEE Symposium on Security and Privacy (SP)*, pages 229–246. IEEE.

Food for Thought: How can we exploit contextual embeddings in the translation of idiomatic expressions?

Lukas Santing[1], **Ryan Sijstermans**[1], **Giacomo Anerdi**[1],

Pedro Jeuris[1], **Marijn ten Thij**[1] and **Riza Batista-Navarro**[1,2]

[1]Department of Advanced Computing Sciences, Maastricht University, The Netherlands
[2]Department of Computer Science, The University of Manchester, UK

Abstract

Idiomatic expressions (or idioms) are phrases where the meaning of the phrase cannot be determined from the meaning of the individual words in the expression. Translating idioms between languages is therefore a challenging task. Transformer models based on contextual embeddings have advanced the state-of-the-art across many domains in the field of natural language processing. While research using transformers has advanced both idiom detection as well as idiom disambiguation, idiom translation has not seen a similar advancement. In this work, we investigate two approaches to fine-tuning a pretrained Text-to-Text Transfer Transformer (T5) model to perform idiom translation from English to German. The first approach directly translates English idiom-containing sentences to German, while the second is underpinned by idiom paraphrasing, firstly paraphrasing English idiomatic expressions to their simplified English versions before translating them to German. Results of our evaluation show that each of the approaches is able to generate adequate translations.

1 Introduction

In the past decade, we have seen an increase in the accuracy of machine translation (MT) approaches (Wang et al., 2021). Some of the contributing factors to this increase is the introduction of the attention mechanism and contextual embedding models (Liu et al., 2020), as well as the wider availability of datasets. According to Škvorc et al. (2022) however, the same increase in accuracy has not been achieved for idiom translation. Idioms are defined as "a group of words established by usage as having a meaning not deducible from those of the individual words" (University of Oxford, 2022).

Since datasets used for MT are, in general, not rich in idioms (Fadaee et al., 2018; Saxena and Paul, 2020; Zhou et al., 2022; Škvorc et al., 2022; Eryiğit et al., 2022), MT models can suffer from this by not being able to distinguish between an idiom and an expression that can be interpreted literally. This can result in a wrong or meaningless translation, as can be seen in Figure 1. However, there are also idioms which can be interpreted literally, depending on the context in which it was used. For instance, the idiom "breaking the ice" could have an idiomatic meaning "to get a conversation started", but its literal meaning is also valid, e.g., in the context of someone breaking ice cubes for a cocktail. Such idiomatic expressions make it even more challenging for models to correctly translate sentences containing them. To further complicate the issue, some multi-word expressions (MWEs) such as "to pass on" and "to come out", are often used in their idiomatic sense but can also be used in their literal sense.

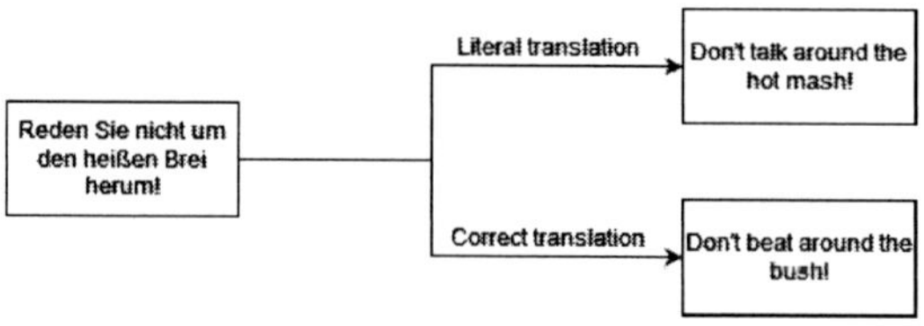

Figure 1: Example of an idiom-containing German sentence with its wrong (literal) and correct translations in English.

With the emergence of the attention mechanism (Yu et al., 2020), transformer models and contextual embeddings (Devlin et al., 2018) came the rapid advancement of the state of the art in many NLP tasks, e.g., question answering and machine translation (Raffel et al., 2020). In this work, we aim to improve the translation of idiomatic expressions by employing contextual embeddings.

We focus on investigating two different approaches for fine-tuning transformer models for the translation of sentences containing idiomatic expressions. Parallel corpora containing idiomatic expressions are scarce (Fadaee et al., 2018; Saxena and Paul, 2020; Zhou et al., 2022; Škvorc et al.,

Proceedings of the 3rd Workshop on Figurative Language Processing (FLP), pages 100 - 110
December 8, 2022 ©2022 Association for Computational Linguistics

2022; Eryiğit et al., 2022), but owing to the availability of a parallel corpus of idiom-containing English sentences and their corresponding German translations (Fadaee et al., 2018), we have chosen English and German as our source and target languages, respectively. The first approach utilises this dataset for idiom-to-idiom translation, i.e., translation of an idiom-containing sentence in English to its equivalent idiom-containing sentence in German. The second approach, meanwhile, is based on idiom paraphrasing, i.e., conversion of an English idiom-containing sentence to its paraphrase, followed by translation of the latter to German. On top of assessing the performance of these approaches based on evaluation metrics, we designed a strategy for human-based evaluation to determine: (1) how fluent their translations are in German, and (2) how well their translations preserve the meaning of source sentences.

To the best of our knowledge, ours is the first work to investigate the extent to which transformer models, specifically the Text-to-Text Transfer Transformer (T5) kind (Raffel et al., 2020), can translate idiom-containing sentences from one language to another. Based on the transformer encoder-decoder architecture (Vaswani et al., 2017), T5 provides a unified framework for casting many NLP problems (e.g., text classification, question answering) as a sequence-to-sequence learning task, and thus lends itself well to the problem of translating idiomatic expressions.

2 Related Work

Neural machine translation (NMT) models (Isabelle et al., 2017) and statistical machine translation (SMT) models (Salton et al., 2014a) have shown difficulty in translating idiomatic expressions (Chakrawarti et al., 2017; Dankers et al., 2022). The meaning of an idiom is generally different from the joint meaning of the words composing it, and therefore translation models tend to make errors from the literal translation of individual words.

In recent years, a number of transformer models, e.g., BERT (Devlin et al., 2018), BART (Lewis et al., 2019) and T5 (Raffel et al., 2020), have been successfully applied to a wide range of natural language processing tasks. The advantage of these models is that, for any word (token), they use a contextual embedding representation which is based not only on the word itself, but also on its context (i.e., surrounding words to the left and right). They have achieved ground-breaking results in almost every NLP task (Liu et al., 2020). Context is key for the comprehension of idiomatic expressions, hence such contextual embeddings could potentially be helpful in understanding them. While the use of transformer models to understand idiomatic expressions has been explored in several papers (Kurfali and Östling, 2020; Zhou, 2021; Zhou et al., 2022; Tan and Jiang, 2021; Škvorc et al., 2022), very little research has been done on idiom translation based on these models.

There are multiple tasks involved in the translation of idiom-containing sentences. The first one involves the identification of idiomatic expressions within a sentence (Fazly et al., 2009). Škvorc et al. (2022), for instance, showed that transformer models can be used to successfully identify idiomatic expressions. Idiom identification is followed by sense disambiguation, which involves determining whether an idiom is used literally or idiomatically in the containing sentence (Sporleder and Li, 2009; Kurfali and Östling, 2020; Tan and Jiang, 2021). Transformers have also advanced the state of the art in this task (Kurfali and Östling, 2020; Tan and Jiang, 2021). A further task is the translation or paraphrasing of idioms, depending on the intended application. Much research has been shown to attempt paraphrasing idioms to replace them with their literal meaning (Liu and Hwa, 2016; Zhou, 2021; Zhou et al., 2022; Tien-Ping and Jia Jun, 2021). The work of Zhou et al. (2022) demonstrated how BART can be used for this purpose.

With respect to datasets for idiom paraphrasing, there are various mono-lingual English idiom datasets (Saxena and Paul, 2020; Zhou et al., 2021; Adewumi et al., 2021). Among these datasets, the PIE dataset (Zhou et al., 2021) stands out, as it contains both idiomatic expressions and their non-idiomatic counterparts.

When it comes to translation to another language rather than paraphrasing within a single language, Salton et al. (2014b) employed SMT to firstly substitute idioms with their simplified meanings before translation to the target language, after which the translated expressions were substituted with idioms in the target language.

Little research can be found when it comes to the direct translation of idiomatic expressions from a source to a target language. A major contributing factor to this could be the scarcity of parallel corpora suitable for this task. A few papers on translation introduced their own datasets. An example is the work of Agrawal et al. (2018) where the authors introduced a parallel corpus of idiom-containing sentences in seven Indian languages and English, on which NMT and SMT models were trained. Fadaee et al. (2018) similarly created an English-German parallel corpus of sentences with idiomatic expressions, and evaluated the performance of NMT and SMT models based on it. Other corpora that support the development of idiom translation include a Russian-English (Aharodnik et al., 2018) and a Chinese-English dataset (Tang, 2022).

3 Methodology

The focus of this work is idiom translation. We thus consider idiom identification as outside of our scope, and make the assumption that input sentences contain idiomatic expressions. Furthermore, in some of our models (described below), the idiomatic expression itself is included as part of the input.

Below, we describe each of the two approaches we propose for idiom translation, one underpinned by idiom-to-idiom translation from the source to target language, and the other based on idiom paraphrasing within the source language followed by translation to the target language. In both cases, a T5 model was fine-tuned for a sequence-to-sequence learning task, where the input is provided in the form of a sequence of tokens and the model produces another sequence as its output. The task that the model needs to learn, is defined by prepending a prefix to the input sequence.

T5 models come in different sizes. In this work, we employed the `t5-small` implementation[1] which has around 60 million parameters and yet is feasible to train with limited computational resources. It comes pretrained for language modelling based on the Colossal Clean Crawled Corpus (Raffel et al., 2020) and fine-tuned for a number of downstream NLP tasks including translation.

3.1 Idiom-to-idiom Translation

In this approach, a model was developed to translate an idiom-containing sentence from the source language (English) to the target language (German).

[1]`https://huggingface.co/t5-small`

Dataset. The dataset used in training and evaluating our single translation model is the IdiomTranslationDS dataset by Fadaee et al. (2018). It consists of English-German sentence pairs where each of the sentences is an idiom-containing translation of the other. The idioms contained in each sentence pair are also provided. The dataset contains a total of 3498 sentence pairs sourced from the WMT training set (Bojar et al., 2017), distributed between a training and test set with 1998 and 1500 sentence pairs, respectively. Our analysis showed that certain idiomatic expressions appeared very frequently in this dataset. For instance, "to pass on", "to be in the know" and "in a nutshell" are contained in 513, 120 and 84 sentence pairs, respectively.

Data Cleaning. Manual inspection of the sentence pairs (carried out by two conversational German speakers) showed that some of the provided German sentences are not correct translations of their corresponding English sentences. To eliminate noise from the training and test sets, these pairs were manually removed, reducing the size of the training and test sets by 13.3% (265 pairs removed) and 15.2% (228 pairs removed), respectively. Furthermore, Unicode characters from other languages (Arabic and Mandarin) which appeared in some of the source and target sentences, were automatically removed.

As the original dataset did not provide predefined training and validation subsets, 15% of the pairs in the training set were randomly selected and held out to comprise a validation set.

Model Training. A T5 model was fine-tuned in different ways in order to develop different versions of our idiom-to-idiom translation model. This was carried out by varying the prefix prepended to the input sequence and/or specifying the pre-identified idiomatic expression within a given sentence.

The authors of T5 already provide a model that had been fine-tuned for a number of downstream tasks, including English-to-German translation (Raffel et al., 2020). As a starting point, the T5 model was further fine-tuned for the existing English-to-German translation task using our cleansed IdiomTranslationDS dataset. This required prepending the input sequences with the prefix *"translate English to German:"*. Additionally, we sought to define a new task for which to fine-tune T5, hence we trained another model whereby the input sequences were prepended with a custom prefix, *"translate English to German with idiom:"*.

For both of the above fine-tuning tasks, we also investigated the effect of specifying the idiom contained within a given sequence. To this end, a suffix indicating the pre-identified idiom was appended to an input sequence. For example, the suffix *"idiom: to be in the picture"* was appended to the original input sequence *"She's not in the picture."* Four different translation models were obtained by fine-tuning the `t5-small` model for 50 epochs, for each of the following tasks: (1) Predefined translation: based on continuing to fine-tune T5 for the already existing English-to-German translation task, using the original input format; (2) Idiom-aware predefined translation: similar to task (1) but with the idiom appended at the end of the input sequence; (3) Custom translation: based on defining a new downstream task for T5, whereby we introduced the custom prefix *"translate English to German with idiom:"*; and (4) Idiom-aware custom translation: similar to task (3) but with the idiom appended at the end of the input sequence. Table 1 presents some examples that illustrate the different ways in which we fine-tuned the T5 model.

3.2 Idiom Paraphrasing and Translation

The second approach consists of a pipeline divided into two sub-tasks, each underpinned by a different model. The first sub-task is concerned with converting English idiom-containing sentences to their English paraphrases by training a paraphrasing model. This is followed by the second sub-task of translating the resulting paraphrases to German. It is worth noting that in the context of this approach, we define *paraphrase* as a simplification of the original idiom-containing sentence, allowing a reader to understand its meaning even if they are unfamiliar with the idiom. For example, a paraphrase of the sentence *"He feels he can paddle his own canoe after turning 18"* is *"He feels he can be self-reliant after turning 18."*

Dataset. To train the paraphrasing model, the PIE dataset (Zhou et al., 2021) was used. This dataset consists of English idiom-containing sentences as well as their corresponding paraphrases (also in English). Additionally, the dataset also specifies which tokens in a sentence corresponds to an idiom, as well as the meaning (sense) of that idiom. A total of 823 (non-unique) idioms are included in the dataset with a total of 5170 sentences, where each idiom has at least five sentence pairs per sense (as some idioms have multiple senses).

Data Cleaning. Although our analysis of the dataset showed that the data is mostly clean, several pre-processing operations were nevertheless applied. Some extraneous characters (e.g., ¾, ™) were removed. Also, variations in punctuation (e.g., different types of quotation marks) were normalised. Tokenisation seems to have been applied (by the dataset creators) on the data, e.g., "don't" appears as "do n't". However, this seems to be have been done inconsistently across the samples. Tokenised contractions were therefore merged again, considering that T5 does not require input sequences to be tokenised, as it comes with its own tokeniser.

The dataset was subdivided into training, validation and test sets following a 70-15-15% split.

Model training: Idiom paraphrasing. We explored a number of ways to fine-tune a T5 model for paraphrasing, while also exploiting the fact that a `t5-small` model fine-tuned specifically for general paraphrasing, is already available. This model, `t5-small-tapaco`[2], was fine-tuned on the TaPaCo dataset (Scherrer, 2020).

As our baseline, the original `t5-small` model was fine-tuned by introducing a new task specified by a custom prefix *"id_par:"* (short for "idiom paraphrasing"). This was necessary as none of the downstream tasks that T5 was originally fine-tuned for, were concerned with paraphrasing. To make the model aware of the idiom contained in a given sentence, we also appended the idiomatic expression itself, as supplied in the dataset.

Meanwhile, the `t5-small-tapaco` model which had already been fine-tuned for general paraphrasing, already recognises the predefined prefix *"paraphrase:"*. To fine-tune this specific model, we prepared the input sequences in our dataset by prepending the said prefix.

In summary, fine-tuning for the following tasks was performed (for 50 epochs), resulting in three types of paraphrasing models (exemplified in Table 2): (1) Custom paraphrasing with `t5-small`: based on fine-tuning `t5-small` whereby we introduced a custom prefix *"id_par:"* and appended the idiom at the end of the input sequence; (2) Predefined paraphrasing with `t5-small-tapaco`: based on conti-

[2]`https://huggingface.co/hetpandya/t5-small-tapaco`

Model Variant	Example Input Sequence
Predefined	*translate English to German: She's not in the picture*
Idiom-aware predefined	*translate English to German: She's not in the picture. idiom: to be in the picture*
Custom	*translate English to German with idiom: She's not in the picture.*
Idiom-aware custom	*translate English to German with idiom: She's not in the picture. idiom: to be in the picture*

Table 1: Examples showing how `t5-small` was fine-tuned for different tasks resulting in four translation model variants.

nuing to fine-tune `t5-small-tapaco` for paraphrasing, with the predefined prefix *"paraphrase:"* prepended to input sequences; and (3) Custom paraphrasing with `t5-small-tapaco`: based on fine-tuning `t5-small-tapaco` with the custom prefix *"id_par:"* and the idiom appended at the end of each input sequence.

Translation. The second sub-task is concerned with the translation of the English paraphrases (resulting from the first sub-task) to German. As the paraphrase model is presumed to have performed simplification of the idiomatic expressions contained in the input sentences, this sub-task can be cast as general translation from English to German. We leveraged the original `t5-small` model for this purpose, as it had already been fine-tuned for the English-to-German translation task.

4 Evaluation and Results

In order to evaluate our approaches, both automatic and human-based evaluation were conducted. Below, we first discuss the results of automatically evaluating each of the idiom-to-idiom translation and idiom paraphrasing models, followed by the results of human-based evaluation.

4.1 Automatic Evaluation

As part of our automatic evaluation, the following metrics were used: BLEU (Papineni et al., 2002), METEOR (Denkowski and Lavie, 2014) and COMET (Rei et al., 2020). COMET, in particular, has a variant known as Referenceless COMET, that we also used to estimate the quality of a generated translation even without a gold standard translation to compare with.

It is worth noting that an absolute score obtained by any of the above metrics is difficult to interpret on its own. Nevertheless, when viewed relative to each other, such scores are helpful in comparing the performance of different models and approaches (bearing in mind that for each of BLEU, METEOR and COMET, higher scores are desirable).

4.1.1 Idiom-to-idiom Translation

The BLEU, METEOR, COMET and Referenceless COMET scores obtained by our different idiom-to-idiom translation models on the cleansed IdiomTranslationDS test set are presented in Table 3. According to all metrics, the best results were obtained by the model that was based on continuing to fine-tune T5 for the predefined English-to-German translation task using the IdiomTranslationDS training set, without the idiomatic expression specified in the input sequence. To investigate whether the performance improvement obtained by this model (over the baseline model) is statistically significant, a paired t-test was performed for all scores. This resulted in p-values of 0.010, 0.056, 0.016 and 0.546 for BLEU, METEOR, COMET and Referenceless COMET, respectively. Considering a significance threshold of 0.05, we can say that the performance improvement based on BLEU and COMET is significant.

4.1.2 Idiom Paraphrasing and Translation

To evaluate the performance of our second approach, we firstly conducted a comparison of our different models for the idiom paraphrasing sub-task. On the basis of that, the best-performing paraphrasing model was selected and integrated with our chosen English-to-German translation model to form a pipeline, whose performance was evaluated separately.

Shown in Table 4 are the results of evaluating our idiom paraphrasing models on our cleansed PIE validation set using the BLEU and METEOR metrics. Based on both scores, the best-performing paraphrasing model is the one that was based on fine-tuning `t5-small-tapaco` for our custom task using the cleansed PIE training set.

To realise the pipeline for our second approach, our Custom `t5-small-tapaco` model was integrated with the original `t5-small` model that was already fine-tuned for general English-to-German translation. This combination was evaluated on the cleansed PIE test set, the results of which are shown

Model Variant	Example Input Sequence
Custom t5-small	*id_par: The comedian had the audience in stitches. idiom: in stitches*
Predefined t5-small-tapaco	*paraphrase: The comedian had the audience in stitches.*
Custom t5-small-tapaco	*id_par: The comedian had the audience in stitches. idiom: in stitches*

Table 2: Examples showing how different paraphrasing model variants based on t5-small and t5-small-tapaco were fine-tuned based for different tasks.

Translation Model	BLEU	METEOR	COMET	Ref. COMET
Pretrained t5-small (Baseline)	0.145	0.493	0.241	0.100
Fine-tuned for Predefined task	**0.151**	**0.498**	**0.257**	**0.101**
Fine-tuned for Idiom-aware predefined task	0.146	0.495	0.255	0.097
Fine-tuned for Custom task	0.147	0.489	0.052	0.052
Fine-tuned for Idiom-aware custom task	0.142	0.492	0.242	0.095

Table 3: Evaluation results based on the cleansed IdiomTranslationDS test set. Referenceless COMET (Ref. COMET) scores were obtained by averaging over all test sentences. Each of the fine-tuned translation models is based on t5-small.

in Table 5. Compared to a baseline approach of translating an English idiom-containing sentence to German using the original t5-small model, our proposed pipeline-based approach obtained improved performance based on the Referenceless COMET metric. A paired t-test was performed and resulted in a p-value of 0.013, confirming that the improvement is statistically significant.

4.2 Human-based Evaluation

To complement the automatic evaluation carried out (described in Section 4.1), we sought the help of volunteer human participants in evaluating the outputs of our two approaches to idiomatic expression translation. To this end, a survey was built (using the Qualtrics platform[3]) to evaluate: (1) the extent to which each of our approaches generated fluent German sentences; and (2) how well each of our approaches generated German sentences that preserved the meaning of the original idiom-containing English sentences.

Survey design. The survey begins with a self-assessment section, which enabled us to ensure that responses were collected only from participants who are at least proficient/conversational in both English and German[4].

The core of the survey consists of two sections, each one intended to evaluate each of our two approaches. In each section, five questions were presented to a participant, where each question (described in more detail below) is intended to assess the quality of a generated German translation of an English idiom-containing sentence. Out of these five questions, two were fixed, i.e., shown to every participant, to allow us to calculate agreement between participants. The other three questions were based on random selection from a pool of 12 English idiom-containing sentences which were automatically translated by each of our approaches.

The first section was designed to evaluate the outputs of our best-performing idiom-to-idiom translation model. Each question presents an English idiom-containing sentence (drawn from the cleansed IdiomTranslationDS test set) and the German translation generated by the said model. A participant is asked to rate the translation in terms of fluency and meaning preservation on a scale of 1 to 5, with the values corresponding to: (1) "Very bad/Incomprehensible", (2) "Bad", (3) "Adequate", (4) "Good", and (5) "Very good/Flawless". An option for "I don't know" was also made available. An example question is shown in Appendix A.

The second section was designed similarly to the first section, except for the English idiom-containing sentences having been drawn from the cleansed PIE test set and their translations having been generated by our pipeline-based approach.

The survey, containing a total of 10 translation quality assessment questions spread across the two sections, was published for one week and obtained responses from a total of 53 participants.

[3] https://www.qualtrics.com

[4] We did not collect any personal information hence ethics approval of the survey was not required.

Paraphrasing Model	BLEU	METEOR
Custom `t5-small` (Baseline)	0.755	0.843
Predefined `t5-small-tapaco`	0.768	0.856
Custom `t5-small-tapaco`	**0.774**	**0.859**

Table 4: Results of evaluating our idiom paraphrasing models based on the cleansed PIE validation set.

	Paraphrasing		Translation
	BLEU	METEOR	Ref. COMET
Pretrained `t5-small` (Baseline)	NA	NA	0.0075
Custom `t5-small-tapaco`+Pretrained `t5-small`	0.768	0.852	**0.0147**

Table 5: Results of evaluating our combined idiom paraphrasing and translation approach, on the PIE test dataset. Referenceless COMET (Ref. COMET) scores were obtained by averaging over all test sentences.

Inter-rater agreement. In order to assess the reliability of the ratings collected through the survey, inter-rater agreement was calculated based on the fixed questions[5] that were presented to all participants. As a preliminary step, we removed any responses where the "I don't know" option was selected instead of a rating from 1 to 5, eliminating only two responses. We then calculated the value of Krippendorff's alpha (Hayes and Krippendorff, 2007) with the help of an implementation available from PyPi[6]. A value of 0.22 for alpha was obtained, which can be interpreted as fair agreement between our participants (Hughes, 2021). We do acknowledge that this implies that the rating task was not straightforward, and that a much higher agreement could have been obtained had we recruited only native German speakers (who also speak English), which we did not have access to at the time of this study.

Results. For each question in each section of the survey, the ratings given by participants were collected and analysed. The results for the idiom-to-idiom translation approach and the pipeline-based approach are visualised[7] in Figures 2 and 3, respectively. Each of the figures shows a box plot for every question, with the box ranging from the first to the third quartile and the whiskers extending to the minimum and maximum scores. It is worth noting that the set of 14 questions used in assessing the first approach (idiom-to-idiom translation) is different from the set of 14 questions used to assess the second approach (pipeline consisting of idiom paraphrasing and translation).

The median for every question is given by a vertical line, while the mean rating[8] is indicated by a star ($\star$). The dotted line represents the average score over all questions. The idiom-to-idiom translation model obtained an average fluency of 3.73, while that obtained by the pipeline-based approach is 3.65 (out of 5). In terms of meaning preservation, very similar average scores were obtained, i.e., 3.30 and 3.29 (out of 5) for the idiom-to-idiom translation and pipeline-based approaches, respectively.

5 Discussion

With respect to the first approach underpinned by idiom-to-idiom translation, our results showed that the best-performing model is the one that was based on continuing to fine-tune `t5-small` for the predefined English-to-German translation task. This shows that a T5 model that was fine-tuned for the predefined translation task, is better at translating English idiom-containing sentences to their idiom-containing German counterparts, compared to a model that was trained for a completely new idiom translation task. This is unsurprising considering that T5 was fine-tuned for general translation on the WMT 2014 English-German dataset with 4.5 million sentence pairs (Vaswani et al., 2017), while the cleansed IdiomTranslationDS dataset that we used to fine-tune T5 for the new, custom idiom translation task, includes only 1733 pairs.

When it comes to the second approach which is based on a pipeline of idiom paraphrasing and translation models, our results demonstrate that fine-

[5]There were a total of four fixed questions given that two were included in each of the two sections.

[6]`https://pypi.org/project/krippendorff/`

[7]The box plots were produced based on code from `https://github.com/mctenthij/CDS_paper`

[8]The average number of ratings collected for the randomly selected questions is 13.25.

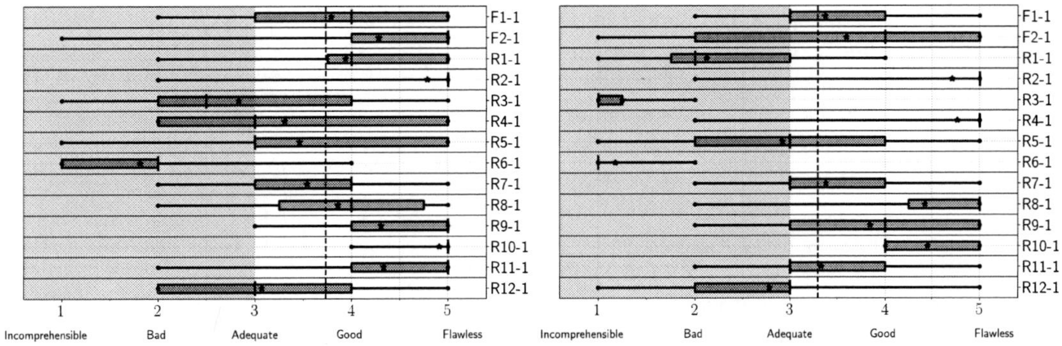

(a) Fluency scores

(b) Meaning preservation scores

Figure 2: Box plots of the scores provided by participants for each survey question assessing the quality of the outputs of our idiom-to-idiom translation model. Questions are denoted using the convention *F#-1* or *R#-1*, where *F* and *R* indicate a fixed and randomly selected question, respectively, and *1* means that the question was used to evaluate the first approach.

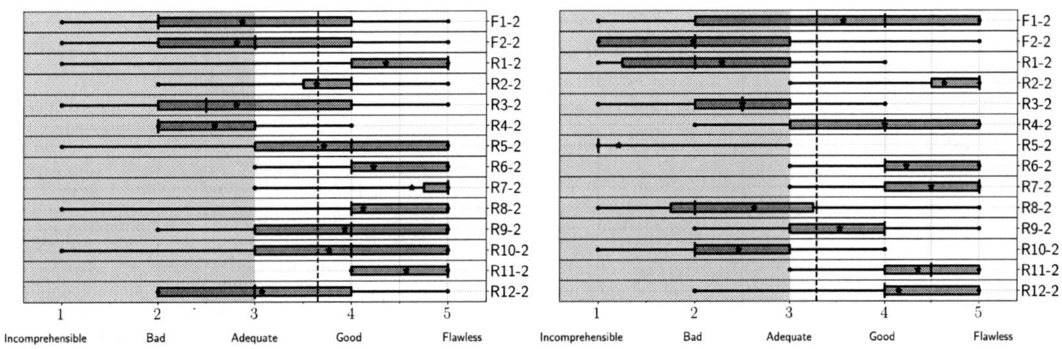

(a) Fluency scores

(b) Meaning preservation scores

Figure 3: Box plots of the scores provided by participants for each survey question assessing the quality of the outputs of the pipeline-based approach. Questions are denoted using the convention *F#-2* or *R#-2*, where *F* and *R* indicate a fixed and randomly selected question, respectively, and *2* means that the question was used to evaluate the second approach.

tuning `t5-small-tapaco` (a T5 model that had already been trained for general English paraphrasing) for our newly proposed custom paraphrasing task, leads to improved performance. Moreover, when this paraphrasing model is combined with the original T5 model for general English-to-German translation, better performance on the translation task is obtained, in comparison with using only the original T5 model.

Although the two approaches are not directly comparable with each other (i.e., the first approach is aimed at keeping the idiom in a German translation while the second one is aimed at generating a German translation of a non-idiomatic English paraphrase), our human-based evaluation shows that the first approach—the one based on idiom-to-idiom translation—seems to produce outputs which are marginally better that those of the second. This can be expected: as the second approach is based on a pipeline of paraphrasing and translation sub-tasks, any errors from the paraphrasing model would have been propagated to the translation model, affecting the quality of the final outputs. This is an issue that does not apply to the first approach since it performs direct translation.

6 Conclusions and Future Work

In this paper, we demonstrate how T5 models can be exploited in idiom translation: by fine-tuning them for idiom-to-idiom translation (first approach) and idiom paraphrasing (second approach). On the one hand, automatic evaluation showed that continuing to fine-tune the original T5 model for the predefined translation task on an idiom translation dataset, yielded optimal performance for idiom-to-idiom translation. On the other hand, fine-tuning a T5 model that had already been trained on a general paraphrasing task, for a custom idiom paraphrasing task, led to the best performance for idiom paraphrasing. Combining the said paraphrasing model with the original T5 model for general translation, resulted in improved results for idiom translation, compared with using just the latter. Human-based evaluation showed that both approaches produce translations of adequate quality.

To further advance research in idiom translation, we propose possible directions that can be pursued in the future. Firstly, a high-quality dataset with a much larger number of idiom-containing sentence pairs can be developed to facilitate better fine-tuning of T5 models for a custom idiom-to-idiom translation task. Moreover, it would be beneficial to create one dataset that can support the development of both idiom-to-idiom translation and idiom paraphrasing approaches. For instance, one can enrich the IdiomTranslationDS dataset by including paraphrases of idioms in English and German. Furthermore, our work has highlighted the fact that idiom translation datasets are scarce. When more such datasets become available, one can assess the extent to which our approaches can be applied to other language pairs.

To mitigate the current lack of large datasets for idiom translation, one could cast the idiom translation problem as a prompt-based learning task (Liu et al., 2021): a framework that makes it possible to apply pretrained language models to downstream tasks (such as translation) without the need for large amounts of data for fine-tuning.

References

Tosin P Adewumi, Saleha Javed, Roshanak Vadoodi, Aparajita Tripathy, Konstantina Nikolaidou, Foteini Liwicki, and Marcus Liwicki. 2021. Potential idiomatic expression (PIE)-english: Corpus for classes of idioms. *arXiv preprint arXiv:2105.03280.*

Ruchit Agrawal, Vighnesh Chenthil Kumar, Vigneshwaran Muralidharan, and Dipti Misra Sharma. 2018. No more beating about the bush: A step towards idiom handling for Indian language NLP. In *Proceedings of the Eleventh International Conference on Language Resources and Evaluation (LREC 2018).*

Katsiaryna Aharodnik, Anna Feldman, and Jing Peng. 2018. Designing a Russian idiom-annotated corpus. In *Proceedings of the Eleventh International Conference on Language Resources and Evaluation (LREC 2018)*, Miyazaki, Japan. European Language Resources Association (ELRA).

Ondřej Bojar, Rajen Chatterjee, Christian Federmann, Yvette Graham, Barry Haddow, Shujian Huang, Matthias Huck, Philipp Koehn, Qun Liu, Varvara Logacheva, Christof Monz, Matteo Negri, Matt Post, Raphael Rubino, Lucia Specia, and Marco Turchi. 2017. Findings of the 2017 conference on machine translation (WMT17). In *Proceedings of the Second Conference on Machine Translation*, pages 169–214, Copenhagen, Denmark. Association for Computational Linguistics.

Rajesh Kumar Chakrawarti, Himani Mishra, and Pratosh Bansal. 2017. Review of machine translation techniques for idea of Hindi to English idiom translation. *International journal of computational intelligence research*, 13(5):1059–1071.

Verna Dankers, Christopher G Lucas, and Ivan Titov. 2022. Can Transformer be Too Compositional? Analysing Idiom Processing in Neural Machine Translation. *arXiv preprint arXiv:2205.15301.*

Michael Denkowski and Alon Lavie. 2014. Meteor Universal: Language Specific Translation Evaluation for Any Target Language. In *Proceedings of the Ninth Workshop on Statistical Machine Translation*, pages 376–380, Baltimore, Maryland, USA. Association for Computational Linguistics.

Jacob Devlin, Ming-Wei Chang, Kenton Lee, and Kristina Toutanova. 2018. BERT: Pre-training of deep bidirectional transformers for language understanding. *arXiv preprint arXiv:1810.04805.*

GülŞen Eryiğit, Ali Şentaş, and Johanna Monti. 2022. Gamified crowdsourcing for idiom corpora construction. *Natural Language Engineering*, page 1–33.

Marzieh Fadaee, Arianna Bisazza, and Christof Monz. 2018. Examining the Tip of the Iceberg: A Data Set for Idiom Translation. In *Proceedings of the Eleventh International Conference on Language Resources and Evaluation (LREC 2018).* European Language Resources Association (ELRA).

Afsaneh Fazly, Paul Cook, and Suzanne Stevenson. 2009. Unsupervised type and token identification of idiomatic expressions. *Computational Linguistics*, 35(1):61–103.

Andrew F Hayes and Klaus Krippendorff. 2007. Answering the call for a standard reliability measure for coding data. *Communication methods and measures*, 1(1):77–89.

John Hughes. 2021. krippendorffsalpha: An R package for measuring agreement using Krippendorff's alpha coefficient. *arXiv preprint arXiv:2103.12170.*

Pierre Isabelle, Colin Cherry, and George Foster. 2017. A challenge set approach to evaluating machine translation. *arXiv preprint arXiv:1704.07431.*

Murathan Kurfali and Robert Östling. 2020. Disambiguation of potentially idiomatic expressions with contextual embeddings. In *Joint Workshop on Multiword Expressions and Electronic Lexicons, Barcelona, Spain (Online), December 13, 2020*, pages 85–94.

Mike Lewis, Yinhan Liu, Naman Goyal, Marjan Ghazvininejad, Abdelrahman Mohamed, Omer Levy, Ves Stoyanov, and Luke Zettlemoyer. 2019. BART: Denoising sequence-to-sequence pre-training for natural language generation, translation, and comprehension. *arXiv preprint arXiv:1910.13461*.

Changsheng Liu and Rebecca Hwa. 2016. Phrasal substitution of idiomatic expressions. In *Proceedings of the 2016 Conference of the North American Chapter of the Association for Computational Linguistics: Human Language Technologies*, pages 363–373, San Diego, California. Association for Computational Linguistics.

Pengfei Liu, Weizhe Yuan, Jinlan Fu, Zhengbao Jiang, Hiroaki Hayashi, and Graham Neubig. 2021. Pre-train, prompt, and predict: A systematic survey of prompting methods in natural language processing. *arXiv preprint arXiv:2107.13586*.

Qi Liu, Matt J Kusner, and Phil Blunsom. 2020. A survey on contextual embeddings. *arXiv preprint arXiv:2003.07278*.

Kishore Papineni, Salim Roukos, Todd Ward, and Wei-Jing Zhu. 2002. BLEU: a Method for Automatic Evaluation of Machine Translation. In *Proceedings of the 40th Annual Meeting of the Association for Computational Linguistics*, pages 311–318, Philadelphia, Pennsylvania, USA. Association for Computational Linguistics.

Colin Raffel, Noam Shazeer, Adam Roberts, Katherine Lee, Sharan Narang, Michael Matena, Yanqi Zhou, Wei Li, and Peter J Liu. 2020. Exploring the Limits of Transfer Learning with a Unified Text-to-Text Transformer. *Journal of Machine Learning Research*, 21:1–67.

Ricardo Rei, Craig Stewart, Ana C Farinha, and Alon Lavie. 2020. COMET: A neural framework for MT evaluation. In *Proceedings of the 2020 Conference on Empirical Methods in Natural Language Processing (EMNLP)*, pages 2685–2702, Online. Association for Computational Linguistics.

Giancarlo Salton, Robert Ross, and John Kelleher. 2014a. An empirical study of the impact of idioms on phrase based statistical machine translation of English to Brazilian-Portuguese. In *Proceedings of the 3rd Workshop on Hybrid Approaches to Machine Translation (HyTra)*, pages 36–41, Gothenburg, Sweden. Association for Computational Linguistics.

Giancarlo Salton, Robert Ross, and John Kelleher. 2014b. Evaluation of a substitution method for idiom transformation in statistical machine translation. In *Proceedings of the 10th Workshop on Multiword Expressions (MWE)*, pages 38–42, Gothenburg, Sweden. Association for Computational Linguistics.

Prateek Saxena and Soma Paul. 2020. EPIE dataset: a corpus for possible idiomatic expressions. In *23rd International Conference on Text, Speech, and Dialogue*, pages 87–94, Brno, Czech Republic. Springer.

Yves Scherrer. 2020. TaPaCo: A corpus of sentential paraphrases for 73 languages. In *Proceedings of the 12th Language Resources and Evaluation Conference*, pages 6868–6873, Marseille, France. European Language Resources Association.

Caroline Sporleder and Linlin Li. 2009. Unsupervised recognition of literal and non-literal use of idiomatic expressions. In *Proceedings of the 12th Conference of the European Chapter of the ACL (EACL 2009)*, pages 754–762, Athens, Greece. Association for Computational Linguistics.

Minghuan Tan and Jing Jiang. 2021. Does BERT understand idioms? A probing-based empirical study of BERT encodings of idioms. In *Proceedings of the International Conference on Recent Advances in Natural Language Processing (RANLP 2021)*, pages 1397–1407.

Kenan Tang. 2022. PETCI: A Parallel English Translation Dataset of Chinese Idioms. *arXiv*, abs/2202.09509.

Tan Tien-Ping and Dong Jia Jun. 2021. Translating idioms using paraphrasing, machine translation and rescoring. *Turkish Journal of Computer and Mathematics Education (TURCOMAT)*, 12(3):1942–1946.

University of Oxford. 2022. Oxford Learner's Dictionaries. Available online: `https://www.oxfordlearnersdictionaries.com/definition/english/idiom?q=idiom`.

Ashish Vaswani, Noam Shazeer, Niki Parmar, Jakob Uszkoreit, Llion Jones, Aidan N Gomez, Łukasz Kaiser, and Illia Polosukhin. 2017. Attention is all you need. *Advances in neural information processing systems*, 30.

Haifeng Wang, Hua Wu, Zhongjun He, Liang Huang, and Kenneth Ward Church. 2021. Progress in Machine Translation. *Engineering*.

Xiao-mei Yu, Wen-zhi Feng, Hong Wang, Qian Chu, and Qi Chen. 2020. An attention mechanism and multi-granularity-based Bi-LSTM model for Chinese Q&A system. *Soft Computing*, 24(8):5831–5845.

Jianing Zhou. 2021. Idiomatic sentence generation and paraphrasing. Master's thesis, University of Illinois.

Jianing Zhou, Hongyu Gong, and Suma Bhat. 2021. PIE: A parallel idiomatic expression corpus for idiomatic sentence generation and paraphrasing. In *Proceedings of the 17th Workshop on Multiword Expressions (MWE 2021)*, pages 33–48, Online. Association for Computational Linguistics.

Jianing Zhou, Ziheng Zeng, Hongyu Gong, and Suma Bhat. 2022. Idiomatic Expression Paraphrasing without Strong Supervision. In *Proceedings of the AAAI Conference on Artificial Intelligence*, volume 36, pages 11774–11782.

Tadej Škvorc, Polona Gantar, and Marko Robnik-Šikonja. 2022. MICE: Mining Idioms with Contextual Embeddings. *Knowledge-Based Systems*, 235:107606.

A Appendix

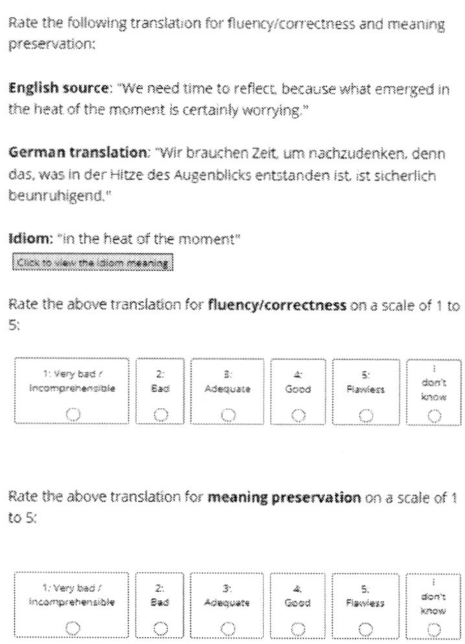
Rate the following translation for fluency/correctness and meaning preservation:

English source: "We need time to reflect, because what emerged in the heat of the moment is certainly worrying."

German translation: "Wir brauchen Zeit, um nachzudenken, denn das, was in der Hitze des Augenblicks entstanden ist, ist sicherlich beunruhigend."

Idiom: "in the heat of the moment"

Click to view the idiom meaning

Rate the above translation for **fluency/correctness** on a scale of 1 to 5:

1: Very bad / Incomprehensible	2: Bad	3: Adequate	4: Good	5: Flawless	I don't know
○	○	○	○	○	○

Rate the above translation for **meaning preservation** on a scale of 1 to 5:

1: Very bad / Incomprehensible	2: Bad	3: Adequate	4: Good	5: Flawless	I don't know
○	○	○	○	○	○

An example of a survey question presented to participants as part of our human-based evaluation.

EUREKA: EUphemism Recognition Enhanced Through KNN-based Methods and Augmentation

Sedrick Scott Keh*[1], Rohit Bharadwaj*[2], Emmy Liu†[1], Simone Tedeschi†[3,4], Varun Gangal[1], Roberto Navigli[3]
[1]Carnegie Mellon University, [2]Mohamed bin Zayed University of Artificial Intelligence, [3]Sapienza University of Rome, [4]Babelscape, Italy
{skeh,mengyan3,vgangal}@cs.cmu.edu, rohit.bharadwaj@mbzuai.ac.ae
{tedeschi,navigli}@diag.uniroma1.it

Abstract

We introduce EUREKA, an ensemble-based approach for performing automatic euphemism detection. We (1) identify and correct potentially mislabelled rows in the dataset, (2) curate an expanded corpus called *EuphAug*, (3) leverage model representations of Potentially Euphemistic Terms (PETs), and (4) explore using representations of semantically close sentences to aid in classification. Using our augmented dataset and kNN-based methods, EUREKA[1] was able to achieve state-of-the-art results on the public leaderboard of the Euphemism Detection Shared Task, ranking first with a macro F1 score of 0.881.

1 Introduction

Euphemisms are mild or indirect expressions used in place of harsher or more direct ones. In everyday speech, euphemisms function as a means to politely discuss taboo or sensitive topics (Danescu-Niculescu-Mizil et al., 2013), to downplay certain situations (Karam, 2011), or to mask intent (Magu and Luo, 2018). The Euphemism Detection task is a key stepping stone to developing natural language systems that are able to process (Tedeschi et al., 2022; Liu et al., 2022; Jhamtani et al., 2021) and generate non-literal texts.

In this paper, we detail our methods to the Euphemism Detection Shared Task at the EMNLP 2022 FigLang Workshop[2]. We achieve performance improvements on two fronts:

1. **Data** – We explore various data cleaning and data augmentation (Shorten and Khoshgoftaar, 2019; Feng et al., 2021; Dhole et al., 2021) strategies. We identify and correct potentially mislabelled rows, and we curate a new dataset called *EuphAug* by extracting sentences from a large unlabelled corpus using semantic representations of the sentences or euphemistic terms in the initial training corpus.

2. **Modelling** – We explore various representational and design choices, such as leveraging the LM representations of the tokens for euphemistic expressions (rather than the `[CLS]` token) and incorporating sentential context through kNN augmentation and deep averaging networks.

Using these methods, we develop a system called EUREKA which achieves a macro F1 score of 0.881 on the public leaderboard and ranks first among all submissions. We found the data innovations to be more significant in our case, indicating that euphemistic terms can be classified with some accuracy if potentially euphemistic spans are identified earlier in the pipeline.

2 Task Settings and Dataset

2.1 Task Settings

The task and dataset are specified by the Euphemism Detection Shared Task, which uses a subset of the euphemism detection dataset of Gavidia et al. (2022). The goal of the task is to classify a Potentially Euphemistic Term (PET) enclosed within delimiter tokens as either literal or euphemistic in that context. The training set contained 207 unique PETs and 1571 samples, of which 1106 are classified as euphemisms.

2.2 Data Cleaning

Gavidia et al. (2022) characterize common sources of ambiguity and disagreement among annotators. However, while exploring the data, we also spotted some rows which were, beyond a reasonable doubt, mislabelled (Table 1). This is an artifact of many human-annotated datasets (Frenay and Verleysen, 2014) and is a potential source of noise that could negatively affect performance (Nazari et al., 2018).

* Equal contribution by S. Keh and R. Bharadwaj
† Equal contribution by E. Liu and S. Tedeschi
[1]Our code is available at https://github.com/sedrickkeh/EUREKA
[2]https://sites.google.com/view/figlang2022/home?authuser=0

Proceedings of the 3rd Workshop on Figurative Language Processing (FLP), pages 111 - 117
December 8, 2022 ©2022 Association for Computational Linguistics

Sentence Containing PET	Sense (Euph.)	Sense (Non-Euph.)	Label (Original)	Label (Corrected)
Does your software collect any information about me, my listening or my surfing habits? Can it be <disabled>?	Handicapped	Switched off	1	0
Europe developed rapidly [...] Effective and <economical> movement of goods was no longer a maritime monopoly.	Prudent or frugal	Related to the economy	0	1
The Lancers continued to hang on to the <slim> one-point line as Golden West started a possession following [...]	Thin (physical appearance)	Thin (non-physical)	1	0

Table 1: Examples of incorrectly labelled sentences identified by our data cleaning pipeline. The label is 1 if the term is used euphemistically, 0 otherwise.

Motivated by this, we design a data cleaning pipeline to quickly identify and correct such errors (Figure 1). Since the goal is simply to correct as many errors as possible (rather than to be perfectly accurate), we take a few heuristic liberties in our design choices. First, to maximize yield and avoid dealing with less impactful PETs, we filter out PETs which appear <10 times or are classified as positive/negative >80% of the time. This leaves us with 33 PETs. We then manually curate a sense inventory (euphemistic vs. non-euphemistic senses) using context clues and BabelNet definitions (Navigli and Ponzetto, 2012, v5.0). To ensure the quality of the sense inventory, we have multiple members of our team look through the assigned euphemistic and non-euphemistic senses and verify their appropriateness. Next, for each sentence, we replace the PET with its euphemistic meaning and calculate the BERTScores (Zhang* et al., 2020) between the initial sentences and PET-replaced sentences. Replacing euphemistic PETs should not change the semantics drastically and hence should result in a high BERTScore, while replacing non-euphemistic PETs would lead to a low BERTScore. To identify potentially misclassified sentences, we therefore look for positively-classified sentences with low BERTScores or negatively-classified sentences with high BERTScores. We heuristically set this threshold at the halfway mark: if a sentence is among the top half of BERTScores and has a negative label (or among the bottom half and has a positive label), then we flag it as "potentially mislabelled". We end up with 203 potentially mislabelled sentences.

Once these potentially mislabelled sentences have been identified, we go through them manually and correct the ones which we identify as incorrectly labelled, such as the ones in Table 1. In cases where we are unsure of what the label should be (e.g. ambiguous cases as mentioned in Gavidia et al. (2022)), we leave the original label. As was done with the sense inventories, multiple members of our team then verify that the corrections made are appropriate. Although this still involves some human labor, it is much more tractable as compared to having to go through the entire dataset. Out of the 203 potentially mislabelled rows, we modify the labels of 25 of them.

2.3 *EuphAug* Corpus

In addition to data cleaning, we also use data augmentation techniques to gather an extended corpus, which we call *EuphAug*. We explore two variants of *EuphAug*, as outlined below:

1. **Representation-Based Augmentation** – We search in an external corpus for additional sentences in which specific PETs appear, then assign a label to these PETs based on their vector representations. We call this procedure *EuphAug-R*.

Let our training set (provided by task organizers) be S. Consider a PET p, which appears in sentences $s_1, s_2, \dots s_k \in S$, with corresponding labels $l_{s_1}, l_{s_2}, \dots l_{s_k} \in \{0, 1\}$. We search in an external corpus C (i.e., WikiText) for n sentences $c_1, \dots, c_n$ containing the PET p. Finally, for each sentence $c_1, \dots, c_n$ we assign label l_{c_j} as follows:

Algorithm 1 EuphAug-R

Task: Given sentence c_j containing PET p, assign l_{c_j}.
for $s_i \in \{s_1, s_2, \dots s_k\}$ **do**
  Find $\text{dist}_i = \text{dist}(s_i, c_j)$
Find $M = \arg\max\{\text{dist}_1, \text{dist}_2, \dots, \text{dist}_k\}$.
Find $m = \arg\min\{\text{dist}_1, \text{dist}_2, \dots, \text{dist}_k\}$.
if $\text{dist}_M \geq \delta \wedge (|\ \text{dist}_M - \delta\ | > |\ \text{dist}_m - \epsilon\ |)$ **then**
  Add c_j to augmented corpus with label $l_{c_j} = l_{s_M}$
else if $\text{dist}_m \leq \epsilon \wedge (|\ \text{dist}_m - \epsilon\ | > |\ \text{dist}_M - \delta\ |)$ **then**
  Add c_j to augmented corpus with label $l_{c_j} = 1 - l_{s_M}$
else
  Do not add c_j to augmented corpus.
end if

where δ and ϵ are manually-tuned thresholds, and $\text{dist}(a, b)$ represents the cosine distance between the sentential embeddings [3] of a and b. In other

[3]https://www.sbert.net/

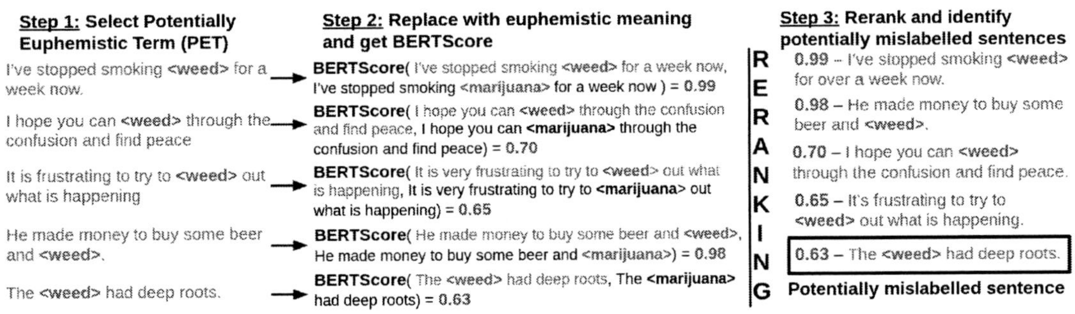

Figure 1: Example of our data cleaning pipeline to automatically identify potentially mislabelled sentences. Red indicates positively classified sentences and blue indicates negatively classified sentences.

words, we augment our corpus with a sentence c_j only if it is sufficiently similar to, or sufficiently different from, all sentences containing the PET in S. We set $n = 20$ as the maximum number of sentences extracted from C for a PET p, and obtain a corpus of around 4700 additional examples.

2. **Sense-Based Augmentation** – While *EuphAug-R* aims to augment the dataset by finding existing sentences which already contain the PETs, this sense-based approach, instead, considers sentences which contain the senses of the PETs. This is done using the sense inventories created in Section 2.2 and searching the WikiText corpus. For instance, to find new sentences containing "disabled", we do not search directly for appearances of "disabled". Rather, we search for instances of "handicapped" and replace these occurrences with "disabled" to obtain our positive examples. We then search for instances of "switched off" and replace those occurrences with "disabled" to obtain our negative examples. We call this expanded corpus *EuphAug-S*. We sample at most 20 new sentences for each sense (if there are less than 20 occurrences in WikiText, we take all of those present). In addition, some words have senses which cannot be summarized concisely in a single expression (e.g. "slim" in Table 1), so we drop these from our search terms. The final *EuphAug-S* contains 950 rows.

3 Methodology

For our baseline model, we use a pretrained RoBERTa-large model (Liu et al., 2019). For evaluation, we use the macro F1-score, as specified by the shared task description.

3.1 PET Embeddings

We leverage the embeddings of PET expressions. While models usually perform classification by passing the `[CLS]` token embedding to a final classifier layer, we instead pass the embeddings of PET tokens. If there are multiple tokens within the PET, we take the sum of these tokens. We hypothesize that `[CLS]` embeddings lose out on the discriminatory power due to pooling of all the embeddings in a sentence, and that using the PET embeddings as signals can better allow the model to focus specifically on the PET senses.

3.2 Making use of context

Additionally, we explore using context outside of the PET embeddings. Intuitively, euphemistic and non-euphemistic terms tend to be used in slightly different contexts, with euphemistic terms often being used to discuss sensitive topics. We experiment with two ways to make use of this additional context, as detailed below.

3.2.1 kNN Augmentation

Inspired by work on retrieval-based language models (Alon et al., 2022; Khandelwal et al., 2019), we augment the baseline model with a kNN store of the training set, and interpolate the classification probabilities of the base model and a kNN-based model. We follow the usual setup for such a model, with the exception that y is a binary variable indicating euphemistic/non-euphemistic rather than a token from the vocabulary.

In Equation 1, $\mathcal{N}$ refers to the 5 closest neighbours to x in the training set retrieved through cosine similarity with the `[CLS]` token generated by RoBERTa, or $f(x)$. (k_i, v_i) refers to the key and value, in this case `[CLS]` tokens for other sentences, and a binary variable, respectively. In Equa-

Feature Tested	Model	Dataset	P	R	F1
-	RoBERTa-large	Original	0.8756	0.8168	0.8399
1) Data Cleaning	RoBERTa-large	Cleaned	0.8617	0.8300	0.8435
2) Data Augmentation	RoBERTa-large	Original+*EuphAug-R*	0.8529	0.8388	0.8452
	RoBERTa-large	Original+*EuphAug-S*	0.8728	0.8306	0.8481
3) PET Embedding	RoBERTa-large+PET	Original	0.8694	0.8408	0.8533
4) Additional Context	RoBERTa-large+KNN	Original	0.8769	0.8210	0.8411
	RoBERTa-large+DAN	Original	0.8481	0.7983	0.8181
Final Models	RoBERTa-large+PET	Cleaned	0.8728	0.8471	0.8582
	RoBERTa-large+PET	Cleaned+*EuphAug-S*	0.8692	0.8584	0.8633
	RoBERTa-large+PET+KNN	Cleaned	0.8792	0.8517	0.8635
Final Ensemble	Model 1 + Model 2 + Model 3	-	**0.8994**	**0.8788**	**0.8884**

Table 2: We independently test 4 features. The final models leverage one or more of these features, and the final ensemble combines the 3 final models. Results are averaged over 10 random seeds. For the final ensemble, since we are just interested in the best possible model, we pick the best random seeds from each model instead of averaging. The three best seeds have F1-scores of 0.8734, 0.8864, and 0.8842, which is slightly improved by our ensembling.

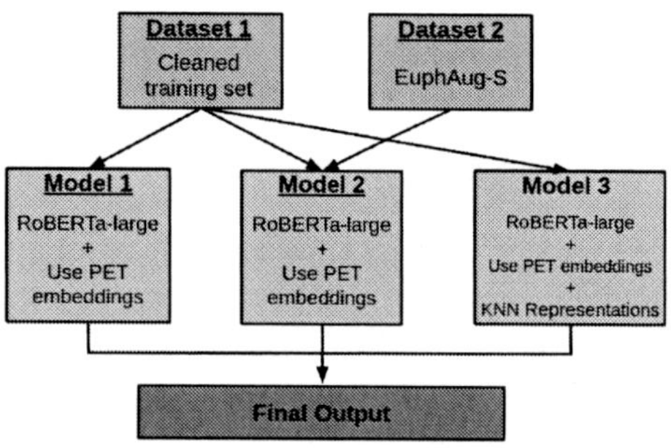

Figure 2: Models and datasets used in the ensemble.

tion 2, this value is combined with the probabilities from the base PET model.

$$p_{\text{kNN}}(y|x) \propto \sum_{(k_i,v_i)\in\mathcal{N}} \mathbb{1}(y_i{=}v_i)\exp\left(-d(k_i,f(x))\right) \quad (1)$$

$$p(y|x)=\lambda p_{kNN}(y|x)+(1-\lambda)p_{PET}(y|x) \quad (2)$$

3.2.2 Deep Averaging Network

Additionally, we experiment with a Deep Averaging Network (DAN) over embeddings for all the tokens of the sentence (Iyyer et al., 2015). For a sentence with tokens $x_1, ..., x_N$, we take the mean vector for the entire sentence: $z = \frac{1}{N}\sum_{i=1}^{N} x_i$. We then pass the mean vector through a linear layer with dropout before a second linear layer which outputs to $\mathbb{R}^2$. Note that unlike the original DAN, we do not drop out tokens, as this was found to hurt performance in preliminary experiments.

3.3 Ensembling

Our final model consists of an ensemble of 3 different models, as shown in Figure 2 and Table 2. For this ensemble, we simply consider a majority vote of the outputs of the 3 models.

4 Experiments and Results

4.1 Implementation Settings

We split our dataset into train-validation-test splits with an 80-10-10 ratio. Note that this splitting is done before any data cleaning or augmentation, so the validation and test sets are not affected by these processes. Further implementation details are provided in Appendix A.

4.2 Automatic Evaluation Results

The main results are shown in Table 2. We independently test 4 features, namely data cleaning, data augmentation, PET embedding, and kNN. Based on the results of these tests, our final models then use combinations of some or all of these features. From the results in Table 2, we make the following observations:

1. **The data augmentation methods lead to slight increases in performance.** This is true for both data cleaning and augmentation, demonstrating the usefulness of reducing noise and adding high-quality training data. In general, augmentation methods lead to larger gains because adding more data is especially useful in our task, where each PET may appear in the original training data only a few times.

2. **Using embeddings of the PET embeddings (instead of the `[CLS]` classifier token) significantly increases performance.** As hypothesized, this is likely because the `[CLS]` token may have too wide of a scope since it needs to represent the entire sentence, while the PET tokens can specifically give us information about the PET terms we are trying to classify.

3. **KNN models lead to slight increase, while DAN models lead to significant decrease, in performance.** In general, our changes in the data side have much greater effects than our changes in the modelling side. For kNN, we think that the neighbors may provide slight signals but are likely drowned out by the original logits, which leads to incremental changes.

We note that the advantages of the kNN method may increase with more data, as this method benefits greatly from a larger datastore. However, as *EuphAug-S* has a relatively large number of examples compared to the training data, we decided to construct the datastore based on only the original training data, as we did not know if there was any significant domain shift between the test data and *EuphAug-S*, and we did not judge the additional samples to be worth this risk.

These three observations motivate our choices for final models to ensemble. In addition, we submit our final ensembled model to the Shared Task leaderboard, and it received an F1 score of 0.881, ranking first place among all submissions.

5 Related Work

Euphemism detection is a relatively underexplored task. In this paper, we use the euphemism PET dataset gathered by Gavidia et al. (2022). Lee et al. (2022) also use this dataset, but for the task of extracting PETs from a given sentence. In the past, other methods have focused specifically on certain types of euphemisms, such as drugs (Zhu et al., 2021), firing/lying/stealing (Felt and Riloff, 2020), and hate speech (Magu and Luo, 2018).

Below, we further detail some of the methods and techniques previously explored in this area. Zhu et al. (2021) use BERT and the masked language model objective to create candidate euphemisms based on input target keywords of sensitive topics. Zhu and Bhat (2021) extend this to multi-word euphemistic phrases using SpanBERT. Similar to the previous paper, they also generate and filter a list of euphemistic phrase candidates, then rank these candidates using probabilities from the masked language model. Meanwhile, Felt and Riloff (2020) use sentiment analysis methods to detect euphemisms, exploring various properties associated with sentiment such as affective polarity, connotation, and intensity.

Other studies contextualize euphemism detection in a specific use case. For instance, Magu and Luo (2018) train models to detect hateful content or euphemistic hate speech. They employ word embeddings and network analysis, creating clusters of euphemisms by using eigenvector centralities as a ranking metric. Furthermore, euphemism detection can also be used in crime detection. Yuan et al. (2018) analyze jargon from cybercrime marketplaces to find patterns in phrases or code words commonly used in underground communications. However, these two methods use static word embeddings, which do not take into account the context. This may affect performance, as context is very important for euphemisms. In contrast, our method uses context-aware embeddings of transformer-based models.

6 Conclusion and Future Work

We proposed EUREKA, a method for classifying euphemistic usage in a sentence. This is an ensemble model that uses ideas such as data cleaning, data augmentation, representations of Potentially Euphemistic Terms (PETs), and k-nearest-neighbor predictions. Our EUREKA system achieves a score of 0.881 and ranks first on the public leaderboard for the Shared Task.

In the future, we hope to extend our methods to dysphemisms or other figurative language instances. It is also interesting to consider a zero-shot setting for euphemism detection, where euphemisms during test time are unseen during training. Figurative language generation, rather than detection, could also be a fruitful area to explore.

Limitations

Our current model and classifer are deficient in terms of their interpretability on certain aspects, and it would be interesting to explore more interpretable models to ensure that the features used to classify euphemisms can transfer to other scenarios. The models and datasets are limited to English (Bender and Friedman, 2018), and euphemisms in other languages are definitely worth exploring. However, this was not in the scope of the shared task

Due to computational resources, we were not able to explore larger models. For example, it is possible that larger models such as GPT-J or GPT-Neo would perform better on this task. However, we leave this to future work.

Acknowledgments

The authors gratefully acknowledge the support of the ERC Consolidator Grant MOUSSE No. 726487 under the European Union's Horizon 2020 research and innovation programme.

Thanks to Graham Neubig for discussion and helpful suggestions.

References

Uri Alon, Frank Xu, Junxian He, Sudipta Sengupta, Dan Roth, and Graham Neubig. 2022. Neuro-symbolic language modeling with automaton-augmented retrieval. In *International Conference on Machine Learning*, pages 468–485. PMLR.

Emily M Bender and Batya Friedman. 2018. Data statements for natural language processing: Toward mitigating system bias and enabling better science. *Transactions of the Association for Computational Linguistics*, 6:587–604.

Cristian Danescu-Niculescu-Mizil, Moritz Sudhof, Dan Jurafsky, Jure Leskovec, and Christopher Potts. 2013. A computational approach to politeness with application to social factors. In *Proceedings of the 51st Annual Meeting of the Association for Computational Linguistics (Volume 1: Long Papers)*, pages 250–259, Sofia, Bulgaria. Association for Computational Linguistics.

Kaustubh D Dhole, Varun Gangal, Sebastian Gehrmann, Aadesh Gupta, Zhenhao Li, Saad Mahamood, Abinaya Mahendiran, Simon Mille, Ashish Srivastava, Samson Tan, et al. 2021. Nl-augmenter: A framework for task-sensitive natural language augmentation. *arXiv preprint arXiv:2112.02721*.

Christian Felt and Ellen Riloff. 2020. Recognizing euphemisms and dysphemisms using sentiment analysis. In *Proceedings of the Second Workshop on Figurative Language Processing*, pages 136–145, Online. Association for Computational Linguistics.

Steven Y Feng, Varun Gangal, Jason Wei, Sarath Chandar, Soroush Vosoughi, Teruko Mitamura, and Eduard Hovy. 2021. A survey of data augmentation approaches for nlp. *arXiv preprint arXiv:2105.03075*.

Benoit Frenay and Michel Verleysen. 2014. Classification in the presence of label noise: A survey. *IEEE Transactions on Neural Networks and Learning Systems*, 25(5):845–869.

Martha Gavidia, Patrick Lee, Anna Feldman, and Jing Peng. 2022. Cats are fuzzy pets: A corpus and analysis of potentially euphemistic terms. *CoRR*, abs/2205.02728.

Mohit Iyyer, Varun Manjunatha, Jordan Boyd-Graber, and Hal Daumé III. 2015. Deep unordered composition rivals syntactic methods for text classification. In *Proceedings of the 53rd Annual Meeting of the Association for Computational Linguistics and the 7th International Joint Conference on Natural Language Processing (Volume 1: Long Papers)*, pages 1681–1691, Beijing, China. Association for Computational Linguistics.

Harsh Jhamtani, Varun Gangal, Eduard Hovy, and Taylor Berg-Kirkpatrick. 2021. Investigating robustness of dialog models to popular figurative language constructs. In *Proceedings of the 2021 Conference on Empirical Methods in Natural Language Processing*, pages 7476–7485.

Savo Fouad Karam. 2011. Truths and euphemisms: How euphemisms are used in the political arena.

Urvashi Khandelwal, Omer Levy, Dan Jurafsky, Luke Zettlemoyer, and Mike Lewis. 2019. Generalization through memorization: Nearest neighbor language models.

Patrick Lee, Martha Gavidia, Anna Feldman, and Jing Peng. 2022. Searching for PETs: Using distributional and sentiment-based methods to find potentially euphemistic terms. In *Proceedings of the Second Workshop on Understanding Implicit and Underspecified Language*, pages 22–32, Seattle, USA. Association for Computational Linguistics.

Emmy Liu, Chenxuan Cui, Kenneth Zheng, and Graham Neubig. 2022. Testing the ability of language models to interpret figurative language. In *Proceedings of the 2022 Conference of the North American Chapter of the Association for Computational Linguistics: Human Language Technologies*, pages 4437–4452, Seattle, United States. Association for Computational Linguistics.

Yinhan Liu, Myle Ott, Naman Goyal, Jingfei Du, Mandar Joshi, Danqi Chen, Omer Levy, Mike Lewis, Luke Zettlemoyer, and Veselin Stoyanov. 2019. Roberta: A robustly optimized bert pretraining approach. Cite arxiv:1907.11692.

Rijul Magu and Jiebo Luo. 2018. Determining code words in euphemistic hate speech using word embedding networks. In *Proceedings of the 2nd Workshop on Abusive Language Online (ALW2)*, pages 93–100, Brussels, Belgium. Association for Computational Linguistics.

Roberto Navigli and Simone Paolo Ponzetto. 2012. Babelnet: The automatic construction, evaluation and application of a wide-coverage multilingual semantic network. *Artificial Intelligence*, 193(0):217 – 250.

Zahra Nazari, Masoom Nazari, Mir Sayed Shah, and Dongshik Kang. 2018. Evaluation of class noise impact on performance of machine learning algorithms.

Connor Shorten and Taghi M Khoshgoftaar. 2019. A survey on image data augmentation for deep learning. *Journal of big data*, 6(1):1–48.

Simone Tedeschi, Federico Martelli, and Roberto Navigli. 2022. ID10M: Idiom identification in 10 languages. In *Findings of the Association for Computational Linguistics: NAACL 2022*, pages 2715–2726, Seattle, United States. Association for Computational Linguistics.

Thomas Wolf, Lysandre Debut, Victor Sanh, Julien Chaumond, Clement Delangue, Anthony Moi, Pierric Cistac, Tim Rault, Remi Louf, Morgan Funtowicz, Joe Davison, Sam Shleifer, Patrick von Platen, Clara Ma, Yacine Jernite, Julien Plu, Canwen Xu, Teven Le Scao, Sylvain Gugger, Mariama Drame, Quentin Lhoest, and Alexander Rush. 2020. Transformers: State-of-the-art natural language processing. In *Proceedings of the 2020 Conference on Empirical Methods in Natural Language Processing: System Demonstrations*, pages 38–45, Online. Association for Computational Linguistics.

Kan Yuan, Haoran Lu, Xiaojing Liao, and Xiaofeng Wang. 2018. Reading thieves' cant: Automatically identifying and understanding dark jargons from cybercrime marketplaces. In *USENIX Security Symposium*.

Tianyi Zhang*, Varsha Kishore*, Felix Wu*, Kilian Q. Weinberger, and Yoav Artzi. 2020. Bertscore: Evaluating text generation with bert. In *International Conference on Learning Representations*.

Wanzheng Zhu and Suma Bhat. 2021. Euphemistic phrase detection by masked language model. In *Findings of the Association for Computational Linguistics: EMNLP 2021*, pages 163–168, Punta Cana, Dominican Republic. Association for Computational Linguistics.

Wanzheng Zhu, Hongyu Gong, Rohan Bansal, Zachary Weinberg, Nicolas Christin, Giulia Fanti, and Suma Bhat. 2021. Self-supervised euphemism detection and identification for content moderation. In *42nd IEEE Symposium on Security and Privacy*.

Appendix A Implementation Settings

For most methods, we use a batch size of 4, learning rate of 5e-6, and we train for 10 epochs. Training was done mostly on a Google Colaboratory environment using Tesla V100, P100 GPUS, and on a workstation having NVIDIA Quadro RTX 6000 with 24GB of VRAM. With RoBERTa-large, training for 10 epochs took around 30-40 minutes. We use the HuggingFace library (Wolf et al., 2020) for model implementation, as well as for implementing the Trainer function. All other hyperparameters (e.g. learning rate decay, warmup steps, etc.) follow the default ones used by the Trainer function in HuggingFace.

An insulin pump? Identifying figurative links in the construction of the drug trafficking lexicon

Antonio Reyes† ‡ and **Rafael Saldívar**†
†Autonomous University of Baja California
School of languages
‡ Autonomous University of Queretaro
School of Languages and Literature
antonio.reyesp@uaq.mx, rafaelsaldivar@uabc.edu.mx

Abstract

One of the remarkable characteristics of the drug trafficking lexicon is its elusive nature. In order to communicate information related to drugs or drug trafficking, the community uses several terms that are mostly unknown to regular people, or even to the authorities. For instance, the terms jolly green, joystick, or jive are used to refer to marijuana. The selection of such terms is not necessarily a random or senseless process, but a communicative strategy in which figurative language plays a relevant role. In this study, we describe an ongoing research to identify drug-related terms by applying machine learning techniques. To this end, a data set regarding drug trafficking in Spanish was built. This data set was used to train a word embedding model to identify terms used by the community to creatively refer to drugs and related matters. The initial findings show an interesting repository of terms created to consciously veil drug-related contents by using figurative language devices, such as metaphor or metonymy. These findings can provide preliminary evidence to be applied by law agencies in order to address actions against crime, drug transactions on the internet, illicit activities, or human trafficking.

1 Introduction

Drug trafficking is a sensitive issue, apart from being a social taboo to some people. Unfortunately, this is a growing phenomenon that is impacting our lives on different layers. Our language is a sample of such impact. Nowadays, it is common to hear or read about drugs everywhere, but the words to name them are not necessarily the ones we are used to hear. Terms such as cocaine, marijuana, crack, or heroine have been replaced by new items, which at first glance seem to be totally unconnected to the context of drugs. Joy, candy, horse, or insulin are new labels used by the community to refer to drug-related contents. Some of them turn quite frequent in mass media and, consequently, in our daily communication; therefore, one can find them registered in specialized dictionaries or lexicons. Some others, on the other hand, are completely obscure to regular people, or even to the authorities.

In this context, the drug trafficking lexicon does not refer exclusively to the jargon to name drugs, but also to the terms used to refer to matters related to them. For instance, production of illegal substances (*colitas* (joint)), criminal gangs (*tacuaches*), or even, political speech (*sembrar* (use/fabricate false evidence)). In this respect, the drug trafficking lexicon is not only used by drug traffickers or by drug addicts. It has reached all social strata and is used by different actors. Furthermore, the drug trafficking lexicon underlines how this phenomenon permeates society through language: The fact of constantly being exposed to such lexicon makes this phenomenon something natural to everyone. Therefore, the consequences of violence, corruption, or institutional collapse derived from the use and sale of illegal drugs tend to be normalized.

Given this context, below we describe an ongoing research to identify drug-related terms by applying machine learning techniques. Our focus is on making explicit what people consciously (creatively) aim to veil regarding the drug trafficking lexicon. Specifically, we are interested in applying NLP techniques to identify figurative devices, such as metaphor or metonymy, as they are understood in Cognitive Grammar (see Langacker (1990)). To this end, we built a data set about drug trafficking in Spanish. This data set contains documents from different sources, such as press, blogs, song lyrics, or political speech. All of them were retrieved from Mexican sites; thus, the data set could be regarded as representative of the Mexican dialect and setting. The data set was used to train a simple word embedding model to identify links between the known terms and the ones created by means of figurative language. For instance, items such as cocaine, heroine, or drug (known terms)

Proceedings of the 3rd Workshop on Figurative Language Processing (FLP), pages 118 - 124
December 8, 2022 ©2022 Association for Computational Linguistics

share similar representations with the ones found in woman, or insulin (figurative terms).

With this study, we aim to provide preliminary evidence that can be applied by law agencies, for instance, to address actions against crime, drug transactions on the internet, illicit activities, human trafficking, among others.

The rest of the article is organized as follows: In Section 2 we describe and exemplify the notion of drug trafficking lexicon. Likewise, we provide a brief review about the scientific papers about the topic. In Section 3 we introduce the data set and detail the experiments that we carried out. In Section 4 we report the results and discuss the possible implications. Finally, in Section 5 we present the final remarks and some pointers to address the future work.

2 The drug trafficking lexicon

At first glance, the drug trafficking lexicon could be regarded as slang, or even as a non-standard vocabulary. Either way, it is common to think that it is only used by some isolated social groups. However, this type of language has gone from marginalization to daily speech in several countries. Mexico is a fair example of it. For instance, in the Mexican context, it is quite natural to hear in the news about *levantones* to refer to someone that has been kidnapped, and likely killed, by a criminal gang. In fact, the Dictionary of Mexican Spanish (El Colegio de México) has registered the term *levantón*, from the verb *levantar* (to lift up) as the action of kidnapping someone violently.

As noted from the example, the drug trafficking lexicon describes more than drug names. It used to depict a reality in which violence, corruption, and institutional collapse predominate; everything derived from the phenomenon of drug trafficking.

With respect to its features, it is necessary to specify that the drug trafficking lexicon is not a language properly; i.e. as far as it has been reported, it has no linguistic particularities to be considered an independent system. It is featured, on the contrary, by a set of lexical items (some of them neologisms) and phrases, whose meaning is often completely obscure to most people.

In this regard, the drug trafficking lexicon has compiled an interesting linguistic inventory, which has been fed from different sources, such as mass and social media, literature, political speech, and popular folklore. In this respect, in the field of Linguistics, some researchers have addressed their approaches from lexicographical perspectives. In particular, some of them have focused on the Latin American context. For instance, Acosta and Mora (2008) conducted a study about the criminal slang and drugs in Colombian prisons. They showed how such criminal jargon is characterized by a frequent use of linguistic devices, such as metaphors and metonymies (this seems to be repeated in the language of drug trafficking in Mexico, since the technical lexicon associated with crime is impregnated with metaphorical expressions (see Mattiello (2008)). More recently, in a research about the phenomenon of drug trafficking in the North American context, Saldívar (2022) described that one of the semantic fields in which this type of lexicon changes constantly is that of drug names. He stressed that this fact is evident in the creation of new terms, as well as in the reassignment of new meanings to the existing ones, both in English and Spanish. Likewise, Pressacco (2022) described violence and drug trafficking in Mexico from the so called narco language. The author distinguishes two classes to categorize this language: literal and figurative. Finally, she provides an interesting list of terms, phrases and constructions to exemplify the drug dealers argot.

In different locations and specialized areas, Sanmartín (1998) analyzed the jargon of the criminals in Spain. She described some linguistic mechanisms to characterize this lexicon, in particular, synonymy and polysemy. On the other hand, Torregrosa and Sánchez-Reyes (2015), in their study about English law enforcement, analyzed the use of conceptual metaphors related to drugs for educational purposes in the training of lawyers. Finally, in a computational approach, Reyes and Saldívar (2022) worked with narco language from a NLP perspective. They suggested a representation of narco-related concepts by identifying triggers of criminal content in corpus.

3 Unveiling figurative language

In this section, we firstly describe the data set used to build the word embedding model; then, we detail the processes to identify the figurative terms.

3.1 Data set

In order to train a vector model to represent the linguistic characteristics of this phenomenon, we gathered a specialized data set about drug trafficking in Spanish. It is worth noting that, given the particularities of the topic (see Section 1), it is unlikely to find a large and public data set to be used. That is why we built a data set with documents of different genres to cover, as much as possible, a broad scenario about the topic. As we have previously pointed out, the documents come from Mexican sources only. This fact could be understood as a local application rather than a generic one. However, according to Bender and Friedman (2018) when explaining the notion of data statements, this reduction could provide the necessary context to allow the community to better understand how the experimental results could be generalized.

Table 1: General statistics per category.

Category	Tokens	Types
Blogs	229,338	29,585
Political	399,006	20,891
Essays	543,718	43,601
Literature	370,794	38,726
Narcocorridos	79,664	12,554
Press	728,165	83,514

The data set is divided in six categories according to the genres that we took into consideration to gather the documents: Blogs, political speech, essays, literature, *narcocorridos* (song lyrics about drug dealers), and press. Due to the linguistic differences across genres, the data set is imbalanced. For instance, with respect to the amount of documents, we collected a few set of texts for the categories *essays* and *literature*, compared to the amount of texts for the category *blogs* and *press*. This impacts on the size of each category. Thus, an essay about drug trafficking is more extensive (and elaborated) than a post in a blog; likewise, the specificity of information devoted to this phenomenon by the politicians in their speeches is completely different to the one reported by the journalists in the news. In addition, the amount of drug-related content is not necessarily the same across the six categories. For instance, compared to the *narcocorridos*, *literature* contains lesser specific information. This is due to the documents in the latter category are stories about drug trafficking within a narrative plot, while the former contains lyrics specifically written to drug dealers.

In order to balance the data set, we randomly select 50,000 words per category. In Table 1, we provide some statistics for each category based on the distinction type/token.

The data set is available upon request for academic purposes.

3.2 Word embeddings representation

In the past years, one of the most effective learning techniques employed in Machine Learning is word embeddings. They could be defined as representations of words in a vector space by grouping similar items (see Mikolov et al. (2013b)). This technique has been used to model linguistic information with excellent outcomes. For instance, Bakarov (2018) has explained that word embeddings are able to efficiently predict syntactic and semantic properties in natural language.

Almeida and Xexéo (2019) divide this technique into two main models: Prediction-based (local data models) and count-based (global data models). Although the use of word embeddings is growing in Machine Learning and other fields, some authors have reported a few drawbacks regarding their implementation in fine-grained tasks. One of the most important drawbacks is the unclear differentiation between semantic relatedness and semantic similarity (Bakarov, 2018).

Given the efficiency to represent linguistic properties, there are various word embeddings implementations. For instance, Word2Vec, FastText, or GloVe. In this study, we have adopted the Word2Vec algorithm, as described by Mikolov et al. (2013a,b).

The Word2Vec algorithm emphasizes the meaning and semantic relations between words by computing their co-occurrence in different documents. In this respect, Dessì et al. (2021) highlight that this algorithm is focused on modeling the context of words by exploiting ML and statistics in such a way the word vectors that share some regularities, regardless of the document they come from, are located nearly in the vector space. Therefore, the resulting representations allow the recognition of relatedness between words. This is why we have selected the algorithm to carry out the vector representation.

This algorithm can be trained using Continuous Bag-Of-Words (CBOW) or Skip-grams. We trained different models using the Skip-gram representation and modifying the vector dimension, window distance, and word frequency. It is worth mentioning that we also trained some models using a

CBOW representation in a preliminary setup; however, the outcomes were not as informative as with the skip-grams. Finally, in order to tune the vectors and come up with an integral model, we trained a final average model by finding the centroid of all the skip-grams representations. To this end, the Spearman's correlation coefficient was used to calculate the models' similarity (Hellrich and Hahn, 2016). The centroid model was used to run the experiments reported below.

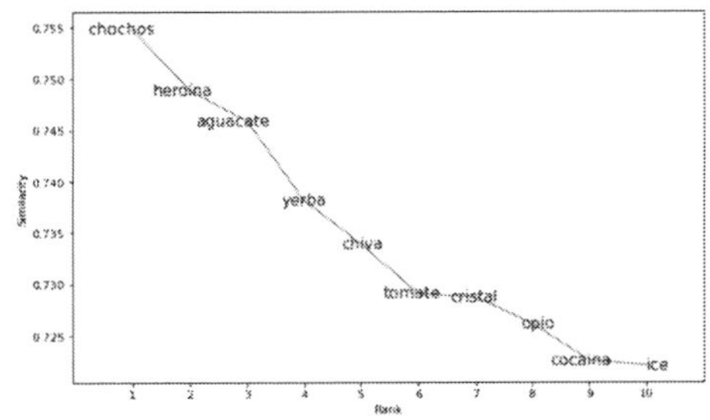

Figure 1: 10 most similar terms for the term *coca*.

3.3 Figurative terms identification

According to Saldívar (2022), apart from its crypticity, one of the characteristics of the drug trafficking lexicon is its speed of change. This fact makes it elusive. Therefore, in order to identify the figurative terms, we firstly decided to use some known terms to build a dictionary. This resource groups items reported in the specialized literature as prototypical of the domain. Thus, they are used as seeds to identify a set of unrelated terms. For instance, a known term registered in the dictionary is *dinero* (money), this term is a seed to locate what others items appear close to it in the vector space. Some of the items are known terms (*morralla* (cash)), but there are others apparently unrelated (*cabezón* (big head)). The latter terms are the ones we are interested in, since they are likely figurative terms to refer to the known term. *Cabezón* is a metonymy to refer to the 100 dollars bills because Franklin's head in these bills is bigger. So, an utterance such as *Antes contaba morralla, ahora puros cabezones* (I was used to cash counting, now big heads counting only) makes sense both semantically and pragmatically.

The dictionary contains 439 terms. According tho the previous explanation, the first step was to look for the 439 terms in our data. Of those terms, only 183 appeared in our documents. The second step consisted in reducing the range of search. Thus, for each known term, we retrieved its 10 most similar words. This produces a total of 1,830 possible figurative terms to be analyzed. In Figure 1, we show the 10 most similar words for the term *coca* (abbreviation of cocaine).

In this figure, we can observe some known terms linked to the drug trafficking context: *Yerba* (marijuana), *cristal*, *chochos*, *ice* (cocaine), *heroína* (heroine), and *opio* (opium), which most people relate automatically to the drug trafficking lexicon. However, there are other items that, at first glance, are totally unconnected to drugs: *tomate* (tomato), *aguacate* (avocado), or *chiva* (female goat). Initially, these items should be discarded due to they do not belong to the drug trafficking context. Nonetheless, given our interest in identifying figurative terms, they become the spotlight. If the vectors of these items are similar to the vectors of the known terms, then this could hypothetically be a sign about some semantic similarity.

In order to confirm this hypothesis, we focused on retrieving the vectors for each unknown term in such a way we could map the figurative usages. For instance, considering the information depicted in Figure 1, we first removed the known terms (*yerba*, *cristal*, *chochos*, *heroína*, *opio*, and *cocaína*); then, we retrieved the vectors for the unrelated terms (*tomate*, *aguacate*, and *chiva*). Finally, given the seed term (*coca* in this example), we mapped the known term and the unknown terms considering their distributional patterns in the vector space. In Figure 2, we show the 10 most similar terms for the presumably unrelated terms *aguacate* and *chiva*.

4 Results

The result of the previous processes is a set of 505 drug-related terms; i.e. an average of 3 unrelated items per known term.

Subsequently, we analyzed the vectors of the 505 candidates in order to recognize elements to connect them to the drug trafficking context. This is clearer if we observe Figure 2: From the 10 most similar words for *aguacate*, the items *churros* (marijuana), *mulas* (drug trafficker), *tachas* (cocaine), and *fuman* (inflectional form of the verb to smoke) are totally drug-related. The same fact for *chiva*. The words *inyecto*, *meto* (inflectional forms of the verbs to inject and to do drugs, respectively), and *chochos* are commonly used by the community to refer to drugs. This fact corroborates that some

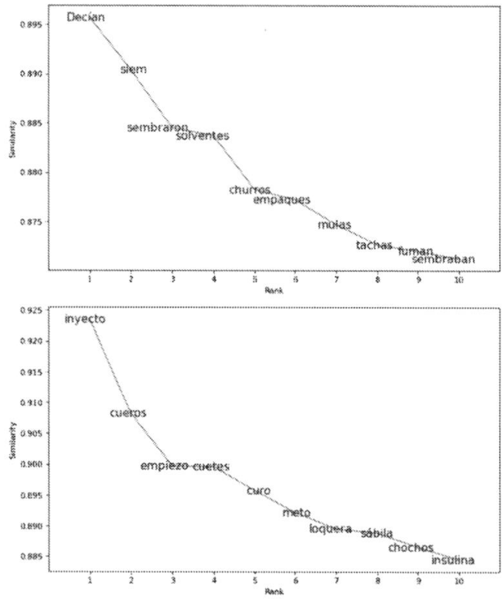

Figure 2: 10 most similar terms for *aguacate* and *chiva.*

of the unconnected items are closely linked to the context of drugs. However, there were others items whose vectors proved the contrary. For instance, *tomate*, from Fig. 1, whose 10 most similar words referred to food only.

Given this result, it could be stated that some unconnected items are, in fact, figurative terms to implicitly express drug-related content. Nonetheless, such assumption should be assessed by the experts; i. e. we could identify some unrelated terms regarding drug trafficking; however, we are not capable of saying that they mean anything to the community. In addition, there is not labeled data to compare our findings. Therefore, in order to provide arguments to validate our findings, we contacted an expert on the topic in Mexico. This expert has published several academic papers and some books about narco and, specifically, about narco language.

Prior to contacting the expert, we grouped the unrelated terms in clusters with the purpose of identifying an underlying semantic structure. To this end, we ran a similarity analysis for the 505 terms considering their co-occurrences in the whole data set. Figure 3 shows a sample of the clusters presented to the expert.

4.1 Evaluation

Once we contacted the expert, we asked him to revise the 505 terms to check whether or not they are terms used in a drug-related context. If so, to confirm, as far as he knows, whether or not they are used to refer or name any term cryptically.

The feedback provided by the expert is summarized as follows: With respect to the first task, he validated all the 505 terms as part of the domain. However, regarding the second task, he marked only 151 terms as terms used to refer to drug-related content in a cryptic manner; i. e. around 70% are already terms in usage in that context, although we did not know (it is worth stressing that we are not part of the community), and only 30% are items, cryptic enough, to be considered figurative terms. In addition, the expert provided the equivalents for the unknown terms. For instance, terms such as *cuete* (gun) and *insulina* (insulin), or *yongo* (yongo) were translated to syringe and place to do drugs, respectively[1].

4.2 Discussion

The feedback given by the expert confirmed that this approach is identifying drug-related terms efficiently. Although some of the 505 terms are already known in the domain, their usage is not very frequent to be registered in some lexical resource. For instance, they are not part of the terms we used to build our dictionary (see 3.3). In this respect, this is evidence about the dynamism of any language. The drug trafficking lexicon, in particular, must be very dynamic due to it expresses outlaw issues mainly.

With respect to the 151 cryptic terms, they confirm such dynamism. They are obscure enough to be able to determine what they mean in the drug trafficking context. However, beyond the fact that they can be considered as figurative terms, it is necessary to identify what kind of figurative device underlies them. In this regard, we are in the process of manually analyzing the linguistic contexts of the 151 terms in order to recognize patterns to explain their usage in this domain. Nonetheless this is work in progress, we have noticed that some of the terms, in fact, rely on figurative language to create an implicit link between the unrelated terms and the known term. For instance, considering the information depicted in Figure 3, terms

[1]To better understand the information given in Figure 3, we provide the translations (not the equivalents) for the known terms in each cluster: *aspirina* (aspirin), *cobija* (blanket), *raya* (line), *cajuela* (trunk), *cocinar* (to cook), *polvo*, *polvito* (dust), *hierba* (grass), *dulce* (candy), *hielo* (ice), *nieve* (snow), *cristal* (glass), *hielera* (icebox), *narcomensaje* (narco-message), *sabanas* (sheets), *goma* (gum), *enteipar* (to apply masking tape on someone), *arete* (earring), *bajón* (downer).

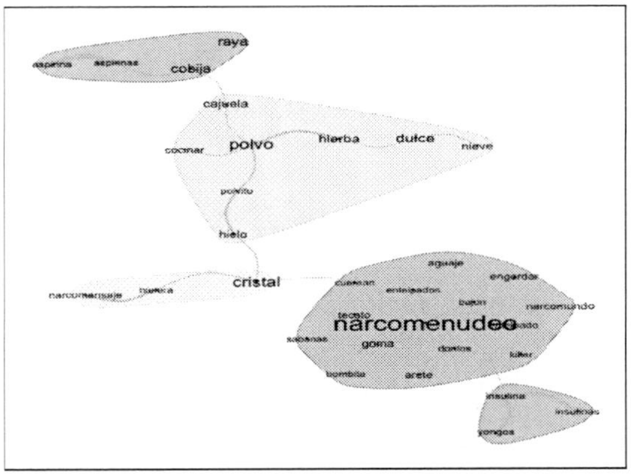

Figure 3: Sample of clusters given the similarity analysis.

such as *nieve* (referring to the drug named crystal) or *insulina* (referring to a syringe and/or the action of being injected) in the green and purple clusters, respectively, are understandable if we assume a metaphoric and metonymic frame. Thus, the term *nieve* (snow) is metaphorically mapped to *polvo* (powder) and then to *cristal* (crystal). First, a feature like the color is the link to secure the comparison. Subsequently, a component *(polvo)* of the whole (crystal) is used to connect to the same drug by profiling its rock-like appearance. Something similar happens to the second term. The *insulina* (insulin) is a legal drug to be injected into the diabetic patients. Many drugs are supposed to be injected to enhance the effect. Therefore, by using this term, the speaker is metonymically connecting a component (syringe) of the whole action (to be injected with one of such drugs).

It is also necessary to highlight that not all the terms can be explained by means of an underlying figurative device. There are terms that appear from other linguistic mechanisms. However, as have been reported by some experts on the topic, figurative language (especially metaphor, metonymy, and analogy) is quite frequent to create terms within the domain, either for cryptic purposes, attenuation, or as a simple exercise of creativity (see (Saldívar, 2022; Torregrosa and Sánchez-Reyes, 2015; Mattiello, 2008)).

5 Conclusions and future work

In this study we have approached an unusual phenomenon in Natural Language Processing: the drug trafficking lexicon. Our focus was on automatically identifying possible figurative terms to refer to drug-related contents in Spanish. To this end, we used a data set about drug trafficking in Mexico and built a word embedding model to identify the terms. The results showed that the model could identify a set of supposed unrelated terms to the domain. Those terms were validated by a human expert; however, only 30% of them are cryptic terms. This means, although they are known by the community, people out of the drug trafficking context do not know them. Therefore, they can be used to veil criminal content. Finally, we have outlined a possible explanation about their successful usage within the domain. In this respect, although this is still work in progress, we have suggested that this can be explained in terms of figurative devices, such as metaphor and metonymy, which according to the Cognitive Linguistics foundations (Langacker, 1990), are part of our conceptual structure.

As future work, it is planned to collect data from other variants to extend the scope of this approach, as well as to deepen the analysis of the linguistic mechanisms to better understand how this lexicon works to successfully communicate veiled information within a complex linguistic system. Thus, the insights could shed light on how this social phenomenon has linguistically permeated our society in broader terms. To conclude, we consider that works like this one could provide evidence to be applied to address actions against different illicit activities.

Limitations

Some of the limitations of this study rely on the data. As mentioned in the manuscript, the data set built to carry out the experiments was gathered considering only one specific dialect. Although the insights could be representative of the phenomenon, they cannot be generalized to the entire system. This is manly due to the social particularities of drug trafficking. For instance, the drug names or gangs depend on social elements extracted from the culture. However, the underlying figurative mechanism is consistent from dialect to dialect, and from language to language, as reported in the literature (see Lakoff (1987); Lakoff and Johnson (1980); Langacker (1987); Goldberg (1997), and others). Another issue regarding the data is the lack of labeled data to compare the results, as well as to use them to prove how our approach performs. In this regard, it is worth highlighting that topics like this one can represent a major challenge when collecting data in some countries. Given the corruption and lawless of some governments, it could be very risky to find proper data and collect a representative corpus.

The human validation is also a limitation. It is unusual to have only one vision to validate the outcomes; however, it is very difficult to find specialists about the topic. This impacts on the number of available experts to assess our findings.

Finally, the manual analysis of the results must be concluded in order to provide a complete description of the figurative devices present in the data. In addition, although we have focused on the figurative terms, we notice that several of the known terms were generated by means of figurative language. Therefore, they should be explained to present a more comprehensive description of the phenomenon.

References

D. Acosta and C. Mora. 2008. Subcultura carcelaria. Diccionario de la jerga canera. *Escuela Penitenciaria Nacional.*

Felipe Almeida and Geraldo Xexéo. 2019. Word embeddings: A survey. *CoRR*, abs/1901.09069.

Amir Bakarov. 2018. A survey of word embeddings evaluation methods. *CoRR*, abs/1801.09536.

Emily M. Bender and Batya Friedman. 2018. Data statements for natural language processing: Toward mitigating system bias and enabling better science. *Transactions of the Association for Computational Linguistics*, 6:587–604.

Danilo Dessì, Diego Reforgiato Recupero, and Harald Sack. 2021. An assessment of deep learning models and word embeddings for toxicity detection within online textual comments. *Electronics*, 10(7).

El Colegio de México. Diccionario del español de México. `http://dem.colmex.mx`. Online on February, 2022.

A. Goldberg. 1997. Construction grammar. In E.K. Brown and J.E. Miller, editors, *Concise Encyclopedia of Syntactic Theories*. Elsevier Science Limited.

Johannes Hellrich and Udo Hahn. 2016. Bad Company—Neighborhoods in neural embedding spaces considered harmful. In *Proceedings of COLING 2016, the 26th International Conference on Computational Linguistics: Technical Papers*, pages 2785–2796, Osaka, Japan. The COLING 2016 Organizing Committee.

G. Lakoff. 1987. *Women, Fire and Dangerous Things: What Categories Reveal About the Mind.* University of Chicago Press, Chicago.

G. Lakoff and M. Johnson. 1980. *Metaphors we live by.* University of Chicago Press, Chicago.

R. Langacker. 1987. *Foundations of Cognitive Grammar.* Stanford University Press.

R. Langacker. 1990. *Concept, Image and Symbol. The Cognitive Basis of Grammar.* Mounton de Gruyter.

E Mattiello. 2008. An introduction to english slang: a description of its morpholgy, semantics and sociology. *Polimetrico.*

Tomas Mikolov, Kai Chen, Gregory S. Corrado, and Jeffrey Dean. 2013a. Efficient estimation of word representations in vector space. In *ICLR*.

Tomas Mikolov, Ilya Sutskever, Kai Chen, Greg S Corrado, and Jeff Dean. 2013b. Distributed representations of words and phrases and their compositionality. In *Advances in neural information processing systems*, pages 3111–3119.

Coralie Pressacco. 2022. *La violencia del narcotráfico en México. Análisis lexicológico.* Universidad de Colima.

A. Reyes and R. Saldívar. 2022. Figurative language in atypical contexts: Searching for creativity in narco language. *Appl. Sci.*, 12, pages = 3: 1642, note = DOI: 10.3390/app12031642.

R. Saldívar. 2022. Metáforas y metonimias conceptuales en nombres de drogas en inglés y en español. *Forma y Función*, 35(1).

J Sanmartín. 1998. *Lenguaje y cultura marginal. El argot de la delincuencia.* Universitat de Valencia.

G Torregrosa and S Sánchez-Reyes. 2015. Raising metaphor awareness in english for law enforcement. *Procedia Soc. Behav. Sci.*, 212:304–308.

Can Yes–No Question-Answering Models be Useful for Few-Shot Metaphor Detection?

Lena Dankin
School of Computer Science
Tel Aviv University
lenadank@tau.ac.il

Kfir Bar
School of Computer Science
Reichman University
kfir.bar@post.runi.ac.il

Nachum Dershowitz
School of Computer Science
Tel Aviv University
nachum@tau.ac.il

Abstract

Metaphor detection has been a challenging task in the NLP domain both before and after the emergence of transformer-based language models. The difficulty lies in subtle semantic nuances that are required to be able to detect metaphor and in the scarcity of labeled data. We explore few-shot setups for metaphor detection, and also introduce new question-answering data that can enhance classifiers that are trained on a small amount of data. We formulate the classification task as a question-answering one, and train a question-answering model. We perform extensive experiments for few shot on several architectures and report the results of several strong baselines. Thus, the answer to the question posed in the title is a definite "Yes!"

1 Introduction

In the past year, pretrained language models established themselves as the foundation for state-of-the-art solutions for most of the common NLP tasks. Usually, one should fine tune a model on a dataset specific to her task and domain so as to achieve high performance, and this requires labeled data, which is not always available in the necessary quantity. In the past few years, a large body of work has been dedicated to transfer learning between domains and models (Alyafeai et al., 2020), and application of models trained on one task to another task by prompting (Brown et al., 2020; Schick and Schütze, 2021). These techniques reduce the amount of training data needed for a specific task, and enable the sharing of semantic knowledge between models.

Metaphor detection is a highly challenging task in the NLP domain. It relies on word level, delicate semantics that are not trivial even for humans, and, thus, even though pretrained language models do encode some metaphoric information (Aghazadeh et al., 2022), the task is not considered solved. As for languages other than English – high quality language models are already often available (Seker et al., 2021; Antoun et al., 2020), but metaphor detection without appropriate labeled data is very difficult (Schneider et al., 2022), and this is why few-shot is a relevant scenario to study.

As Su et al. (2020) suggest, metaphor detection can be viewed as a reading-comprehension task where one needs to answer a question whether a specific word is metaphoric or literal in the context of a given sentence. They formatted metaphor detection as a classification task of the full sentence (global context), the word in question and a short sentence fragment that contains this query word (local context). The texts, along with POS tags of each word, are fed into the classifier to obtain a prediction. Similar to the vast majority of classification tasks, this classifier is expected to learn how to identify metaphors based on the labels it is provided during training, but the input itself does not suggest that the task is regarding metaphor.

We take the reading-comprehension approach further in two respects: First, we experiment with several phrasings of explicit natural-language questions about whether the query token is metaphoric within the context of the sentence. Thus we employ the capability of large language models to understand delicate semantics (at least up to some point) by querying the models directly. Second, we design our classifier with a backbone of a yes–no question-answering model. Given the context sentence, we ask explicitly, "Is the word in question metaphoric in this context?" We evaluate our

Proceedings of the 3rd Workshop on Figurative Language Processing (FLP), pages 125 - 130
December 8, 2022

model in a few-shot scenario and compare it to several baselines.

2 Related Work

Over the past few years, as in other fields in NLP, transformer-based architectures have dominated the models for metaphor detection. Leong et al. (2020) report the results of the 2020 shared task, and can be referred to for prior models that are not transformer based.

DeepMet (Su et al., 2020), the highest-scoring system in that shared task, transforms metaphor detection into a reading comprehension task, querying for the label of each token given its context in the sentence. The classification model is a siamese network that encodes two contexts for the token – the entire sentence and the sentence fragment wherein the token is located. The model is also fed with the POS tag of the token in question.

MelBERT (Choi et al., 2021) is a transformer-based model that applies two theoretical concepts of metaphor identification: (1) A metaphor's literal meaning is different from its metaphorical meaning in the sentence. (2) The metaphor is unusual in the context of the sentence. MrBERT (Song et al., 2021) employs a similar architecture to MelBERT, adding the encoded grammatical local context of the query token.

Few-shot learning refers to learning from a small number of training examples. One few-shot technique for NLP is pattern exploiting training (PET) (Schick and Schütze, 2021) over the RoBERTa architecture. PET, requiring task-specific unlabeled data, uses natural language patterns to represent the inputs as cloze style questions. Answers are then filled in by the predictions of the language model. ADAPET (Tam et al., 2021) extends PET by providing denser supervision during fine-tuning, outperforming PET without the need of unlabeled data.

GPT-3 (Brown et al., 2020) takes few-shot abilities forward and demonstrates strong performance without directly fine-tuning on task-specific data. Instead, in the few-shot scenario, at inference time it is presented with a few labeled instances as a part of the query.

3 Metaphor Detection Model

Metaphor detection can be regarded as a token-classification task within a sentence. The word in question in a given sentence can be classified either as metaphoric or literal.

In this work, we experiment with the formulation of metaphor detection as a yes–no question answering (QA) task with two concatenated inputs: a *question* and a *passage*, that is, a text segment to which the question refers. For each word in question, we suggest several different constructions of *questions* and *passages*. These formulations are shown in Table 1 and are referred to as f1–f3. We add f4 to assess the contribution of a question-like phrasing.

Our suggested architecture for metaphor detection is presented in Figure. 1. We begin by fine-tuning a RoBERTa base model (Liu et al., 2019) on QA data (see Section 4.1). Next, this model is fine-tuned on different sizes of metaphor data, phrased as questions.

The results are compared to the RoBERTa base model and to DeepMet. Since we are aiming to analyse the advantages of the QA model in a few-shot scenario, rather than to outperform the state of the art, our baseline models are ones that are similar in terms of architecture and additional resources. Training on the entire VUA dataset we are experimenting with, the RoBERTa baseline achieves the F1 score of 71.4, while MelBERT, the current state of the art, attains an F1 of 72.3.

4 Data

4.1 Yes–No Question-Answering Datasets

BoolQ. BoolQ (Clark et al., 2019) is a reading comprehension dataset comprised of 13K yes–no questions on various topics, each question relates to a different passage. The train split consist of 9.4K instances, with a ratio of 0.62 positive:negative labels.

WordNet. We utilize WordNet (Fellbaum, 1998) to extract yes–no questions to train a question answering model. WordNet curates a large collection of English lexemes, along with their different senses and different usage examples for each. When the different meanings are completely unrelated (like the word *bank* used for a financial institution or for sloping land), we rely on the context to determine the right meaning. This is somewhat related to the task of metaphor detection due to the fact that the model needs to address the alternative meanings a word may have.

For each *word* and *sentence example*, we con-

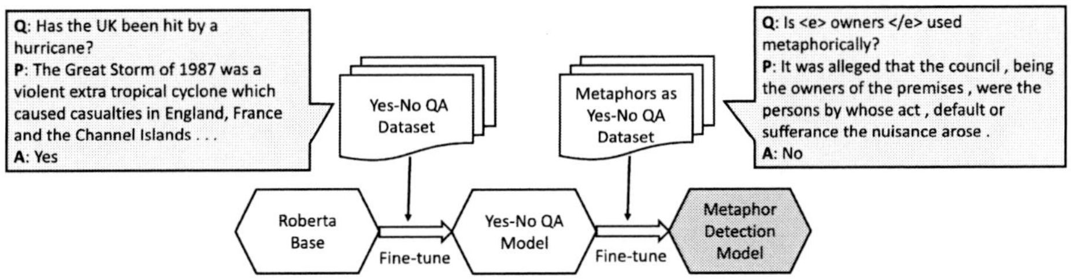

Figure 1: Our suggested metaphor detection model is fine-tuned on top of a yes–no question answering model.

	Question	Passage
f1	Is <e> *word* </e> used metaphorically?	*sentence*
f2	Is <e> *word* </e> used metaphorically in <s> *sentence* </s>?	*metaphor definition*
f3	Does <e> *word* </e> mean as if or like *word*?	*sentence*
f4	*word*	*sentence*

Table 1: Different formulations of questions for metaphor detection. For *metaphor definition* we use, "Metaphor is a figure of speech in which a word or phrase is applied to an object or action to which it is not literally applicable", taken from Merriam-Webster.

struct two sets of questions and passages using the following pattern:

Question: Does <e> *word* </e> mean *definition*?

Passage: *sentence example*

The correct definition is used to form a pair of question and passage with a "Yes" answer, and a random definition is chosen from the rest of the glosses for *word* to form a question with a "No" answer. This construction requires WordNet entries with more than one definition. We split the dataset into a training set of 32K instances and evaluation set of 7.5K instances. Both splits are fully balanced in respect to positive and negative labels. Note that there is no overlap of *words* between the two splits.

4.2 VUA Metaphor Dataset

We train and evaluate on the widely used VUA corpus (Steen et al., 2010), with the splits provided in (Leong et al., 2020); see Table 2 for details. The metaphoric tokens that are annotated in this corpus are of four parts of speech: nouns, verbs, adjectives and adverbs. We use VUA in two different formats: the original, token classification format, and the yes–no question answering format, denoted VUA_{qa}.

5 Experiments

5.1 QA Models

We begin by training several QA models, each on a different dataset: (a) The **BoolQ** model is trained on the entire BoolQ data. (b) **WordNet** is trained on the entire WordNet. (c) **Mix** is trained on both the BoolQ and WordNet datasets.

	Sentences	Tokens	Positive fraction
Train	12109	72611	18%
Test	4080	22198	17%

Table 2: Number of sentences, tokens and percentage of positive tokens in the VUA dataset.

The models are RoBERTa-base fine-tuned on two inputs – a question, followed by a passage (Devlin et al., 2019). We train for 10 epochs with batch size 32 and learning rate 1×10^{-5}. The number of training epochs is selected over the validation splits.

5.2 Metaphor Detection Models

We fine-tune each QA model on different subsets of VUA_{qa}, each subset of a different size, up to 500 sentences. Since each sentence contains multiple query tokens, for each sentence from VUA there are several training instance in VUA_{qa}, and thus 500 sentences annotated for metaphors on a token level transform into a few thousand training examples for all models that perform sequence classification for the single token in question. Each experiment is repeated four times with different random seeds, and we report the average F1 score and its standard deviation. In these experiments,

(a) BoolQ model (b) WordNet model (c) Mix model

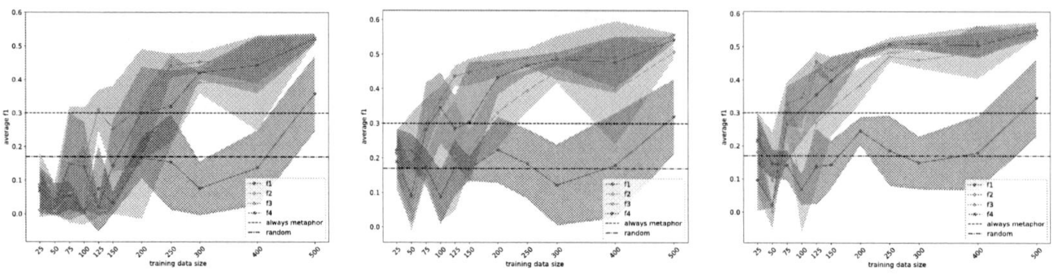

Figure 2: Average F1 score over different training-set sizes, averaged over random seeds. Shaded areas indicate the standard deviation.

our aim is to analyze the competence of the underlying QA models in a zero- and few-shot scenario. We use a single set of parameters for all QA-based models. Specifically, a learning rate of 1×10^{-5}, batch size of 32, and 2 epochs. Following (Chen et al., 2020), we balance the weight at a ratio of 1:3 in favor of the positive label.

We use the following two baselines:
(a) A RoBERTa based sequence classifier that is fine-tuned on top of the RoBERTa pretrained model, similar to the baseline in (Choi et al., 2021). The input to this model is the concatenation of the sentence and the token in question, with the separation token in between. This baseline evaluates the contribution of the underlying question model. Note that this input is different than f4, since for f4, the token in question is the first input to the classifier. Since f4 is an input to a QA underlying model that accepts the question first, we maintain this order. However, for the baseline, since there is no QA model involved, we keep the recommended order for such classification tasks.
(b) DeepMet. For each dataset size, we fine tune four models with different random seeds and the results are averaged, similarly as for the QA-based models.

For the RoBERTa baseline, we tune hyper-parameters for each training data size with the technique suggested by (Zheng et al., 2022). Specifically, we experimented with batch size of 32, learning rate in $\{1\times10^{-5}, 3\times10^{-5}\}$ and number of training epochs in $\{2, 3\}$. DeepMet is evaluated with its default hyper-parameters. We also experimented with a RoBERTa token base classification, a baseline suggested in (Chen et al., 2020). While performing similarly to the sequence classifier when both were trained on the full data (Choi et al., 2021), for the few-shot scenario it is inferior to the sequence based classifier, and thus we omit it from the figures. We include the score of a classifier that randomly predicts "Metaphor" with the probability of the positive class over the entire dataset (18%), and the score of the classifier that always predicts "Metaphor".

We begin with the evaluation of the different input patterns for our three models. Figure 2 shows the performance of the four patterns for each model. There is a clear advantage to all question-based patterns, with pattern f3 being the dominant one. Zero-shot is only relevant for our models, since the RoBERTa baseline is fine-tuned over a pretrained model and not a classification model. For all our models, the results in zero-shot mode are lower than the "always metaphor" baseline; thus, our architecture is not appropriate for this scenario.

Next, we assess the contribution of the underlying QA models. From Figure 2, we conclude that there is an overall advantage to the WordNet model over the BoolQ one across most patterns, and the Mix model is the best of all three.

In Figure 3, we compare our best model, namely, Mix with f3, with the best RoBERTa baseline and with DeepMet. Our model outperforms both baselines by a significant margin. In addition, we see a smaller standard deviation for our model, indicating that this architecture is more stable for small training datasets.

6 Conclusions and Future Work

QA-based models were shown to be effective for metaphor detection when training data is very limited. We analyzed the contribution of the question-like phrasing and the underlying QA model, and

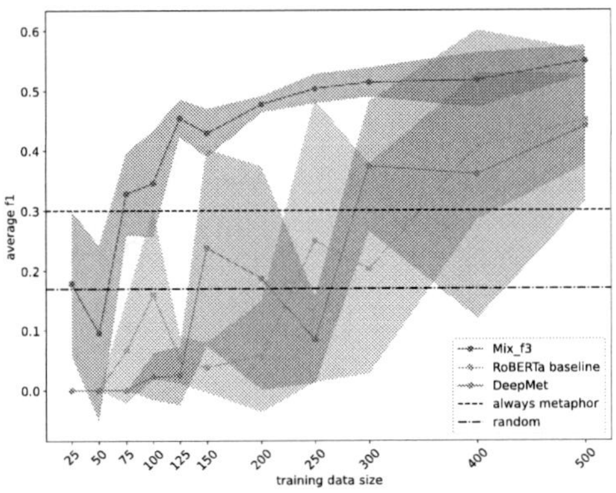

Figure 3: Mix model compared with the two baselines, RoBERTa and DeepMet.

report strong baselines for the few-shot scenario.

Another contribution is the use of WordNet. Transformer-based language models are pretrained on unlabeled data, thus many linguistic resources that were previously extensively used are less needed now. We have shown how the high-quality annotated data from WordNet can be utilized to train a QA model that can answer questions about semantics. We believe that similar techniques can generate high-quality datasets for training models for other NLP tasks.

As future work, we suggest exploring natural language inference models as underlying models for metaphor detection. Those models have been shown to be strong zero-shot models for various NLP tasks, so they can probably be of assistance in the metaphor domain. Another direction we aim to explore is the combination of our QA based technique with models such as DeepMet and MelBERT.

References

Ehsan Aghazadeh, Mohsen Fayyaz, and Yadollah Yaghoobzadeh. 2022. Metaphors in pre-trained language models: Probing and generalization across datasets and languages. In *Proceedings of the 60th Annual Meeting of the Association for Computational Linguistics*, volume 1: Long Papers, pages 2037–2050, Dublin, Ireland. Association for Computational Linguistics.

Zaid Alyafeai, Maged Saeed AlShaibani, and Irfan Ahmad. 2020. A survey on transfer learning in natural language processing. *arXiv preprint arXiv:2007.04239*.

Wissam Antoun, Fady Baly, and Hazem Hajj. 2020. AraBERT: Transformer-based model for Arabic language understanding. In *LREC 2020 Workshop Language Resources and Evaluation Conference*, pages 9–15, Marseille, France. European Language Resource Association.

Tom Brown, Benjamin Mann, Nick Ryder, Melanie Subbiah, Jared D Kaplan, Prafulla Dhariwal, Arvind Neelakantan, Pranav Shyam, Girish Sastry, Amanda Askell, Sandhini Agarwal, Ariel Herbert-Voss, Gretchen Krueger, Tom Henighan, Rewon Child, Aditya Ramesh, Daniel Ziegler, Jeffrey Wu, Clemens Winter, Chris Hesse, Mark Chen, Eric Sigler, Mateusz Litwin, Scott Gray, Benjamin Chess, Jack Clark, Christopher Berner, Sam McCandlish, Alec Radford, Ilya Sutskever, and Dario Amodei. 2020. Language models are few-shot learners. In *Advances in Neural Information Processing Systems*, volume 33, pages 1877–1901. Curran Associates, Inc.

Xianyang Chen, Chee Wee (Ben) Leong, Michael Flor, and Beata Beigman Klebanov. 2020. Go figure! Multi-task transformer-based architecture for metaphor detection using idioms: ETS team in 2020 metaphor shared task. In *Proceedings of the Second Workshop on Figurative Language Processing*, pages 235–243, Online. Association for Computational Linguistics.

Minjin Choi, Sunkyung Lee, Eunseong Choi, Heesoo Park, Junhyuk Lee, Dongwon Lee, and Jongwuk Lee. 2021. MelBERT: Metaphor detection via contextualized late interaction using metaphorical identification theories. In *Proceedings of the 2021 Conference of the North American Chapter of the Association for Computational Linguistics: Human Language Technologies*, pages 1763–1773, Online. Association for Computational Linguistics.

Christopher Clark, Kenton Lee, Ming-Wei Chang, Tom Kwiatkowski, Michael Collins, and Kristina Toutanova. 2019. BoolQ: Exploring the surprising difficulty of natural yes/no questions. In *Proceedings of the 2019 Conference of the North American Chapter of the Association for Computational Linguistics: Human Language Technologies*, volume 1 (Long and Short Papers), pages 2924–2936, Minneapolis, MN. Association for Computational Linguistics.

Jacob Devlin, Ming-Wei Chang, Kenton Lee, and Kristina Toutanova. 2019. BERT: Pre-training of deep bidirectional transformers for language understanding. In *Proceedings of the 2019 Conference of the North American Chapter of the Association for Computational Linguistics: Human Language Technologies*, volume 1 (Long and Short Papers), pages 4171–4186, Minneapolis, MN. Association for Computational Linguistics.

Christiane Fellbaum. 1998. *WordNet: An Electronic Lexical Database*. Bradford Books.

Chee Wee Leong, Beata Beigman Klebanov, Chris Hamill, Egon Stemle, Rutuja Ubale, and Xianyang Chen. 2020. A report on the 2020 VUA and TOEFL metaphor detection shared task. In *Proceedings of the Second Workshop on Figurative Language Processing*, pages 18–29, Online. Association for Computational Linguistics.

Yinhan Liu, Myle Ott, Naman Goyal, Jingfei Du, Mandar Joshi, Danqi Chen, Omer Levy, Mike Lewis, Luke Zettlemoyer, and Veselin Stoyanov. 2019. RoBERTa: A robustly optimized BERT pretraining approach. *ArXiv*, 1907.11692.

Timo Schick and Hinrich Schütze. 2021. Exploiting cloze-questions for few-shot text classification and natural language inference. In *Proceedings of the 16th Conference of the European Chapter of the Association for Computational Linguistics*, volume Main, pages 255–269, Online. Association for Computational Linguistics.

Felix Schneider, Sven Sickert, Phillip Brandes, Sophie Marshall, and Joachim Denzler. 2022. Metaphor detection for low resource languages: From zero-shot to few-shot learning in Middle High German. In *LREC Workshop on Multiword Expression (LREC-WS)*, pages 75–80, Marseille, France. European Language Resources Association.

Amit Seker, Elron Bandel, Dan Bareket, Idan Brusilovsky, Shaked Refael Greenfeld, and Reut Tsarfaty. 2021. AlephBERT: A pre-trained language model to start off your Hebrew NLP application. *ArXiv*, 2104.04052.

Wei Song, Shuhui Zhou, Ruiji Fu, Ting Liu, and Lizhen Liu. 2021. Verb metaphor detection via contextual relation learning. In *Proceedings of the 59th Annual Meeting of the Association for Computational Linguistics and the 11th International Joint Conference on Natural Language Processing*, volume 1: Long Papers, pages 4240–4251, Online. Association for Computational Linguistics.

Gerard J. Steen, Aletta G. Dorst, J. Berenike Herrmann, Anna Kaal, Tina Krennmayr, and Trijntje Pasma. 2010. *A Method for Linguistic Metaphor Identification: From MIP to MIPVU*, volume 14 of *Converging Evidence in Language and Communication Research*. John Benjamins Publishing.

Chuandong Su, Fumiyo Fukumoto, Xiaoxi Huang, Jiyi Li, Rongbo Wang, and Zhiqun Chen. 2020. DeepMet: A reading comprehension paradigm for token-level metaphor detection. In *Proceedings of the Second Workshop on Figurative Language Processing*, pages 30–39, Online. Association for Computational Linguistics.

Derek Tam, Rakesh R. Menon, Mohit Bansal, Shashank Srivastava, and Colin Raffel. 2021. Improving and simplifying pattern exploiting training. In *Proceedings of the 2021 Conference on Empirical Methods in Natural Language Processing*, pages 4980–4991, Online and Punta Cana, Dominican Republic. Association for Computational Linguistics.

Yanan Zheng, Jing Zhou, Yujie Qian, Ming Ding, Chonghua Liao, Li Jian, Ruslan Salakhutdinov, Jie Tang, Sebastian Ruder, and Zhilin Yang. 2022. FewNLU: Benchmarking state-of-the-art methods for few-shot natural language understanding. In *Proceedings of the 60th Annual Meeting of the Association for Computational Linguistics*, volume 1: Long Papers, pages 501–516, Dublin, Ireland. Association for Computational Linguistics.

An Exploration of Linguistically-Driven and Transfer Learning Methods for Euphemism Detection

Devika Tiwari and **Natalie Parde**
Natural Language Processing Laboratory
Department of Computer Science
University of Illinois Chicago
{dtiwari, parde}@uic.edu

Abstract

Euphemisms are often used to drive rhetoric, but their automated recognition and interpretation are under-explored. We investigate four methods for detecting euphemisms in sentences containing potentially euphemistic terms. The first three linguistically-motivated methods rest on an understanding of (1) euphemism's role to attenuate the harsh connotations of a taboo topic and (2) euphemism's metaphorical underpinnings. In contrast, the fourth method follows recent innovations in other tasks and employs transfer learning from a general-domain pre-trained language model. While the latter method ultimately (and perhaps surprisingly) performed best (F_1 = 0.74), we comprehensively evaluate all four methods to derive additional useful insights from the negative results.

1 Introduction

Euphemism is a ubiquitous figurative language tool, wherein the speaker refers to taboo topics in indirect, metaphorical terms to convey politeness or formality. Identifying euphemism can reveal tacit facts about the speaker's intention and the context of the utterance (Gómez, 2009), but there has been minimal work exploring how this might be done computationally (Felt and Riloff, 2020; Gavidia et al., 2022). In this paper, we compare the performance of four methods for automated euphemism detection. The first two methods identify euphemism based on expected sentiment differences between euphemisms and their automatically generated non-euphemistic paraphrases. The third method exploits the metaphorical underpinnings of euphemism, following the hypothesis that the euphemism's root word will have more possible senses than its single-word literal paraphrase. In contrast to these linguistically-driven methods, the last method fine-tunes a popular pre-trained language model (Devlin et al., 2019, BERT) for the task of euphemism detection. We find strong, and perhaps surprising, evidence that the last method outperforms the alternatives.

Our contribution in this paper is twofold. First, we demonstrate the utility of pre-trained language models for novel figurative language processing tasks. Second, we demonstrate our process of translating linguistic theory of euphemism into empirical models. Although our results show that those methods need to be refined, it is our hope that this transparency will minimize redundancy in future research. Thus, our work is well-aligned with Nissim et al. (2017)'s position that reporting negative results in shared tasks can produce useful insights.

2 Related Work

2.1 Linguistic Theories of Euphemism

We frame our study of euphemism detection through the lens of established linguistic theory. Gómez (2009) explains euphemism from a cognitive and pragmatic perspective, emphasizing that euphemism suspends the negative connotations of taboo concepts to serve a discursive purpose within a given context. It is not merely a lexical substitution at the linguistic level; rather, it is a socially-motivated cognitive strategy that has the effect of signaling politeness to the interlocutor. Euphemism is thus characterized by both the speaker's intentional indirectness and the hearer's recognition of their attempt to veil the concept's offensiveness.

Fernández (2008) highlights that euphemism is almost always predicated on a metaphor. Using metaphor to express a taboo concept makes discussion of the taboo more permissible in public discourse. Hence, the function of euphemism is to neutralize a topic by speaking of it in vague terms. The ambiguity of the individual words in a euphemistic expression masks the overtly unacceptable features of the concept for which it stands.

These two theories delineate two hallmarks of euphemism: It produces a change in perceived sen-

Proceedings of the 3rd Workshop on Figurative Language Processing (FLP), pages 131 - 136
December 8, 2022

timent, and it relies on an abstract metaphor to stand for a concrete concept. We use these linguistic facts as the foundation for our sentiment- and word sense-based solutions.

2.2 Euphemism Detection in NLP

Zhu and Bhat (2021) presented the first attempt at euphemistic phrase detection. From a raw text corpus of online posts, they mine euphemistic phrase candidates that represent target keywords and then apply a masked language model (MLM) based on SpanBERT (Joshi et al., 2019) to rank the candidate phrases in order of confidence. Their work was limited to euphemisms in the drug domain, with downstream applications in content moderation. In contrast, we designed our models to generalize to euphemism at large, independent of topic. We also employ MLMs in two of our methods, but for the purpose of generating single-word paraphrases, not to compute model confidence.

Recently, Gavidia et al. (2022) created the first corpus of sentences containing potentially euphemistic terms (PETs). To do so, they compiled a list of 184 PETs on a variety of taboo topics such as death, sexual activity, and substances. Then, they extracted sentences from the U.S.-dialect subsection of the Corpus of Global Web-Based English (Davies and Fuchs, 2015, GloWbE) that contained an instance of one of those PETs. PETs either did or did not function as a euphemism, dependent on context. They used RoBERTa-based sentiment analysis (Liu et al., 2019) to show that PETs function as euphemisms when replacing them with literal paraphrases causes an increase in negative and offensive sentiment. This work informed the sentiment-based technique in two of our methods. Subsequently, Lee et al. (2022) expanded on their work by developing a method that mines single and multi-word expressions, filters them based on similarity to sensitive topics, and identifies the euphemistic PETs based on the phrases that caused the greatest sentiment shift when paraphrased.

3 Dataset and Task Description

Our work was conducted as part of a shared task with the goal of creating a system that determines whether or not a given sentence containing a PET is euphemistic. The data was sourced from Gavidia et al. (2022)'s corpus of PETs. The training dataset consisted of 1572 utterances, with PETs demarcated within angled brackets. An *utterance* was defined as the sentence containing the PET along with the preceding and following sentences to provide additional context. Utterances were assigned labels of 1 or 0, with 1 indicating that the PET was euphemistic and 0 indicating that it was not. A condensed example of an entry in the training dataset is shown in Table 1. The test dataset consisted of 393 unlabeled utterances. Similar to the training data, each utterance included three sentences, with the PET denoted within angle brackets.

Index	Utterance	Label
81	...locked up in a military <detention camp> on vague charges of being a Terrorist sympathizer...	1

Table 1: Sample entry from the training dataset.

4 Methods

We explored four methods for euphemism detection, broadly categorized by their reliance on engineered, linguistically-driven features or transfer learning. In the first two methods, we expected that if the original sentence contained a euphemism, then substituting the PET with a synonymous non-euphemistic term should produce a difference in the sentiment between the original and the generated, paraphrased sentence. The third approach relies on the premise that euphemisms are metaphorical extensions of the head of the phrase, while their non-euphemistic paraphrases have more specific semantic scope. The fourth approach employs BERT, a popular transformer-based model that we fine-tuned to detect euphemism. We provide further details regarding the intuition and implementation guiding each of these approaches in §4.1-4.3.

4.1 Sentiment-based Methods

Consider the PET *armed conflict* for which the non-euphemistic paraphrase is *war. Armed conflict*, more indirect and ambiguous, evokes less negative and offensive sentiment than its synonym *war*, which is more direct and richer in emotional content. On the other hand, consider the sentence *Her ideas were <underdeveloped>*. In this context, the PET *underdeveloped* is not functioning as a euphemism. Substituting it with a non-euphemistic paraphrase such as *weak* has little effect on the sentence's sentiment. Following this, the underlying

Feature	Description
NEGATIVE_DIFF	SENTDIFF(o, p) when measuring $S_d(\cdot)$ along the *negative* dimension (*d=negative*).
NEUTRAL_DIFF	SENTDIFF(o, p) when *d=neutral*.
POSITIVE_DIFF	SENTDIFF(o, p) when *d=positive*.
OFFENSIVE_DIFF	SENTDIFF(o, p) when *d=offensive*.

Table 2: Sentiment-based features computed based on measured differences in negative, neutral, positive, and offensive sentiment between the original and paraphrased versions of the sentence.

intuition guiding our sentiment-based methods was that there may be a greater difference in sentiment between the original sentence and the paraphrase when the original PET was euphemistic.

4.1.1 Paraphrasing Using Back-Translation

We used back-translation between English and German to generate the paraphrase for each utterance, implemented using Ma (2019)'s NLP augmentation (`nlpaug`) library. We anticipated that the original sentence would lose many figurative elements through the process of back-translation, leading the PET to be replaced by a semantically consistent but literal paraphrase. We then computed the difference in sentiment between the original sentence o and back-translated paraphrase p, where $S_d(\cdot)$ is a measure of sentiment for a given input along a specific dimension d:

$$\text{SENTDIFF}(o, p) = S_d(o) - S_d(p) \quad (1)$$

Sentiment was measured along five dimensions (Lee et al., 2022, negative, neutral, positive, non-offensive, and offensive) using the RoBERTa (Liu et al., 2019) sentiment and offensiveness models. We used differences in negative, neutral, positive, and offensive sentiment as features (Table 2) for a logistic regression model to classify sentences as euphemistic or non-euphemistic. We used Python's `scikit-learn` library[1] to implement our classifier, leaving all hyperparameters at their default values.

4.1.2 Paraphrasing Using MLM

As an alternative to back-translation, we also generated paraphrases using MLM and masking out PETs. Because MLM accounts for sentence context, we expected that the tokens replacing the PET would be influenced by the overall sentiment of the sentence. Thus, if the context was indicative of taboo or sensitive content, then the MLM's suggestions should reflect that sentiment. From the set of suggested replacements for each PET, we selected the token that was most similar in meaning to the original PET. To do this, we generated an embedding for the original PET and each of the token suggestions using the Sentence Transformers framework (Reimers and Gurevych, 2019). We ignored MLM tokens that were either stopwords or identical to the original PET.

We selected the MLM token that had the highest cosine similarity to the PET, with the expectation that this token would be a non-euphemistic paraphrase of it. The selected token was substituted for the PET in the original sentence. We then calculated negative, neutral, positive, and offensive sentiment differences between the original sentence and the paraphrase as explained in §4.1.1, using those shifts as features for classification.

4.2 Word Sense-based Method

In the third approach, rather than analyzing sentiment differences, we compared the number of word senses between the syntactic head of the PET and its single-word non-euphemistic paraphrase. Consider the euphemism *expecting* used instead of *pregnant*. *Expect*, the lemma of the euphemism, has much wider semantic scope than *pregnant*. In replacing a very specific term with a more vague, metaphorical one, euphemism functions to reduce the explicitly taboo undertones of the target concept (Fernández, 2008). We captured this apparent ambiguity of the euphemistic term compared to the concreteness of its non-euphemistic paraphrase through measured polysemy. The euphemism is expected to be built on a word with more senses than the non-euphemistic word it replaces.

The non-euphemistic paraphrase of the PET in each utterance was determined using the same MLM technique described in §4.1.2. Because the PET can be a multi-word expression, and senses are counted for individual words, we extracted the syntactic head of each PET. If the PET was a single word, then the head was the word itself. Otherwise,

[1] `https://scikit-learn.org/stable/`

the head was identified as the root token of the PET's dependency parse (predicted using Python's spaCy[2] library). For example, if the euphemism *lay off* was used in the context of firing employees, then the head of the PET would be the verb *lay*.

We used WordNet (Fellbaum, 1998) to find the number of word senses for the lemmas of both the chosen MLM token and the head of the original PET. If a lemma did not appear in the WordNet dictionary, then its number of senses was set to one. The number of word senses of the head of the PET and of the chosen MLM token were used as features for a logistic regression model to classify the test utterances as euphemistic or non-euphemistic. Similarly to our first approach, we used Python's scikit-learn library[3] to implement our logistic regression classifier, with default hyperparameters.

4.3 Transfer Learning Method

Our final method was a fine-tuned BERT (Devlin et al., 2019) model. Specifically, we fine-tuned the bert-base-cased pre-trained model from Hugging Face[4] for euphemism detection using the Trainer API. The model was pretrained on data from BookCorpus (Zhu et al., 2015) and English Wikipedia.[5] We anticipated that this model would offer a strong baseline to which the other models could be compared, while also facilitating study into the extent that general-domain pre-training data can be leveraged for this task. Input was tokenized using AutoTokenizer, also from the Hugging Face library. We set the model to pad shorter input sequences to the maximum sequence length, and truncate longer input sequences to the maximum acceptable input length for the model (512 tokens).

5 Evaluation

We compared the performance of all methods using precision, recall, and F_1-measure, following task guidelines. The sentiment-based methods described in §4.1 were excluded from our shared task submission and thus not evaluated on the test data, due to their observed under-performance during validation experiments. Our validation experiments were evaluated using a withheld subset of 20% of the training data. In Table 3, we report all models' performance on the the validation set, enabling comparison between all techniques described in §4. In Table 4, we report the performance of the two top-performing methods, *Word Sense* (§4.2) and *BERT* (§4.3), on the test dataset as evaluated by the shared task submission portal.

Method	P	R	F_1
Sentiment-BT	0.34	0.50	0.41
Sentiment-MLM	0.35	0.50	0.41
Word Sense	0.59	0.51	0.44
BERT	**0.83**	**0.92**	**0.87**

Table 3: Performance comparison among all models on a held-out validation subset of the training data.

Method	P	R	F_1
Word Sense	0.50	0.55	0.43
BERT	**0.74**	**0.75**	**0.74**

Table 4: Performance comparison among shared task submissions on the test data.

6 Discussion

The results show that *BERT* unquestionably outperforms the sentiment- and word sense-based methods. This illustrates that a fine-tuned model pre-trained on general-domain data can be successfully leveraged for euphemism detection. Close inspection of the predictions from the three linguistically-driven methods revealed that they overwhelmingly classified sentences as euphemistic. We suspect that they learned to reliably detect the presence of figurative language but require further refinement to discriminate between euphemism and other figurative language phenomena (e.g., metaphor).

Sentiment-BT likely under-performed because we found that PETs remained surprisingly intact through the process of back-translation. Hence, there were few sentiment differences between the original and paraphrased sentences. Similarly, the tokens selected in *Sentiment-MLM* may have fit the sentence context but were not literal paraphrases of the PET. Beyond *Sentiment-MLM*, this may also explain the failure of *Word Sense* relative to *BERT*. If the paraphrases themselves are unreliable, then it entails that subsequent downstream comparisons of sentiment or polysemy between the original and paraphrased sentences will also be inaccurate.

[2] https://spacy.io/
[3] https://scikit-learn.org/stable/
[4] https://huggingface.co/bert-base-cased
[5] https://en.wikipedia.org/

7 Conclusion

In this paper, we explored linguistically-driven and transfer learning methods to detect euphemism. Our linguistically-driven methods drew upon differences in sentiment and word sense frequency between euphemisms and their paraphrases. Our transfer learning method fine-tuned BERT for euphemism detection and proved to be the most successful. We motivate our sentiment- and word sense-based methods using linguistic theory and report their results despite under-performance to highlight the scope for future improvement. In our next steps, we aim to devise techniques for more accurately paraphrasing euphemisms (simultaneously driving the dial forward towards *euphemism understanding*), allowing us to further investigate linguistically-driven approaches. We will also study whether fine-tuning source models intended for metaphor detection or sentiment analysis will further improve upon our transfer learning results.

Limitations

We acknowledge that the linguistically-driven models in this paper are only applicable to data where the PET has been explicitly demarcated. To deploy these models in a real-world setting, we would have to create a system that is capable of not only detecting the presence of a euphemism but can identify it from data that has not been annotated.

Furthermore, in addition be being limited to euphemisms in English, our proposed models are trained only on American dialectal data. This calls into question the cross-cultural validity of our models. Specifically, the target concepts that necessitate euphemism and the metaphors that those euphemisms are built upon are culturally-dependent constructs, posing a challenge for building generalizable euphemism detection models.

Acknowledgments

We thank the anonymous reviewers for their helpful feedback, and the shared task organizers for encouraging research on this exciting and challenging problem. This work was completed as part of an Honors College capstone project at the University of Illinois Chicago.

References

Mark Davies and Robert Fuchs. 2015. Expanding horizons in the study of world englishes with the 1.9 billion word global web-based english corpus (glowbe). *English World-Wide*, 36(1):1–28.

Jacob Devlin, Ming-Wei Chang, Kenton Lee, and Kristina Toutanova. 2019. BERT: Pre-training of deep bidirectional transformers for language understanding. In *Proceedings of the 2019 Conference of the North American Chapter of the Association for Computational Linguistics: Human Language Technologies, Volume 1 (Long and Short Papers)*, pages 4171–4186, Minneapolis, Minnesota. Association for Computational Linguistics.

Christiane Fellbaum. 1998. *WordNet: An Electronic Lexical Database*. Bradford Books.

Christian Felt and Ellen Riloff. 2020. Recognizing euphemisms and dysphemisms using sentiment analysis. In *Proceedings of the Second Workshop on Figurative Language Processing*, pages 136–145, Online. Association for Computational Linguistics.

Eliecer Crespo Fernández. 2008. Sex-related euphemism and dysphemism: An analysis in terms of conceptual metaphor theory. *Atlantis*, 30(2):95–110.

Martha Gavidia, Patrick Lee, Anna Feldman, and JIng Peng. 2022. Cats are fuzzy pets: A corpus and analysis of potentially euphemistic terms. In *Proceedings of the Language Resources and Evaluation Conference*, pages 2658–2671, Marseille, France. European Language Resources Association.

Miguel Gómez. 2009. Towards a new approach to the linguistic definition of euphemism. *Language Sciences*, 31:725–739.

Mandar Joshi, Danqi Chen, Yinhan Liu, Daniel S. Weld, Luke Zettlemoyer, and Omer Levy. 2019. Spanbert: Improving pre-training by representing and predicting spans.

Patrick Lee, Martha Gavidia, Anna Feldman, and Jing Peng. 2022. Searching for PETs: Using distributional and sentiment-based methods to find potentially euphemistic terms. In *Proceedings of the Second Workshop on Understanding Implicit and Underspecified Language*, pages 22–32, Seattle, USA. Association for Computational Linguistics.

Yinhan Liu, Myle Ott, Naman Goyal, Jingfei Du, Mandar Joshi, Danqi Chen, Omer Levy, Mike Lewis, Luke Zettlemoyer, and Veselin Stoyanov. 2019. Roberta: A robustly optimized BERT pretraining approach. *CoRR*, abs/1907.11692.

Edward Ma. 2019. NLP augmentation. https://github.com/makcedward/nlpaug.

Malvina Nissim, Lasha Abzianidze, Kilian Evang, Rob van der Goot, Hessel Haagsma, Barbara Plank, and Martijn Wieling. 2017. Last words: Sharing is caring: The future of shared tasks. *Computational Linguistics*, 43(4):897–904.

Nils Reimers and Iryna Gurevych. 2019. Sentence-bert: Sentence embeddings using siamese bert-networks. *CoRR*, abs/1908.10084.

Wanzheng Zhu and Suma Bhat. 2021. Euphemistic phrase detection by masked language model. In *Findings of the Association for Computational Linguistics: EMNLP 2021*, pages 163–168, Punta Cana, Dominican Republic. Association for Computational Linguistics.

Yukun Zhu, Ryan Kiros, Rich Zemel, Ruslan Salakhutdinov, Raquel Urtasun, Antonio Torralba, and Sanja Fidler. 2015. Aligning books and movies: Towards story-like visual explanations by watching movies and reading books. In *Proceedings of the IEEE international conference on computer vision*, pages 19–27.

Back to the Roots: Predicting the Source Domain of Metaphors using Contrastive Learning

Meghdut Sengupta and **Milad Alshomary** and **Henning Wachsmuth**
Leibniz University Hannover, Hannover, Germany
Institute of Artificial Intelligence
{m.sengupta, m.alshomary, h.wachsmuth}@ai.uni-hannover.de

Abstract

Metaphors frame a given target domain using concepts from another, usually more concrete, source domain. Previous research in NLP has focused on the identification of metaphors and the interpretation of their meaning. In contrast, this paper studies to what extent the source domain can be predicted computationally from a metaphorical text. Given a dataset with metaphorical texts from a finite set of source domains, we propose a contrastive learning approach that ranks source domains by their likelihood of being referred to in a metaphorical text. In experiments, it achieves reasonable performance even for rare source domains, clearly outperforming a classification baseline.

1 Introduction

Metaphors foster meaning in language by establishing a mapping between two conceptual domains, where concepts rooted in a usually rather concrete *source domain* are projected to a usually rather abstract *target domain* (Lakoff and Johnson, 2003). In other words, metaphors explain one concept in terms of another concept. For example, in the sentence "the sales tax would generate \$12 billion in annual tax revenues", the target domain *taxation* is described through concepts from the source domain *machine*, as indicated by the verb "generate".

Recent research suggests that even state-of-the-art NLP models face problems with making inferences on figurative language such as metaphors (Chakrabarty et al., 2021). To better comprehend the meaning intended by metaphorical language, additional levels of understanding need to be incorporated. So far, past research in natural language processing has focused on the distinction of literal from metaphorical text (Shutova et al., 2010) as well as on the interpretation of metaphors in terms of understanding their literal meaning from their intended meaning and vice versa (Shutova et al., 2012; Stowe et al., 2021). For these tasks, the mapping between source and target domain has often been used as an effective cue. To the best of our knowledge, however, no work directly attempts the actual identification of the conceptual domains of metaphors from a given sentence. A reason behind may lie in the theoretical unboundedness of the number of concepts (and, as a result, the space of metaphors) associated with a single concept.

In this paper, we study to what extent source domains can be predicted computationally from given metaphorical sentences. We restrict our view to the slightly simplified setting in which a set of possible source domains is predefined (but possibly large). Conceptually, this makes the task a classification problem: Given the sentence, assign it to the correct source domain.

However, for larger numbers of source domains, it may be hard to learn a reliable classification model, particularly when annotated metaphor data is limited. Instead, we therefore propose a contrastive learning approach (Zhang et al., 2022) based on our hypothesis that the source domain and the metaphorical sentences are related linguistically. The approach ranks all source domains based on the similarity of their embeddings to the embedding of the given sentence. At inference time, it then chooses the top-ranked source domain.

We evaluate our approach on the corpus of Gordon et al. (2015), covering 1429 English metaphorical sentences and 138 source domains. With an accuracy of 0.619, our approach clearly outperforms transformer-based classification baselines, especially on rare source domains. Even though the unboundedness problem remains, we thereby contribute towards a better computational understanding of metaphorical language. To go beyond, we expect that modeling external knowledge about source domains will be needed.

2 Related Work

As stated above, past NLP research has tackled the study of metaphors mostly in the form of two

Proceedings of the 3rd Workshop on Figurative Language Processing (FLP), pages 137 - 142
December 8, 2022

Sentence	Metaphor	Src. Domain
The sad news is with the exception of very few no firearm organisation is doing anything of the slightest value in fighting gun control.	fighting	Struggle, War
This is the historical context of Obama's election victory.	victory	Competition, Game, War
They attack ""rich people"" while enjoying all the spoils of their luck, I have zero problems with earned wealth, but these clowns literally lucked out in life.	attack	War

Table 1: Example sentences from the dataset having one or more than one concepts grouped as the source domain.

tasks: metaphor identification (Mao et al., 2018; Do Dinh and Gurevych, 2016) and metaphor interpretation (Beust et al., 2003; Shutova, 2010). Most works in these research fields build on the work of Lakoff and Johnson (2003) on the interpretation of intended meanings in metaphorical expressions. The author theorized different metaphors in terms of mapped concepts (source and target domains). Approaches to metaphor interpretation have particularly witnessed unsupervised extraction of source domains and target domains to interpret the intended meaning of metaphorical expressions (Li et al., 2013; Yu and Wan, 2019). In contrast, we seek to predict the source domain, even if it is not mentioned in the text.

Notable research combining metaphor identification and interpretation has been carried out by Shutova et al. (2013). The authors first identified metaphors by verb and noun clustering, followed by interpreting the intended meaning of the metaphors by addressing it as a paraphrasing task.

Li et al. (2013) modeled explicit conceptual metaphors (where the source domain and the target domain are situated as excerpts of text in the sentence) and implicit conceptual metaphors (where the two domains are not apparent), where they extracted source and target domains in an unsupervised approach. A limitation of their work is that no evaluation is provided regarding how authentic the source domains and the target domains are that are excavated.

Recently Stowe et al. (2021) have interpreted metaphors by extracting source and target domains from the semantic space of their associated concepts in FrameNet (Ruppenhofer et al., 2016), to generate metaphorical expressions. We complement this study in that we assess how well source domain prediction works when the set of domains is known in advance.

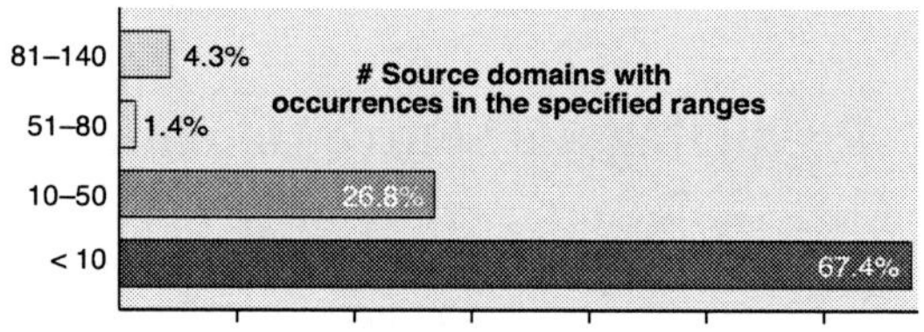

Figure 1: Insights into the distribution of the given data: 67.4% of the source domains are referred to in less than 10 metaphors, 4.3% occur between 81 to 140 times, etc.

Ahrens and Jiang (2020) developed an algorithm to identify source domains from text with the help of lexical resources like WordNet, which partially addressed the unboundedness problem of source domains. However, their work is essentially an annotation procedure for source domain verification.

The only datasets suitable for our purposes are the one of Shutova and Teufel (2010), where source and target domains have been annotated manually, and the one of Gordon et al. (2015) where both conceptual source and target domains and their linguistic triggers are given. We rely on the latter, since the former one has only 761 samples.

3 Data

To study the task of predicting the source domain of metaphors, we need data where source domains are annotated. We employ the dataset of Gordon et al. (2015), which was originally created to explore how the *meaning shift* (Shutova et al., 2013) happens between source and target domains. The dataset contains 1771 metaphorical sentences, spanning 70 source domains annotated for the linguistic metaphors (metaphorical text excerpts in the sentence corresponding to source and target domains). We use the "source linguistic metaphor" and henceforth refer to it simply as *metaphor*. For example, in the sentence "An invasion of wealth may not suit their interests", the metaphor is "invasion" and the annotated source domain is *War*.

Table 1 shows three example metaphors from the dataset. As can be seen, some metaphors pertain to more than one source domain. For example, in the sentence "This is the historical context of Obama's election victory", the metaphor "victory" has the source domains *Competition*, *Game*, and *War*. In

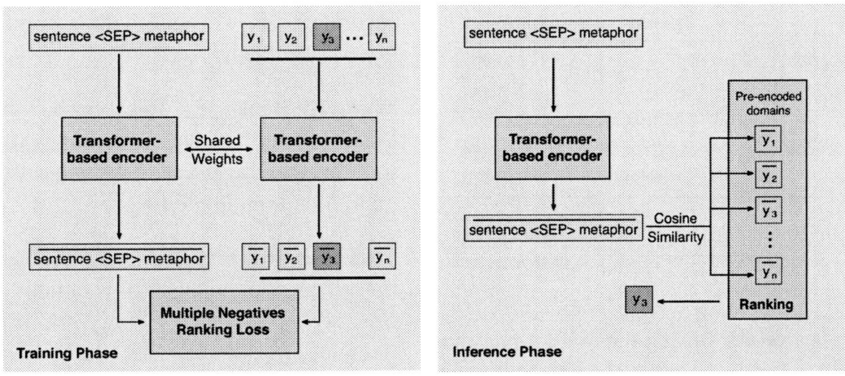

Figure 2: Our contrastive learning approach: During training, we optimize the transformer models based on Multiple Negatives Ranking Loss. At inference, we select the source domain most similar to a given metaphorical sentence.

this paper, we see such cases as composite source domains, that is, if a metaphor in a given sentence has multiple source domains, we treat them as one new source domain. As a result, the total number of source domains in our work is 138. Figure 1 shows the distribution of source domains in the whole dataset, underlining the complexity of the problem and the sparsity of the data.

4 Approach

For a predefined set of domains, we here model source domain prediction as a ranking task. Given a metaphorical sentence as input, we rank all candidate domains by their likelihood of being the source domain based on their semantic similarity to the sentence. Then, we choose the top-ranked domain as the predicted source domain.

To that end, we develop a contrastive learning approach which compares the semantic representations of the input sentence and the candidate domains. Figure 2 gives an overview.

4.1 Training Phase

On a training set, our approach learns to minimize the semantic distance of the correct source domain from the given metaphorical sentence. For representing the data at hand, we build on the recent success of sentence transformers (Reimers and Gurevych, 2019), which leverage efficient representations for different downstream tasks. We fine-tune a sentence transformer as follows:

1. We pass the sentence (concatenated with its metaphor by a separator token) and each source domain through two transformer-based encoders with shared weights, in order to obtain an embedding for each. Our central idea revolved around exploring how our approach works. To test the approach to it's full potential we refrain from using large transformer based encoders like T5 (Raffel et al., 2020) - which we think may affect the model performance to the extent, where understanding what is responsible for a good model performance - the approach or the encoder - would be difficult. Hence, we simply use BERT (Devlin et al., 2019) and DistilBERT (Sanh et al., 2019) [1] as encoders for creating the sentence representations.

2. For a vector of sentences $\mathbf{x}$ and corresponding correct source domains $\mathbf{y}$, that is, with only positive instance pairs (x_i, y_i) with $x_i \in \mathbf{x}$ and $y_i \in \mathbf{y}$ like Reimers and Gurevych (2020) we rely on *Multiple Negatives Ranking Loss* (Henderson et al., 2017), where x_i along with each domain y_j, $j \neq i$, is used as a negative pair. Let $k = |X| = |Y|$ be the number of pairs, then we compute the loss as:

$$
\begin{aligned}
&\mathcal{L}(\mathbf{x}, \mathbf{y}, \theta) \\
= \; & -\frac{1}{k} \cdot \sum_{i=1}^{k} \log P_{\text{approx}}(y_i | x_i) \\
= \; & -\frac{1}{k} \cdot \sum_{i=1}^{k} \left(S(x_i, y_i) - \log \sum_{j=1}^{k} e^{S(x_i, y_j)} \right)
\end{aligned}
$$

In line with Henderson et al. (2017), $S(x, y)$ is the score of an instance computed from the sentence embeddings. The ranking function is defined

[1] Specifically, we use 'bert-base-uncased' and 'distilbert-base-uncased' as the pre-trained checkpoints. These are the variants with the lowest number of parameters of BERT and DistilBERT respectively.

Approach	Encoder	Accuracy
Majority baseline	–	0.063
Classification baseline	BERT	0.421
	DistilBERT	0.473
Contrastive learning	BERT	**0.619**
	DistilBERT	0.612

Table 2: Main results: Accuracy of our approach and the baselines. Using BERT, our approach performs best.

by θ which is a vector storing the current parameters of the transformer-based encoders. Following the idea of contrastive learning, the loss will be minimized, if positive instances get high scores and negative instances low scores.

4.2 Inference Phase

At inference time, the input is just a sentence concatenated with its metaphor. We pass this input through the encoder to obtain its embedding. Using a ranking evaluator, we next compute the cosine similarity in terms of the paired cosine distance between the sentence embedding and the pre-encoded embeddings of each of the candidate source domains. Then, we take the most similar source domain as our predicted output, that is, the one whose embedding has the minimum distance to the sentence embedding.

5 Experiments

This section reports on first experiments that we carried out to evaluate our approach to source domain prediction against different baselines. The goal was to study whether and when contrastive learning provides advantages over standard classification in the given task. [2]

5.1 Experimental Setup

We relied on the following experimental setup:

Data From the dataset described in Section 3, we omitted two instances that were corrupt. We also removed a few duplicates: These instances had the same sentence and source domain, but a different value for some attribute that we did not use (e.g., "schema slot"). Afterwards, we split the remaining 1429 texts randomly into 70% for training (1000 texts), 10% for validation (128 texts), and 20% for testing (301 texts). The split is preserved for reproducibility. We evaluate our model with top-1 accuracy score with our ranking evaluator as mentioned previously.

Majority Baseline To assess how much can be learned from the data, we employ a majority baseline that always predicts the majority source domain found in the training set.

Classification Baselines As discussed initially, the given task conceptually defines a classification problem. Accordingly for baselines, we fine-tune attention-based sequence-to-sequence language transformers in symmetry with the encoders of our contrastive learning approach, namely BERT and DistilBERT, to directly classify the source domains.[3] We report the final score in terms of the average accuracy over 20 iterations of each model. We optimized both models with AdamW (Loshchilov and Hutter, 2017) in six epochs, batches of size 32, a learning rate of 5^{-5}.

Contrastive Learning (Approach) The two configurations of our approach follows the concept discussed in Section 4. Also here, we report the average accuracy over 20 iterations for each model. We optimized both variants in 6 epochs, batches of size 32, and a learning rate of 5^{-5}.

5.2 Main Results

Table 2 presents the results of all evaluated models on the test set. The majority baseline achieves an accuracy of 0.063. While the classifier based on DistilBERT predicts a little less than half of all source domains correctly (0.473), our contrastive learning approaches clearly outperform all baselines, supporting our hypothesis. Still, the highest accuracy (0.619 based on BERT) reveals room for improvement, possibly suggesting a need for more knowledge about source domains and their connections to the concepts being mentioned.

5.3 Results across Source Domains

One major challenge regarding the task is the number of source domains involved and their distribution. As shown in figure 1, 67.4% of the source domains occur in less than 10 metaphors - indicating there are less than 10 instances of these source

[2]The experiment code can be found at `https://github.com/webis-de/FIGLANG-22`.

[3]Due to the high number of source domains (i.e., classes here) in the data, we considered grouping similar source domains and performing the classification in a two step process. We decided against, though, since many of the source domains occur rarely only (see Figure 1), so we would lose a substantial amount of information during grouping.

		# Src. Domain Occurrences			
Approach	**Encoder**	**< 10**	**10–50**	**51–80**	**81–140**
Classification baseline	BERT	0.000	0.214	0.504	0.823
	DistilBERT	0.000	0.376	**0.522**	**0.856**
Contrastive learning	BERT	0.480	**0.694**	0.511	0.632
	DistilBERT	**0.512**	0.664	0.500	0.615

Table 3: Result analysis: Accuracy on different subsets of the test set, partitioned based on the occurrences of the source domains in accordance with Figure 1.

domains in the dataset. This is particularly important because this represents the real-life scenario about how source domains occur in metaphors. Ideally, an approach for identifying source domains should be able to perform well in this scenario.

To see how our approach compares to the classification baseline across the distribution of the source domains in the dataset, we partitioned the test instances into four subsets depending on the occurrences of source domains (using the ranges from Figure 1).

Table 3 reports the average accuracy over 5 iterations on each subset, keeping all other hyperparameters same as discussed previously. As can be seen, our approach consistently outperforms the classification baselines in the case of rarer source domains (*< 10* and *10–50*), which denotes the vast majority of the dataset. In contrast, the classification baselines perform better on the subsets with frequent source domains (*51–80* and *81-140*) While this suggest that more data may make classification suitable, the unboundedness of metaphors renders sufficient data unlikely in general. We thus conclude that our approach generalizes better to real-world scenarios with multiple source domains likely to be present in scanty data distributions.

6 Conclusion

Understanding a metaphor includes the recognition of the source domain from which concepts are projected to the target domain being discussed. In this paper, we have proposed a contrastive learning approach to recognize the source domain from a given metaphorical text computationally, when the set of domains is predefined. Experiments suggest that the approach works reasonably well, particularly for source domains that are represented scarcely, which we expect to likely happen often in real-world situations. However, the obtained results also reveal notable room for improvement. In future work, we plan to investigate the impact of modeling external knowledge about the domains as well as the recognition of source domains in unbounded settings.

Acknowledgments

This work has been supported by the Deutsche Forschungsgemeinschaft (DFG, German Research Foundation), under project number TRR 318/1 2021 – 438445824.

Limitations

In our work, we have formulated our approach on the assumption that a given set of metaphors have a finite predefined set of source domains. In a real-world scenario, however, the possible candidates for a source domain of a metaphor are theoretically unbounded. Hence, while our assumption is a start towards modeling source domain prediction, it definitely leaves questions to be answered in this context. Moreover, we restricted our view to classification and contrastive learning approaches in this paper as an initial investigation of the task. Other NLP techniques may be worth considering, such as few-shot learning and active learning. We plan to investigate these in the future to get a better idea of the capabilities of our approach. Finally, we point that the observations we make in this paper about metaphor may not all generalize to other languages than English. Metaphor use has language-specific peculiarities that we left untouched here.

Ethical Statement

We do not see any immediate ethical concerns with the study presented in this paper. The data we used is freely available, and a potential misuse of the approach we develop for ethically doubtful use cases seems not apparent to us.

References

Kathleen Ahrens and Menghan Jiang. 2020. Source domain verification using corpus-based tools. *Metaphor and Symbol*, 35(1):43–55.

Pierre Beust, Stéphane Ferrari, Vincent Perlerin, et al. 2003. Nlp model and tools for detecting and interpreting metaphors in domain-specific corpora. In *Proceedings of the Corpus Linguistics 2003 conference*, pages 114–123. Citeseer.

Tuhin Chakrabarty, Debanjan Ghosh, Adam Poliak, and Smaranda Muresan. 2021. Figurative language in recognizing textual entailment. In *Findings of the Association for Computational Linguistics: ACL-IJCNLP 2021*, pages 3354–3361, Online. Association for Computational Linguistics.

Jacob Devlin, Ming-Wei Chang, Kenton Lee, and Kristina Toutanova. 2019. BERT: Pre-training of deep bidirectional transformers for language understanding. In *Proceedings of the 2019 Conference of the North American Chapter of the Association for Computational Linguistics: Human Language Technologies, Volume 1 (Long and Short Papers)*, pages 4171–4186, Minneapolis, Minnesota. Association for Computational Linguistics.

Erik-Lân Do Dinh and Iryna Gurevych. 2016. Token-level metaphor detection using neural networks. In *Proceedings of the Fourth Workshop on Metaphor in NLP*, pages 28–33.

Jonathan Gordon, Jerry Hobbs, Jonathan May, Michael Mohler, Fabrizio Morbini, Bryan Rink, Marc Tomlinson, and Suzanne Wertheim. 2015. A corpus of rich metaphor annotation. In *Proceedings of the Third Workshop on Metaphor in NLP*, pages 56–66, Denver, Colorado. Association for Computational Linguistics.

Matthew Henderson, Rami Al-Rfou, Brian Strope, Yun hsuan Sung, László Lukács, Ruiqi Guo, Sanjiv Kumar, Balint Miklos, and Ray Kurzweil. 2017. Efficient natural language response suggestion for smart reply. *ArXiv e-prints*.

George Lakoff and Mark Johnson. 2003. *Metaphors We Live By*. University of Chicago Press.

Hongsong Li, Kenny Q. Zhu, and Haixun Wang. 2013. Data-driven metaphor recognition and explanation. *Transactions of the Association for Computational Linguistics*, 1:379–390.

Ilya Loshchilov and Frank Hutter. 2017. Decoupled weight decay regularization. *arXiv preprint arXiv:1711.05101*.

Rui Mao, Chenghua Lin, and Frank Guerin. 2018. Word embedding and wordnet based metaphor identification and interpretation. In *Proceedings of the 56th annual meeting of the association for computational linguistics*. Association for Computational Linguistics (ACL).

Colin Raffel, Noam Shazeer, Adam Roberts, Katherine Lee, Sharan Narang, Michael Matena, Yanqi Zhou, Wei Li, Peter J Liu, et al. 2020. Exploring the limits of transfer learning with a unified text-to-text transformer. *J. Mach. Learn. Res.*, 21(140):1–67.

Nils Reimers and Iryna Gurevych. 2019. Sentence-bert: Sentence embeddings using siamese bert-networks. *arXiv preprint arXiv:1908.10084*.

Nils Reimers and Iryna Gurevych. 2020. Making monolingual sentence embeddings multilingual using knowledge distillation.

Josef Ruppenhofer, Michael Ellsworth, Myriam Schwarzer-Petruck, Christopher R Johnson, and Jan Scheffczyk. 2016. Framenet ii: Extended theory and practice. Technical report, International Computer Science Institute.

Victor Sanh, Lysandre Debut, Julien Chaumond, and Thomas Wolf. 2019. DistilBERT, a distilled version of BERT: smaller, faster, cheaper and lighter. *CoRR*, abs/1910.01108.

Ekaterina Shutova. 2010. Automatic metaphor interpretation as a paraphrasing task. In *Human Language Technologies: The 2010 Annual Conference of the North American Chapter of the Association for Computational Linguistics*, pages 1029–1037, Los Angeles, California. Association for Computational Linguistics.

Ekaterina Shutova, Lin Sun, and Anna Korhonen. 2010. Metaphor identification using verb and noun clustering. In *Proceedings of the 23rd International Conference on Computational Linguistics (Coling 2010)*, pages 1002–1010, Beijing, China. Coling 2010 Organizing Committee.

Ekaterina Shutova and Simone Teufel. 2010. Metaphor corpus annotated for source - target domain mappings. In *Proceedings of the Seventh International Conference on Language Resources and Evaluation (LREC'10)*, Valletta, Malta. European Language Resources Association (ELRA).

Ekaterina Shutova, Simone Teufel, and Anna Korhonen. 2013. Statistical metaphor processing. *Computational Linguistics*, 39(2):301–353.

Ekaterina Shutova, Tim Van de Cruys, and Anna Korhonen. 2012. Unsupervised metaphor paraphrasing using a vector space model. In *Proceedings of COLING 2012: Posters*, pages 1121–1130, Mumbai, India. The COLING 2012 Organizing Committee.

Kevin Stowe, Nils Beck, and Iryna Gurevych. 2021. Exploring metaphoric paraphrase generation. In *Proceedings of the 25th Conference on Computational Natural Language Learning*, pages 323–336, Online. Association for Computational Linguistics.

Zhiwei Yu and Xiaojun Wan. 2019. How to avoid sentences spelling boring? towards a neural approach to unsupervised metaphor generation. In *Proceedings of the 2019 Conference of the North American Chapter of the Association for Computational Linguistics: Human Language Technologies, Volume 1 (Long and Short Papers)*, pages 861–871, Minneapolis, Minnesota. Association for Computational Linguistics.

Rui Zhang, Yangfeng Ji, Yue Zhang, and Rebecca J. Passonneau. 2022. Contrastive data and learning for natural language processing. In *Proceedings of the 2022 Conference of the North American Chapter of the Association for Computational Linguistics: Human Language Technologies: Tutorial Abstracts*, pages 39–47, Seattle, United States. Association for Computational Linguistics.

SBU Figures It Out: Models Explain Figurative Language

Mohadeseh Bastan*
Stony Brook University
mbastan@cs.stonybrook.edu

Yash Kumar Lal*
Stony Brook University
ylal@cs.stonybrook.edu

Abstract

Figurative language is ubiquitous in human communication. However, current NLP models are unable to demonstrate a significant understanding of instances of this phenomena. FigLang shared task on figurative language understanding posed the problem of predicting and explaining the relation between a premise and a hypothesis containing an instance of the use of figurative language. We experiment with different variations of using T5-large for this task and build a model that significantly outperforms the task baseline. Treating it as a new task for T5 and simply finetuning on the data achieves the best score on the defined evaluation. Furthermore, we find that hypothesis-only models are able to achieve most of the performance.

1 Introduction

Figurative language is an important component of discourse, ranging from daily interactions to books. It is used as a tool to convey complex and deeper emotions that are often difficult to express literally (Ghosh et al., 2015). Despite the fact that Transformer-based pretrained language models (LMs) get even larger, they are still unable to comprehend the physical world, cultural knowledge, or social context in which figurative language is embedded. Large-scale crowdsourced datasets often contain these phenomena inherently. To show true conceptual understanding of figurative language, the model should not only be able to correctly differentiate a figurative instance from its literal counterpart, but also explain its decision. These natural language explanations should be readily comprehensible by an end-user who needs to assert a model's reliability (Camburu et al., 2018; Wiegreffe and Marasovic, 2021).

This paper describes the experiments and submission of the LUNR lab at Stony Brook University, USA to the shared task on Figurative Language Understanding (Chakrabarty et al., 2022b) organized at EMNLP 2022. Given a premise and a hypothesis, the shared task required predicting the relation between them as well as an explanation for the same. We use variations in input format, separator and sequential fine-tuning techniques to build our final model.

Since the task involves predicting the label as well as an explanation for it, in this paper we vary the order of generation of each target in our models. Prior work (Khashabi et al., 2020) highlighted the importance of separator tokens. It helps the model distinguish between different portions of the input. Additionally, since this task is not a common one, variations in input format and keywords dictate how well a model performs. To that end, we experimented with different formats prescribed for T5 models as well as a simple one for an unseen, new task. Finally, we also experimented with sequential fine-tuning on several related datasets to improve performance on the shared task.

Our final model is a simple T5-large model finetuned on the task data, trained to generate the explanation before the label. The input format does not contain any task-specific keys and does not resemble any of the ones described in Raffel et al. (2020). The model uses a "\n" separator, which is a prominent part of how UnifiedQA (Khashabi et al., 2020) was built over T5. It improves significantly over the task baseline. We observe that (1) treating this as a new task leads to best model performance, (2) the dataset contains artifacts that hypothesis-only models use to reach significant performance, and (3) knowing the type of phenomena being encapsulated does not help the model.

2 Related Work

The model's ability to explain decisions has been investigated in previous studies. Rajani et al. (2019) presents a novel Common Sense Explanations

*First two authors have equal contribution

Proceedings of the 3rd Workshop on Figurative Language Processing (FLP), pages 143 - 149
December 8, 2022 ©2022 Association for Computational Linguistics

(CoS-E) dataset to explore commonsense reasoning and propose a novel method, CAGE for automatically generating explanations that achieve state-of-the-art performance. Camburu et al. (2018) introduces a large corpus of human-annotated explanations for the Stanford Natural Language Inference (SNLI) (Bowman et al., 2015a) dataset which is collected to enable research in generation of free-form textual reasoning. Bastan et al. (2022) introduces SuMe dataset which generates relation between entities and an explanation for why this relation exists or how this relation comes about.

None of the previous work explored the possibility of different data formats. In this work we evaluate different combinations of the explanation and label generations. We also study the effect of the pretrained model on similar tasks as a sequential pretraining.

3 Data

The shared task data (Chakrabarty et al., 2022a) contains 9,000 high-quality literal, figurative sentence pairs with entail/contradict labels and the associated explanations. The benchmark spans five types of figurative language: Paraphrase, Sarcasm, Simile, Metaphor, and Idiom. The definition of each type is explained as follows:

Paraphrase is a rephrasing of something that is written. All sentences in this category belongs to the entailment category.

Sarcasm is using phrases which have the opposite meaning from what they are intended to convey. It can be used for creating contradiction labels.

Simile is using a figure of speech to compare something with something else. It can be used for both entailment and contradiction labels.

Metaphor is when a word or phrase used to describe something that it cannot literally describe. It can be used for both entailment and contradiction labels. It can be used for both entailment and contradiction labels.

Idiom is established by usage as having a meaning not derived from their individual meanings. It can be used for both entailment and contradiction labels.

A noteworthy property of this data is that both the entailment/contradiction labels and the explanations are w.r.t the figurative language expression (i.e., metaphor, simile, idiom) rather than other parts of the sentence. The task is challenging because it inherently requires 1) relational reasoning using background commonsense knowledge, and 2) finegrained understanding of figurative language.

We split 7,500 examples into a 80-20 train and dev set randomly. These sets are then used to build models for the overall shared task.

4 Experiment Design

We use the T5 (Raffel et al., 2020) family of models for our submission. Particularly, we build over T5-large.

Since this is a new task for T5, we experiment with various input and output formats. We build models where the label is placed before and after explanation on the target side. Large language models have also been shown to be sensitive to the choice of separators. To this end, we build models that conform to different input/output formats as well as separators.

Prior work has shown that pretraining on large amounts of data similar to the task improves the downstream performance of models. To this end, we use e-SNLI (Camburu et al., 2018) to sequential fine-tuning our model before finetuning on downstream task data to obtain a final model. e-SNLI is an extension of the SNLI dataset (Bowman et al., 2015b) with an additional layer of human-annotated natural language explanations of the entailment relations. Similarly, SuMe Bastan et al. (2022) is a biomedical mechanism explanation dataset which contains a set of supporting sentence about two main entities, the relation between the entities, and a sentence explaining the mechanism behind this relation. They explored the generation of explanation and target label at the same time given the supporting sentences, using different transformer based models. They use [explanation. label] as the output format while we explore all possible orders and separator tokens. We used the model pretrained on SuMe dataset and finetuned on this task.

Poliak et al. (2018) used hypothesis-only models showed that statistical irregularities may allow a model to perform natural language inference in some datasets beyond what should be achievable without access to the context. Motivated by that, we also build hypothesis-only models to analyze whether models require contexts to perform this NLI + explanation task.

5 Results

5.1 Evaluation

To evaluate the performance of each model, we use two generations and three classifications metrics. For generations, we use BLEURT (Sellam et al., 2020) and BERTScore (Zhang et al., 2019) which have been proven to be more effective than tradition ROUGE scores. In order to evaluate the quality of explanations, we compute the average between these two scores. NLI label accuracy is then reported based on three explanation average score thresholds. We compute the accuracy@0 meaning accuracy on all generated data, accuracy@50 meaning accuracy of the generated label for all texts with average explanation score higher than 50, and accuracy@60 which is the accuracy of the generated label for all texts with average explanation score higher than 60. This evaluation scheme has been defined by the task organizers themselves.

5.2 Task Results

The baseline model released for the task is T5-3B finetuned on this dataset (Chakrabarty et al., 2022b). Our best model is a T5-large finetuned on task data in using RTE keywords with the "[SEP]" separator, and predicting the label before the explanation. It significantly improves upon the baseline set for the shared task despite being much smaller in terms of number of parameters. Particularly, we observe that Acc@60 is much lower than Acc@50, which means that the average accuracy of the generated label drops as the average explanation score threshold goes up from 50 to 60 (becomes stricter).

	Acc@0	Acc@50	Acc@60
Our Model	**0.889**	**0.824**	**0.517**
Baseline	0.767	0.691	0.443

Table 1: Results on shared task test set

6 Analysis

We analyse the performance of the numerous models that we have built to understand the impact of various design decisions that we took — input format, sequential fine-tuning, and order of required predictions. Further, we also want to understand the impact of artifacts present in the dataset itself on model performance. We use the evaluation described in subsection 5.1 on the dev set for analysis.

6.1 How does input format affect performance?

The data input formats vary in two aspects — task-specific keywords and the separator. Specifically, the task-specific keywords can correspond to a new task for T5 (no keywords), RTE and MNLI (Appendix D.2 and D.3 of Raffel et al. (2020) respectively). We experiment with three possible separators between pieces of input text - ‘ ’ (whitespace), [SEP] (the sep token), and "\n" (the newline character). Both **\n** and **[SEP]** are predefined to the tokenizer as one unique token before training.

The effects of these design choices can be seen in Table 2. We find that treating this as a new task (and not using any predefined task-specific keywords) yields the best model performance. Furthermore, predicting the label before predicting its explanation is better than the opposite. This is in line with the expected order of performing both tasks — one would predict the relation between the pair before explaining it. We also see that using the [SEP] token is better for the label before explanation setting except when using the MNLI task format.

6.2 Does sequential fine-tuning help?

Prior work has shown that sequential fine-tuning on similar tasks often helps models. Both e-SNLI (Camburu et al., 2018) and SuMe (Bastan et al., 2022) are tasks where models have to predict labels as well as explain it. We built models that were first psequential fine-tuning on one of these datasets and then finetuned on the task data. The results of these two experiments are shown in Table 3.

We found that the sequential fine-tuning paradigm actually hurts model performance significantly, no matter which task is used with the model first. We hypothesize that while these selected tasks are similar in terms of what the model has to predict, they do not capture any aspects of the figurative language phenomena. So, introducing a model to these tasks does not necessarily nudge it towards the right domain.

6.3 Label before explanation vs explanation before label

We explored different order of generation for the label and the explanation. First, for each data, we set the label to be generated before the explanation (*lbe*) then we changed the order and first generated the explanation before the label (*ebl*).

The results are shown in Table 2. We find that

Keyword	Label Position	Seperator	Model Name	Acc@0	Acc@50	Acc@60
-	after	-	ebl-no	0.830	0.778	0.557
-	after	[SEP]	ebl-sep	0.789	0.737	0.513
-	after	\n	ebl-slashn	0.822	0.766	0.557
-	before	-	lbe-no	0.838	0.773	0.531
-	before	[SEP]	lbe-sep	**0.899**	**0.830**	0.584
-	before	\n	be-slashn	0.844	0.789	0.539
mnli	after	-	mnli-ebl-no	0.790	0.737	0.514
mnli	after	[SEP]	mnli-ebl-sep	0.779	0.721	0.512
mnli	after	\n	mnli-ebl-slashn	0.814	0.747	0.540
mnli	before	-	mnli-lbe-no	0.799	0.754	0.537
mnli	before	[SEP]	mnli-lbe-sep	0.711	0.672	0.451
mnli	before	\n	mnli-lbe-slashn	0.788	0.738	0.529
rte	after	-	rte-ebl-no	0.737	0.690	0.486
rte	after	[SEP]	rte-ebl-sep	0.797	0.748	0.537
rte	after	\n	rte-ebl-slashn	0.833	0.767	0.531
rte	before	-	rte-lbe-no	0.797	0.745	0.510
rte	before	[SEP]	rte-lbe-sep	0.891	0.827	**0.590**
rte	before	\n	rte-lbe-slashn	0.741	0.698	0.476

Table 2: Model performance with different input formats on the dev set. The first column shows the task specific keyword we used in finetuning. It's either nothing, the same as 'mnli' task, or 'rte' task. The second column indicates whether the label is generated before or after the explanation. *lbe* means that the model was trained to generate the label before the explanation while *ebl* indicates the opposite. The third column indicates which separator was used between the label and the explanation. We either used no token, [SEP] token, or \n token. Model name comes from the combination of the previous three columns. This notation is used in all other tables as well. Treating the shared task as a new T5 task, using the [SEP] token as separator, and predicting the label before the explanation helps us build the best model.

Model Name	Acc@0	Acc@50	Acc@60
lbe-sep	**0.899**	**0.830**	**0.584**
esnli-mnli-ebl-sep	0.73	0.666	0.413
sume-mnli-ebl-slashn	0.696	0.672	0.502
sume-mnli-lbe-sep	0.729	0.669	0.410

Table 3: Effect of sequential fine-tuning on model performance on shared task data. We only include the best possible model scores obtained in the no-, esnli- and sume- sequential fine-tuning regime. Clearly, sequential fine-tuning only has a negative impact on model performance.

predicting the label before moving on to the explanation is better for the model in both a new task and the RTE task setup. However, the opposite is true for MNLI. Why the pattern does not hold remains an open research issue.

6.4 Presence of artifacts in the dataset

Poliak et al. (2018) showed the presence of artifacts in several popular NLI datasets. We use a similar approach and build hypothesis-only models to test the presence of artifacts in this dataset and task. Ideally, these models should perform very poorly on this data since they do not have access to the premise and have to judge incomplete inputs.

Model Name	Acc@0	Acc@50	Acc@60
lbe-sep	0.672	0.627	**0.423**
mnli-lbe-no	**0.696**	**0.634**	0.418
rte-lbe-no	0.680	0.622	0.416

Table 4: Performance of hypothesis-only models on the task. The table only includes the best performing model from each input format task type (new, mnli and rte).

Table 4 shows that models are able to achieve high enough Acc@0 scores, showing that the overall dataset contains some artifacts. Technically, if a significant portion of the dataset can be correctly classified without looking at the premise (well beyond the most-frequent-class baseline), it shows that it is possible to perform well on the datasets

Model Name	Acc@0	Acc@50	Acc@60
ebl-no	0.854	0.803	0.542
mnli-ebl-no	0.847	0.786	0.567
rte-ebl-no	**0.862**	**0.804**	**0.584**

Table 5: Performance of models when they are also provided the type of phenomena captured in the premise-hypothesis. We only include the best performing model from each input format task type (new, mnli and rte).

without modeling natural language inference hence the data relies on annotation artifacts (Gururangan et al., 2018). However, it is also clear that using Acc@60 shows the weakness of the explanations generated by these models. Overall, we posit that using hypothesis-only models alone are also effective in performing this task.

6.5 Does knowing the type of figurative language phenomena help?

Wang et al. (2019) showed that additional knowledge is useful in improving NLI models. The dataset is annotated with the type of figurative phenomena encapsulated in the premise-hypothesis pair. Using this additional information can help a model predict the relation between the pair better, and nudge it towards the correct explanation.

Performance for such models is listed in Table 5. We find that knowing the type of phenomena hurts the model as compared to just simply finetuning with vanilla task inputs and outputs. It is unclear why this additional knowledge has a negative impact. One assumption can be because this additional information is not available at the test data, we can only use this information during training. This study is done on the development set. We trained a model with this additional information, but at the time of evaluation we didn't use this as this is not available in the test set.

7 Conclusion

Figurative language is an important component of discourse, often used as a tool to convey complex emotions usually difficult to express literally. The shared task is designed to test whether models can predict the relation between a pair of sentences that contains figurative language as well as explain that phenomena. We experiment with building several models based on T5-large varying the input format, order of prediction and sequential fine-tuning.

Our final model is a simple T5-large model fine-tuned on the task data, trained to generate the explanation before the label. The input format does not contain any task-specific keys and does not resemble any of the ones described in Raffel et al. (2020) but uses a "\n" separator. It improves significantly over the task baseline. We observe that (1) treating this as a new task leads to best model performance, (2) the dataset contains artifacts that hypothesis-only models use to reach significant performance, and (3) knowing the type of phenomena being encapsulated does not help the model.

8 Limitations

Our approach is fundamentally limited by the limits of the fine-tuned transformer based models since we only used one specific t5-large model. Further, it might be computationally prohibitive to try larger models since in requires more resources and computational machines. We focus on exploring different preprocessing steps, whereas a significant amount of errors stem from the capacity of the model in generating good explanations.

References

Mohaddeseh Bastan, Nishant Shankar, Mihai Surdeanu, and Niranjan Balasubramanian. 2022. Sume: A dataset towards summarizing biomedical mechanisms. *arXiv preprint arXiv:2205.04652*.

Samuel R Bowman, Gabor Angeli, Christopher Potts, and Christopher D Manning. 2015a. A large annotated corpus for learning natural language inference. *arXiv preprint arXiv:1508.05326*.

Samuel R. Bowman, Gabor Angeli, Christopher Potts, and Christopher D. Manning. 2015b. A large annotated corpus for learning natural language inference. In *Proceedings of the 2015 Conference on Empirical Methods in Natural Language Processing*, pages 632–642, Lisbon, Portugal. Association for Computational Linguistics.

Oana-Maria Camburu, Tim Rocktäschel, Thomas Lukasiewicz, and Phil Blunsom. 2018. e-snli: Natural language inference with natural language explanations. In S. Bengio, H. Wallach, H. Larochelle, K. Grauman, N. Cesa-Bianchi, and R. Garnett, editors, *Advances in Neural Information Processing Systems 31*, pages 9539–9549. Curran Associates, Inc.

Tuhin Chakrabarty, A. Saakyan, Debanjan Ghosh, and Smaranda Muresan. 2022a. Flute: Figurative language understanding through textual explanations.

Tuhin Chakrabarty, Arkadiy Saakyan, Debanjan Ghosh, and Smaranda Muresan. 2022b. Flute: Figurative language understanding and textual explanations. *arXiv preprint arXiv:2205.12404*.

Aniruddha Ghosh, Guofu Li, Tony Veale, Paolo Rosso, Ekaterina Shutova, John Barnden, and Antonio Reyes. 2015. Semeval-2015 task 11: Sentiment analysis of figurative language in twitter. In *Proceedings of the 9th international workshop on semantic evaluation (SemEval 2015)*, pages 470–478.

Suchin Gururangan, Swabha Swayamdipta, Omer Levy, Roy Schwartz, Samuel R Bowman, and Noah A Smith. 2018. Annotation artifacts in natural language inference data. *arXiv preprint arXiv:1803.02324*.

Daniel Khashabi, Sewon Min, Tushar Khot, Ashish Sabharwal, Oyvind Tafjord, Peter Clark, and Hannaneh Hajishirzi. 2020. UNIFIEDQA: Crossing format boundaries with a single QA system. In *Findings of the Association for Computational Linguistics: EMNLP 2020*, pages 1896–1907, Online. Association for Computational Linguistics.

Adam Poliak, Jason Naradowsky, Aparajita Haldar, Rachel Rudinger, and Benjamin Van Durme. 2018. Hypothesis only baselines in natural language inference. In *Proceedings of the Seventh Joint Conference on Lexical and Computational Semantics*, pages 180–191, New Orleans, Louisiana. Association for Computational Linguistics.

Colin Raffel, Noam Shazeer, Adam Roberts, Katherine Lee, Sharan Narang, Michael Matena, Yanqi Zhou, Wei Li, and Peter J. Liu. 2020. Exploring the limits of transfer learning with a unified text-to-text transformer. *Journal of Machine Learning Research*, 21(140):1–67.

Nazneen Fatema Rajani, Bryan McCann, Caiming Xiong, and Richard Socher. 2019. Explain yourself! leveraging language models for commonsense reasoning. In *Proceedings of the 57th Annual Meeting of the Association for Computational Linguistics*, pages 4932–4942, Florence, Italy. Association for Computational Linguistics.

Thibault Sellam, Dipanjan Das, and Ankur P Parikh. 2020. Bleurt: Learning robust metrics for text generation. *arXiv preprint arXiv:2004.04696*.

Xiaoyan Wang, Pavan Kapanipathi, Ryan Musa, Mo Yu, Kartik Talamadupula, Ibrahim Abdelaziz, Maria Chang, Achille Fokoue, Bassem Makni, Nicholas Mattei, et al. 2019. Improving natural language inference using external knowledge in the science questions domain. In *Proceedings of the AAAI Conference on Artificial Intelligence*, volume 33, pages 7208–7215.

Sarah Wiegreffe and Ana Marasovic. 2021. Teach me to explain: A review of datasets for explainable natural language processing. In *Thirty-fifth Conference on Neural Information Processing Systems Datasets and Benchmarks Track (Round 1)*.

Tianyi Zhang, Varsha Kishore, Felix Wu, Kilian Q Weinberger, and Yoav Artzi. 2019. Bertscore: Evaluating text generation with bert. *arXiv preprint arXiv:1904.09675*.

A Sequential Fine-tuning

The extended results of the model pretrained on SuMe (Bastan et al., 2022) is shown in Table 6 and the results of the model pretrained on e-snli (Camburu et al., 2018) and fine-tuned on this task is shown in Table 7. Since the sequential fine-tuning on esnli is time and resource consuming, we only explored a few set of preprocessing on this task.

Model Name	Acc@0	Acc@50	Acc@60
ebl-no	0.606	0.541	0.324
ebl-sep	0.653	0.593	0.379
ebl-slashn	0.648	0.624	0.455
lbe-no	0.674	0.615	0.375
lbe-sep	0.696	0.637	0.388
lbe-slashn	0.687	0.655	0.460
mnli-ebl-no	0.684	0.628	0.408
mnli-ebl-sep	0.701	0.641	0.410
mnli-ebl-slashn	0.696	**0.672**	**0.502**
mnli-lbe-no	0.714	0.643	0.394
mnli-lbe-sep	**0.729**	0.669	0.410
mnli-lbe-slashn	0.689	0.661	0.488
rte-ebl-no	0.676	0.625	0.402
rte-ebl-sep	0.691	0.604	0.347
rte-ebl-slashn	0.680	0.662	0.488
rte-lbe-no	0.713	0.652	0.402
rte-lbe-sep	0.701	0.643	0.397
rte-lbe-slashn	0.682	0.657	0.472

Table 6: SuMe Pretrained Models Performance

Model Name	Acc@0	Acc@50	Acc@60
ebl-no	0.727	0.655	0.375
mnli-ebl-sep	**0.73**	**0.666**	**0.413**

Table 7: ESNLI Pretrained Models Performance

B Hypothesis-only Models

The hypothesis-only experiments show the presence of artifacts in this dataset. The full performance of these models are shown in Table 4.

C Effect of Knowing the Phenomena

The extended results of the model with the *type* information is shown in Table 5.

Model Name	Acc@0	Acc@50	Acc@60
ebl-no	0.638	0.578	0.363
ebl-sep	0.637	0.576	0.381
ebl-slashn	0.676	0.612	0.404
lbe-no	0.684	0.604	0.410
lbe-sep	0.672	0.627	**0.423**
lbe-slashn	0.672	0.611	0.398
mnli-ebl-no	0.639	0.563	0.362
mnli-ebl-sep	0.670	0.596	0.378
mnli-ebl-slashn	0.661	0.593	0.390
mnli-lbe-no	**0.696**	**0.634**	0.418
mnli-lbe-sep	0.676	0.618	0.411
mnli-lbe-slashn	0.674	0.603	0.402
rte-ebl-no	0.632	0.569	0.366
rte-ebl-sep	0.637	0.574	0.363
rte-ebl-slashn	0.634	0.561	0.351
rte-lbe-no	0.680	0.622	0.416
rte-lbe-sep	0.678	0.628	0.398
rte-lbe-slashn	0.679	0.607	0.409

Table 8: Hypothesis Only Performance

Model Name	Acc@0	Acc@50	Acc@60
ebl-no	0.854	0.803	0.542
ebl-sep	0.826	0.766	0.520
ebl-slashn	0.839	0.780	0.543
lbe-no	0.754	0.712	0.490
lbe-sep	0.742	0.690	0.488
lbe-slashn	0.740	0.694	0.496
mnli-ebl-no	0.847	0.786	**0.567**
mnli-ebl-sep	0.834	0.776	0.560
mnli-ebl-slashn	0.819	0.771	0.528
mnli-lbe-no	0.741	0.694	0.503
mnli-lbe-sep	0.756	0.709	0.487
mnli-lbe-slashn	0.755	0.713	0.509
rte-ebl-no	**0.862**	**0.804**	0.584
rte-ebl-sep	0.816	0.786	0.536
rte-ebl-slashn	0.821	0.775	0.533
rte-lbe-no	0.738	0.705	0.485
rte-lbe-sep	0.762	0.713	0.525
rte-lbe-slashn	0.758	0.719	0.509

Table 9: Type Added Performance

NLP@UIT at FigLang-EMNLP 2022: A Divide-and-Conquer System For Shared Task On Understanding Figurative Language

Khoa Thi-Kim Phan, Duc-Vu Nguyen, Ngan Luu-Thuy Nguyen
University of Information Technology, Ho Chi Minh City, Vietnam
Vietnam National University Ho Chi Minh City, Vietnam
{khoaptk, vund, ngannlt}@uit.edu.vn

Abstract

This paper describes our submissions to the EMNLP 2022 shared task on Understanding Figurative Language as part of the Figurative Language Workshop (FigLang 2022). Our systems based on pre-trained language model **T5** are divide-and-conquer models which can address both two requirements of the task: 1) classification, and 2) generation. In this paper, we introduce different approaches in which each approach we employ a processing strategy on input model. We also emphasize the influence of the types of figurative language on our systems.

1 Introduction

Recent years have witnessed the great rise of Artificial Intelligence (AI). Due to the performance of AI, many downstream tasks from any fields are solved efficiently. One of the central topic in AI is Natural Language Understanding (NLU) in which Natural Language Inference (NLI) or Recognizing Textual Entailment (RTE) plays an important role, which was pointed out in (MacCartney and Manning, 2008).

While RTE was defined as a task of determining whether a natural language hypothesis h can be inferred from a given premise p (MacCartney, 2009), Figurative Language Understanding (FLU) was considered as a task of determining whether any figure of speech depends on a non-literal meaning of some or all of the words used (Chakrabarty et al., 2022). Therefore, FLU can be framed as a kind of RTE task (Chakrabarty et al., 2022; Stowe et al., 2022).

In addition, the EMNLP 2022 shared task requires not only to generate the label (entail/contradict), but also to generate a plausible explanation for the prediction, whose example is shown in Table 1. Especially, the entail/contradict label and the exploration are related to the meaning of the figurative language expression. This is a challenging task that require to propose a approach that could tackle both tasks: 1) classification, 2) generation.

Premise	The place looked impenetrable and inescapable
Hypothesis	The place looked like a fortress.
Label	Entailment
Explanation	A fortress is a military stronghold, hence it would be very hard to walk into, or in other words impenetrable and inescapable.

Table 1: Examples of relations between a premise and a hypothesis: E (Entailment), C (Contradiction).

Over the past few years, a number of high-performance systems have been created solving several NLP tasks based on pre-trained transformer models (Vaswani et al., 2017; Devlin et al., 2019; Lewis et al., 2019; Raffel et al., 2020b). However, there have still been very few works related to figurative language due to the lack of high-quality datasets and the challenge of this task.

Therefore, thanks to the exclusive dataset of the shared task, in this paper, we advocate different approaches which are mainly based on pre-trained language model **T5** (Raffel et al., 2020b), combining to employ various input processing strategies to tackle the task.

In this paper, we conduct an investigation into the benefit of using state-of-the-art seq2seq pre-trained language models (T5) to evaluate figurative language understanding task in EMNLP 2022. We also employ a divide-and-conquer model with different potential input processing strategies to improve the performance of our system. Then, we point out the importance of the types of figurative language in this task.

2 System Description

In all our submissions, we considered both two tasks: the NLI task, and the explanation generation task as two seq2seq tasks. Therefore, we fine-tuned

Proceedings of the 3rd Workshop on Figurative Language Processing (FLP), pages 150 - 153
December 8, 2022 ©2022 Association for Computational Linguistics

two tasks jointly as a simultaneous computation model which first predicts label, and then the explanation. In addition, we also used the attribute about types of Figurative Language across the data as a predictor and treated it as seq2seq tasks. Therefore we have 3 component models based on fine-tuning pre-trained model T5 (Raffel et al., 2020b): NLI predictor, Type predictor, and Generator.

2.1 T5

T5 transformer is a encoder-decoder model or sequence-to-sequence model. It is a "unified framework that converts every language problem into a text-to-text format" (Raffel et al., 2020b). Compared to other transformers which take in natural language data by converting to corresponding numerical embeddings, T5 takes in data in the form of text, and also produce the text as an output. This text-to-text nature does not require any the change of hyper-parameters and loss functions when learn NLP tasks (Grover et al., 2020). Furthermore, T5 has been trained on a multi-task mixture of unsupervised and supervised tasks in which include our NLI task and generation task. Therefore, T5 model is one of the most prominent pre-trained models that we can use.

Figure 1: Overview of input and output of T5.

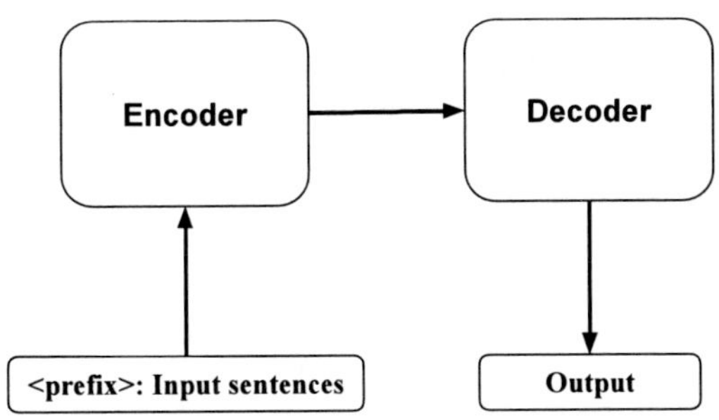

2.2 NLI predictor and Type predictor

In this two component models, the premise and hypothesis sentences are concatenated and fed to the encoder, then while the decoder of NLI task is the label prediction (entail/contradict), the decode of Type predictor is the type prediction (Paraphrase, Sarcasm, Simile, Metaphor, Idiom). The overview of two component models are shown in Fig.2

Figure 2: Overview of two component models. Red diagram is NLI predictor, the green diagram is Type predictor.

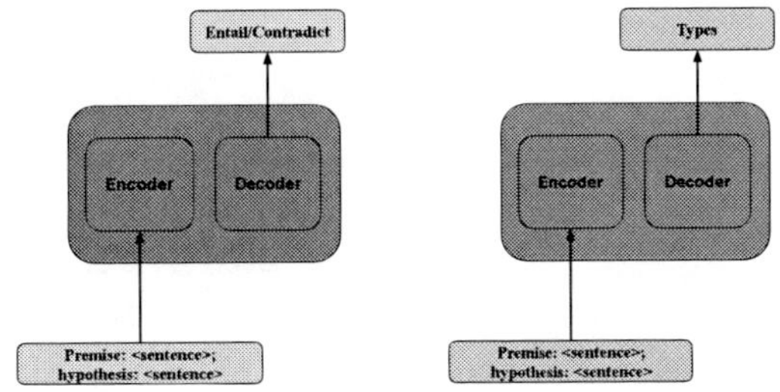

2.3 Generator

We employed different input processing strategies each submission in the Generator. Specifically, in the first submission, we simply used the premise and hypothesis sentences as a input of the encoder as same as NLI predictor did. However, the performance of the model is not too well, so we tried to add valuable attributes such as NLI predictor, and Type predictor to the left of the input of the encoder. Therefore, we conducted experiments for submission 2, 3, 4 by adding a NLI predictor, a Type predictor, and a NLI predictor + a Type predictor to the left of the input, respectively. Besides, The 5th submission is similar to the 3rd submission, except the parameters of the model. The model is depicted in Fig.3.

3 Experiments

3.1 Experimental setting

Following the given evaluation metrics, in all our experiments, we report the Accuracy@60 based on evaluation scripts from the task organizing committee.

As described in **Section 2**, our approaches depends on pre-trained language model T5. We use a model namely $T5_{large}$ downloaded from the Hugging Face library (Raffel et al., 2020a). The network's parameters are optimized using the AdamW (Loshchilov and Hutter, 2017) and a linear learning rate scheduler, which are suggested by the Hugging Face default setup. The hyperparameters that we tune include the number of epochs, batch size, and learning rate. In particular, we set batch size of 32, and learning rate of 3e-4 for all component models. For NLI predictor and Type predictor, we use 20 epochs. For Generator, the model is trained

Figure 3: Overview of submissions. While the component (1), (1)+(2), (1)+(3) is considered as a input model of the 1st, 2nd, 3rd submission respectively, the 4th one has all 3 components as a input model.

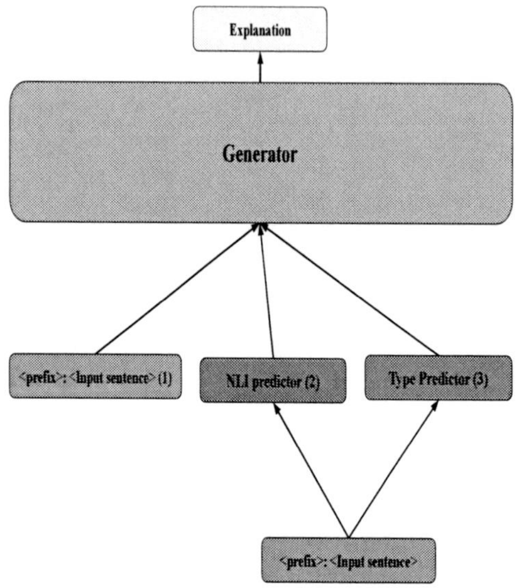

Submissions	Input model	Score	Size (bytes)
1	premise, hypothesis	58.26	39154
2	NLI predictor, premise, hypothesis	57.93	38015
3	Type predictor, premise, hypothesis	60.53	42532
4	NLI predictor, Type predictor, premise, hypothesis	59.80	37763

Table 2: Official results of our system on test dataset.

on 40 epochs. All experiments in this paper are conducted on Google Colab Pro.

3.2 Result and Discussion

For producing the results on the test dataset, we splited the training dataset into the training dataset and development dataset with 7300 samples, and 200 samples respectively for fine-tuning the pre-trained language model $T5_{large}$.

Our latest system achieved the official score 60.53 which ranked 3rd on the shared task. On each of the submissions, the systems obtained scores 58.26, 57.93, 60.53, and 59.80 respectively. Table 2 gives the detailed results of each submissions.

Comparing the detailed scores, we found that our submitted systems varied in performance mainly due to the difference of input model of the submissions. As described in Table 2, the system in which the input of model is the combination of NLI predictor, premise and hypothesis performed the worst, while the one which has the type predictor combining with input sentences (premise and hypothesis) outperformed the rest of our experiments. Therefore, the types of figurative language were indicated to be an integral role in understanding figurative language.

Depending on the input models, the Generator has different outputs, as shown in the Table 3. Compared to the models which add only one component into the input models: NLI predictor or Type predictor, the model of submission 4 had more information that consists of two input sentences, NLI predictor, and Type Predictor. However, the Generator did not produce adequate explanations as we expected. Therefore, the strategy including more information may not be a good choice when generating outputs in this case. Despite that, more efforts are required to explore the real reason behind the results, then we can learn and employ the input processing strategies reasonably to improve the performance of the system.

4 Conclusion and Future Work

In this paper, we have presented our system for the EMNLP 2022 Shared Task on the Figurative Language Understanding. Our systems are built on fine-tuning pre-trained language model T5 with different input processing strategies, which is a divide-and-conquer model which integrated two or three components: NLI predictor, Type predictor,

Sample	Explanation	NLI predictor	Type Predictor
"premise": "I stubbed my toe last night and cursed angrily." "hypothesis": "Stubbing my toe last night and cussing out loud made me so happy." "Predicted Label": Contradiction	"Stubbing one's toe is usually a very painful experience and can result in people feeling angry and cursing loudly which is not a happy feeling."		
	"Stubbing your toe and cursing loudly is not a good thing because it can cause pain and discomfort."	X	
	"Stubbing one's toe and cursing loudly is not a good thing and so being happy about it cannot be justified."		X
	"Stubbing your toe and cursing loudly is not a good way to spend a night in bed and so someone who is happy about it cannot be considered rational."	X	X

Table 3: Examples of explanation produced by the systems.

and Generator. The performance of models are relied how successful the Type predictor is, which means the attribute about types of Figurative Language should be considered as an integral factor of the input of model.

Due to limited time and resources, we had not conducted thorough enough experiments to get better results, but the system and the involvement in this challenge bring us a good groundwork for further study. In the future, we plan to expand the experiment by employing and fine-tuning other pretrained language models. Furthermore, we may also explore different strategies making the most of what we have for the input of models.

References

Tuhin Chakrabarty, A. Saakyan, Debanjan Ghosh, and Smaranda Muresan. 2022. Flute: Figurative language understanding through textual explanations.

Jacob Devlin, Ming-Wei Chang, Kenton Lee, and Kristina Toutanova. 2019. BERT: Pre-training of deep bidirectional transformers for language understanding. In *Proceedings of the 2019 Conference of the North American Chapter of the Association for Computational Linguistics: Human Language Technologies, Volume 1 (Long and Short Papers)*, pages 4171–4186, Minneapolis, Minnesota. Association for Computational Linguistics.

Khushnuma Grover, Katinder Kaur, Kartikey Tiwari, Parteek Kumar, et al. 2020. Deep learning based question generation using t5 transformer. In *International Advanced Computing Conference*, pages 243–255. Springer.

Mike Lewis, Yinhan Liu, Naman Goyal, Marjan Ghazvininejad, Abdelrahman Mohamed, Omer Levy, Ves Stoyanov, and Luke Zettlemoyer. 2019. Bart: Denoising sequence-to-sequence pre-training for natural language generation, translation, and comprehension. *arXiv preprint arXiv:1910.13461*.

Ilya Loshchilov and Frank Hutter. 2017. Decoupled Weight Decay Regularization. *arXiv preprint arXiv:1711.05101*.

Bill MacCartney. 2009. *Natural language inference*. Stanford University.

Bill MacCartney and Christopher D Manning. 2008. Modeling semantic containment and exclusion in natural language inference. In *Proceedings of the 22nd International Conference on Computational Linguistics (Coling 2008)*, pages 521–528.

Colin Raffel, Noam Shazeer, Adam Roberts, Katherine Lee, Sharan Narang, Michael Matena, Yanqi Zhou, Wei Li, and Peter J. Liu. 2020a. Exploring the limits of transfer learning with a unified text-to-text transformer. *Journal of Machine Learning Research*, 21(140):1–67.

Colin Raffel, Noam Shazeer, Adam Roberts, Katherine Lee, Sharan Narang, Michael Matena, Yanqi Zhou, Wei Li, Peter J Liu, et al. 2020b. Exploring the limits of transfer learning with a unified text-to-text transformer. *J. Mach. Learn. Res.*, 21(140):1–67.

Kevin Stowe, Prasetya Utama, and Iryna Gurevych. 2022. Impli: Investigating nli models' performance on figurative language. In *Proceedings of the 60th Annual Meeting of the Association for Computational Linguistics (Volume 1: Long Papers)*, pages 5375–5388.

Ashish Vaswani, Noam Shazeer, Niki Parmar, Jakob Uszkoreit, Llion Jones, Aidan N Gomez, Łukasz Kaiser, and Illia Polosukhin. 2017. Attention is all you need. *Advances in neural information processing systems*, 30.

Adversarial Perturbations Augmented Language Models for Euphemism Identification

Guneet Singh Kohli
Thapar University, Patiala, India
guneetsk99@gmail.com

Prabsimran Kaur
Thapar University, Patiala, India
pkaur_be18@thapar.edu

Jatin Bedi
Thapar University, Patiala, India
jatin.bedi@thapar.edu

Abstract

Euphemisms are mild words or expressions used instead of harsh or direct words while talking to someone to avoid discussing something unpleasant, embarrassing, or offensive. However, they are often ambiguous, thus making it a challenging task. The Third Workshop on Figurative Language Processing colocated with EMNLP 2022 organized a shared task on Euphemism Detection to better understand euphemisms. We have used the adversarial augmentation technique to construct new data. This augmented data was then trained using two language models, namely, BERT and Longformer. To further enhance the overall performance, various combinations of the results obtained using Longformer and BERT were passed through a voting ensembler. We were able to achieve an F1 score of 71.5 using the combination of two adversarial Longformers, two ad- versarial BERT, 1 non adversarial BERT.

1 Introduction

Euphemisms are mild words or expressions used instead of harsh or direct words while talking to someone to avoid discussing something unpleasant, embarrassing, or offensive. They are often used as a sign of politeness while discussing sensitive or taboo topics (Bakhriddionova, 2021), for instance, using the term "Let go" instead of the word "Fired," using "Put down" instead of "euthanized," or any similar phrase that would make it sound less unappealing or unpleasant (Karam, 2011). Euphemism can also be employed to disguise the truth (Rababah, 2014) to minimize a threatening situation to create a favorable image. For instance, when the phrase "enhanced interrogation techniques" is used, they mean "torture" or use "armed conflict" instead of "war". This figurative behavior of euphemisms makes it ambiguous and challenging for natural language processing techniques to handle these words since they can be interpreted literally in some situations. Moreover, humans might disagree with what constitutes a euphemism (Gavidia et al., 2022).

In the past, many computational approaches for processing have been employed. A sentiment analysis-based approach was used by (Felt and Riloff, 2020) to handle x-phemisms (a term used to refer to both euphemisms and dysphemisms). In their work, they found synonym pairs and used a weakly supervised bootstrapping algorithm to generate semantic lexicon. These lexicons were then used to classify phrases as euphemistic, dysphemistic, or neutral. (Zhu et al., 2021) worked on detecting euphemisms used for dug names on the internet and identifying the terms these euphemisms refer to. Similarly, (Magu and Luo, 2018) also worked on a similar problem statement. However, (Zhu et al., 2021) and (Magu and Luo, 2018) interpreted euphemisms as code words, which is different from those of the shared task organizers. Both (Zhu and Bhat, 2021) and (Zhu et al., 2021) considered the detection and identification of euphemism as a masked language model (MLM) problem where they filtered out words that did not fit their list of euphemisms.

This paper defines our participation in the Euphemism Detection shared task (Lee et al., 2022) organized for the Third Workshop on Figurative Language Processing co-located with EMNLP 2022. We have used the adversarial augmentation technique in combination with transformers to detect euphemisms. A detailed explanation of our proposed approach is given in Section 3.

2 Task & Data Description

Euphemism Detection is a binary classification shared task that focuses on detecting euphemisms in a given input statement. This shared task aims to study the performance of Natural Language Models on euphemisms. The data provided in the shared task comprised a Euphemism Corpus created by

Proceedings of the 3rd Workshop on Figurative Language Processing (FLP), pages 154 - 159
December 8, 2022

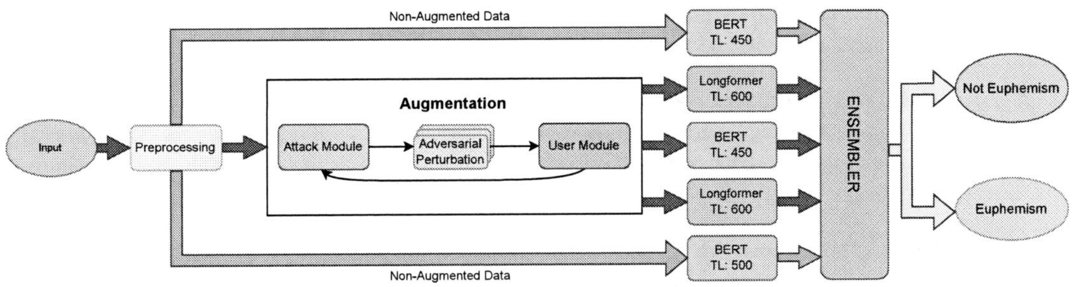

Figure 1: Architecture of the proposed pipeline. Here TL indicates the Token length used for training.

(Gavidia et al., 2022). The raw data used for the creation of this dataset is extracted from the Corpus of Global Web-Based English (GloWbE) (Davies and Fuchs, 2015), which contains text data from websites, blogs, and forums of twenty different English-speaking countries. The training data provided to the participants comprised 1572 sentences, of which 466 were labeled "0," and the rest were labeled "1". The testing data consists of 393 data points. The participants were expected to classify the sentences into "0" (not euphemistic) and "1" (is euphemistic) classes.

3 Methodology

This section gives a detailed description of the pipeline proposed. Section 3.1 and Section 3.2 provides a detailed overview of the preprocessing performed on the data and the augmentation technique used before passing the data through the models. Section 3.4 details the models used for the training.

3.1 Data Pre-Processing

The data in its raw form is often unstructured and comprises punctuations, unusual text, and symbols, which make it unfit for the distillation of correct features causing the model to underperform. Thus, it is essential to preprocess the data before using it. In this paper, we have performed basic preprocessing involving tokenization (splitting the sentences into words), conversion of words into lowercase, removal of stopwords (such as a, the, an), and removal of punctuation and emojis using the NLTK library (Loper and Bird, 2002).

3.2 Augmentation

Deep learning models require a large dataset to produce higher accuracy. However, the training data for the task comprised merely 1572 data points. Moreover, the data was imbalanced (as mentioned in Section 2, which could cause the model to overfit on the predominant label ("1"). Thus, data augmentation was performed for the label "0" of the dataset using the Adversarial attack technique available in TextAttack[1] (Morris et al., 2020). TextAttack iterates through the dataset and generates an adversarial perturbation (changes in the input that causes the model to misclassify) for each correct prediction that the model makes. There are two ways to generate adversarial perturbation:

1. **Visual**: is the method in which a text sequence similar to the original sequence is generated by changing a few characters or introducing realistic "typos" that humans would make.

2. **Semantic**: is the method in which the generated sentence is semantically similar to the original. This is done by paraphrasing the sentence or using synonyms.

TextAttack supports both of these adversarial perturbation techniques. Each attack by TextAttack is built using these four components. The first component is Goal Function that determines whether the attack was successful. Constraints component checks whether the perturbation made preserves the semantics or not.Transformations component generates a set of potential perturbations through deletion, insertion, or substitution of words, characters, and phrases.The Search Method component explores the transformation space to select the best perturbation. The augmentation of the data was done in two steps:

1. **Class Imbalance Removal** : We augment 466 instances of '0' labels with their adversarial representation, which brought the final

[1]https://github.com/QData/TextAttackaugmenting-text-textattack-augment

instance of non-euphemism instances to 932 and total data instances to 2038

2. **Adversarial Augmentation**: We test the dual context training setup discussed in section 3.3. and generate the adversarial version of all the 2038 instances.

3.3 Dual Context training setup

Inspired by the Siamese BERT(Reimers and Gurevych, 2019) , we tried using a dual context setup in which the input given to the language model was as follows:
Input text: *Original instance* $[SEP]$ *Adversarial augmented instance*

Here the input to the language model is the original instance from the training data and the adversarial augmented text instance from the text attack separated by a token $[SEP]$. The following setup aims at leveraging two different perspectives of the same instance to make the model more robust to the other contextual representations of Euphemism. The following structure increased the input length of the system.

In the case of unaugmented data the input text can be understood as follows:
Input text: *Original instance* $[SEP]$ *Original instance*

3.4 Modeling

In this paper, we have used BERT(Devlin et al., 2018) and Longformer (Beltagy et al., 2020) language models to detect euphemisms. This section gives a detailed explanation of their respective architectures.

3.4.1 BERT

Bidirectional Encoder Representations from Transformers (BERT) is used for pre-training deep bidirectional transformers on unlabeled data to develop a language understanding. The sentences are passed through BERT as a sequence of tokens. Before feeding the word sequences, 15% of the words are replaced by [MASK] in each sequence. A [CLS] is appended at the beginning of the first line, and a [SEP] is appended at the end of each sentence. A token, sentence, and positional embedding are added to each token, as shown in Figure 2. The truncation or padding of the sequence is done based on the maximum sequence length used.The maximum sequence length used for each case was determined by finding the average length of the text in the dataset. These encoded sentences are then passed through the transformer model. This pre-trained can then be fine-tuned d by adding the output layer depending on the task at hand.

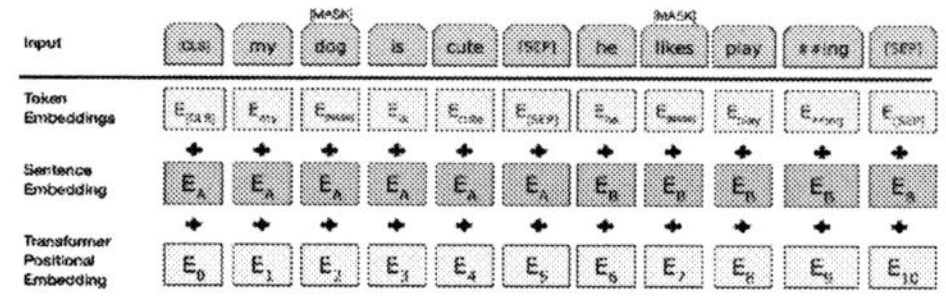

Figure 2: BERT input representations

3.4.2 Longformer

The major drawback of transformer models like BERT is that they cannot attend to sequence lengths longer than 512. This is because the memory and computational requirements of self-attention grow quadratically. Thus Longformer: The Long-Document Transformer, a transformer whose attention pattern rises linearly with the input sequence, was proposed. To achieve this reduced complexity Longformer combines several attention patterns:

1. **Sliding Window**: Each token in the sequence will only attend to tokens that fall under an arbitrary window whose size is assumed to be *"w"* (w/2 tokens on the right and w/2 tokens on the left). If this is done for *"l"* layers, each token would have attended to $(l * w)$ adjacent tokens. This is the reach of the attention for a given token and is known as the receptive field.

2. **Dilated Sliding Window**: To further improve the performance of the sliding window attention a dilatation of size *"d"* is taken. Here "d" represents the number of gaps between each token in the window. The reception field of this dilated sliding window will be $(l * w * d)$.

3. **Global Attention (full self-attention)**: To ensure support for long-term dependencies, the model utilizes global self-attention where, instead of using three different hidden vectors query (Q), key (K), and value (V), two separate sets of vectors *Q_s, K_s, V_s* (for sliding window), and *Q_g, K_g, V_g* (for global attention) are used.

3.5 Ensembler

To enhance the overall performance of the proposed pipeline, the results obtained by training:

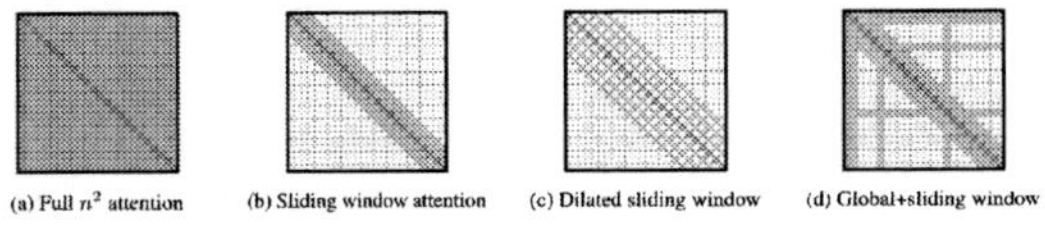

Figure 3: Comparison of transformer self attention and Longformer attention patterns

- Longformer on augmented data with the maximum sequence length of 600
- Longformer on augmented data with the maximum sequence length of 650
- BERT on augmented data with the maximum sequence length of 450
- BERT on the preprocessed data with a maximum sequence length of 450
- BERT on the preprocessed data with a maximum sequence length of 500

are passed through a voting ensembler, and the label with highest frequency is selected as the final label for that sentence, as depicted in Figure 1.

4 Results and Discussion

Euphemism in speech is generally difficult to identify semantically for human beings and thus makes it even more challenging task for the AI to map the understanding and undergo right identification. Our submission aims to handle the task of identifying the Euphemism in a given sentence by modelling Longformer and BERT in an adversarial setup.

4.1 Experimental Setting

To train the language models, we used an 80:10:10 split. We use the default hyperparameters to train BERT and Longformers. We use a learning rate of 1e-5 and an LR scheduler with Polynomial Decay and train the model for three epochs. We use the AdamW optimizer and set the batch size to 4. We trained the models on Tesla P100-PCIE-16GB GPU. The experimentations using the dual context setup yielded lower scores than the other submissions to the leaderboard. We aim to focus more on this proposed methodology and refine our approach for further research into the idea of making a model robust through multiple representation learning.

4.2 BERT Results Analysis

In this section we report our evaluations for the Adversarial Bert and Vanilla BERT. The BERT (TL: 450, UA))[2] yielded the lowest F1 score of 0.667 among all the experimentation. The main aim of our evaluation was to highlight the performance improvement using adversarial augmentation. On close observation in Table 1, it can be noticed that use of augmented data improved the F1 score for BERT to 0.671 (TL:450) and 0.681 (TL:500). The improvement in the F1 scores can be attributed to the robustness introduced by fine tuning the language model on the adversarial examples. It is to be noted that with better hyper parameter tuning the results could have been improved.

4.3 Longformer Results Analysis

The introduction of adversarial augmentation, along with dual context input, increases the average token length of the sentences in the given data set. This increase in average token size highlighted the shortcoming of the BERT model, which can only work up to 512 tokens, and brought about the requirement for Longformers. The results in Table 1 highlight the improvement in the performance of the Longformers. We achieved an F1 score of 0.689 with TL:600 and 0.704 with TL:650. The adversarial examples helped create a more dynamic, robust embedding space for the Longformer to exploit and make better predictions than the BERT. Though Longformer has been known to perform less than BERT in many of the Natural Language Inference tasks in our case, they take the lead and leverage the dual context adversarial setup quite well.

4.4 Ensemble Modelling Results Analysis

We leveraged the individual performance of **Longformers**[3] and **BERT**[4] in a combined way by preparing three different variations of Voting Ensemble to report our results.

1. B(TL:450, UA)+ B(TL:450, A)+B(TL:500, A): The following ensemble yielded a F1 Score of 0.709 which was comparable to the individual performance of the Longformer(TL:650). The ensemble of B perform significantly better than individual B variations by minimum of 4%
2. LF (TL:600, A)+ LF(TL:650, A)+B(TL:500, A): Ensemble of 2 LF and the best individual B variation reported the F1 score of 0.713 which was a slight gain from the LF(TL: 650, A).

[2] 'TL' refers to token length, 'UA' refers to Unaugmented Data, 'A' refers to adversarial augmented data

[3] Longformer has been referred to as 'LF' in section 4.3

[4] BERT has been referred to as 'B' is section 4.3

Model and Technique	Precision	Recall	F1 Score
BERT (TL: 450, UA)	0.655	0.702	0.667
BERT (TL: 450, A)	0.660	0.701	0.671
BERT (TL : 500, A)	0.674	0.693	0.681
Longformer (TL : 600, A)	0.681	0.701	0.689
Longformer (TL : 650, A)	0.714	0.699	0.704
Ensemble (Longformer (TL : 600, A)+Longformer (TL : 650, A)+ BERT (TL: 450, UA)+BERT (TL: 450, A)+BERT (TL: 500, UA)	**0.716**	**0.714**	**0.715**
Ensemble (Longformer (TL : 600, A)+Longformer (TL : 650, A)+ BERT (TL: 500, A)	0.708	0.719	0.713
Ensemble (Longformer (TL : 600, A)+BERT (TL: 450, A)+ BERT (TL: 500, A)	0.723	0.702	0.709

Table 1: Experimentation results of model variations. Here 'TL' is maximum token length. 'A' represents that the model was trained on the adversarial augmented data, and 'UA' indicates the model trained on unaugmented data

3. LF (TL:600, A)+ LF(TL :650, A)+ B(TL:450, UA)+ B(TL:450, A)+ B(TL: 500, UA): This ensemble was the best performing submission in this task for our team. The ensemble reported F1 score of 0.715. The results are comparable to the previous ensemble thus highlighting the dominance of LF in ensemble setup

5 Conclusion

In this paper, we proposed an Adversarial Perturbated (TextAttack) BERT and Longformer model, which aims to create a robust model capable of identifying the Euphemism in text. We experimented with different token lengths and eventually created a voting ensemble model that combined our other experiments into a single encapsulation. The ensemble of two adversarial Longformers, two adversarial BERT, and one non-adversarial produced an F1 score of 0.715, which was our best submission. The use of dual context input to the models falls short of the expected performance boost and motivates us to look further into the concept of using multiple representations. We aim to experiment with different methods to combine these representations into a single exemplary representation that can pass into these language models to solve the downstream tasks.

6 Limitations

In this paper, we propose using dual context input with an adversarial training set up to approach the challenge of Euphemism Detection. The approach currently failed to make a significant impact, as reflected by our system performance on the leaderboard. On further analysis, the lack of high performance can be attributed to a selection non ideal set of hyperparameters while training the system. Combining two different contextual representations requires introducing an Attention module or experimenting with other methods to that can result in a better pair encoding of the input.

References

Dildora Oktamovna Bakhriddionova. 2021. The needs of using euphemisms. *Mental Enlightenment Scientific-Methodological Journal*, 2021(06):55–64.

Iz Beltagy, Matthew E Peters, and Arman Cohan. 2020. Longformer: The long-document transformer. *arXiv preprint arXiv:2004.05150*.

Mark Davies and Robert Fuchs. 2015. Expanding horizons in the study of world englishes with the 1.9 billion word global web-based english corpus (glowbe). *English World-Wide*, 36(1):1–28.

Jacob Devlin, Ming-Wei Chang, Kenton Lee, and Kristina Toutanova. 2018. Bert: Pre-training of deep bidirectional transformers for language understanding. *arXiv preprint arXiv:1810.04805*.

Christian Felt and Ellen Riloff. 2020. Recognizing euphemisms and dysphemisms using sentiment analysis. In *Proceedings of the Second Workshop on Figurative Language Processing*, pages 136–145.

Martha Gavidia, Patrick Lee, Anna Feldman, and Jing Peng. 2022. Cats are fuzzy pets: A corpus and analysis of potentially euphemistic terms. *arXiv preprint arXiv:2205.02728*.

Savo Karam. 2011. Truths and euphemisms: How euphemisms are used in the political arena. *3L, Language, Linguistics, Literature*, 17(1).

Patrick Lee, Martha Gavidia, Anna Feldman, and Jing Peng. 2022. Searching for pets: Using distributional and sentiment-based methods to find potentially euphemistic terms. *arXiv preprint arXiv:2205.10451*.

Edward Loper and Steven Bird. 2002. Nltk: The natural language toolkit. *arXiv preprint cs/0205028*.

Rijul Magu and Jiebo Luo. 2018. Determining code words in euphemistic hate speech using word embedding networks. In *Proceedings of the 2nd workshop on abusive language online (ALW2)*, pages 93–100.

John X Morris, Eli Lifland, Jin Yong Yoo, Jake Grigsby, Di Jin, and Yanjun Qi. 2020. Textattack: A framework for adversarial attacks, data augmentation, and adversarial training in nlp. *arXiv preprint arXiv:2005.05909*.

Hussein Abdo Rababah. 2014. The translatability and use of x-phemism expressions (x-phemization): Euphemisms, dysphemisms and orthophemisms) in the medical discourse. *Studies in Literature and Language*, 9(3):229–240.

Nils Reimers and Iryna Gurevych. 2019. Sentence-bert: Sentence embeddings using siamese bert-networks. *arXiv preprint arXiv:1908.10084*.

Wanzheng Zhu and Suma Bhat. 2021. Euphemistic phrase detection by masked language model. *arXiv preprint arXiv:2109.04666*.

Wanzheng Zhu, Hongyu Gong, Rohan Bansal, Zachary Weinberg, Nicolas Christin, Giulia Fanti, and Suma Bhat. 2021. Self-supervised euphemism detection and identification for content moderation. In *2021 IEEE Symposium on Security and Privacy (SP)*, pages 229–246. IEEE.

FigurativeQA: A Test Benchmark for Figurativeness Comprehension for Question Answering

Geetanjali Rakshit and Jeffrey Flanigan
Computer Science and Engineering Department
UC Santa Cruz
{grakshit,jmflanig}@ucsc.edu

Abstract

Figurative language is widespread in human language (Lakoff and Johnson, 2008), posing potential challenges in NLP applications. In this paper, we investigate the effect of figurative language on the task of question answering (QA). We construct FigurativeQA, a test set of 400 yes-no questions with figurative and non-figurative contexts, extracted from product reviews and restaurant reviews. We demonstrate that a state-of-the-art RoBERTa QA model has considerably lower performance in question answering when the contexts are figurative rather than literal, indicating a gap in current models. We propose a general method for improving the performance of QA models by converting the figurative contexts into non-figurative by prompting GPT-3, and demonstrate its effectiveness. Our results indicate a need for building QA models infused with figurative language understanding capabilities.

1 Introduction

Understanding figurative language can be a challenging task for humans, let alone for machines (Zayed et al., 2020). Although native speakers may effortlessly infer the meaning of similes and metaphors, it may be particularly difficult for non-native speakers to understand. Effects of the presence of figurative language has been studied for various downstream NLP tasks such as machine translation (Dankers et al., 2022), recognizing textual entailment (Chakrabarty et al., 2021), and dialog models (Jhamtani et al., 2021), inter-alia.

To the best of our knowledge, there is no prior line of work investigating question answering (QA) on figurative text. Figurative language has a limited presence in existing question answering (QA) datasets in popular use such as SQuAD (Rajpurkar et al., 2018) and Natural Questions (Kwiatkowski et al., 2019), where the contexts are typically literal and factual, constructed from Wikipedia passages.[1]

While figurative language has a limited presence in many QA datasets, it does occur regularly in some domains, such as the reviews domain. User-written reviews, especially those with highly positive or highly negative ratings tend to use strong opinions and are more likely to contain figurative language (Mohammad et al., 2016). We show that it can be challenging for existing QA models to draw inferences from this kind of figurative text.

We propose a new task of answering questions from text that is figurative, and consequently, more challenging to answer. For this task, we present a test dataset, FigurativeQA, consisting of 400 questions and accompanying figurative contexts constructed from Amazon product reviews (Niculae and Danescu-Niculescu-Mizil, 2014) and Yelp restaurant reviews (Oraby et al., 2017). We leverage existing resources for figurative contexts (Niculae and Danescu-Niculescu-Mizil, 2014; Oraby et al., 2017) and manually construct question-answer pairs from these contexts. Further, we create non-figurative versions of this dataset, both automatically by prompting GPT-3 (Brown et al., 2020) as well as manually. We show that it is harder to answer questions from figurative context for current state-of-the-art models. In fig. 1, we show examples of figurative contexts from Amazon product reviews and Yelp restaurant reviews, a question answer pair for the contexts, along with automatically and manually constructed non-figurative versions of the context.

The contributions of this work are the following:

- FigurativeQA, a test set of 400 yes/no question-answer pairs with figurative and non-figurative contexts. For the 200 figurative contexts, we also provide manually created literal

[1]From a rough check of the SQuAD dev set, we observe that the questions themselves are also mostly non-figurative. We found two examples of figurative questions out of 5,928 answerable questions in the SQuAD dev set, one of them being *"Who is eligible to toss their name in the hat to be First Minister?"*.

Proceedings of the 3rd Workshop on Figurative Language Processing (FLP), pages 160 - 166
December 8, 2022 ©2022 Association for Computational Linguistics

Figurative Context: *The album , like almost everything Krush has released ,* ***slays*** *.*
Question: *Is the album good?*
Answer: *Yes*
Non-fig. version (manually created): *The album is really good, like most of Krush's work.*
Non-fig. version (from GPT-3): *The album is really good, like almost everything Krush has released.*

Figurative Context: *Although, the menu items doesnt* ***SCREAM*** *French cuisine. Most foods looks like you can get at any American place.*
Question: *Is the menu authentic french?*
Answer: *No*
Non-fig. version (manually created): *The menu items aren't typical of French cuisine. Rather, they are common at most American eateries.*
Non-fig. version (from GPT-3): *Although, the menu items doesn't look very French. Most foods look like you can get at any American place.*

Figure 1: Examples of figurative contexts from FigurativeQA. Example 1 is from Amazon product reviews and Example 2 from Yelp restaurant reviews.The figurative text fragments within the contexts are shown in bold and italics.

contexts for comparison.

- We show that it is harder to answer questions from figurative contexts for models trained on QA data with non-figurative contexts, and that manually changing the figurative context to a meaning-preserving non-figurative version improves performance.
- We propose a method to use GPT-3 to automatically produce non-figurative contexts from figurative ones, and demonstrate that it improves our QA system on the FigurativeQA dataset.

The outline of the paper is as follows: after reviewing related work (§2), we introduce our new QA dataset for figurative language (§3). We next introduce a general method for converting figurative language to non-figurative language by prompting GPT-3 (§4), which we use to improve our baseline QA model. We then present our experimental results (§5), and finally conclude (§6).

2 Related Work

Handling of figurative language is of significance in many downstream NLP tasks such as machine translation (Mao et al., 2018; Dankers et al., 2022), recognizing textual entailment (Chakrabarty et al., 2021), sentiment analysis (Qadir et al., 2015), among others. Chakrabarty et al. (2021) investigate the robustness of state-of-the-art entailment models on figurative examples on test sets for similes, metaphors, and irony. Chakrabarty et al. (2022) test figurative language understanding in pre-trained language models by evaluating continuation of text in narratives, while (Liu et al., 2022) investigate non-literal reasoning capabilities of language models on a Winograd-style non-literal language understanding task.

The idea of converting metaphors to their literal counterparts has been previously explored for machine translation by Mao et al. (2018), where metaphors in English text are first identified and then converted to a literal version, by making use of word embeddings and WordNet, before doing machine translation into Chinese. In dialog systems, a similar approach was employed by Jhamtani et al. (2021), where idioms and metaphors in utterances are converted to literal versions using a dictionary lookup-based method. Our work is closest to Jhamtani et al. (2021), except that we explore the robustness of QA systems in a machine comprehension setup, instead of dialog models, to figurative language, which, to the best of our knowledge, is a first. Our automatic approach to creating rephrased non-figurative versions of figurative text is done using pre-trained language models, rather than rule-based methods which have been shown to be error-prone (Jhamtani et al., 2021).

Related QA datasets include the FriendsQA dataset (Yang and Choi, 2019), which is a dialog-based QA dataset constructed from dialogs from the TV series Friends. While it does contain metaphors and sarcasm, it may not be ideal to test figurative language understanding as it is unclear how much of the dataset is actually figurative. The dialogic nature of the dataset further contributes to making it challenging. Another dataset that requires figurative language understanding is the RiddleSense dataset (Lin et al., 2021), which comprises of riddles, but unlike ours, it's modeled as an open domain QA task, rather than a machine comprehension task. Parde and Nielsen (2018) show that questions about novel metaphors from literature are judged to be deeper than non-metaphorical or non-conventional metaphors by humans, but their focus is on generating deep questions, rather than testing the robustness of QA models.

3 FigurativeQA Dataset

The figurative data in FigurativeQA comes from two sources: Amazon product reviews (Niculae and Danescu-Niculescu-Mizil, 2014), and Yelp restaurant reviews (Oraby et al., 2017). For comparison, we also extract non-figurative contexts from each of these sources to form the non-figurative split of FigurativeQA. We construct a question answering dataset on top of these contexts. For simplicity, we only work with yes-no questions. Fig 1 shows examples from the FigurativeQA dataset. The data statistics from each source (Amazon and Yelp) and each split (figurative and non-figurative) are summarized in Table 1.

We select figurative texts for annotation with question-answer pairs from Amazon product reviews using the following procedure. Niculae and Danescu-Niculescu-Mizil (2014) construct a dataset of figurative comparisons extracted using comparator patterns (such as *"like"*, *"as"*, or *"than"*) from Amazon product reviews, and then obtain 3 sets of figurativeness scores (on a scale of 1 to 4) on Amazon Mechanical Turk (with scores of 1–2 binned as literal and 3–4 as figurative). Of the 1260 comparisons in this dataset, we extract the sentences which have an average figurativeness score of greater than 3. This leaves us with 254 sentences, of which we manually pick 100 instances, and construct a yes-no question for each sentence.

We select examples for annotating with question-answer pairs from Yelp reviews using a similar procedure. Oraby et al. (2017) construct a dataset for NLG in the restaurant domain from Yelp reviews, which comes labeled with sentiment information (1-2 rating for negative, 3 for neutral and 4-5 for positive). Since positive or negative reviews are more likely to contain figurative language, from the set of positive and negative reviews, we extract instances using comparator patterns such as *"like"*, *"as"*, or *"than"*, similar to the procedure in Niculae and Danescu-Niculescu-Mizil (2014). We then manually choose 100 instances that contain rich, figurative language, and construct a yes-no question for each.

	avg. context length	**category**	**Yes**	**No**
fig.	9	**Amazon**	52	48
	16	**Yelp**	50	50
non-fig.	10	**Amazon**	50	50
	14	**Yelp**	49	51

Table 1: Number of yes-no questions from Amazon product reviews and Yelp restaurant reviews for figurative and non-figurative contexts, and average length of context (number of words)

The figurative contexts from FigurativeQA tend to contain more *similes*, since comparator patterns (*"like"*, *"as"*, or *"than"*) were used to extract the text. However, we observe that many of these examples also contain other kinds of figurative constructs such as metaphor, idiom, hyperbole, sarcasm, etc, because the nature of the reviews text is such that it is replete with figurative expressions.

For each context in FigurativeQA, we construct a yes-no question. For the figurative contexts, we make sure to pose a question such that answering it would require understanding of the figurative text present in the context. For the non-figurative contexts, we construct questions that look similar to the ones for the figurative contexts. Additionally, for the figurative contexts extracted from Amazon and Yelp, we manually create non-figurative counterparts that preserve the meaning and overall content.

4 Non-Figurative Contexts from GPT-3

We obtain non-figurative versions of the figurative contexts from FigurativeQA by prompting GPT-3 (da-vinci-002). Please refer to Appendix A for model details and the prompts we used.

As an intrinsic evaluation of the effectiveness of our prompting method, we manually evaluate the correctness of the non-figurative/literal contexts generated by prompting GPT-3. Table 2 shows the results from the manual evaluation of the GPT-3 outputs. We observe that GPT-3 performs fairly well in converting figurative language in FigurativeQA to literal, with nearly 81% and 75% of the outputs in Amazon and Yelp, respectively, judged

Amazon	**Context (original, figurative)**: *Second , the final confrontation was more **like a footnote in the story** than a real ending .* **[CORRECT] Non-fig. context (from GPT-3)**: *Second, the final confrontation was less significant than it should have been given its place in the story.*
	Context (original, figurative): *Her misty , vaguely dreamlike writing can pull a reader into the world of 1900s New Orleans and its society , but her heroine sometimes feels more **like a vessel** than a fully-realized person .* **Figurative Context**: *Not a storybook , by any means , this one is more **like a visit to the zoo** .* **[INCORRECT] Non-fig. context (from GPT-3)**: *This story is not like a fairytale, it's more like a visit to the zoo.*
	Context (original, figurative): *The books are **like potato chips** - you **can't eat just one** .* **[SAME] Non-fig. context (from GPT-3)**: *The books are like potato chips - you can't eat just one .*
Yelp	**Context (original, figurative)**: *i had the chicken fajitas , which came with a giant flour tortilla that was **as hot as hades** .* **[CORRECT] Non-fig. context (from GPT-3)**: *i had the chicken fajitas , which came with a really big and hot flour tortilla.*
	Context (original, figurative): *this is as authentic thai **as much as imitation crab is authentic crab** .* **[INCORRECT] Non-fig. context (from GPT-3)**: *this is as inauthentic thai as much as imitation crab is inauthentic crab.*
	Context (original, figurative): *the same thing with the steak and potatoes , it was almost as if they tried to **decorate the plate with salt** .* **[SAME] Non-fig. context (from GPT-3)**: *the same thing with the steak and potatoes , it was almost as if they tried to decorate the plate with salt .*

Figure 2: Examples of non-figurative contexts generated from GPT-3, for Amazon and Yelp. The figurative text fragments within the contexts are shown in bold and italics.

	Amazon	Yelp
correct	81%	75%
incorrect	15%	19%
same	4 %	6%

Table 2: Evaluation of non-figurative outputs from GPT-3. **Correct** means the GPT-3 output is non-figurative and correctly preserves the meaning. **Same** means GPT-3 produced the exact same output as the input (no change). All other outputs are **incorrect**.

to be correct. In fig. 2, we show examples of non-figurative text generated from GPT-3.

5 Experiments and Results

As a baseline, we run RoBERTa-base (Liu et al., 2019) finetuned on the training set of BoolQ (Clark et al., 2019). The performance on FigurativeQA is summarized in Tables 3 and 4. We find that the RoBERTa QA model performs poorly on the figurative contexts compared to the non-figurative contexts, and that manually changing the figurative language to non-figurative language improves performance. This indicates that automatic conversion of figurative language to non-figurative language may improve performance.

	Amazon	Yelp
Fig (orig.)	83.43 ± 1.1	66.84 ± 2.61
Fig (man. non-fig)	93.5 ± 1.12	90 ± 1.44
Non-fig (orig.)	92 ± 1.42	89.6 ± 1.68

Table 3: Accuracy of RoBERTa-base fine-tuned on BoolQ, on the figurative split, manually created non-figurative version of the figurative split, and non-figurative split of FigurativeQA. (We reran experiments 1000 times with bootstrap resampling. The numbers reported are the mean and std-dev.)

To improve upon the baseline model, we pass the automatic non-figurative contexts from GPT-3 (§4) to our RoBERTa-base model. We find that this procedure improves the performance on figurative language split, and has no effect on the non-figurative language split, and improves overall performance on FigurativeQA. As an additional comparison, we also prompt GPT-3 as a QA model and report its performance on FigurativeQA.[2]

	Amazon	Yelp
Baseline: Fig	83.43±1.1	66.84±2.61
Ours: Fig	86.51±1.13	73.5 ±1.66
Baseline: Non-fig	92±1.42	89.6±1.68
Ours: Non-fig	92.45±1.12	89.4±1.69
Baseline: Overall	87.71±0.89	78.21±.6
GPT-3: Overall	64.58±1.71	60.1±3.1
Ours: Overall	**89.5±3.18**	**81.46±1.19**

Table 4: QA performance on FigurativeQA. Our method uses GPT-3 prompting (zero-shot) to convert the figurative contexts to literal (We reran experiments for 1000 times with bootstrap resampling. The numbers reported are the mean and std-dev. The numbers in bold are the best results.)

6 Conclusion and Future Work

We show that current QA models do not perform so well when answering questions from figurative contexts as compared to non-figurative text. On manually created non-figurative versions of these contexts, we are able to show significant improvements. However, the manual annotation being an expensive step, we use an automatic method of prompting of GPT-3 and were still able to achieve performance gains. This highlights a need to build QA models that can handle figurative text. In the future, we would like to do a fine-grained analysis of QA performance on different kinds of figurative constructs, including similes, metaphors, irony, idioms, rhetorical questions, hyperbole, personification, etc.

Limitations

Our dataset contains the specific domains of Amazon and Yelp reviews, and is English-only. Results and conclusions may not generalize to other domains or languages.

References

Tom Brown, Benjamin Mann, Nick Ryder, Melanie Subbiah, Jared D Kaplan, Prafulla Dhariwal, Arvind Neelakantan, Pranav Shyam, Girish Sastry, Amanda Askell, et al. 2020. Language models are few-shot learners. *Advances in neural information processing systems*, 33:1877–1901.

Tuhin Chakrabarty, Yejin Choi, and Vered Shwartz. 2022. It's not rocket science: Interpreting figurative language in narratives. *Transactions of the Association for Computational Linguistics*, 10:589–606.

Tuhin Chakrabarty, Debanjan Ghosh, Adam Poliak, and Smaranda Muresan. 2021. Figurative language in recognizing textual entailment. *arXiv preprint arXiv:2106.01195*.

Christopher Clark, Kenton Lee, Ming-Wei Chang, Tom Kwiatkowski, Michael Collins, and Kristina Toutanova. 2019. Boolq: Exploring the surprising difficulty of natural yes/no questions. *arXiv preprint arXiv:1905.10044*.

Verna Dankers, Christopher G Lucas, and Ivan Titov. 2022. Can transformer be too compositional? analysing idiom processing in neural machine translation. *arXiv preprint arXiv:2205.15301*.

Harsh Jhamtani, Varun Gangal, Eduard Hovy, and Taylor Berg-Kirkpatrick. 2021. Investigating robustness of dialog models to popular figurative language constructs. *arXiv preprint arXiv:2110.00687*.

Tom Kwiatkowski, Jennimaria Palomaki, Olivia Redfield, Michael Collins, Ankur Parikh, Chris Alberti, Danielle Epstein, Illia Polosukhin, Jacob Devlin, Kenton Lee, et al. 2019. Natural questions: a benchmark for question answering research. *Transactions of the Association for Computational Linguistics*, 7:453–466.

George Lakoff and Mark Johnson. 2008. *Metaphors we live by*. University of Chicago press.

Bill Yuchen Lin, Ziyi Wu, Yichi Yang, Dong-Ho Lee, and Xiang Ren. 2021. Riddlesense: Reasoning about riddle questions featuring linguistic creativity and commonsense knowledge. *arXiv preprint arXiv:2101.00376*.

Emmy Liu, Chen Cui, Kenneth Zheng, and Graham Neubig. 2022. Testing the ability of language models to interpret figurative language. *arXiv preprint arXiv:2204.12632*.

Yinhan Liu, Myle Ott, Naman Goyal, Jingfei Du, Mandar Joshi, Danqi Chen, Omer Levy, Mike Lewis, Luke Zettlemoyer, and Veselin Stoyanov. 2019. Roberta: A robustly optimized bert pretraining approach. *arXiv preprint arXiv:1907.11692*.

Rui Mao, Chenghua Lin, and Frank Guerin. 2018. Word embedding and wordnet based metaphor identification and interpretation. In *Proceedings of the 56th annual meeting of the association for computational linguistics*. Association for Computational Linguistics (ACL).

[2]Please refer to Appendix B for details about prompting GPT-3 as a QA system.

Saif Mohammad, Ekaterina Shutova, and Peter Turney. 2016. Metaphor as a medium for emotion: An empirical study. In *Proceedings of the Fifth Joint Conference on Lexical and Computational Semantics*, pages 23–33.

Vlad Niculae and Cristian Danescu-Niculescu-Mizil. 2014. Brighter than gold: Figurative language in user generated comparisons. In *Proceedings of the 2014 conference on empirical methods in natural language processing (EMNLP)*, pages 2008–2018.

Shereen Oraby, Sheideh Homayon, and Marilyn Walker. 2017. Harvesting creative templates for generating stylistically varied restaurant reviews. *arXiv preprint arXiv:1709.05308*.

Natalie Parde and Rodney Nielsen. 2018. Automatically generating questions about novel metaphors in literature. In *Proceedings of the 11th International Conference on Natural Language Generation*, pages 264–273.

Ashequl Qadir, Ellen Riloff, and Marilyn A Walker. 2015. *Learning to recognize affective polarity in similes*.

Pranav Rajpurkar, Robin Jia, and Percy Liang. 2018. Know what you don't know: Unanswerable questions for squad. *arXiv preprint arXiv:1806.03822*.

Zhengzhe Yang and Jinho D Choi. 2019. Friendsqa: Open-domain question answering on tv show transcripts. In *Proceedings of the 20th Annual SIGdial Meeting on Discourse and Dialogue*, pages 188–197.

Omnia Zayed, John Philip McCrae, and Paul Buitelaar. 2020. Figure me out: a gold standard dataset for metaphor interpretation. In *Proceedings of the 12th Language Resources and Evaluation Conference*, pages 5810–5819.

A Appendix A: Prompting GPT-3 for figurative text

We use the da-vinci-002 model with temperature set to 0.3 and max-length set to 100. We used a prompt with 5 examples, as shown in Fig. 3.

For the following inputs, if the text contains figurative language, convert it to a literal version. Otherwise, output the same text as the input.

Input: It's inevitable. Their love was built on sand and this is why their marriage has landed on the rocks.
Output: It's inevitable. Their love was unstable and this is why their marriage has failed.

Input: The weather forecast predicted a heatwave this week across most of the country.
Output: The weather forecast predicted a heatwave this week across most of the country.

Input: During the heatwave, the entire house was like a furnace.
Output: During the heatwave, the entire house was uncomfortably hot.

Input: The brisket is nothing to write home about.
Output: There is nothing particularly remarkable about the brisket.

Input: The fries were served cold.
Output: The fries were served cold.

Input: The lamb had a melt in the mouth texture.
Output: The lamb was soft and well-cooked.

Input: The adapter worked like a charm.
Output: The adapter worked perfectly.

Figure 3: GPT-3 prompt to generate non-figurative versions of the figurative contexts.

B Appendix B: Prompting GPT-3 for QA

We use the da-vinci-002 model with temperature set to 0.3 and max-length set to 100. We used a prompt with 2 examples, as shown in Fig. 4.

Based on the passage, answer the following question with a yes or a no.

Passage:
Windows Movie Maker (formerly known as Windows Live Movie Maker in Windows 7) is a discontinued video editing software by Microsoft. It is a part of Windows Essentials software suite and offers the ability to create and edit videos as well as to publish them on OneDrive, Facebook, Vimeo, YouTube, and Flickr.
Question: Is windows movie maker part of windows essentials?
Answer: yes

Passage:
Both Jersey and Bank of England notes are legal tender in Jersey and circulate together, alongside the Guernsey pound and Scottish banknotes. The Jersey notes are not legal tender in the United Kingdom but are legal currency, so creditors and traders may accept them if they so choose.
Question: Is jersey currency legal tender in the uk?
Answer: no

Figure 4: GPT-3 prompt to get yes-no answers.

Exploring Euphemism Detection in Few-Shot and Zero-Shot Settings

Sedrick Scott Keh
Carnegie Mellon University
skeh@cs.cmu.edu

Abstract

This work builds upon the Euphemism Detection Shared Task proposed in the EMNLP 2022 FigLang Workshop, and extends it to few-shot and zero-shot settings. We demonstrate a few-shot and zero-shot formulation using the dataset from the shared task, and we conduct experiments in these settings using RoBERTa and GPT-3. Our results show that language models are able to classify euphemistic terms relatively well even on new terms unseen during training, indicating that it is able to capture higher-level concepts related to euphemisms.

1 Introduction

Euphemisms are figures of speech which aim to soften the blow of certain words which may be too direct or too harsh (Magu and Luo, 2018; Felt and Riloff, 2020). In the EMNLP 2022 FigLang Workshop Euphemism Shared Task, participating teams are given a set of sentences with potentially euphemistic terms (PETs) enclosed in brackets, and the task is to classify whether or not the PET in a given sentence is used euphemistically.

In this task/dataset, however, there are many PETs which are repeated throughout both the training and testing sets (more details in Section 3). In addition, several PETs are classified as euphemistic almost 100% of the time during training. This raises an important question: is the model actually learning to classify what a euphemism is, or is it simply reflecting back things it has seen repeatedly during training? How do we know if the model we train can truly capture the essence of what a euphemism is? Even among humans, this is a very nontrivial task. If one hears the phrase "lose one's lunch" for the first time, for example, it may not be immediately obvious that it is a euphemism for throwing up. However, when used in a sentence, the context clues together with an understanding of the meanings of the words "lose" and "lunch" will allow a human to piece together the meaning. For a machine to be able to do this, however, is not trivial at all.

To this end, we test this by checking whether a model can correctly classify PETs it has never seen during training. This leads us to our few-shot/zero-shot setting. The two key contributions of our paper are as follows: 1) We propose and formulate the few-shot and zero-shot euphemism detection settings; and 2) We run initial baselines on these euphemisms using RoBERTa and GPT-3, and we present a thorough analysis of our results.

2 Related Work

Compared to other figures of speech like similes (Chakrabarty et al., 2020) and metaphors (Chakrabarty et al., 2021), work on euphemisms has been limited. Recently, Gavidia et al. (2022); Lee et al. (2022) released a new dataset of diverse euphemisms and conducted analysis on automatically identifying potentially euphemistic terms. In the past, Felt and Riloff (2020) used sentiment analysis techniques to recognize euphemistic and dysphemistic phrases. Other studies also focused on specific euphemistic categories such as hate speech (Magu and Luo, 2018) and drugs (Zhu et al., 2021).

In terms of zero-shot figurative language detection, the existing literature has also been quite limited. The few existing studies (Schneider et al., 2022) mostly focus on metaphors and on low-resource settings. This leaves out less common figures of speech such as euphemisms, and the low-resource formulation is also not exactly identical to the zero-shot setting we explore in this paper.

3 Task and Dataset

Our task is similar to the FigLang 2022 Workshop Shared Task on Euphemism Detection. Given a sentence containing a potentially euphemistic term (PET), we want to determine whether the PET is used euphemistically. The key difference with our task is that we perform the binary classification on

Proceedings of the 3rd Workshop on Figurative Language Processing (FLP), pages 167 - 172
December 8, 2022 ©2022 Association for Computational Linguistics

	Ave. Test Size	Ave. # of unique PETs in test
Standard	295.0	93.3
Few-Shot (k=1)	279.6	35.0
Few-Shot (k=3)	281.2	35.4
0-shot (random)	280.6	34.3
Death	174.0	14.9
Sexual Activity	45.0	10.4
Employment	176.0	23.5
Politics	161.0	20.9
Bodily Functions	26.0	7.0
Physical/Mental	299.0	36.0
Substances	88.0	9.1

Table 1: Dataset statistics for the few-shot and zero-shot settings. Because there is some stochasticity involved in dataset creation, we take averages over 10 samples.

a few-shot/zero-shot setting. Similarly, we use the dataset proposed by Gavidia et al. (2022), which contains 1965 sentences with PETs, split across 129 unique PETs and 7 different euphemistic categories (e.g. death, employment, etc.) Furthermore, the dataset also contains additional information such as the category and the status of the PET ("always euph" vs "sometimes euph").

4 Methodology

4.1 Constructing the Few-Shot Setting

For the k-shot setting, we want the PETs in the validation/test set to have appeared in the training set only k times. Let our set of PETs be $P = \{p_1, p_2, \dots p_N\}$. We construct the test set as follows. First, we randomly sample a PET p_i from P, then find all sentences $s_1, s_2, \dots s_M$ containing PET p_i. Out of these M sentences, we sample k sentences $s_{j_1}, s_{j_2}, \dots s_{j_k}$ to keep in our training set, moving all the $(M - k)$ remaining sentences s_j to our test set. We repeat this process until we reach the desired size for our validation/test set. In our case, we stop when the validation and test each reach around 15% of our entire dataset ($\pm 2\%$ to account for the fact that it's unlikely to reach 15% exactly). In practice, we sample 30% for the validation+test set combined, then randomly split this 30% into two sets of 15% in order to increase the PET diversity in both the validation and the test splits. For the k-shot setting, we use $k = 1$ and $k = 3$. The dataset statistics for the k-shot datasets can be found in Table 1.

4.2 Constructing the Zero-Shot Setting

For the zero-shot setting, we want the PETs in the validation/test set to never have appeared in the training set. There are two ways to achieve this:

1. **Random Sampling** – The construction for this is similar to that of the few-shot setting, except here, we don't sample $s_{j_1}, s_{j_2}, \dots s_{j_k}$ to keep in the training set but rather move all M sentences $s_1, s_2, \dots s_M$ to our validation/test set.

2. **Type-based** – Rather than randomly choosing assorted PETs to holdout into our test set, we instead choose the test set PETs to all come from a single category, while the training set will come from the remaining categories. These categories are provided alongside the sentences in the dataset by Gavidia et al. (2022), and there are 7 categories in total. Because some categories may contain more sentences (and more PETs) than others, then the sizes of the training splits of these categories will be different. To address this, we subsample from the training splits of the categories with excess rows to match the training category with the least number of rows. This way, we ensure that all categories have an equal number of rows of training data, and so any changes in performance will be likely due to the data quality (rather than due to simply having more/less data). At the end, this gives us a training size of 1367 rows for each category. For the test splits, different categories also have different sizes, but we choose to leave the test split sizes unchanged and opted not to do the sampling like we did for the training step because the smallest testing category has size 26 ("bodily functions"), while some other categories had test sizes of 200+ ("physical/mental"), so we found it impractical to force the test sizes to be identical. Statistics for these datasets can be found in Table 1. In theory, having larger test sets will mostly affect the variance, but the mean should not be affected that much. We comment more on this in Section 6.

4.3 Models

We consider two different types of baseline models. First, we consider networks which we can reasonably fine-tune. For this group, we select RoBERTa (Liu et al., 2019), covering both the RoBERTa-base model and the RoBERTa-large model, which have been extensively used for classification. The rationale behind choosing RoBERTa was twofold. First, RoBERTa is a commonly used standard for various classification tasks and has generally been shown to perform better than other simple transformer-based models such as BERT (Devlin et al., 2019). Second, it has empirically been shown to work sufficiently well when dealing with euphemisms, as Lee et al.

(2022) used RoBERTa-based sentiment and offensiveness models to search for euphemisms.

In addition, we also try out large language models such as GPT-3 (davinci) (Brown et al., 2020), which has been known to work well on zero-shot and few-shot settings. We are interested to find out whether the large-scale pretraining provides GPT-3 with the capability to implicitly model the concept of "euphemism-hood", which is built from several other adjacent concepts such as politeness and tone. We hence explore using both zero-shot and few-shot prompts for GPT-3.

5 Experiment Setup

5.1 RoBERTa Implementation Settings

For both RoBERTa-base and RoBERTa-large, we fine-tune for 10 epochs, taking the model with the best validation performance (F1) as our final model. For RoBERTa-base, we use a learning rate of 1e-5 and a batch size of 16, while for RoBERTa-large, we use a learning rate of 5e-6 and a batch size of 4. All other hyperparameters such as learning rate decay and warmup steps are according to the default settings of HuggingFace's trainer function.

5.2 GPT-3 Implementation Settings

We use the largest version of GPT-3 (davinci). For the zero-shot settings, we prompt it with the phrase "Is the word [PET] used euphemistically in the following sentence: [SENT]", where [PET] and [SENT] represent the euphemistic term and current sentence in question. Here, we conduct a small amount of prompt engineering. For instance, we also tried out "Does this sentence contain a euphemism: [SENT]" or adding "(Yes/No)" before or after our current formulation. We found that our current formulation performs the best among these variations, which is why we choose to report that in Table 2. Meanwhile, for few-shot settings, we simply repeated our zero-shot prompt, followed by either "Yes" or "No" corresponding to the label, and a line break to separate different examples.

Another key challenge with GPT-3 is mapping the responses to 0/1 binary classes. Because GPT-3 is a generative model, it may not necessarily just answer yes/no; instead, it may generate long paragraphs or unrelated characters. To do this mapping, we use a rule-based method. First, if the first 3 characters of the response is "yes" or if the first 2 characters are "no", then we can immediately map them. Next, we gather a list of "1-class" phrases and a list of "0-class" phrases. Here, "1-class" phrases include "is a euphemism", "is used euphemistically", "can be considered a euphemism", "it seems like it", etc. In other words, when these phrases appear in a sentence, then the label is most likely a 1. This likewise holds for "0-class" phrases which are indicative of the label being 0. This includes phrases such as "not a euphemism" or "does not appear to be euphemistic". Lastly, GPT-3 sometimes generates random noise, irrelevant sentences, or says something like "I'm not sure" or "I can't answer that". For these remaining cases, we choose to just ignore them from our scoring. Based on our experiments, this happened only around 4% of the time, so we believe the change to be not that significant. The full list of "1-class" and "0-class" phrases can be found in the Appendix.

6 Results and Analysis

Table 2 shows the results of running all 3 models on both the zero-shot and the few-shot settings. We make the following observations below:

1. **The overall results are generally quite good.** The standard RoBERTa-large setting (i.e. no k-shot/zero-shot) attains an F1 score of 0.836, while a zero-shot model attains an F1 score of 0.740, which is a relatively high F1 score, considering that all the examples during test time were unseen during training. This shows that the model is able to learn something beyond simply just memorizing the PETs during training, and that it is able to somewhat capture the essence of what makes a phrase euphemistic. Perhaps it is able to track discrepancies in sentiment (Lee et al., 2022) or discrepancies in other features such as politeness. At this point, it is difficult to discern exactly why the zero-shot performance is good, and it is an interesting point to explore further in the future.

2. **The "bodily functions" category performs quite poorly, while the "substances" category performs quite well.** For the "bodily functions", this can easily be explained by the dataset size and test set quality. Among the categories, "bodily functions" by far had the least number of test examples at 26 (see Table 1). In fact, there appears to be some correlation between the performance and the size of the test set, as the "sexual activity" category (second-smallest test set) also exhibits relatively poor performance. In addition, the "bodily functions" category has a disproportionately high

		RoBERTa-base			RoBERTa-large			GPT-3 (davinci)		
		P	R	F1	P	R	F1	P	R	F1
Standard Model	-	0.850	0.799	0.824	0.877	0.812	0.836	-	-	-
Few-Shot	k=1	0.802	0.744	0.759	0.818	0.748	0.769	0.565	0.551	0.546
	k=3	0.834	0.795	0.808	0.879	0.798	0.825	0.624	0.599	0.617
Zero-Shot (Random)	-	0.770	0.699	0.715	0.798	0.726	0.740	0.537	0.543	0.507
Zero-Shot (Type-based)	Death	0.782	0.735	0.742	0.803	0.748	0.761	0.453	0.457	0.448
	Sexual Activity	0.647	0.606	0.622	0.633	0.603	0.615	0.533	0.550	0.477
	Employment	0.778	0.790	0.781	0.782	0.817	0.792	0.537	0.532	0.479
	Politics	0.754	0.622	0.645	0.826	0.645	0.688	0.537	0.558	0.484
	Bodily Functions	0.500	0.240	0.324	0.500	0.416	0.480	0.500	0.192	0.278
	Physical/Mental	0.757	0.663	0.689	0.750	0.680	0.693	0.517	0.510	0.489
	Substances	0.897	0.858	0.878	0.913	0.883	0.895	0.553	0.551	0.486

Table 2: Experiment results for RoBERTa-base, RoBERTa-large, and GPT-3 (davinci). Results are averaged over 5 experiments with different dataset splits.

number of items with label 1 (i.e. euphemistic usage), which can skew the F1-score quite a bit. Observe that the macro precision is 0.5 for all 3 models, which tends to happen when the distribution is very skewed and gets a precision of exactly 1.0 for one class and exactly 0.0 for the other class. Meanwhile, for the "substances" category performing well, we speculate that this could be because a lot of these words are quite common. Words like "weed" and "sober" are used quite commonly, as opposed to other euphemisms, which are less commonly used in everyday conversations (e.g. "ethnic cleansing" is a rare phrase).

3. **GPT-3 generally performed quite poorly. Furthermore, GPT-3 performance seems to be independent of category.** For all 7 categories, as well as the randomly sampled zero-shot set, the GPT-3 model has F1 scores between 0.47 and 0.50 for almost all of them. This is a sharp contrast with the RoBERTa model, which varies quite significantly depending on the category. In addition, the GPT-3 performance is much lower than the RoBERTa performance. We hypothesize that this can be solved with additional prompt engineering or prompt tuning (Li and Liang, 2021; Lester et al., 2021). This poor performance can also be a possible cause for the lack of category dependence – perhaps the model is not good enough to discern the subtle differences between these categories in the same way that the RoBERTa models do.

4. **The few-shot performance is better than the zero-shot performance. The 3-shot performance for RoBERTa is almost at level of training the standard model.** This should not come as a surprise, since having at least 1 appearance in the training set is already quite a lot of information provided to the model. Furthermore, the initial dataset had 1965 sentences split across 129 unique PETs, which averages out to around 15 sentences per PET. It is thus notable that being shown 3 examples gives almost the same performance as being shown 15 examples. This suggests that maybe a lot of the learning happens in the early stages, or that many sentences are actually redundant for training purposes. Another interesting area for future exploration would be in trying to find which sentences are the most "instructive" and hence best included within the training set for few-shot settings.

5. **The GPT-3 model greatly benefited from the few-shot setting.** Comparing the $k = 1$ and $k = 3$ GPT-3 results with the zero-shot results, we see that there is a marked increase in performance when a few examples were given as prompts to GPT-3. This is consistent with the findings of Brown et al. (2020) regarding GPT-3's capacity to perform in-context learning. This also makes intuitive sense, as simply providing GPT-3 with a single sentence to classify with no additional context can be quite difficult. In the first place, the GPT-3 model may not even fully know the task from a zero-shot setting. With just 3 examples, the F1 score increases from 0.507 to 0.617, which is a significant increase.

7 Conclusion and Future Work

In this paper, we explored zero-shot and few-shot settings for the Euphemism Detection task. We formulated the problem settings and crafted zero-shot and few-shot datasets from the EMNLP 2022 FigLang Workshop Euphemism Shared Task dataset. We tried two type of models, namely RoBERTa and GPT-3. We found promising results that these language models (especially fine-tuned RoBERTa) were able to perform quite well, even on completely unseen euphemistic terms.

While our results were overall good, the results for GPT-3 were quite poor. In the future, we believe that further prompt engineering or prompt tuning will definitely be helpful in improving the performance of GPT-3 (Li and Liang, 2021; Lester et al., 2021). Furthermore, this idea of few-shot and zero-shot detection is not exclusive to euphemisms. We believe that checking the performance of language models to classify unseen examples is something that will be important to check for a lot of figures of speech and will be important in our quest to process and generate figurative text.

Limitations

As mentioned in the body, a key limitation to our work is the lack of prompt engineering or prompt tuning. We tried some manually crafted prompts, but this does not seem to be enough to get GPT-3 to perform at the level it is expected to.

References

Tom B. Brown, Benjamin Mann, Nick Ryder, Melanie Subbiah, Jared Kaplan, Prafulla Dhariwal, Arvind Neelakantan, Pranav Shyam, Girish Sastry, Amanda Askell, Sandhini Agarwal, Ariel Herbert-Voss, Gretchen Krueger, Tom Henighan, Rewon Child, Aditya Ramesh, Daniel M. Ziegler, Jeffrey Wu, Clemens Winter, Christopher Hesse, Mark Chen, Eric Sigler, Mateusz Litwin, Scott Gray, Benjamin Chess, Jack Clark, Christopher Berner, Sam McCandlish, Alec Radford, Ilya Sutskever, and Dario Amodei. 2020. Language models are few-shot learners. *CoRR*, abs/2005.14165.

Tuhin Chakrabarty, Smaranda Muresan, and Nanyun Peng. 2020. Generating similes effortlessly like a pro: A style transfer approach for simile generation. In *Proceedings of the 2020 Conference on Empirical Methods in Natural Language Processing (EMNLP)*, pages 6455–6469, Online. Association for Computational Linguistics.

Tuhin Chakrabarty, Xurui Zhang, Smaranda Muresan, and Nanyun Peng. 2021. MERMAID: Metaphor generation with symbolism and discriminative decoding. In *Proceedings of the 2021 Conference of the North American Chapter of the Association for Computational Linguistics: Human Language Technologies*, pages 4250–4261, Online. Association for Computational Linguistics.

Jacob Devlin, Ming-Wei Chang, Kenton Lee, and Kristina Toutanova. 2019. BERT: Pre-training of deep bidirectional transformers for language understanding. In *Proceedings of the 2019 Conference of the North American Chapter of the Association for Computational Linguistics: Human Language Technologies, Volume 1 (Long and Short Papers)*, pages 4171–4186, Minneapolis, Minnesota. Association for Computational Linguistics.

Christian Felt and Ellen Riloff. 2020. Recognizing euphemisms and dysphemisms using sentiment analysis. In *Proceedings of the Second Workshop on Figurative Language Processing*, pages 136–145, Online. Association for Computational Linguistics.

Martha Gavidia, Patrick Lee, Anna Feldman, and Jing Peng. 2022. Cats are fuzzy pets: A corpus and analysis of potentially euphemistic terms. *CoRR*, abs/2205.02728.

Patrick Lee, Martha Gavidia, Anna Feldman, and Jing Peng. 2022. Searching for PETs: Using distributional and sentiment-based methods to find potentially euphemistic terms. In *Proceedings of the Second Workshop on Understanding Implicit and Underspecified Language*, pages 22–32, Seattle, USA. Association for Computational Linguistics.

Brian Lester, Rami Al-Rfou, and Noah Constant. 2021. The power of scale for parameter-efficient prompt tuning. In *Proceedings of the 2021 Conference on Empirical Methods in Natural Language Processing*, pages 3045–3059, Online and Punta Cana, Dominican Republic. Association for Computational Linguistics.

Xiang Lisa Li and Percy Liang. 2021. Prefix-tuning: Optimizing continuous prompts for generation. In *Proceedings of the 59th Annual Meeting of the Association for Computational Linguistics and the 11th International Joint Conference on Natural Language Processing (Volume 1: Long Papers)*, pages 4582–4597, Online. Association for Computational Linguistics.

Yinhan Liu, Myle Ott, Naman Goyal, Jingfei Du, Mandar Joshi, Danqi Chen, Omer Levy, Mike Lewis, Luke Zettlemoyer, and Veselin Stoyanov. 2019. Roberta: A robustly optimized bert pretraining approach. Cite arxiv:1907.11692.

Rijul Magu and Jiebo Luo. 2018. Determining code words in euphemistic hate speech using word embedding networks. In *Proceedings of the 2nd Workshop on Abusive Language Online (ALW2)*, pages 93–100, Brussels, Belgium. Association for Computational Linguistics.

Felix Schneider, Sven Sickert, Phillip Brandes, Sophie Marshall, and Joachim Denzler. 2022. Metaphor detection for low resource languages: From zero-shot to few-shot learning in middle high german. In *LREC Workshop on Multiword Expression (LREC-WS)*, pages 75–80, Marseille, France. European Language Resources Association.

Wanzheng Zhu, Hongyu Gong, Rohan Bansal, Zachary Weinberg, Nicolas Christin, Giulia Fanti, and Suma Bhat. 2021. Self-supervised euphemism detection and identification for content moderation. In *42nd IEEE Symposium on Security and Privacy*.

A GPT3 Implementation: Positive and negative phrases

Note that all sentences are converted to lowercase first before doing a search with these phrase lists. The “1-class” phrases and “0-class” phrases are shown below:

“1-class”: ["is used euphemistically", "can be used euphemistically", "is being used euphemistically", "may be used euphemistically", "might be used euphemistically", "is a euphemism", "is used as a euphemism", "is being used as a euphemism", "can be used as a euphemism", "may be used as a euphemism", "might be used as a euphemism", "appears to be a euphemism", "appears to be used euphemistically", "could be used euphemistically", "could be used as a euphemism", "could be a euphemism", "is considered a euphemism", "could be considered a euphemism", "can be considered a euphemism", "could be seen as a euphemism", "can be seen as a euphemism", "could be considered euphemistic", "can be considered euphemistic", "i think so", "i believe so"]

“0-class”: ["not used euphemistically", "not being used euphemistically", "not a euphemism", "not used as a euphemism", "not being used as a euphemism", "does not appear to be a euphemism", "does not appear to be used euphemistically", "i don’t think so", "i don’t believe so", "i do not think so"]

On the Cusp of Comprehensibility: Can Language Models Distinguish Between Metaphors and Nonsense?

Bernadeta Griciūtė[1,2], Marc Tanti[1], and Lucia Donatelli[2]
[1]University of Malta
[2]Saarland University
{bernadeta.griciute.21, marc.tanti}@um.edu.mt
donatelli@coli.uni-saarland.de

Abstract

Creative texts can sometimes be difficult to understand as they balance on the edge of comprehensibility. However, good language skills and common sense can allow advanced language users to both interpret creative texts and reject some linguistic input as nonsense. The goal of this work is to evaluate whether current language models can make the distinction between creative language use and nonsense. To test this, we have computed the mean rank and pseudo-log-likelihood score (PLL) of metaphorical and nonsensical sentences. We have also fine-tuned RoBERTa for binary classification between the two categories. There was a significant difference in the mean ranks and PLL scores of the categories, and the classifier reached around 75-88% accuracy. The results raise interesting questions on what could have led to such satisfactory performance.

1 Introduction

The ultimate goal of Natural Language Understanding (NLU) models is to reach a human-like level of language comprehension. However, a good command of language manifests itself not only in being able to interpret advanced usages of a language, but also in discriminating the uninterpretable, erroneous cases. While automatic grammar checkers are already in place, semantic incongruity is more difficult to trace. The task is further complicated by the existence of figurative language, where a listener is required to go an extra step (when compared to literal language) in order to decode the meaning. The borderline between creative, but still understandable text, and nonsense can be seen as the cusp of comprehensibility.

One of the types of figurative language is metaphors, which are convenient to research due to their ubiquity. Linguistic **metaphors** can be defined as expressions of an understanding of one concept in terms of another, where there is some similarity between the two. While metaphor per se signifies a shift in meaning, they do vary in the degree of metaphoricity and creativity. The most threadbare metaphors which are so commonly used that they become unnoticeable are **conventional metaphors**, for example, "he *takes* a few moments to reply". On the other side of the scale of metaphoricity there are **creative metaphors**, where a novel meaning emerges in a sentence, for example, "the ATM *coughed up* my card" (Cardillo et al., 2010). However, even when it comes to novel metaphors, language users should still be able to infer the meaning - otherwise, they are just **nonsense**.

Professor Irving Massey has suggested that distinguishing between a metaphor and nonsense could be a new Turing test (Massey, 2021). The professor claims that switching between literal and metaphorical senses is an aesthetic gesture inaccessible for computers, and that "the ability to experience metaphor is the very definition of the human". While admittedly for the time being there is no way to track aesthetic experiences of a computer, the (in)ability of computational models to make the distinction between a metaphor and mere nonsense might be worth looking at.

While we sometimes deify metaphors as "a hallmark of human intelligence" (Cardillo et al., 2010), and assume that the interpretation of metaphors, especially of novel metaphors, demands human cognitive skills and real world experiences, it is also possible that there are enough clues encoded at the linguistic level that they would help a non-human to distinguish between metaphors and nonsense.

In order to test whether the ability to demystify metaphors is a skill exclusively possessed by mortals, we are going to measure and compare the PLL scores of metaphors and nonsense, as well as use mean ranks of predictions on masked words to test how well the nonsensicality can be explained by plausibility (language model probability). Finally, a binary classifier based on a pre-trained lan-

Proceedings of the 3rd Workshop on Figurative Language Processing (FLP), pages 173 - 177
December 8, 2022 ©2022 Association for Computational Linguistics

guage model is going to be trained in order to check whether the current language models are able to distinguish between metaphors and nonsense.

2 Related Works

A study by Pedinotti et al. (2021) hints that language models might already have acquired a human-like intuition of sentence plausibility. The authors of the study have found out that the pseudo-log-likelihood scores (PLL) of sentences obtained using BERT (Devlin et al., 2019) correlated with the plausibility ratings of human annotators. The best performing model in the Corpus of Linguistic Acceptability (CoLA) (Warstadt et al., 2019) task in the GLUE benchmark (Wang et al., 2018), ERNIE, surpasses even the human baseline (75.5 vs. 66.4 MCC), discriminating linguistically unacceptable sentences better than human participants.

However, another study conducted by Gupta et al. (2021) found that the BERT family of models are easily susceptible to adversarial examples and fail to even recognize incoherent, ungrammatical utterances, giving similarly confident scores to input that was perturbed to be nonsensical as to its meaningful counterpart. Findings like this are evidence that, when discriminating between meaningful and nonsensical sentences, the models might be relying on some spurious correlations or annotator artifacts rather than the targeted divergence in comprehensibility.

3 Data and Experiments

3.1 Dataset

To the best of our knowledge, there's only one dataset that is annotated for both metaphors and nonsense - the one by Pedinotti et al. (2021), which the authors have kindly agreed to share. The dataset consists of 300 matched sentences, 100 for each of the three categories: metaphors (47 conventional and 53 creative), literal sentences, and nonsensical sentences.

In order to have more input sentences for the experiments, the dataset was further extended by adding 200 pairs of matched metaphorical and literal sentences from Cardillo et al. (2010) and Cardillo et al. (2016). These datasets were originally aimed at aiding the research of human metaphor comprehension, and contains 400 pairs (280 in Cardillo et al. (2010) and 120 in Cardillo et al. (2016)) of matched literal and metaphorical sentences, which had been carefully normalized along a number of dimensions, including length, naturalness, and figurativeness.

Type	Example
Met-Ped	I could almost taste victory.
Non-Ped	I could almost wash victory.
Met-Car	Her orders were a sharp bark.
Non-Gen	His orders were a sharp crust.
Non-BEL	Our homework buys more sky.

Table 1: Metaphor and nonsense examples from *Ped* (Pedinotti et al., 2021), *Car* (Cardillo et al., 2010), *BEL* (O'Neill et al., 2020) and the automatically *Gen*erated datasets.

Since the Cardillo et al. datasets do not include nonsense sentences, to have a balanced dataset, 200 nonsensical sentences were added. 100 of them were automatically generated (and manually handpicked from several options) by shuffling either subjects (for nominal metaphors) or subject complements (for predicate metaphors) across the sentences. Another 100 were generated with the help of BackTranslationAugmenter perturbation technique from the TextAttack framework (Morris et al., 2020), or by swapping places of verb arguments in a sentence.[1]

By generating the nonsense sentences from the metaphorical ones, we hoped to create a normalized dataset where the sentences between the categories would have similar syntactical structures and similarly plausible words. However, part of our experiments was also repeated on an extended dataset where we added the rest of the sentences (200 pairs) from the Cardillo et al. datasets, and randomly picked 200 nonsensical sentences from a corpus of sentences "without semantic context" by O'Neill et al. (2020). See Table 1 for example sentences from each dataset.

3.2 Experiments

With the chosen set of data, several experiments have been conducted. The first two explore properties of the dataset and whether the plausibility of the data can be a sufficient indicator for nonsense classification, and in the third set of experiments, a binary classifier has been trained.

3.2.1 Experiment 1: Plausibility

Following the Pedinotti et al. (2021) study, a pseudo-log-likelihood score (PLL) has been com-

[1] Our code and data are available at `https://github.com/bgriciute/Metaphors-vs-Nonsense`.

puted for every sentence in the picked datasets. This was done in order to check whether the same tendencies as pointed in the Pedinotti et al. (2021) paper, could be observed on a larger scope, as well as for comparing the datasets.

Since models like BERT are bidirectional, they cannot be used for computing sentence probability. An alternative way to get a probability-like score is to use PLL (Wang and Cho, 2019). The PLL score is computed by masking one token at a time, calculating its probability given all the other context words, and then summing the log-probabilities of all the words in the sentence. For the scoring, an *MLM* Python library by Salazar et al. (2020) has been used.

3.2.2 Experiment 2: Mean Ranks

Another strategy chosen to test how probable a string is according to a language model was to see, what rank a masked target word would get among the predictions of a model.

In the sentences from the Pedinotti et al. (2021) dataset, the target words (single words that are used metaphorically or nonsensically) were masked. The masked sentences were then fed to the BERT (Devlin et al., 2019) language model. To compare the predictability of the target words, we looked at which ranking position the target word that was masked would appear when sorted by probability.

3.2.3 Experiment 3: Classifier

For the classification experiments, we chose to fine-tune a pre-trained RoBERTa (Liu et al., 2019) language model. It has been chosen after conducting some primary experiments where it did perform better than BERT or MultiBERT. The `roberta-base` version by HuggingFace(Wolf et al., 2020) was fine-tuned with Adam optimizer and a learning rate of 1e-6 for 8 epochs, picking afterwards a model from the best epoch for testing. The classification was performed on different combinations between metaphorical, literal, and nonsensical sentences.

Additionally, we have also trained a Naive Bayes classifier in order to validate that the classification task on the target dataset requires a more complex method than a bag-of-words approach.

4 Results

Experiment 1

Table 2 indicates average PLL scores of each type of sentences (where applicable) for each of the aforementioned datasets that have been chosen for

	Pedinotti	Cardillo	O'Neill
Literal	-17.8	-17.8	-
Metaphor	-26.4	-23.5	-
Nonsense	-33.1	-30.13	-44.7

Table 2: Average PLL score of the different categories across datasets (the nonsense sentences in the Cardillo column are automatically generated).

the final training. Additionally, Figure 1 illustrates the distribution of the scores within each category. The PLL scores reveal, in accordance with the results of the Pedinotti et al. (2021) experiments, a difference between the three categories, the literal sentences being most plausible, followed by the metaphors, and nonsense sentences, meaning that the RoBERTa model finds nonsense sentences the least plausible.

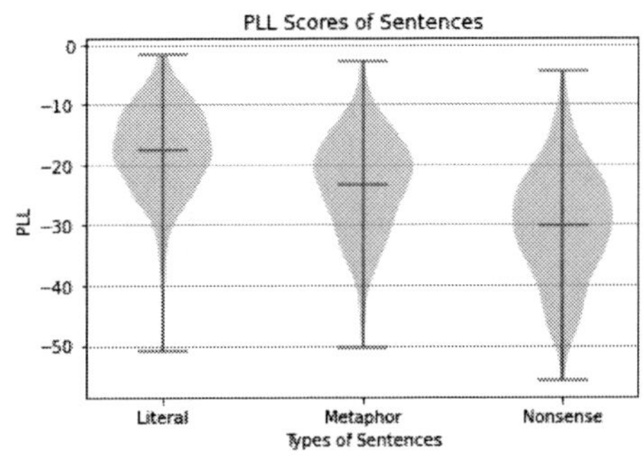

Figure 1: PLL scores of the literal and metaphorical sentences from Cardillo et al. (2010, 2016) datasets, and nonsensical sentences automatically generated from them.

It is interesting to note that the metaphorical sentences from the Pedinotti et al. (2021) dataset were on average less probable than the ones from Cardillo et al. (2010) (-26.4 versus -23.5 PLL), even though both conventional and creative metaphors were scored together. On the other hand, the nonsensical sentences manually created by Pedinotti et al. (2021) were evaluated by the model as way more probable than the sentences from the O'Neill et al. (2020) dataset which have been created by automatically shuffling words in the sentences (-33.1 vs. -44.7 PLL).

Experiment 2

In Experiment 2, we could also observe a significant difference between the ranks of sentences from different categories. Figure 2 gives a violin plot of the ranks of sentences from different categories.

Categories	Accuracy
lit-non	92.5%
lit-met	85.0%
met-non	75.0%
met-non (ext.)	88.0%

Table 3: Accuracy of the fine-tuned RoBERTa classifier between the different categories: *lit* - literal, *met* - metaphorical, and *non* - nonsense. The last experiment was also repeated on an extended dataset.

One can observe that the median ranks of nonsensical sentences were way higher than the ones of target words in literal or metaphorical sentences, meaning that the target words were less predictable.

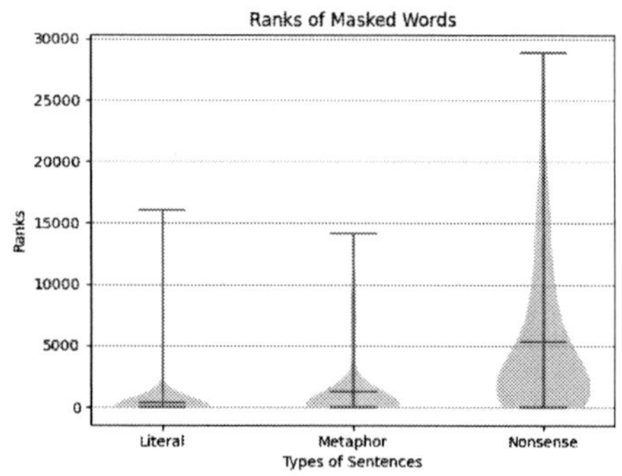

Figure 2: Ranks of target words among mask predictions sorted by probability of the sentences from Pedinotti et al. (2021) dataset.

Experiment 3

Table 3 summarizes the accuracy of the trained classifiers. We run several combinations categories. The three first numbers report the accuracy of models trained on the joined dataset consisting of 100 sentences for each category from Pedinotti et al. (2021) and 200 sentences from Cardillo et al. (2010) (or automatically generated) with 80/10/10 split for train/dev/test sets. The last experiment was conducted on a dataset with additional 200 metaphorical sentences from Cardillo et al. (2010) and 200 nonsensical from (O'Neill et al., 2020).

The Naive Bayes classifier received 22.5% accuracy when discriminating between metaphors and nonsense, suggesting that bag-of-words approach for the target classification task is not sufficient.

5 Discussion

The experiment results have demonstrated that language models can see the difference in plausibility between nonsense and metaphorical sentences. Such finding can be a useful probe when investigating what do models know about the language. The ability of models to distinguish between nonsense and metaphors (especially creative ones) suggest that the language models have an intuition that even highly unusual phrases/sentences can make sense.

The findings can also be brought up in a discussion about the nature of metaphors. While it could seem that, in order to understand some metaphor (and, it this way, to distinguish it from nonsense), extensive world-knowledge and an associative thinking is needed, our results suggest that, unless the models have also already acquired the aforementioned assets, metaphors can be distinguished from nonsense based on their linguistic form as well.

Furthermore, using a metaphor vs. nonsense classifier could be useful in ranking translated (literary) sentences, to see if the metaphors have been used correctly.

6 Future Work

While we were trying our best to ensure the training and testing data is free of unintended biases, further research would be needed to find out whether there really are no artifacts left. It is not clear whether the models are really relying on semantic acceptability in the case of our classifiers. It can also be that models are taking advantage of annotation artifacts when making decisions. One way to test for this would be to remove the target word from the sentences and try to train a classifier on the rest of the sentence.

7 Conclusion

The conducted experiments have shown that the current language models are able to pick the difference in plausibility between metaphorical and nonsensical sentences. The classifier between these two categories is also performing well, reaching about 75-88% accuracy (depending on the size of the training dataset). However, further research is needed to see whether this classification performance comes from distinguishing the semantic acceptability of the sentences, or if it is due to linguistic artifacts in the sentences that models can rely on when making the decision.

Limitations

For reliable results, the classification experiments should be repeated on a larger, more varied dataset, with extensive hyperparameter tuning and model comparison.

Acknowledgments

We would like to thank Reviewers 1 & 2 for taking the time and effort necessary to review the paper, and for their valuable suggestions.

References

Eileen Cardillo, Gwenda Schmidt-Snoek, Alexander Kranjec, and Anjan Chatterjee. 2010. Stimulus design is an obstacle course: 560 matched literal and metaphorical sentences for testing neural hypotheses about metaphor. *Behavior research methods*, 42:651–64.

Eileen Cardillo, Christine Watson, and Anjan Chatterjee. 2016. Stimulus needs are a moving target: 240 additional matched literal and metaphorical sentences for testing neural hypotheses about metaphor. *Behavior Research Methods*, 49.

Jacob Devlin, Ming-Wei Chang, Kenton Lee, and Kristina Toutanova. 2019. BERT: Pre-training of deep bidirectional transformers for language understanding. In *Proceedings of the 2019 Conference of the North American Chapter of the Association for Computational Linguistics: Human Language Technologies, Volume 1 (Long and Short Papers)*, pages 4171–4186, Minneapolis, Minnesota. Association for Computational Linguistics.

Ashim Gupta, Giorgi Kvernadze, and Vivek Srikumar. 2021. Bert amp; family eat word salad: Experiments with text understanding. *Proceedings of the AAAI Conference on Artificial Intelligence*, 35(14):12946–12954.

Yinhan Liu, Myle Ott, Naman Goyal, Jingfei Du, Mandar Joshi, Danqi Chen, Omer Levy, Mike Lewis, Luke Zettlemoyer, and Veselin Stoyanov. 2019. Roberta: A robustly optimized BERT pretraining approach. *CoRR*, abs/1907.11692.

Irving Massey. 2021. A new turing test: metaphor vs. nonsense. *AI & society*, 36(3):677–684.

John Morris, Eli Lifland, Jin Yong Yoo, Jake Grigsby, Di Jin, and Yanjun Qi. 2020. Textattack: A framework for adversarial attacks, data augmentation, and adversarial training in nlp. In *Proceedings of the 2020 Conference on Empirical Methods in Natural Language Processing: System Demonstrations*, pages 119–126.

Erin O'Neill, Morgan Parke, Heather Kreft, and Andrew Oxenham. 2020. Development and validation of sentences without semantic context to complement the basic english lexicon sentences. *Journal of Speech, Language, and Hearing Research*, 63:3847–3854.

Paolo Pedinotti, Eliana Di Palma, Ludovica Cerini, and Alessandro Lenci. 2021. A howling success or a working sea? testing what BERT knows about metaphors. In *Proceedings of the Fourth BlackboxNLP Workshop on Analyzing and Interpreting Neural Networks for NLP*, pages 192–204, Punta Cana, Dominican Republic. Association for Computational Linguistics.

Julian Salazar, Davis Liang, Toan Q. Nguyen, and Katrin Kirchhoff. 2020. Masked language model scoring. In *Proceedings of the 58th Annual Meeting of the Association for Computational Linguistics*, pages 2699–2712, Online. Association for Computational Linguistics.

Alex Wang and Kyunghyun Cho. 2019. BERT has a mouth, and it must speak: BERT as a Markov random field language model. In *Proceedings of the Workshop on Methods for Optimizing and Evaluating Neural Language Generation*, pages 30–36, Minneapolis, Minnesota. Association for Computational Linguistics.

Alex Wang, Amanpreet Singh, Julian Michael, Felix Hill, Omer Levy, and Samuel Bowman. 2018. GLUE: A multi-task benchmark and analysis platform for natural language understanding. In *Proceedings of the 2018 EMNLP Workshop BlackboxNLP: Analyzing and Interpreting Neural Networks for NLP*, pages 353–355, Brussels, Belgium. Association for Computational Linguistics.

Alex Warstadt, Amanpreet Singh, and Samuel R. Bowman. 2019. Neural network acceptability judgments. *Transactions of the Association for Computational Linguistics*, 7:625–641.

Thomas Wolf, Lysandre Debut, Victor Sanh, Julien Chaumond, Clement Delangue, Anthony Moi, Pierric Cistac, Tim Rault, Rémi Louf, Morgan Funtowicz, Joe Davison, Sam Shleifer, Patrick von Platen, Clara Ma, Yacine Jernite, Julien Plu, Canwen Xu, Teven Le Scao, Sylvain Gugger, Mariama Drame, Quentin Lhoest, and Alexander M. Rush. 2020. Transformers: State-of-the-art natural language processing. In *Proceedings of the 2020 Conference on Empirical Methods in Natural Language Processing: System Demonstrations*, pages 38–45, Online. Association for Computational Linguistics.

A Report on the FigLang 2022 Shared Task on Understanding Figurative Language

Arkadiy Saakyan[1] **Tuhin Chakrabarty**[1] **Debanjan Ghosh**[2] **Smaranda Muresan**[1]
[1]Department of Computer Science, Columbia University
[2]Educational Testing Service
a.saakyan@columbia.edu, tuhin.chakr@cs.columbia.edu, dghosh@ets.org, smara@cs.columbia.edu

Abstract

We present the results of the Shared Task on Understanding Figurative Language that we conducted as a part of the 3rd Workshop on Figurative Language Processing (FigLang 2022) at EMNLP 2022. The shared task is based on the FLUTE dataset (Chakrabarty et al., 2022), which consists of NLI pairs containing figurative language along with free text explanations for each NLI instance. The task challenged participants to build models that are able to not only predict the right label for a figurative NLI instance, but also generate a convincing free-text explanation. The participants were able to significantly improve upon provided baselines in both automatic and human evaluation settings. We further summarize the submitted systems and discuss the evaluation results.

1 Introduction

Figurative language such as metaphors, similes or sarcasm plays an important role in enriching human communication, allowing us to express complex ideas and emotions in an implicit way (Roberts and Kreuz, 1994; Fussell and Moss, 1998). However, understanding figurative language still remains a bottleneck for natural language processing (Shutova, 2011). In spite of the fact that Transformer-based language models (LMs) get larger (Brown et al., 2020; Raffel et al., 2020), they are still incapable of comprehending the physical world, cultural knowledge, or social context of figurative language (Bisk et al., 2020).

In recent years, there have been several benchmarks dedicated to figurative language understanding, which generally frame "understanding" as a recognizing textual entailment (a.k.a natural language inference (NLI)) task — deciding whether one sentence (premise) entails/contradicts another (hypothesis) (Chakrabarty et al., 2021; Stowe et al., 2022; Srivastava et al., 2022). However, similar to general NLI datasets, these benchmarks suffer from spurious correlations and annotation artifacts (McCoy et al., 2019; Poliak et al., 2018). These can allow large language models (LLMs) to achieve near human-level performance on in-domain test sets, yet turn brittle when evaluated against out-of-domain or adversarial examples (Glockner et al., 2018; Ribeiro et al., 2016, 2020). To tackle these problems, research in NLI has argued that it is not enough to correctly predict the entail/contradict labels, but also to explain the decision using natural language explanations that are comprehensible to an end-user assessing model's reliability (Camburu et al., 2018; Majumder et al., 2021; Wiegreffe et al., 2021), leading to novel datasets such as e-SNLI (Camburu et al., 2018).

In this paper, we report on the shared task that aim to test the ability of models to not only predict the right label, but also provide a free-text explanation to the instance. This task was conducted as part of the 3rd Workshop on Figurative Language Processing (FigLang 2022) at EMNLP 2022. Section 2 provides a description of the shared task, datasets, and evaluation metrics. Section 3 contains brief summaries of each of the participating systems whereas Section 4 reports a comparative analysis of the participating systems.

2 Datasets and Task Description

As stated earlier, this shared task is based on the FLUTE dataset that was released by Chakrabarty et al. (2022). FLUTE consists of pairs of premises (literal sentences) and hypotheses (figurative sentences), with the corresponding entailment or contradiction labels (NLI instances), along with explanations for each instance (Table 1). This dataset is based on four types of figurative language - idiom, metaphor, sarcasm, and simile. Note, given sarcasm is the opposite of the literal meaning, we would only have contradictions in the dataset, thus we also generate a literal hypothesis that entails the literal premise. Table 1 contains a few examples

Proceedings of the 3rd Workshop on Figurative Language Processing (FLP), pages 178 - 183
December 8, 2022 ©2022 Association for Computational Linguistics

Type	Premise (literal)	Hypothesis (figurative*)	Label	Explanation
Paraphrase + Sarcasm	My next door neighbors are *always arguing* in our shared hallway.	It's *so annoying* to have to hear my next door neighbors *argue all the time* in our shared hallway.	E	The sound of arguing neighbors can often be very disruptive and if it happens all the time in a common space like a shared hallway it is natural to find it annoying.
		It's *so pleasant* to have to hear my next door neighbors *argue all the time* in our shared hallway.	C	The sound of arguing neighbors can often be very disruptive and so someone considering it to be pleasant is not really accurate.
Simile	The assembly hall was now *hot and moist*, more so than usual.	In fact, the assembly hall was now *like a steam sauna.*	E	A sauna is a hot and moist environment, so the simile is saying that the hall is even hotter and more moist than usual.
	The assembly hall was now *cold and dry*, more so than usual.		C	A steam sauna is a small room or hut where people go to sweat in steam, so it would be hot and humid, not cold and dry.
Metaphor	He *mentally assimilated* the knowledge or beliefs of his tribe.	He *absorbed the knowledge* or beliefs of his tribe.	E	To absorb something is to take it in and make it part of yourself.
	He *utterly decimated* his tribe's most deeply held beliefs.		C	Absorbed typically means to take in or take up something, while "utterly decimated" means to destroy completely.
Idiom	Lady Southridge was wringing her hands, *trying hard and desperately to salvage* the bleak and miserable situation so that it somehow looks positive.	Lady southridge was wringing her hands, trying *to grasp at straws.*	E	To grasp at straws means to make a desperate attempt to salvage a bad situation, which is exactly what Lady Southridge is trying to do.
	Lady Southridge was wringing her hands, *doing absolutely nothing to overturn* the bleak and miserable situation so that it somehow looks positive.		C	To grasp at straws means to make a desperate attempt to salvage a bad situation, but the sentence describes not doing anything to change the situation

Table 1: FLUTE examples of figurative text (hypothesis) and their respective literal entailment (E) and contradiction (C) premises, along with the associated explanations. * For simile, metaphor, and idiom, figurative examples are the hypothesis whereas for sarcasm, we have both figurative and literal hypotheses.

	Entails	Contradicts	Total
Paraphrase	1339	-	1339
+ Sarcasm	-	2678	2678
Simile	750	750	1500
Metaphor	750	750	1500
Idiom	1000	1000	2000

Table 2: Dataset statistics showing distribution of Figurative Language across FLUTE.

taken fro the dataset. FLUTE contains 9,000 high quality <literal, figurative> sentence pairs with entail/contradict labels and the associated examples. Please refer to Table 2 for the dataset statistics.

2.1 Evaluation Setup

To evaluate the participant models, we built a test set by randomly selecting 750 instances (i.e., <premise, hypothesis> pairs with associated explanations) from the sarcasm dataset, and 250 examples each from simile, metaphor and idiom datasets, for a total of 1,500 instances. Below we describe several automatic metrics and human evaluations we consider to assess the models' ability to understand figurative language.

Automatic Metrics To judge the quality of the explanations we compute the average between BERTScore (Zhang et al., 2020) [1] and BLEURT (Sellam et al., 2020), which we refer to as *explanation score* (between 0 and 100). Instead of reporting only label accuracy, we report label accuracy at three thresholds of explanation score (0, 50, and 60). Accuracy@0 is equivalent to simply computing label accuracy, while Accuracy@50 counts as correct only the correctly predicted labels that achieve an explanation score greater than 50.

Human Evaluation We also measure the quality of the generated textual explanations via the MTurk platform. We recruit crowd workers with at least 98% HIT approval rate. We compute human judgement scores (H_{score}), identical to the e-ViL score in Kayser et al. (2021). We used instances that were used for evaluation in (Chakrabarty et al., 2022), and selected those on which all systems predicted correctly (a total of 150 samples, around 50 per figurative language type). We present five

[1] We use the DeBERTa-mnli version that has shown to have highest correlation with human judges (He et al., 2020).

textual explanations generated by the models and ask three workers the following question: *Given the two sentences, does the explanation justify the answer above?* We provide four options: *Yes* (1), *Weak Yes* ($\frac{2}{3}$), *Weak No* ($\frac{1}{3}$), and *No* (0). For each explanation, we average the scores by the three annotators and report the sample average in Table 4 as H_{score}.

3 Participants and Results

Training Phase The shared task started on July 10, 2022, when the training data and the auxiliary scripts were made available to all the registered participants. Participants were allowed to choose to partition the training data further to a validation set for tuning the hyper parameters. Likewise, they can also elect to use the training data to perform cross-validation.

Evaluation Phase In this phase, test instances for evaluation are released. We released the test data on August 15, 2022. Submissions were accepted until August 20, 2022. Out of all the submissions, five shared task system papers are accepted to the Workshop. Predictions are submitted to the Codalab site and evaluated against the gold labels of the test instances. We used Codalab for the shared task because it is easy to use, provided easy communication with the participants (e.g., allow mass-emailing to the participants), as well as tracks all the submissions updating the leader-board in real-time. We allowed up to five submissions per day for each participant team. We did setup our own GPU-based evaluation using a custom Docker architecture. The leader-board displayed the accuracy@60 scores on the descending order.

In total we have five participating teams alongside the organizing team of shared task. We describe the participating systems in the following section.

Team	Acc@60	H_{score}
TeamCoolDoge	**63.33 (1)**	*74.98 (2)*
rachneet	**63.33 (1)**	**75.28 (1)**
vund	*60.73 (2)*	71.82 (5)
yklal95	51.73 (3)	73.73 (4)
baseline	48.33 (4)	74.39 (3)

Table 3: Automatic (Accuracy@60) and Human evaluation results (H_{score}) by team with rank in parenthesis.

Baseline (Chakrabarty et al., 2022) The baseline is the system described in Chakrabarty et al. (2022). This system is trained to predict labels and rationales jointly using a T5-3B model (Raffel et al., 2020). Unlike other teams (Chakrabarty et al., 2022) verbalized inputs using natural language instruction: *Does the sentence "P" entail or contradict the sentence "H"? Please answer between "Entails" or "Contradicts" and explain your decision in a sentence.*

TeamCoolDoge (Gu et al., 2022b) present *DREAM-FLUTE* which first uses DREAM (Gu et al., 2022a) to generate an elaboration of the situation in the premise and hypothesis (separately), then uses this additional context for classification and explanation generation. They hypothesize that such additional, pertinent details could also improve a model's ability to judge whether it is an entailment or contradiction between the premise and hypothesis. This posit this could be especially helpful for the instances that use figurative language, where the underlying meaning might be opaque to the model and that further elaborating the context can make certain inferences more explicit. They take as input *<Premise> <Premise-elaboration-from-DREAM> <Hypothesis> <Hypothesis-elaboration-from-DREAM>* and fine-tune a T5-3B model to then jointly generate Label and Explanation. While the scene elaboration dimensions from DREAM can vary across the categories of *consequence, emotion, motivation, social norm* the winning submission is based on consequence elaboration dimension. It should be noted that the underlying model is similar to the baseline model (ablation without using DREAM), however the performance differs due to different hyperparameters.

Rachneet (Bigoulaeva et al., 2022) focus their efforts on the transfer of information from multiple related tasks for improved performance on FLUTE. They compare the effectiveness of *Sequential Fine Tuning* with that of *MultiTask Learning* in a context where one of the target tasks is dependent on the other. Their final submission which led to the highest Acc@60 on the FLUTE test set is a T5 (Raffel et al., 2020) based model where the label and rationales are predicted jointly. In particular their best submission is a sequentially fine-tuned model where they first finetune on eSNLI (Camburu et al., 2018) followed by IMPLI (Stowe et al., 2022) and

Team	idiom	metaphor	sarcasm	simile
TeamCoolDodge (AI2)	**74.85 (1)**	72.47 (3)	**75.71 (1)**	*77.33 (2)*
rachneet (UKP)	72.22 (3)	**77.27 (1)**	73.13 (4)	**79.11 (1)**
vund (UIT)	70.76 (4)	71.46 (4)	72.09 (5)	73.78 (3)
yklal95 (SBU)	70.76 (4)	*76.01 (2)*	73.64 (3)	73.78 (3)
debanjan (us)	*73.98 (2)*	*76.01 (2)*	*74.68 (2)*	71.11 (4)

Table 4: Human evaluation results (H_{score}) by team by figurative language type with rank in parenthesis.

finally FLUTE (Chakrabarty et al., 2022).

Vund (Phan et al., 2022) considered both the tasks: the NLI task, and the explanation generation task as two seq2seq tasks. They fine-tuned the two tasks separately as a simultaneous computation model. In addition, they also used the attribute about types of Figurative Language across the data as a predictor and treated it as seq2seq tasks. Therefore they have 3 component models based on fine-tuning pre-trained model T5 (Raffel et al., 2020) : NLI predictor, Type predictor, and Generator. Unlike other teams that predict label and rationale jointly here the team uses T5-large model in a pipeline fashion.

yklal (Lal and Bastan, 2022) propose a simple T5-large model fine-tuned on the FLUTE data, trained to generate the explanation before the label. The input format does not contain any task-specific keys and does not resemble any of the ones described in Raffel et al. (2020). The model uses a newline separator, which is a prominent part of how UnifiedQA (Khashabi et al., 2020) was built over T5.

4 Analysis

The best performing teams according to both human and automatic evaluation were TeamCoolDoge, rachneet, and vund (Table 3). For automatic metric we report Accuracy@60, i.e., accuracy score that counts as correct only the correctly predicted labels that achieve an explanation score greater than 60. We notice in Table 3 that TeamCoolDoge and rachneet have attain the highest score in case of accuracy score where team vund is slightly behind.

Likewise, human evaluation results (Table 4) show relatively small difference between teams, indicating plausibility of explanations across systems and across different types of figurative language. These results support the high automatic evaluation scores the teams have achieved. Some discrepancies in human and automatic evaluation are present (e.g., the team TeamCoolDodge did not achieve the highest human score for metaphors and similes). This can be explained by high standard deviation in the human score (around 0.3, or one step increment in the answer), however, future work may explore spurious cues and lack of correlation in automatic metrics.

Across types of figurative language, explanations for similes and metaphors achieve higher human scores for the best submissions. This could be explained by the visual nature of comparisons drawing from commonsense property identification which can benefit from elaboration as used in the DREAM framework used by TeamCoolDoge.

5 Conclusion

This paper summarizes the results of the shared task on understanding figurative language organized as part of the 3rd Workshop on the Figurative Language Processing at EMNLP 2022 (FigLang 2022). This shared task aimed to not only predict the correct label for a figurative NLI instance but also generate a convincing explanation for the same. We provided basic description of each of the participating systems who submitted a shared task system paper (i.e. four qualifying submissions). All of the submitted systems by the participants attain higher accuracy than the baseline. We also conducted human evaluation via MTurk platform that shows the quality of explanations generated by the systems is comparable. Finally, to conclude, we hope the shared task will promote further exploration into figurative language understanding.

References

Irina Bigoulaeva, Rachneet Singh Sachdeva, Harish Tayyar Madabushi, Aline Villavicencio, and Iryna Gurevych. 2022. Effective cross-task transfer learning for explainable natural language inference with t5. In *Proceedings of the Third Workshop on Figurative Language Processing*. Association for Computational Linguistics.

Yonatan Bisk, Ari Holtzman, Jesse Thomason, Jacob Andreas, Yoshua Bengio, Joyce Chai, Mirella Lapata, Angeliki Lazaridou, Jonathan May, Aleksandr Nisnevich, Nicolas Pinto, and Joseph Turian. 2020. Experience grounds language. In *Proceedings of the 2020 Conference on Empirical Methods in Natural Language Processing (EMNLP)*, pages 8718–8735, Online. Association for Computational Linguistics.

Tom Brown, Benjamin Mann, Nick Ryder, Melanie Subbiah, Jared D Kaplan, Prafulla Dhariwal, Arvind Neelakantan, Pranav Shyam, Girish Sastry, Amanda Askell, et al. 2020. Language models are few-shot learners. *Advances in neural information processing systems*, 33:1877–1901.

Oana-Maria Camburu, Tim Rocktäschel, Thomas Lukasiewicz, and Phil Blunsom. 2018. e-snli: Natural language inference with natural language explanations. In *Advances in Neural Information Processing Systems*, volume 31. Curran Associates, Inc.

Tuhin Chakrabarty, Debanjan Ghosh, Adam Poliak, and Smaranda Muresan. 2021. Figurative language in recognizing textual entailment. In *Findings of the Association for Computational Linguistics: ACL-IJCNLP 2021*, pages 3354–3361, Online. Association for Computational Linguistics.

Tuhin Chakrabarty, A. Saakyan, Debanjan Ghosh, and Smaranda Muresan. 2022. Flute: Figurative language understanding through textual explanations.

Susan R Fussell and Mallie M Moss. 1998. Figurative language in emotional communication. *Social and cognitive approaches to interpersonal communication*, pages 113–141.

Max Glockner, Vered Shwartz, and Yoav Goldberg. 2018. Breaking NLI systems with sentences that require simple lexical inferences. In *Proceedings of the 56th Annual Meeting of the Association for Computational Linguistics (Volume 2: Short Papers)*, pages 650–655, Melbourne, Australia. Association for Computational Linguistics.

Yuling Gu, Bhavana Dalvi, and Peter Clark. 2022a. DREAM: Improving situational QA by first elaborating the situation. In *Proceedings of the 2022 Conference of the North American Chapter of the Association for Computational Linguistics: Human Language Technologies*, pages 1115–1127, Seattle, United States. Association for Computational Linguistics.

Yuling Gu, Yao Fu, Valentina Pyatkin, Ian Magnusson, Bhavana Dalvi Mishra, and Peter Clark. 2022b. Just-dream-about-it: Figurative language understanding with dream-flute. In *Proceedings of the Third Workshop on Figurative Language Processing*. Association for Computational Linguistics.

Pengcheng He, Xiaodong Liu, Jianfeng Gao, and Weizhu Chen. 2020. Deberta: Decoding-enhanced bert with disentangled attention. *arXiv preprint arXiv:2006.03654*.

Maxime Kayser, Oana-Maria Camburu, Leonard Salewski, Cornelius Emde, Virginie Do, Zeynep Akata, and Thomas Lukasiewicz. 2021. E-vil: A dataset and benchmark for natural language explanations in vision-language tasks. In *Proceedings of the IEEE/CVF International Conference on Computer Vision (ICCV)*, pages 1244–1254.

Daniel Khashabi, Sewon Min, Tushar Khot, Ashish Sabharwal, Oyvind Tafjord, Peter Clark, and Hannaneh Hajishirzi. 2020. UNIFIEDQA: Crossing format boundaries with a single QA system. In *Findings of the Association for Computational Linguistics: EMNLP 2020*, pages 1896–1907, Online. Association for Computational Linguistics.

Yash Kumar Lal and Mohaddeseh Bastan. 2022. Sbu figures it out: Models explain figurative language. In *Proceedings of the Third Workshop on Figurative Language Processing*. Association for Computational Linguistics.

Bodhisattwa Prasad Majumder, Oana-Maria Camburu, Thomas Lukasiewicz, and Julian McAuley. 2021. Rationale-inspired natural language explanations with commonsense. *arXiv preprint arXiv:2106.13876*.

Tom McCoy, Ellie Pavlick, and Tal Linzen. 2019. Right for the wrong reasons: Diagnosing syntactic heuristics in natural language inference. In *Proceedings of the 57th Annual Meeting of the Association for Computational Linguistics*, pages 3428–3448, Florence, Italy. Association for Computational Linguistics.

Khoa Thi Kim Phan, Duc-Vu Nguyen, and Ngan Luu-Thuy Nguyen. 2022. Nlp@uit at figlang-emnlp 2022: A divide-and-conquer system for shared task on understanding figurative language. In *Proceedings of the Third Workshop on Figurative Language Processing*. Association for Computational Linguistics.

Adam Poliak, Jason Naradowsky, Aparajita Haldar, Rachel Rudinger, and Benjamin Van Durme. 2018. Hypothesis only baselines in natural language inference. *arXiv preprint arXiv:1805.01042*.

Colin Raffel, Noam Shazeer, Adam Roberts, Katherine Lee, Sharan Narang, Michael Matena, Yanqi Zhou, Wei Li, and Peter J Liu. 2020. Exploring the limits of transfer learning with a unified text-to-text transformer. *Journal of Machine Learning Research*, 21:1–67.

Marco Tulio Ribeiro, Sameer Singh, and Carlos Guestrin. 2016. " why should i trust you?" explaining the predictions of any classifier. In *Proceedings of the 22nd ACM SIGKDD international conference on knowledge discovery and data mining*, pages 1135–1144.

Marco Tulio Ribeiro, Tongshuang Wu, Carlos Guestrin, and Sameer Singh. 2020. Beyond accuracy: Behavioral testing of NLP models with CheckList. In *Proceedings of the 58th Annual Meeting of the Association for Computational Linguistics*, pages 4902–4912, Online. Association for Computational Linguistics.

Richard M Roberts and Roger J Kreuz. 1994. Why do people use figurative language? *Psychological science*, 5(3):159–163.

Thibault Sellam, Dipanjan Das, and Ankur Parikh. 2020. BLEURT: Learning robust metrics for text generation. In *Proceedings of the 58th Annual Meeting of the Association for Computational Linguistics*, pages 7881–7892, Online. Association for Computational Linguistics.

Ekaterina V Shutova. 2011. Computational approaches to figurative language. Technical report, University of Cambridge, Computer Laboratory.

Aarohi Srivastava, Abhinav Rastogi, and Abhishek Rao. 2022. Beyond the imitation game: Quantifying and extrapolating the capabilities of language models. In *In preparation*.

Kevin Stowe, Prasetya Utama, and Iryna Gurevych. 2022. IMPLI: Investigating NLI models' performance on figurative language. In *Proceedings of the 60th Annual Meeting of the Association for Computational Linguistics (Volume 1: Long Papers)*, pages 5375–5388, Dublin, Ireland. Association for Computational Linguistics.

Sarah Wiegreffe, Jack Hessel, Swabha Swayamdipta, Mark Riedl, and Yejin Choi. 2021. Reframing human-ai collaboration for generating free-text explanations. *arXiv preprint arXiv:2112.08674*.

Tianyi Zhang, Varsha Kishore, Felix Wu, Kilian Q. Weinberger, and Yoav Artzi. 2020. Bertscore: Evaluating text generation with bert. In *International Conference on Learning Representations*.

A Report on the Euphemisms Detection Shared Task

Patrick Lee and **Anna Feldman** and **Jing Peng**
Montclair State University
New Jersey, USA
{leep6,feldmana,pengj}@montclair.edu

Abstract

This paper presents The Shared Task on Euphemism Detection for the Third Workshop on Figurative Language Processing (FigLang 2022) held in conjunction with EMNLP 2022. Participants were invited to investigate the euphemism detection task: given input text, identify whether it contains a euphemism. The input data is a corpus of sentences containing potentially euphemistic terms (PETs) collected from the GloWbE corpus (Davies and Fuchs, 2015), and are human-annotated as containing either a euphemistic or literal usage of a PET. In this paper, we present the results and analyze the common themes, methods and findings of the participating teams.

1 Introduction

Euphemisms are mild or indirect expressions that are used in place of other ones when discussing potentially offensive or sensitive topics. Their linguistic functions include (politeness, concealment, and neutralization of unappealing words/phrases). Despite being an important element of language use, their figurative nature poses a challenge for natural language processing (NLP).

There are numerous challenges to working with euphemisms. One is the phenomenon of the "euphemism treadmill", by which words/phrases gain or lose euphemistic meanings over time (Pinker, 2003). Another is that researchers may not agree on what euphemisms are. For example, Zhu and Bhat (2021); Zhu et al. (2021) treat code words as euphemisms, but our working definition does not. Even when restricted to our working definition, however, annotators were found to sometimes disagree in the task of labeling example sentences as euphemistic (Gavidia et al., 2022). For all these reasons, the words/phrases in this shared task are referred to as potentially euphemistic terms (PETs). The main challenge, which is the focus of this shared task, is the ambiguity of PETs: the same words/phrases that may be euphemistic in one context may be literal in another. For example,

Asked to choose between jobs and the environment, a majority – at least in our warped, first-past-the-post system – will pick jobs. (non-euphemistic)

This summer, the budding talent agent was between jobs and free to babysit pretty much any time. (euphemistic)

We propose the Shared Task on Euphemism Detection: given input text, identify whether it contains a euphemism; i.e., distinguish between euphemistic and literal usages of the same PETs in different contexts. The data used is a corpus of texts containing PETs, collected by Gavidia et al. (2022), which contains parallel euphemistic and literal examples for a range of PETs. 46 participants spanning 13 teams attempted the task, and we received 9 system descriptions.

Due to a lack of extensive research in this area, it is unclear how NLP techniques, such as language models (LMs), will perform on euphemism detection. The purpose of this shared task is to (1) explore the ability of NLP techniques for this task and (2) investigate what methods could further improve upon their performance.

2 Related Work

There is not much work on automatic detection of euphemisms. The most directly related work is by Magu and Luo (2018), Felt and Riloff (2020), Kapron-King and Xu (2021), Zhu et al. (2021) and Zhu and Bhat (2021). Felt and Riloff (2020) present the first effort to recognize euphemisms and dysphemisms (derogatory terms) using NLP. The authors use the term *x-phemisms* to refer to both. They first identify three sensitive topics (lying, stealing, and firing). They use a weakly supervised algorithm for semantic lexicon induction (Thelen

Proceedings of the 3rd Workshop on Figurative Language Processing (FLP), pages 184 - 190

and Riloff, 2002) to generate lists of near-synonym phrases for each topic semi-automatically. Felt and Riloff (2020) experiment with two methods to classify phrases as euphemistic, dysphemistic, and neutral: 1) dictionary-based method addressing affect, connotation, intensity, arousal, and dominance; 2) contextual sentiment analysis to classify x-phemisms. The important product of this work is a gold-standard dataset of human x-phemism judgements. The important lesson here is that Felt and Riloff (2020) show that sentiment connotation and affective polarity are useful for identifying x-phemisms, but not sufficient. While the performance of Felt and Riloff (2020)'s system is relatively low and the range of topics is very narrow, this work certainly inspires further investigations.

Zhu et al. (2021) define two tasks: 1) euphemism detection (based on the input keywords, produce a list of candidate euphemisms) 2) euphemism identification (take the list of candidate euphemisms produced in (1) and output an interpretation). Zhu et al. (2021) select sentences matched by a list of keywords, create masked sentences (mask the keywords in the sentences) and apply the masked language model proposed in BERT (Devlin et al., 2018) to filter out generic (uninformative) sentences and then generate expressions to fill in the blank. These expressions are ranked by relevance to the target topic.

Euphemisms are also related to the language of politeness (e.g., Danescu-Niculescu-Mizil et al. (2013); Rababah (2014)), which plays a role in applications involving dialogue and social interactions in different contexts.

Other shared tasks have proposed a similar classification task on other types of figurative language. Ghosh et al. (2020) report on a sarcasm detection task run on conversation data from Twitter and Reddit, while Madabushi et al. (2022) report on an idiom detection and embedding task.

3 Task Setting

Participants were given a dataset of PET-containing texts created by Gavidia et al. (2022). In this section, we describe the dataset and the classification task.

3.1 Dataset Description

The corpus of PETs was formed by taking a list of PETs (single and multi-word expressions, collected from a variety of sources) and extracting texts from the GloWBe corpus (Davies and Fuchs, 2015) (only the US-English portion) which contained them. Each text sample comprised up to 3 sentences: the sentence that the PET appeared in, as well as the preceding and following sentences, if available. In total, the dataset contains 1,965 text samples spanning 129 different PETs and 7 topics/categories. Of these, 1,382 were annotated to contain a euphemistic usage of a PET, and the remaining 583 a literal usage. Thus, the dataset is imbalanced (an aspect which multiple teams explicitly considered in their approaches). The full details of the data, including the distribution amongst the PETs and topics, can be found in the original paper (Gavidia et al., 2022).

The training and test sets were created using an 80-20 split. The range of PETs which appeared in each split was balanced as much as possible, given that several PETs only appeared once as a euphemistic or literal example. Details of the split are summarized in Table 1.

Split	Rows	Euphemistic		Literal	
		Rows	PETs	Rows	PETs
Train	1572	1106	122	466	54
Test	393	276	121	117	55

Table 1: Train-Test Split Details

A simplified version of the dataset was created for the participants, where each row contained only (1) the text sample with the PET denoted in brackets, and (2) its label (a '1' for euphemistic, and a '0' for literal). This version omitted information about each row, such as meta-information about the PET: the specific morphological variant present in the row, the topic category (e.g., "death", "politics", etc.), and whether it always appeared in the dataset as a euphemism ("always-euphs") or only sometimes ("sometimes-euphs"). This information, however, was available to the participants via a Github link to the full dataset (which several teams chose to leverage).

3.2 Task Description

The shared task was set up as a competition on Codalab[1]. Participants were invited to develop systems trained on the training data (see Table 2 for some examples) and submit answer labels on the test set, which would be compared to the labels in

[1] https://codalab.lisn.upsaclay.fr/competitions/5726

the original dataset for evaluation. The evaluation metric used to rank submissions was the macro-F1 score.

Text	Label
More likely it'll harm them. With less products to make, Foxxcom will have to <lay off> workers. With more workers seeking jobs those other factories will be able to resist demands for higher wages.	1
We do NOT need some self-imposed book cop telling us what to read or not to read. <Lay off>. Get over it.	0
After about 30 minutes of waiting, a fight broke out between an older African American man and an African American woman of <a certain age>. After making a lot of noise and landing a few blows to their respective bodies, the armed security guards escorted them out of the terminal.	1

Table 2: Example Rows from the Dataset

4 Participants and Results

8 teams that participated in the task also submitted descriptions of their systems, with one author additionally exploring a zero-shot/few-shot variant of the task. A summary of their performances is shown in Table 3. In this section, we describe the methods used by the best-performing teams, and analyze the common themes between the approaches and motivations of all the submissions.

4.1 Best Submissions

The best-performing team (Keh et al., 2022) (macro-F1 0.881) explores a variety of data and modeling modifications, and combine the best-performing ones into an ensemble of three models to improve upon a baseline RoBERTa-large model (Liu et al., 2019). On the data side, they explore two methods of data augmentation, and find that adding examples containing similar/opposite word senses to PETs (for positive and negative examples) works best; this highlights the potential significance of sense-based approaches for this task. They also explore identifying and correcting 25 potentially mislabeled rows from the dataset, reporting an improvement of 0.0036 points over the base model and a final score ~0.007 higher when using their "cleaned" dataset. While it is unclear how this cleaning would affect other systems in general, their investigation hints at the potential for not only human disagreement but also human error in labeling figurative language. On the modeling side, they find that classifying on the tokens of the PETs, rather than the [CLS] token, yields significant a performance increase. They also experiment with two methods of incorporating extra context and find that k-Nearest Neighbor (kNN) (5NN in this case) augmentation yields slight improvements. They report the best improvement by combining the following three models: (1) a RoBERTa-large model classifying on the PET token(s), (2) the same, but using their sense-augmented dataset, and (3) the same as (1), but interpolating the classification probabilities of its base model and the 5NN classifier.

The second-best performing team (Kesen et al., 2022) achieved a macro-F1 of 0.872 using additional supervision and, interestingly, incorporating visual imagery into their approach. Using DeBERTa-v3 (He et al., 2021) as their baseline (the "large" version of which performs best), they incorporate additional supervision by including PETs themselves, as well as their (manually collected) literal descriptions, in their inputs. The authors found this to greatly improve performance, reasoning that such direct supervision could help mitigate ambiguity inherent to the task. This is a similar result to (Keh et al., 2022), where extra attention on the PETs themselves is effective. They then obtain imageries of both the PETs and their literal descriptions using a text-to-image model, and obtain image embeddings using a pretrained visual encoder. These are incorporated into training, and yields statistically significant performance improvements. Qualitative analysis of the images for each PET reveals insights into how LMs might understand figurative expressions.

4.2 Analysis of Methods

Below, we describe approaches that we observed in multiple submissions. Since the objective was to explore different aspects of this task, we find these insights to be valuable, even if they did not score high.

4.2.1 Using PET Embeddings Directly

Multiple teams found that explicitly involving the tokens of the PET for classification led to significant improvement. Kesen et al. (2022) and Wang et al. (2022) include the PET in their inputs by con-

Rank	Username	Macro-F1	Title of Paper
1	vgangal	0.88	EUREKA: Euphemism Recognition Enhanced Through KNN-based Methods and Augmentation (Keh et al., 2022)
2	ilker	0.87	Detecting Euphemisms with Literal Descriptions and Visual Imagery (Kesen et al., 2022)
3	Wanderer	0.85	A Prompt Based Approach for Euphemism Detection (Maimaitituoheti, 2022)
4	liuyiyi	0.84	Euphemism Detection by Transformers and Relational Graph Attention Network (Wang et al., 2022)
5	peratham.bkk	0.82	TEDB System Description to a Shared Task on Euphemism Detection 2022 (Wiriyathammabhum, 2022)
6	PaulTrust	0.79	Bayes at FigLang 2022 Euphemism Detection shared task: Cost-Sensitive Bayesian Fine-tuning and Venn-Abers [...] (Trust and Kadusa, 2022)
7	devika	0.74	An Exploration of Linguistically-Driven and Transfer Learning Methods for Euphemism Detection (Tiwari and Parde, 2022)
8	gunetsk99	0.72	Adversarial Perturbations Augmented Language Models for Euphemism Identification (Kohli et al., 2022)

Table 3: Results of submitted systems to the Shared Task on Euphemism Detection

catenating it to each input text prior to learning. Keh et al. (2022) run their final classification on the PET embedding, rather than that of the [CLS] token. These changes were a significant feature of these teams' best approaches. It appears that providing direct supervision/focusing the modeling procedure on the PET helps, perhaps because the PET is the semantic focus of the task (rather than other words in the data, which are not always important).

4.2.2 Using the Literal Meanings of PETs

Each PET is detailed in Gavidia et al. (2022) to have a literal meaning or paraphrase, which is the more offensive or unpleasant "real meaning" that the PET substitutes. Several teams chose to integrate literal meanings of each input PET into their methods, though they opted to generate their own literal meanings, rather than use the ones from the original paper. This seemed to be effective, as the two best-performing teams found it to improve performance — Kesen et al. (2022) appended literal meanings to their inputs and used them to generate image embeddings, while Keh et al. (2022)(b) used literal meanings to select examples for data augmentation — in conjunction with direct supervision on the PET (4.2.1). Tiwari and Parde (2022) paraphrased PETs with their literal meanings in attempt to obtain sentiment shifts, but this did not work well for classification, likely because the paraphrasing mechanism did not produce quality paraphrases that could serve as literal meanings for the PETs.

4.2.3 Addressing Data Imbalance/Inadequacy

Multiple teams addressed the fact that the dataset was imbalanced (see 1). Maimaitituoheti (2022) found that their approach scored an F1 of 0.914 versus 0.789 on the euphemistic and literal examples, respectively, suggesting that the model performance could indeed be skewed towards the higher-volume euphemistic examples.

(Trust and Kadusa, 2022) experimented with multiple modeling enhancements, such as Bayesian modeling, exclusively to address the imbalance issue and found that they improved performance. Kohli et al. (2022) sought to address the imbalance by using adversarial perturbations to augment the '0' label, and found it to increase performance slightly. As aforementioned, Kesen et al. (2022) augment the dataset by strategically selecting sentences from other corpora (albeit for general augmentation, rather than to achieve a balance) and similarly report slight performance increases, but, like Kohli et al. (2022), they do not exclusively use the augmented data in their final approach. These results generally support the intuition that addressing data inadequacies helps models learn, but only partially for this shared task.

4.2.4 Incorporating Additional Context

While this task necessitates making use of contextual differences between input texts, several teams attempted to incorporate additional information from the context. Wang et al. (2022) model syntactic connections between the PET and other words in the text as a relational graph, finding that using this as an input to BERT is effective (though no baseline or example parse is provided). As aforementioned in Section 4.1, Kesen et al. (2022) slightly improve performance by using the k-nearest neighbors for each input as additional context. Kohli et al. (2022) finds that simply using longer input sequence lengths than standard BERT allows for (512) generally improves performance, although it is not clear at what sequence length this would cease to be the case. All these methods to incorporate more input context seemed to generally improve performance.

4.2.5 Linguistic Transparency

Some teams attempted solutions that would promote model explainability. Kesen et al. (2022) claim that images of PETs and their literal meanings are a way to gain insight into how models interpret PETs, but while this is an interesting way to probe models' current understanding of figurative expressions, it is unclear how models might use these images to enhance classification in an understandable way. The two-model ensemble used by Wang et al. (2022) attempt to incorporate linguistic (semantic and syntactic) information of the PET and its context, though without compelling examples of how these may help classification, the improvements seem somewhat unexplainable. Finally, Tiwari and Parde (2022) interestingly pursued an approach that is based exclusively on the linguistic intuition that euphemisms produce sentiment shifts, but using these shifts alone for this task was ineffective.

On the other hand, methods which found success using transformers are not very transparent. Wiriyathammabhum (2022) test various transformers and obtain their best result by combining a CNN variant with the highest-performing one, but it is not clear what this network is learning, as is typically the case with neural networks. Furthermore, Keh (2022) find that transformers work decently for this task in the zero-shot setting (see 4.2.6), but admit that it's not clear what BERT is learning in order to do so.

4.2.6 Zero/Few-shot Learning

Maimaitituoheti (2022) train a RoBERTa model using prompt-tuning because it has been shown to work well (better than regular fine-tuning) with few-shot examples. While our task was not formulated as a zero/few-shot task, several PETs appeared only a few times in the data and were effectively few-shot examples. Keh (2022) notably re-formulate the task for the zero/few-shot setting. When PETs were randomly selected to be zero-shot examples, RoBERTa-large achieved a score of 0.740, showing that the model was able to "learn" something about euphemisms (not simply memorizing) and apply it to examples with PETs unseen during training. They also show that few-shot examples benefit the model greatly, with 3-shot performance (0.825) nearly matching the baseline performance (0.836). Furthermore, they found that GPT3, which typically works well in the zero/few-shot setting, worked badly for this task.

5 Discussion and Findings

Here, we describe some common findings of the submitted systems that may be useful for future work.

5.1 More Data is Better

Having more examples of each PET generally led to better performance. Kesen et al. (2022) and Keh et al. (2022) improved performance by augmenting the dataset. Maimaitituoheti (2022) showed that performance on the euphemistic label is better, likely because there were many more examples than the non-euphemistic label. Compellingly, Keh (2022) showed in their zero/few-shot task that 3-shot learning was much better than 1-shot. The results of this task call for larger datasets of euphemisms, perhaps from a variety of different sources.

5.2 BERT Works

All teams experimented with some variation of BERT and reported decent scores using unmodified BERT models, the highest being 0.839 (Kesen et al., 2022) using RoBERTa-large. The zero-shot investigation by Keh (2022), too, shows that RoBERTa picks up something during training that is generalizable to other euphemisms. Overall, pre-trained transformers seem to provide a solid baseline from which to launch euphemism work.

5.3 Linguistic Intuitions

Because euphemisms (as well as other types of figurative language) are often commonly used expressions, it is likely that large language models have some existing "knowledge" about these collocations. One could interpret the success of using PET embeddings directly (Kesen et al., 2022; Wang et al., 2022) as evidence that models can leverage this knowledge for the task.

Another linguistic notion is that euphemisms' function may lead to changes in sentiment, which has been found to potentially be useful for identifying euphemisms (Felt and Riloff, 2020; Lee et al., 2022), but it remains somewhat unclear whether it is useful for the disambiguation proposed in this task. Wiriyathammabhum (2022) do find that transformers pre-trained specifically on sentiment were more helpful than those pre-trained on other tasks (e.g., sarcasm or hate speech detection). Tiwari and Parde (2022) try a non-transformer-based approach based on the intuition that PETs should produce higher sentiment shifts in euphemistic sentences when paraphrased with its literal meaning, but found it was difficult to generate such paraphrases. This corroborates our own past experimentation (?), and it seems that future approaches based on sentiment shifts have to address the need for better paraphrasing mechanisms, or consider using them to supplement a larger input feature set.

6 Conclusions and Future Work

We present the results of "The Shared Task on Euphemism Detection for the Third Workshop on Figurative Language Processing" and summarize the various systems submitted, as well as common findings. Overall, we find that results are promising: even when dealing with the difficult issue of an especially polite and indirect form of figurative language, current NLP techniques such as transformers and augmentation seem to work quite well. Teams explored a variety of intriguing methods to enhance the baseline performance of these models, some of which were even linguistically transparent. If one considers that labeling euphemisms is subject to human disagreement, the F1-scores achieved by the teams are even more compelling since they may be near, if not already at, the level of human agreement on the task. The results of this shared task establish a baseline for future work on euphemisms and figurative language in general.

Future work on this task could be expanding on the dataset to include more examples and a wider range of PETs, testing further enhancements, and improving performance by ensembling various combinations of the best-performing improvements. Future work for euphemism detection in general could be to expand from the disambiguation task; e.g. identifying where euphemisms are in a text, providing interpretations of a euphemism, or even euphemistic language generation.

Limitations

While the data used denoted where the target PET was in each text sample, this information is not provided in raw text. Identifying the PET in a text sample is a challenge that future approaches, especially those seeking to focus models on the PET, will need to consider. Additionally, this shared task was run on a dataset that could be significantly expanded and balanced. The dataset also contained potentially subjective labels that were only made by two human annotators; this could be made more robust by ensembling more annotators. Finally, this task was based on a dataset comprising only of texts of US English, and it is unclear how these results would transfer cross-lingually to other kinds of euphemisms.

Ethics Statement

When we created the shared task, we tried to be compliant with the ACL Ethics Policy. Euphemisms are expressions that 'hide' prejudices by using softened language. Models capable of recognizing and interpreting euphemisms should be better at detecting biases related to gender, age, race, or socioeconomic background, detrimental to the society.

Acknowledgements

This material is based upon work supported by the National Science Foundation under Grants No. 1704113 and No. 2226006.

References

Cristian Danescu-Niculescu-Mizil, Moritz Sudhof, Dan Jurafsky, Jure Leskovec, and Christopher Potts. 2013. A computational approach to politeness with application to social factors. *arXiv preprint arXiv:1306.6078*.

Mark Davies and Robert Fuchs. 2015. Expanding horizons in the study of world englishes with the 1.9 billion word global web-based english corpus (glowbe). *English World-Wide*, 36(1):1–28.

Jacob Devlin, Ming-Wei Chang, Kenton Lee, and Kristina Toutanova. 2018. Bert: Pre-training of deep bidirectional transformers for language understanding. *arXiv preprint arXiv:1810.04805*.

Christian Felt and Ellen Riloff. 2020. Recognizing euphemisms and dysphemisms using sentiment analysis. In *Proceedings of the Second Workshop on Figurative Language Processing*, pages 136–145.

Martha Gavidia, Patrick Lee, Anna Feldman, and Jing Peng. 2022. Cats are fuzzy pets: A corpus and analysis of potentially euphemistic terms.

Debanjan Ghosh, Avijit Vajpayee, and Smaranda Muresan. 2020. A report on the 2020 sarcasm detection shared task.

Pengcheng He, Jianfeng Gao, and Weizhu Chen. 2021. Debertav3: Improving deberta using electra-style pretraining with gradient-disentangled embedding sharing. *arXiv preprint arXiv:2111.09543*.

Anna Kapron-King and Yang Xu. 2021. A diachronic evaluation of gender asymmetry in euphemism. *arXiv preprint arXiv:2106.02083*.

Sedrick Scott Keh. 2022. Exploring Euphemism Detection in Few-Shot and Zero-Shot Settings. In *Proceedings of the 3rd Workshop on Figurative Language Processing*. Association for Computational Linguistics.

Sedrick Scott Keh, Rohit K. Bharadwaj, Emmy Liu, Simone Tedeschi, Varun Gangal, and Roberto Navigli. 2022. EUREKA: EUphemism Recognition Enhanced through Knn-based methods and Augmentation. In *Proceedings of the 3rd Workshop on Figurative Language Processing*. Association for Computational Linguistics.

Ilker Kesen, Aykut Erdem, Erkut Erdem, and Iacer Calixto. 2022. Detecting Euphemisms with Literal Descriptions and Visual Imagery. In *Proceedings of the 3rd Workshop on Figurative Language Processing*. Association for Computational Linguistics.

Guneet Kohli, Prabsimran Kaur, and Jatin Bedi. 2022. Adversarial Perturbations Augmented Language Models for Euphemism Identification. In *Proceedings of the 3rd Workshop on Figurative Language Processing*. Association for Computational Linguistics.

Patrick Lee, Martha Gavidia, Anna Feldman, and Jing Peng. 2022. Searching for pets: Using distributional and sentiment-based methods to find potentially euphemistic terms. *arXiv preprint arXiv:2205.10451*.

Yinhan Liu, Myle Ott, Naman Goyal, Jingfei Du, Mandar Joshi, Danqi Chen, Omer Levy, Mike Lewis, Luke Zettlemoyer, and Veselin Stoyanov. 2019. Roberta: A robustly optimized bert pretraining approach. *arXiv preprint arXiv:1907.11692*.

Harish Tayyar Madabushi, Edward Gow-Smith, Marcos Garcia, Carolina Scarton, Marco Idiart, and Aline Villavicencio. 2022. Semeval-2022 task 2: Multilingual idiomaticity detection and sentence embedding.

Rijul Magu and Jiebo Luo. 2018. Determining code words in euphemistic hate speech using word embedding networks. In *Proceedings of the 2nd workshop on abusive language online (ALW2)*, pages 93–100.

Abulimiti Maimaitituoheti. 2022. A Prompt Based Approach for Euphemism Detection. In *Proceedings of the 3rd Workshop on Figurative Language Processing*. Association for Computational Linguistics.

Steven Pinker. 2003. *The Blank Slate: The modern denial of human nature*. Penguin.

Hussein Abdo Rababah. 2014. The translatability and use of x-phemism expressions (x-phemization): Euphemisms, dysphemisms and orthophemisms) in the medical discourse. *Studies in literature and language*, 9(3):229–240.

Michael Thelen and Ellen Riloff. 2002. A bootstrapping method for learning semantic lexicons using extraction pattern contexts. In *Proceedings of the 2002 conference on empirical methods in natural language processing (EMNLP 2002)*, pages 214–221.

Devika Tiwari and Natalie Parde. 2022. An Exploration of Linguistically-Driven and Transfer Learning Methods for Euphemism Detection. In *Proceedings of the 3rd Workshop on Figurative Language Processing*. Association for Computational Linguistics.

Paul Trust and Provia Kadusa. 2022. Bayes at FigLang 2022 Euphemism Detection shared task: Cost-Sensitive Bayesian Fine-tuning and Venn-Abers Predictors for Robust Training under Class Skewed Distributions. In *Proceedings of the 3rd Workshop on Figurative Language Processing*. Association for Computational Linguistics.

Yuting Wang, Yiyi Liu, Ruqing Zhang, Yixing Fan, and Jiafeng Guo. 2022. Euphemism Detection by Transformers and Relational Graph Attention Network. In *Proceedings of the 3rd Workshop on Figurative Language Processing*. Association for Computational Linguistics.

Peratham Wiriyathammabhum. 2022. TEDB System Description to a Shared Task on Euphemism Detection 2022. In *Proceedings of the 3rd Workshop on Figurative Language Processing*. Association for Computational Linguistics.

Wanzheng Zhu and Suma Bhat. 2021. Euphemistic phrase detection by masked language model.

Wanzheng Zhu, Hongyu Gong, Rohan Bansal, Zachary Weinberg, Nicolas Christin, Giulia Fanti, and Suma Bhat. 2021. Self-supervised euphemism detection and identification for content moderation. *arXiv preprint arXiv:2103.16808*.

Author Index

Association for Computational Linguistics
209 N. Eighth Street
Stroudsburg, Pennsylvania 18360

ISBN 978-1-7138-9110-9

CURRAN ASSOCIATES INC.
proceedings.com